'Every student of Christian truth should be aware of the doctrinal contribution of each of the persons treated in this volume. The authors, experts in their field of contribution, have given substantial treatment to the thought of each individual, highlighting their major and enduring contribution to Christian thought, but including their thinking on a wide spectrum of subjects. Brad Green's editorial conception of how each chapter should progress and the overall contribution it should make to the whole makes this an eminently useful book as a text. But its text-book quality does not mean that it is not just as desirable for pleasure reading. The combination of explanatory narrative, interaction with other scholars, and primary source references creates both relevance and credibility for an important discussion of vital foundational issues in the history of Christian Doctrine.'

Tom Nettles, The Southern Baptist Theological Seminary

'These substantial essays are clear and scholarly introductions to some of the main Patristic and early medieval theologians. It is not possible to understand the theology of the Reformation or of the Puritan movement, or of evangelicalism more generally, without recognizing that these movements consciously built not only upon Scripture, but on a Conciliar, Patristic and early medieval foundation. At the Reformation this tradition was deliberately purified, not overthrown. The editor and the other contributors are to be congratulated on providing fine studies of those whose writings helped to form the orthodox Protestant identity.'

Paul Helm, Teaching Fellow, Regent College (Vancouver, British Columbia)

'One of the most encouraging developments in evangelical theology over the last few years has been the increasing awareness among its theologians of the fact that the roots of much evangelical belief predates the Reformation; yet it remains the case that there are few entry-level guides to the great thinkers of the early and medieval church which are specifically designed to help evangelicals come to a better understanding of the origins of their thinking. For this reason, this collection of essays is most welcome, as it provides the reader not only with helpful introductions to the thought of key theologians

but also opens up avenues of further exploration for those interested in probing deeper into the great resources of the wider Christian tradition.'

Carl Trueman, Westminster Theological Seminary

'The church did not spring up yesterday; as the community of Christ, it stretches across the landscapes of time. Shapers of Christian Orthodoxy introduces us to the pioneering thinkers of the faith, including figures as diverse as fiery Tertullian, speculative Origen, heroic Athanasius, awesome Augustine, and (from the Middle Ages) the brilliant Thomas Aquinas. A team of skilled modern scholars provides rich, sometimes controversial, always stimulating interpretations of their lives and writings. I can think of few comparable resources for learning how to do theology from some of the most enduring giants of Christian thought.'

Nick Needham, Highland Theological College

'A winsome introduction to many of the towering minds of the Christian tradition, and a welcome invitation to join our minds to their searching efforts to enter more fully into the mystery of Christ.'

R. R. Reno, Creighton University

'This is a superb collection of essays on the greatest theologians of the Great Tradition during the first thirteen centuries of church history. It is encouraging to see such fresh and creative engagement with the development of Christian doctrine seen through the prism of its major shapers. Highly recommended!'

Timothy George, founding Dean of Beeson Divinity School, Samford University

'For those evangelicals who are seeking to advance their understanding of how Christianity evolved before the Reformation, this collection of essays offers a valuable means of doing so. The reader will see clearly how Protestantism, indebted to its predecessors, is part of a larger and older continuum of faith.'

D. H. Williams, Baylor University

SHAPERS OF CHRISTIAN ORTHODOXY

Engaging with Early and Medieval Theologians

Edited by BRADLEY G. GREEN

An imprint of InterVarsity Press
Downers Grove, Illinois

InterVarsity Press
P.O. Box 1400, Downers Grove, IL 60515-1426
Internet: www.ivpress.com
E-mail: email@ivpress.com

Published in the United States of America by InterVarsity Press, Downers Grove, Illinois, with permission from Apollos, Nottingham, England.

InterVarsity Press® is the book-publishing division of InterVarsity Christian Fellowship/USA®, a movement of students and faculty active on campus at hundreds of universities, colleges and schools of nursing in the United States of America, and a member movement of the International Fellowship of Evangelical Students. For information about local and regional activities, write Public Relations Dept., InterVarsity Christian Fellowship/USA, 6400 Schroeder Rd., P.O. Box 7895, Madison, WI 53707-7895, or visit the IVCF website at <www.intervarsity.org>.

ISBN 978-0-8308-3886-8

Printed in Canada ∞

InterVarsity Press is committed to protecting the environment and to the responsible use of natural resources. As a member of Green Press Initiative we use recycled paper whenever possible. To learn more about the Green Press Initiative, visit <www.greenpressinitiative.org>.

Library of Congress Cataloging-in-Publication Data

Shapers of Christian orthodoxy/edited by Bradley G. Green.
p. cm.
Includes bibliographical references and indexes.
ISBN 978-0-8308-3886-8 (USA: paper: alk. paper)—ISBN 978-1-87784-436-7 (UK: paper: alk. paper)
1. Theology, Doctrinal—History—Early church, ca. 30-600. 2. Theology, Doctrinal—History—Middle Ages, 600-1500. 3. Theologians. I. Green, Bradley G., 1965-
BT23.S52 2010
230.092'2—dc22

2010019898

P 21 20 19 18 17 16 15 14 13 12 11 10 9 8 7 6 5 4 3 2 1
Y 28 27 26 25 24 23 22 21 20 19 18 17 16 15 14 13 12 11 10

CONTENTS

CONTRIBUTORS

Carl Beckwith is Associate Professor of Divinity at Beeson Divinity School, Samford University, Birmingham, Alabama. His research interests include the trinitarian and Christological thought of the early church fathers and the appropriation of patristic thought by the Reformers. His books are *Hilary of Poitiers on the Trinity: From 'De Fide' to 'De Trinitate'*, Early Christian Studies (Oxford University Press, 2008); and a translation of Johann Gerhard's *Handbook of Consolations for the Fears and Trials that Oppress Us in the Struggle with Death* (Wipf & Stock, 2009).

Gerald Bray did post-doctoral work in Cambridge and taught at Oak Hill College in London before going to Beeson Divinity School in 1993. He was Anglican Professor of Divinity there until 2006, when he became Research Professor. He also works for the Latimer Trust in London. His books include *The Doctrine of God* (IVP, 1993) and *Biblical Interpretation, Past and Present* (IVP, 1996); and he has edited a number of major texts for the Church of England Record Society. He has also edited several volumes in the Ancient Christian Commentary on Scripture (IVP), Ancient Christian Texts (IVP) and Ancient Christian Doctrine (IVP) series.

Mark W. Elliott is Senior Lecturer in Church History at the University of St Andrews. He has written *The Song of Songs and Christology in the Early Church*

(Mohr Siebeck, 2000), *The Reality of Biblical Theology* (Peter Lang, 2007) and edited *Isaiah 40–66*, vol. 11 of the Ancient Christian Commentary on Scripture series (IVP, 2007).

Bradley G. Green teaches theology at Union University in Jackson, Tennessee, and helped found Augustine School, also in Jackson. He is the author of *Colin Gunton and the Failure of Augustine: The Theology of Colin Gunton in Light of Augustine* (Wipf & Stock, 2010) and *The Gospel and the Mind: Recovering and Shaping of the Intellectual Life* (Crossway, 2010).

David S. Hogg is Associate Professor of Theology and Medieval Studies at Southeastern Baptist Theological Seminary. He is the author of *Anselm of Canterbury: The Beauty of Theology* (Ashgate, 2004).

Robert Letham is a minister in the Evangelical Presbyterian Church in England and Wales, Senior Tutor in Systematic and Historical Theology at Wales Evangelical School of Theology and Adjunct Professor of Systematic Theology, Westminster Theological Seminary, Philadelphia. He is the author of *The Work of Christ* (IVP, 1993), *The Lord's Supper* (Presbyterian & Reformed, 2001), *The Holy Trinity* (Presbyterian & Reformed, 2004), *Through Western Eyes* (Mentor, 2007) and *The Westminster Assembly: Reading its Theology in Historical Context* (Presbyterian & Reformed, 2009).

Bryan Litfin is Professor of Theology at Moody Bible Institute in Chicago, Illinois. He has written *Getting to Know the Church Fathers: An Evangelical Introduction* (Brazos, 2007) and a novel, *The Sword* (Crossway, 2010), the first volume in a trilogy.

W. Brian Shelton is Associate Professor of Theology and Dean of the School of Christian Studies at Toccoa Falls College, Georgia, US. He is the author of *Martyrdom from Exegesis in Hippolytus: An Early Church Presbyter's Commentary on Daniel* (Paternoster, 2008), and recently contributed on patristic responses to cultural opposition in *The Contemporary Church and the Early Church: Case Studies in Ressourcement* (Wipf & Stock, 2010).

INTRODUCTION

Bradley G. Green

Whether you have studied academic theology or not, if you have an interest in Christian thought or theology, it is likely that along the way you have stumbled across a thinker or writer to whom you have been attracted. It may have been a line of text, a lengthy theological tome, a polemical work or a devotional treatise. Nonetheless, most of us at some point find our 'heroes' from amidst the writings of the last two thousand years.

This volume has its origin in a similar experience, or set of experiences. In the writing of my doctoral dissertation, I was trying to work through Augustine's *De Trinitate* (*The Trinity*). This work is in some ways one of Augustine's most seminal and mature theological works, although *The City of God* rightfully and understandably should be called his *magnum opus*. But as I worked through *De Trinitate* I found myself swimming in completely different waters from my contemporary milieu. It was difficult initially to follow Augustine's train of thought, to understand perhaps why he was arguing the way he was, and to foresee where he might be headed with his argument. I read and reread many sections, particularly the opening sections, and continued to plod along. But a wonderful thing happened. As I stayed the course, Augustine began to become a bit less foreign to me, and I began to grasp his logic. I believe I even began to understand why he was arguing the way he was. A volume that initially had been a bit off-putting – if not downright intimidating – began to appear as a friend and ally.

Plus I gained more than simply additional ammunition with which to buttress my systematic theology. As I read and reread Augustine I was learning how to think theologically. I saw Augustine making theological connections that I might not naturally have made. I saw Augustine wrestling with certain analogies for the Trinity – as if he were inviting the reader to wrestle with an analogy along with him – only to discard most of the analogies before the journey was complete, for most of the analogies ultimately proved unhelpful.

In short, by watching one of the greatest theologians of the Christian church theologize, *I* was learning how to theologize. And although I already knew that historical theology, the history of Christian thought, is important, I was now learning first-hand why it is so important. Now, it is easy to quote Santayana, 'He who is ignorant of the past is doomed to repeat it,' or Richard Weaver, 'Ideas Have Consequences.' It is quite another thing to walk with a great thinker, and begin to understand why they argued the way they did.

I teach systematic theology for a living and love it. I enjoy quoting Charles Hodge when he speaks about how the human mind yearns for order, and how the mind inherently and intuitively seeks to order the data it receives.[1] I think Hodge is right. I passionately affirm that Scripture is inherently theological at its core, and that systematic theology is a proper *and necessary* end flowing from the reality of the nature of Scripture itself. We must learn to think theologically. In the best theology courses students are taught the background of theological battles, and the historical exigencies that led to a construal of a doctrine in a certain way. But at times we learn, or teach, theology by giving a 'bullet point' summary of the orthodox position, and students are left knowing they are supposed to believe XYZ – say, the Chalcedonian Formula – but have little understanding of the gravitas and significance of such conclusions. And they do not simply lack this sense of gravitas or significance, but fail to understand how key thinkers came to such conclusions in the first place. As a result, I suspect many students conclude that they know they should believe the Chalcedonian Formula, if only because Dr Smith says so, and perhaps they admire, or at least somewhat trust, Dr Smith (you fill in the name).

I happily and passionately affirm the full authority, sufficiency and perspicuity of Scripture. And I passionately affirm that all thinkers in the Christian tradition must be judged against the bar of Scripture. God has given us Scripture, and it is certainly sufficient for our needs. At the same time, we would be wrong to suggest that God simply departed from his church either at the point the last New Testament document was written, or at the point when

1. Charles Hodge, *Systematic Theology* (Grand Rapids: Eerdmans, repr. 1968), vol. 1.

the New Testament was seen as canonical (367, with Athanasius, or earlier). Rather, is it not wiser to suspect that God might have been leading certain persons in the history of the church to articulate something in a helpful way, to forge a helpful argument, to discover an insightful theological axiom or principle?

The best theology is simply an attempt to make sense of Scripture. As others have noted, the eighty-year-old woman in the pew, with the worn Bible, marked and ragged from years of reading, wrestling and Sunday school teaching, is certainly a theologian in an important sense of the word. And by standing on the shoulders of the key theologians of the Christian tradition, we can see how they attempted to make sense of Scripture in their own time. We may find the occasional interpretation outlandish, or a logical move to be a howling non sequitur, but we do see faithful people genuinely trying to wrestle with holy Writ. As C. S. Lewis writes, 'People were no cleverer then than they are now; they made as many mistakes as we. But not the *same* mistakes.'[2] Our modern lenses can perhaps be skewed, so this allows us to gain an insight into Scripture we might otherwise have missed. If we have not read Athanasius, we might miss the very natural way in which Athanasius in *On the Incarnation* sees the theological interrelatedness between the incarnation and atonement. Similarly, if we have not read Anselm's *Cur Deus homo*, we might not see the logic of the atonement as being something so thoroughly God-centred.

Now, although the above insights from Athanasius and Anselm are fundamentally biblical, why not just stick to the Bible, and save our money for something other than buying all those old dusty books? I think the answer is to be found in two interrelated propositions: (1) First, through reading the great theologians we come to see the logic of why they reached the conclusions they did, why they felt that with certain issues the very gospel was at stake, and we see the significance of central theological conclusions from the last two thousand years. (2) Secondly, and perhaps just as significant, we learn how to think theologically – how to theologize – by reading the theologizing of the great theologians of Christian history. Let it be said clearly, we should be reading the great theologians, and every theologian should be one who is constantly saturating himself or herself in Scripture. And we should be willing to conclude that certain moves made by certain theologians were wrong-headed, inappropriate, fundamentally unbiblical and so on. But I believe the training received by grasping and understanding the theologizing of the great

---

2. C. S. Lewis, 'On the Reading of Old Books', in *God in the Dock: Essays on Theology and Ethics* (Grand Rapids: Eerdmans, 1970), p. 202.

theologians is invaluable, and would strengthen both the faith and work of contemporary theological students. There are many other benefits that could be mentioned – and will be in due course – not the least of these simply being the joy of studying pre-modern theology, and not constantly becoming bogged down in the often sterile and mind-numbing world of contemporary theology. Many nights (and early mornings) spent with Augustine were life-giving in comparison with the task of plodding through the latest theological tome hot off the press.

The best evangelical theology has always paid attention to the past, to the key thinkers, issues and doctrinal developments in the history of the church. Evangelicals have affirmed that Scripture is the *norm normans non normata* (the norming norm that is not normed). When evangelicals affirm *sola scriptura*, we are affirming that the Christian canon is the only infallible word we have from God. Thus Christian theology should always be returning to Scripture, be immersing itself in Scripture, and seeking to understand God, his ways and will through attention to his Word. Given the proper and sustained attention evangelicals have given – and should continue to give – to Scripture, it is understandable that one temptation for us *might* be an inattention to the seminal thinkers of some two thousand years of church history. But this is an unnecessary error for evangelicals, and, even more centrally, it is one that is inconsistent with an affirmation of the full trustworthiness and reliability of holy Writ. The Christian faith contends that all of reality hinges on certain first-century events: the incarnation, life and teachings, and death, resurrection and ascension of Jesus, and the sending of the Holy Spirit and spread of the gospel in the first century. Thus Christians – who affirm that all reality hinges on such first-century events – have reason to give attention to the *past*. It is part of the DNA of the Christian faith to recognize that our lives and destinies are inextricably related to a long history of God's actions in history. And thus Christians should have not only a future focus, because we are confident that God is going to keep his promises and provide for his people; we should also have a certain *past* orientation in that we know that what God has done in the past is key to understanding who we are and how we are to live.

When this volume was being organized and contributors were asked to be a part, the purpose of the book was summarized in the following three key points:

1. To strengthen the faith of Christian students (and other readers), by helping them to understand the riches of the church's theological reflection.

2. To introduce theological students to the key theologians of the Christian church.
3. To help readers learn how to think theologically, by seeing how the central early and medieval theologians thought.

Undergirding these three goals is an overarching commitment to the evangelical tradition articulated during the Protestant Reformation, and clarified and elaborated since that time. There has been a type of renaissance of interest in evangelical circles since the 1990s or so in the church fathers. I remember as a seminary student discovering Tom Oden's *Agenda for Theology: After Modernity . . . What?* (Grand Rapids: Zondervan, 1990). There Oden traces his own journey from being a 'movement theologian' (in which he went from fad to fad – feminism, Freudianism, Marxism, etc.) to being an orthodox Protestant theologian. He recounts how he began to read two types of theological works that helped in his journey to orthodoxy: (1) the works of evangelical theologians and (2) the works of the church fathers. It is difficult not to be infected with a desire to read the church fathers after having read of Oden's experience. While I have never been a 'movement theologian', it was during the often soul-withering experience of doctoral studies that I discovered my own church father, Augustine, leading eventually to a doctoral dissertation that focused in part on Augustine's doctrine of the Trinity.

It seems to me that this renaissance of interest in the church fathers is a healthy one. And at the risk of oversimplifying, there are two mistaken trajectories one might take in returning to a study of the fathers. First, one might conclude that the greatest light shines in the first five to eight centuries of the church's history, and then see subsequent developments as less illuminating. Secondly, one might see theology as really beginning in the fifteen-hundreds with the Protestant Reformation. Both of these trajectories are properly rejected, and this is clearly a false dichotomy. Instead evangelicals should read all the fathers and gain as much exegetical insight, theological helpfulness and pastoral wisdom from them as possible. The riches are vast and worthy of attention. At the same time, evangelicals can glean much from the developments of the sixteenth century too.

I also suspect that a study of the riches of the church fathers (as well as of the medieval theologians) need not incline one to depart from the Protestant tradition. For some, it appears that the study of the church fathers leads to a loosening of Reformation commitments. I have found that a study of the church fathers (and medieval theologians), when combined with the study of Scripture and the continued study of evangelical theology, has strengthened my love for and commitment to evangelical theology. A couple of comments are in order.

First, the Reformers themselves often saw themselves as in fundamental continuity with much of the tradition that preceded them, even if they believed a need for reform had arisen. Secondly, I wonder if certain evangelicals who make sweeping generalizations about some deficiency in the evangelical tradition have immersed themselves in the tradition – particularly in the Reformers themselves. When I spent a summer reading Calvin's *Institutes* from cover to cover I did not find a dry, soulless dispenser of theological propositions. Instead, I found straightforward Bible-soaked theology and a pastoral heart. I suspect such delving would help evangelicals not only to recover the wealth of the early and medieval theologians, but that of the Reformers and their heirs too.

In the light of the above, contributors were asked in their respective chapters to offer (1) an insightful theological analysis and commentary on each theologian; and (2) a critical assessment of each theologian that asks how evangelicals should view and appropriate (or not) the insights of the theologian. It is hoped that this volume might contribute to a passion for thinking theologically and, ultimately, for acting in the light of what is known. Augustine could argue that it is right to try to say something about God, as long as we approach him a certain way. Augustine writes, 'there is no effrontery in burning to know, out of faithful piety, the divine and inexpressible truth that is above us, provided the mind is fired by the grace of our creator and savior, and not inflated by arrogant confidence in its own powers'.[3] It is hoped that these chapters will indeed lead to the cultivation of minds 'fired by the grace of our creator and savior', and that readers will be helped to think rightly about our good and great God.

3. *The Trinity* 5.1. In *The Works of Saint Augustine: A Translation for the 21st Century*, vol. 11, ed. John E. Rotelle, O. S. A., tr. Edmund Hill (Hyde Park, NY: New City, 1992).

1. IRENAEUS

W. Brian Shelton

Introduction

Many historians and theologians consider Irenaeus to be the most important figure in the second-century church. He receives more attention than any other figure in the development of early Christianity, because he verbalizes an advanced, articulate theology in a formative era and a geographical location that offer us few voices. Mary Ann Donovan declares, 'The second century was *the* century for the construction of Christian identity. One of the principal architects of that identity was Irenaeus of Lyons.'[1] As an important founder of orthodoxy and as inspiration for the Christian faith, Irenaeus deserves much attention in church history. However, the honour and notice come to Irenaeus with just as much scrutiny and criticism. In an era in which historical criticism of Christianity is alive and well in the academy, and in which sources of antiquity become available in new ways, both archaeologically and technologically, a new competition for traditional and alternative Christianities is waging.[2]

---

1. Mary Ann Donovan, *One Right Reading: A Guide to Irenaeus* (Collegeville, Minn.: Liturgical, 1997), p. 3; italics original.
2. Contemporary historical and theological critical scholarship maintains that one form of Christianity emerged from the second to the fourth centuries, the product

As bishop of Lyons in Roman Gaul, now southern France, Irenaeus was a staunch defender of emerging Christian orthodoxy, an advocate of persecuted Christianity, an important link between East and West, a vital heir to the apostolic tradition, a fan of the Scriptures that the church later calls canonical, and an opponent of gnostic doctrine. The latter is of utmost concern to Irenaeus, as Gnosticism constituted a major movement of mystical religious thought and practice in antiquity. Recently, the rise of interest in gnostic studies, texts and history comes with late twentieth-century access to the Nag Hammadi library of gnostic manuscripts. The controversial references to the *Gospel of Mary* and *Gospel of Philip* in the best-seller *The Da Vinci Code* have fuelled gnostic curiousity on a popular level.

In fact, at times contemporary scholarship offers unwarranted criticism to orthodox tradition, but uncritical latitude to gnostic tradition. Irenaeus is right in the centre of the mêlée. Bart Ehrman accuses him of 'defamatory descriptions' of gnostic churches, calls him a 'heresy hunter', and posits that Nag Hammadi scholars dispute whether Irenaeus 'knew what he was talking about'. At the same time, Ehrman claims that a gnostic gospel with its radically different view for 'understanding of God, the world, Christ, salvation, human existence . . . will open up new vistas for understanding Jesus and the religious movement he founded'.[3] In a sense of fiat, writers like Elaine Pagels claim that writings like the gnostic *Gospel of Thomas* are valid as a 'perspective offered by one of the *other* Christian gospels composed in the first century'.[4]

Footnote 2 (*cont.*)

of polemical attacks and political tactics. Thus one favoured tradition of Jesus prevailed by politically ostracizing other traditions. This finds significant momentum in Walter Bauer's *Orthodoxy and Heresy in the Earliest Centuries*, ed. Robert A. Kraft and Gerhard Krodel (Philadelphia: Fortress, 1971). The reader should watch for the theological battle between Irenaeus and second-century heresies reported here and recognize how truth, faithfulness to the teaching of the apostles, and unity are central to Irenaeus' argument – not a dishonest scrutiny of doctrine and not primarily political methods. For a sample challenge to the Bauer thesis, see Darrell L. Bock, *The Missing Gospels: Unearthing the Truth Behind Alternative Christianities* (Nashville: Thomas Nelson, 2006), which challenges claims of prejudiced early doctrinal unity.

3. Bart D. Ehrman, 'Christianity Turned on Its Head: The Alternative Vision of the Gospel of Judas', in Rodolphe Kasser, Marvin Meyer and Gregor Wurst (eds.), *The Gospel of Judas* (Washington, DC: National Geographic Society, 2006), pp. 82–83, 88.
4. Elaine H. Pagels, *Beyond Belief: The Secret Gospel of Thomas* (New York: Vintage, 2003), p. 29; italics original.

She softens their antithetical doctrine by declaring Gnostics to be 'outsiders' who were 'attracted to the presence of a group joined by spiritual power into an extended family', a feeling paralleling her own personal spiritual crisis.[5] Eric Osborn points out how contemporary scholars make the Gnostics look innocent, like 'good chaps, active in local government and Rotary International, with a devotion to home and garden'.[6] Irenaeus would be appalled to learn that the ancient heresy he helped to defeat is on the road to revival and legitimacy.

Biography

Although the details of Irenaeus' personal history are few, a basic framework of this church father's life can be deduced from sparse details mostly in the historical commentary of Eusebius and in autobiographical material of Irenaeus.[7] Additional ancient and medieval figures referenced him and his work in a way that offers a few additional pieces of information.

Irenaeus hailed from Asia Minor, probably the city of Smyrna because of his claim to have sat under Polycarp. 'We ourselves saw him in our early youth, for he lived long.'[8] Eusebius adds to his testimony, 'For I [Irenaeus] saw thee [Florinus] when I was yet a boy in the lower Asia with Polycarp . . . I can tell also the very place where the blessed Polycarp was accustomed to sit and discourse' as he conversed with people in teaching.[9] This is confirmed by his intimate familiarity with Polycarp's interactions with Roman bishop Anicetus and with Marcion.

Before his arrival in Lyons, Irenaeus may have studied and even taught at Rome under Bishop Anicetus. This cannot be known for certain, but probably (1) later diplomatic visits to Rome entail some familiarity with the Roman church, and (2) Polycarp's own visits may have served as a link or even an

5. Ibid., p. 6.
6. Eric Osborn, 'Irenaeus: Rocks in the Road', *Expository Times* 14 (2003), p. 255.
7. Eusebius, *Ecclesiastical History*, tr. C. F. Cruse (Peabody: Hendrickson, 2000), 5.4–8, 20, 26.
8. *Against Heresies* 3.3.4. All quotations of *Against Heresies* are taken from the translation of Robert M. Grant, *Irenaeus of Lyons*, The Early Church Fathers (New York: Routledge, 1997), unless otherwise noted, where usually they will be taken from the still popularly used *Against Heresies*, in Alexander Roberts and James Donaldson (eds.), *The Ante-Nicene Fathers* [*ANF*], vol. 1 (Edinburgh: T. & T. Clark, 1866; repr. Grand Rapids: Eerdmans, 1953).
9. Eusebius, *Ecclesiastical History* 5.20.5–6.

escort for Irenaeus.[10] What is certain is that the presence of his leadership there serves as an important link between East and West. With a Greek Christian mindset and a legacy of the apostolic tradition come to the West, Irenaeus can be called a scion of the East.[11] This East–West link enhances his potential for insight and influence, as well as his important principle of the universality of the church.

Certainly by about 175, Irenaeus is in or near Lyons and is a well-established figure in the church there under the bishopric of Pontinus. At the time, Lyons was an important centre of government, as well as for travel and trade. The language was still Celtic (Gallic), and it even had a significant population of immigrants from the East. Scholars suggest that he may already have been bishop of Vienne, about twenty miles south of Lyons,[12] when a tragic and formative event took place: severe persecution by Roman authorities broke out against the church there. Its bishop, Pontinus, was martyred under horrific persecution, and the church citizens there immediately appointed Irenaeus bishop of Lyons.

Eusebius reports the episode of persecution with great detail, including named individuals, graphic description of their suffering, and citations of their testimony of their faith.[13] A sample offers an insight into the world in which Irenaeus ministered:

> The greatness, indeed, of the tribulation, and the extent of the madness exhibited by the heathen against the saints, and the sufferings which the martyrs endured in this country, we are not able fully to declare, nor is it indeed possible to describe them . . . clamors and blows, plundering and robberies, stonings and imprisonments . . . the holy martyrs finally endured tortures, beyond all description; Satan striving with all his power, that some blasphemy might be uttered by them.[14]

---

10. *Against Heresies* 3.3.4; Eusebius, *Ecclesiastical History* 5.24.16–18.
11. J. A. Cerrato employs the term 'scion' as an attribution to Hippolytus, another figure who probably emigrated to the West. I first suggested that Irenaeus also deserves the designation in my review of Cerrato, *Hippolytus between East and West: The Commentaries and the Provenance of the Corpus*, in *Journal of Early Christian Studies* 12 (2004), p. 362.
12. Eric Osborn, *Irenaeus of Lyons* (New York: Cambridge University Press, 2001), p. 4.
13. Eusebius, *Ecclesiastical History* 5.1–3. The account is followed by a recognition of Irenaeus as carrier of the persecution report to Bishop Eleutherus (5.4). Reference to the death of Pontinus lies in Eusebius, *Ecclesiastical History* 5.4.1, 5.5.8, and is usually dated 177/178.
14. Ibid. 5.1.

Scholars believe that this historic account may have been written by Irenaeus himself.[15]

In an era of less distinction between a bishop and a presbyter, Irenaeus' seat of administration was a pastoral one. His role as spiritual and administrative leader becomes important in understanding the polemical activities of his tenure and his contribution to orthodoxy. Jeffrey Soboson describes Irenaeus' role as presbyter: 'He is the leader of the Christian community assigned the task of preserving the faith, teaching it, and making sure to defend it against error.'[16] The expanse of his role as bishop of Vienne and Lyons leads historians to identify him as an early monarchial bishop, and commonly date him as flourishing AD 175–95. Two recorded occasions show Irenaeus appealing to the bishop of Rome that may demonstrate the early nature of Roman authority and of regional bishops.

First, in 177, he mediated before Eleutherus about Montanism. Controversy arose in some churches in Asia Minor around the teaching of Montanus, including visions, signs and awaiting Christ's return in the desert. It seems that Irenaeus represented the churches of southern Gaul in defending them by calling for unity in the church.[17] Seeing the conflict as far as Rome causes Robert Lee Williams to conclude that the Montanist 'New Prophecy' contained 'patterns that were less than worthy of the long standing Roman traditions of scholastic churches'.[18]

Secondly, in the late 180s, he mediated before Victor about Asian Quarodecimians. Victor had threatened to break off communion with these churches of Asia for celebrating Easter on 14 Nisan rather than the Sunday following. Irenaeus reminded Victor that previous bishops had never broken off fellowship with one another. Despite their disagreement, they seemed to depart in peace and communion.[19] Eusebius cannot pass up the opportunity to recognize a play off his name: 'Irenaeus, who was truly well-named, became a peacemaker in this matter, exhorting and negotiating on behalf of the peace of the churches.'[20]

---

15. Claudio Moreschini and Enrico Norelli, *Early Christian Greek and Latin Literature. Vol. 1: From Paul to the Age of Constantine* (Peabody: Hendrickson, 2005), p. 223; Eusebius, *Ecclesiastical History* 5.4.
16. Jeffrey G. Soboson, 'The Role of the Presbyter: An Investigation of the *Adversus Haereses* of Saint Irenaeus', *Scottish Journal of Theology* 27 (1974), pp. 129–146.
17. Eusebius, *Ecclesiastical History* 5.1–4.
18. Robert Lee Williams, '"Hippolytan" Reactions to Montanism: Tensions in the Churches of Rome in the Early Third Century', *Studia patristica* 39 (2006), p. 138.
19. Moreschini and Norelli, *Greek and Latin Literature*, p. 224.
20. Eusebius, *Ecclesiastical History* 5.23–25, viz. 5.24.18.

Irenaeus then fades from the annals of history. 'Last heard of about 190, addressing letters to various bishops', like the one to Victor.[21] The tradition of his martyrdom cannot be strongly substantiated or controverted, and seems to be based on Gregory of Tours' Frankish history.[22] In his Isaiah commentary, Jerome makes a passing but interesting comment about 'Irenaeus, bishop of Lyons and martyr', but scholars suspect it to be a redaction, given the silence of Jerome in his biographical entry of Irenaeus in *Lives of Illustrious Men* and the lack of any other patristic mention.[23]

Writings

During his stay at Lyons, Irenaeus crafted his significant work *Detection and Overthrow of Falsely-Named Knowledge*, commonly known as *Against Heresies*.[24] A large work in five books, this anti-heretical polemic is rich in both systematic and biblical theology. Written about AD 190 to a 'dear friend' mentioned at the beginning of each book, this work has proved invaluable in understanding gnostic theology, early ecclesiastical conflict, and the overall position of orthodox doctrine at the end of the second century. Furthermore, its influence on future patristic writers seems to be immeasurable, although historians should be quick to acknowledge that Irenaeus represents contemporary theology as much as he informs it.

The Greek text of *Against Heresies* survives only in extracts. However, the work can be reconstructed from a Latin translation produced before 421, an Armenian version of Books 4–5, and several Syriac fragments. Occasionally, the work receives critical evaluation. For example, recently Joel Kalvesmaki has argued that Irenaeus wrote Book 1 in two phases. The first part aimed to refute only the Valentinians before being turned into a global heresiology, in

---

21. Richard Norris, 'Irenaeus', in Patrick W. Carey and Joseph T. Lienhard (eds.), *Biographical Dictionary of Christian Theologians* (Peabody: Hendrickson, 2002), p. 267.
22. Gregory of Tours, *The History of the Franks* 1.29, tr. and introduction by Lewis Thorpe (Harmonsworth: Penguin, 1985).
23. Jerome refers to him: *S. Irenaeus, episcopus Lugdunensis et martyr* (Jerome, *Commentary on Isaiah* 64, José van der Straeten, 'Saint Irénéee fut-il martyr?', in *Les Martyrs de Lyon (177)* [Paris: Centre national de la Recherche scientifique, 1978], p. 150).
24. First shortened to 'Against Heresies' by Eusebius himself, *Ecclesiastical History* 5.7.1. Titles find different translations, such as *Exposure and Rebuttal of the 'Knowledge' Falsely So Named*, in Norris, 'Irenaeus', p. 267.

which Simon the Magician is the basis of them all. Such an analysis explains 'a number of peculiar features of *Against Heresies*'.[25]

Scholars have logically hypothesized the geographical locale of the original readers confronted with Ptolemaean and Marcosian Gnosticism. His constant focus on Valentinian Gnosticism suggests a Western audience, as Valentinus arrived in Rome about 140. Irenaeus' repeated appeal to the apostolic fathers may suggest an Eastern audience, but on the other hand his narration seems to introduce, rather than presume, these Eastern figures for his audience. For example, 'a deacon of ours from Asia' implies audience unfamiliarity with Polycarp of Asia Minor.[26] His reference to 'living among the Celts' with their 'barbarous tongue' and 'lack of elegant style' suggests he is not writing to one of their own.[27] However, this does not preclude the work's recipient from being a newcomer to the Rhône Valley; in fact, perhaps he is another transplant from the East like Irenaeus himself. Certainly the Marcosion gnostic dissent was very real to the region. Thus Dominic Unger suggests that Rome itself may be a good possibility for receipt of Irenaeus' *Against Heresies*.[28] Its authorship in Greek does not prevent an AD 190 provenance, the heresy could easily have infiltrated a neighbouring area, and Irenaeus wrote and visited Rome on several other occasions. Additionally, his reference to Marcellina's influence in Rome may be a point of context for that audience – but does not necessitate it. He displays impressive humility in his writing and persuasion: 'You cannot expect rhetorical art, which we have never learned, or the craft of writing, in which we have not had practice, or elegant style and persuasiveness, with which we are not familiar.'[29] He likewise lacks classical philosophical training, like one sees in Justin, and the legal training one sees in Tertullian. But Irenaeus earns his own place among the apologists in his theological assault against those who seek to redefine the teachings of the apostles and the Scriptures.

The only other extant major work by Irenaeus is *Demonstration of the Apostolic Preaching*, authored during this same time period. Written to a fellow believer,

---

25. Joel Kalvesmaki, 'The Original Sequence of Irenaeus, *Against Heresies* 1: Another Suggestion', *Journal of Early Christian Studies* 15 (2007), p. 407.
26. *Against Heresies* 1.13.5; cf. 4.32.1, also thought to refer to Polycarp: 'After this fashion also did a presbyter, a disciple of the apostles, reason with respect to the two testaments, proving that both were truly from one and the same God' (*ANF*).
27. Ibid. 1.pref.3 (*ANF*).
28. Dominic J. Unger, 'Introduction', in *St. Irenaeus of Lyons: Against the Heresies*, Ancient Christian Writers 55 (Mahwah, NJ: Paulist, 1992), pp. 5–6.
29. *Against Heresies* 1.pref.3, tr. Unger.

Marcianus, whose locale is unknown,[30] it is catechetical and apologetic, functioning as a proof of the apostolic writers by using Christological proofs from the Old Testament to explain Christian doctrine. It is a summary of the same material contained in *Against Heresies*, but lacks the voluminous detail on gnostic doctrines and the accompanying polemic against them. It is a positive depiction of the faith, showing how faith and right belief find logical support, centring on the truth that comes in Christ incarnate. Iain MacKenzie describes it as 'the very distillation of Irenaean thought'.[31] It was probably written after *Against Heresies* because of its summative quality.

The *Demonstration of the Apostolic Preaching* was rediscovered in an Armenian translation in 1904. Besides the text being readily available, it has recently received new attention and new translations. Since it echoes *Against Heresies*, the work was probably designed as a tool for catechumens or, without naming Gnosticism, a resource against what the church perceived to be heresy.

Patristic historians list additional works by Irenaeus that are now lost. Some fragments are preserved in other writers, such as his *Commentary on the Ogdoad*, preserved only in Eusebius, in which he challenges gnostic theology centred on the significance of the number eight in their system. The work may not be so different from the other two, however. Eusebius describes the work, 'In which book he also showed that he was the first who received the original succession from the apostles.'[32] These other lost works attributed to him are listed in the table below.

Reading Irenaeus can be difficult. His style is technical, and many details focus on a gnostic system of theology foreign to the contemporary reader. Although probably not trained formally in philosophy or rhetoric, he knows their methods and employs them. Meanwhile, the Gnosticism he targets is cosmic and mythological, but it shares much theology and rhetoric with Judaism and Christianity. A given gnostic passage can seem vague because it reflects on the mystical dimensions of historical and biblical realities. A passage

---

30. *Demonstration* 1. MacKenzie speculates it may be a recipient in his well-known Smyrna, based only on the reference of distance between author and recipient (Iain M. MacKenzie, *Irenaeus's* Demonstration of the Apostolic Preaching: *A Theological Commentary and Translation*, tr. J. Armitage Robinson [Burlington, VT: Ashgate, 2002], p. 37). All quotations of the *Demonstration of the Apostolic Preaching* are from MacKenzie.

31. Ibid., p. 31.

32. Eusebius, *Ecclesiastical History* 5.20.1.

Lost works referenced in Eusebius	*Lost works referenced in Jerome*	*Explanation of References*
Against Heresies and *Refutation and Overthrow of False Doctrine*	*Against Heresies*	Eusebius: 'It may suffice to prove by the testimony of two witnesses . . . maintaining sound doctrine in the church, may surely be regarded as worthy of all credit: and such were Irenaeus and Clement of Alexandria.'
Demonstration of the Apostolic Preaching	*On Apostolic Preaching*	A letter to fellow believer Marcianus that is a proof of the apostolic preaching.
Ogdoad	*Commentary on the Ogdoad*	Eusebius: 'on the number eight', 'in which he showed that he was the first who received the original succession from the apostles'.
On Knowledge	*Against the Nations*	Eusebius: against the Greeks
On Schism	*On Schism* *On Discipline*	To Blastus
(Various disputes)	(Various treatises)	Eusebius: 'a book of various disputes in which is mentioned the Epistle to the Hebrews'. *Probably* the same work referenced between them.
Wisdom of Solomon		Eusebius: 'quoting certain passages from them'
On Sovereignty	*On Monarchy*	Eusebius: 'or the truth that God is not the author of evil' to Florinus, who 'appeared to maintain this opinion'. Eusebius mentions three letters of Irenaeus 'against those at Rome who were counterfeiting the sound ordinance of the church', providing pieces of two of them. Jerome: *That God Is Not the Author of Evil* to Florinus

can also sound bizarre, as its mysterious elements use biblical rhetoric but speak of an inverse of biblical values at times because of its negative attitude towards the earthly body and the physical world. Irenaeus is quick to criticize and mock the seeming illogical, unbiblical and preposterous theology, silently moving in and out of gnostic facts and claims to orthodox criticism and correction. Finally, Irenaeus branches out at various lengths to relate other gnostic points, writings or rationale – often without explicit reference to his opponents' position – easily confusing the inattentive reader. Contemporary English translations usually have section headings that are immensely helpful in keeping up with Irenaeus.

Still, a first-time reader of Irenaeus may be overwhelmed or disappointed. In an encouraging article entitled 'Irenaeus: Rocks in the Road', Eric Osborn argues that the exposition in this church father's writings 'flows like a great highway', but many an idea 'strikes in turn a series of rocks or problems which Irenaeus must answer'.[33] Context and perspective help to keep the obstacles and distractions in perspective. Osborn breaks the contribution of Irenaeus, mainly from *Against Heresies*, into four theological concepts and two criteria for operating them. 'To this text [Scripture] he applies the classical criteria of logi (what is true) and aesthetics (what is fitting) to draw out his four concepts of divine Intellect, economy, recapitulation, and participation.'[34] A reader might be advised to watch for these themes as a useful aid in understanding the master of Lyons.

However, the reward in reading Irenaeus is great. His theological contribution is multifarious, ranging from creation to eschatology, from sin to salvation, from heresy to orthodoxy, and from the Old Testament tabernacle to the New Testament church. His adamancy about true doctrine is a call for right belief for God's people because of the threat that false gnostic doctrine poses to the Christian faith. Thus, although his appeal is systematic and polemical as it targets heretical theology, this church father is just as pastoral and devotional of the object of his doctrine. Irenaeus says himself that he lays out the Valentinian gnostic system because 'it was necessary to provide clear proof and bring their teachings to light. Perhaps some of them will repent and by returning to the only God, the Creator and Maker of the universe can be saved.'[35]

---

33. Osborn, 'Rocks', p. 256.
34. Osborn, *Irenaeus*, p. xi.
35. *Against Heresies* 1.31.3.

Theological analysis

In two preserved works numbering more than 250 pages, Irenaeus treats a wide range of doctrinal issues. The sections below summarize and analyse some of his most important topics – most important to Irenaeus, most important in reading Irenaeus and most important to the development of orthodoxy in the early church.

Gnostic context/heresiology

It is already apparent how the theology, efforts and contribution of Irenaeus are irrevocably contextualized in the gnostic controversy. A basic understanding of Gnosticism is essential for understanding and certainly appreciating the case against it laid out in *Against Heresies*. Readers of the work should realize that unfamiliarity with Gnosticism will be like watching the sequel to a movie that relies heavily on the storyline of the initial episode. Kurt Rudolph lays out four essential characteristics that serve as a brief guide for us. Gnosticism displays these qualities:[36]

- *Strong dualism.* The material world is a blend of good and evil, with the good associated with an unknowable, transcendent God and the bad associated with lesser gods, including the Old Testament Creator.
- *Salvation not resurrection.* While the flesh is not redeemable but evil, a spark of light is contained in each person that can be liberated through gnosis. While the soul or spirit is eternally saved, there is no physical resurrection of the dead, and Christ's own resurrection did not have to be physical and usually is not.
- *Different cosmology.* Creation is also dualistic. Sparks of divinity, associated with light, have been encapusluated in certain people. These represent all things good, including spirit, soul and knowledge. Darkness symbolizes evil, expressed through matter, flesh and ignorance.
- *Eschatology in the* plērōma. Salvation is recognition of where the soul will finally reside, in the place absolutely disconnected to the physical world.

---

36. Kurt Rudolph, *Gnosis: The Nature and History of Gnosticism*, tr. Robert McLachlan Wilson (Edinburgh: T. & T. Clark, 1983), pp. 57–59. For a more recent overview of Gnosticism, see Christoph Markschies, *Gnosis: An Introduction*, tr. John Bowden (New York: T. & T. Clark, 2003).

In particular, Irenaeus wrote in reaction to the church activities of the disciples of Valentinus in the region of Lyons. An influential figure in Roman ecclesiastical life in the mid-second century, this gnostic leader may have competed for the office of bishop of Rome itself. In Valentinian gnostic theology, salvation's goal was to re-enter the *plērōma*, the divine realm, which is opposed to the created world and physical matter in a strongly Platonic fashion. Experiencing the *plērōma* is often symbolized by terms such as 'union' or 'unity'. This led gnostic leaders such as the followers of Marcus towards physical indulgence as an act of transcendence of the physical realm. For them, spiritual awareness seems to have been transferred through sexual activity outside marriage. Irenaeus accused Mark the Magician of seducing women under the ruse of instructing them in the faith.[37]

Irenaeus' great work *Against Heresies* contains most of his theological thought. *Against Heresies* is laid out over five books, and an overview of this work will assist the reader in imagining his case against Gnosticism. Book 1 lays out the system of theology taught by Ptolemy, disciple of Valentinus, who was a leading gnostic writer in the mid-second century. Chapters 9 and 10 are particularly important, as Irenaeus critiques the gnostic exegetical method and posits the unity of the faith of the church, respectively. In Book 2 Irenaeus engages the gnostic teaching he laid out in the first book. Rational and theological arguments attack the gnostic view of the divine world, the *plērōma*, the aeons, dualism and numerology, as well as gnostic exegesis, Christology and eschatology. Book 3 hosts Irenaeus employing the Scriptures to refute gnostic theology. Extremely important here is how the Christian Scriptures contain and correlate to the apostolic teaching and ecclesiastical tradition in a 'rule of faith'. The unity and progress of the history of salvation finds explanation in Book 4, establishing the Creator to be the same God as the Father, one with the Son. Book 5 is a completion of his refutation, again centring on the teachings of Jesus and Paul.

Irenaeus tends to refute the Gnostics straightforwardly based on logic, Scripture and theology, and the effect of exposing the gnostic doctrines contributed to refuting them in a subordinate way.[38] In particular, he tends to employ a three-part epistemological case against the Gnostics: apostolic tradition, Scripture and a common rejection of them to solidify the true revelation

37. *Against Heresies* 1.8.1–7.

38. Ibid. 1.31.3. See Gérard Vallée, *A Study in Anti-Gnostic Polemics: Irenaeus, Hippolytus, and Epiphanius*, Studies in Christianity and Judaism 1 (Ontario: Wilfrid Laurier University Press, 1981), pp. 51–54, concerning Hippolytus' 'uncovering' approach against Irenaeus' 'engaging' approach.

of God in Christ. There is no room for esoteric vision and gnostic salvation in Christian belief.

Although *Against Heresies* and *Demonstration* contain most of his theological thought, it should also be viewed as representing the theology of the early church at least in the West (but also shared with the churches throughout the empire that came to be known as 'catholic', over against those called 'gnostic' that the work seeks to refute and disqualify from the true church). The expression 'knowledge falsely so called' in its title seems to come from Paul's exhortation in 1 Timothy 6:20: 'O Timothy, guard what has been entrusted to you, avoiding worldly and empty chatter and the opposing arguments of what is falsely called "knowledge"' (NASB).

Epistemology: tradition, rule, Scripture, catholicity

Irenaeus appealed to several sources of knowledge as authoritative, but clearly saw them as one larger revelation of God. The tradition of the apostles handed down to the churches combines with the Scripture read and studied in the churches to establish a rule of doctrine, which he saw as uniting all true believers everywhere.

Apostolic tradition and the rule of faith

His most effective theological tool was the apostolic tradition – the teachings of the apostles that had come down to the churches through written and commonly understood forms. This source of authority existed, over against subjective and unorthodox gnostic writings and scriptures that promote an esoteric vision from Jesus himself. The faith common to all churches everywhere descended from a direct line of elders in the church back to the apostles. Irenaeus declares, 'The Church, though dispersed throughout the world to the ends of the earth, received from the apostles and their disciples this faith in one God, the Father Almighty . . .'[39] He elaborates:

> One must hear the presbyters who are in the church, those who have the succession from the apostles, as we have shown, and with the succession of the episcopate have received the sure spiritual gift of truth according to the good pleasure of the Father. As for all the others who are separate from the original succession, in whatever place they gather, they are suspect. They are heretics with false doctrine or schismatics full of pride and audacity and self-willed or, again, hypocrites looking only for vain and vainglory.[40]

---

39. *Against Heresies* 1.10.1.
40. Ibid. 4.26.2–43.

Irenaeus establishes a theory of theological truth that we call his 'rule of faith'.[41] Generally speaking, this standard is the tradition of the apostles, evidenced in the church and recorded in an early notion of Scripture that was handed down to all true churches and her leaders everywhere. To speak more specifically is the topic of much scholarly debate.[42] However, O'Keefe and Reno rightly caution against any assumption that second-century use of Scripture 'was nothing more than an exhaustive exercise in proof-texting animated by an anti-intellectual submission to doctrinal authority'.[43] Instead, it was an intentional, thoughtful and faithful effort by church leaders to employ Scripture and the apostolic tradition against what they viewed as inferior and dangerous false doctrine.

This 'rule of faith' principle occurs throughout his writings and is the basis for the faith of every believer: 'Having therefore the truth itself as our rule and the testimony concerning God set clearly before us . . . we should exercise ourselves in the investigation of the mystery and administration of the living God.'[44] Likewise, this is the thesis for his minor work *Demonstration of the Apostolic Teaching*. This 'rule of faith' or 'rule of truth' is the standard of the apostolic teaching. It also has a sense of catholicity, as it is the standard of faith and truth celebrated wherever churches follow the instructions of the apostles.

John Lawson condenses Irenaeus' rule of faith to three elements: (1) the assent to truth, (2) the self-committal to the truth, and (3) the surrender of oneself to God as seen in Jesus Christ.[45] Thus there is a belief, dedication and

---

41. The Latin *regula veritatis* corresponds to the Greek *ho kanōn alētheias* (the canon of truth). Often the rule receives the technical name *regula fidei* or *regula veritatis*.
42. Concerning the differences between rules of faith and truth, Osborn explains, 'Generally the term rule of faith was preferred for internal use within the church and rule of truth was preferred when argument was directed to heretics' (Osborn, *Irenaeus*, p. 145, n. 17). Concerning charges of the orthodox abuse of the rule, see Bart D. Ehrman, *The Orthodox Corruption of Scripture: The Effect of Early Christological Controversies on the Text of the New Testament* (New York: Oxford University Press, 1993), esp. pp. 3–32, 120–165 and 274–280.
43. John J. O'Keefe and R. R. Reno, *Sanctified Vision: An Introduction to Early Christian Interpretation of the Bible* (Baltimore: Johns Hopkins University Press, 2005), p. 126.
44. *Against Heresies* 2.28.1 (*ANF*). Ammundsen renders this to be a genitive of apposition, for definition and explanation (Vladamar Ammundsen, 'The Rule of Truth in Irenaeus', *Journal of Theological Studies* 13 [1912], p. 576).
45. John Lawson, *The Biblical Theology of Saint Irenaeus* (London: Epworth, 1948), pp. 240–243.

response aspect that is built into the rule of faith that ultimately legitimizes the rule as true and divinely approved. Irenaeus declares, 'For to yield assent to God, and to follow his Word, and to love Him above all, and one's neighbor as one's self, and to abstain from every evil deed, and all other things of a like nature which are common to both [covenants], do reveal one and the same God.'[46] The table below shows the relationship between tradition, Scripture and catholicity in Irenaeus:

Rule of faith from *apostolic tradition*	'But Polycarp also was not only instructed by apostles, and conversed with many who had seen Christ, but was also, by apostles in Asia, appointed bishop of the Church in Smyrna, whom I also saw in my early youth, for he tarried [on earth] a very long time, and, when a very old man, gloriously and most nobly suffering martyrdom, departed this life, having always taught the things which he had learned from the apostles, and which the Church has handed down, and which alone are true' (*Against Heresies* 3.3.2–4 [*ANF*])
Rule of faith from *Scriptural connection* to apostolic tradition	'True knowledge is [that which consists in] the doctrine of the apostles, and the ancient constitution of the Church throughout all the world, and the distinctive manifestation of the body of Christ according to the successions of the bishops, by which they have handed down that Church which exists in every place, and has come even unto us, being guarded and preserved without any forging of Scriptures, by a very complete system of doctrine' (*Against Heresies* 4.33.6 [*ANF*])
Rule of faith as confirmed by *universal church*	'As I have already observed, the Church, having received this preaching and this faith, although scattered throughout the whole world, yet, as if occupying but one house, carefully preserves it . . . the Churches which have been planted in Germany do not believe or hand down anything different, nor do those in Spain, nor those in Gaul, nor those in the East, nor those in Egypt, nor those in Libya, nor those which have been established in the central regions of the world' (*Against Heresies* 1.10.2 [*ANF*])

46. *Against Heresies* 4.13.4 (*ANF*).

There are numerous references to these three categories of data in his *Against Heresies*.[47]

This unbroken chain both confirms the catholic Scriptures but also constructs the catholic Scriptures. Twenty-first-century readers of Irenaeus should recognize that the apostles' writings are primarily represented by what becomes the New Testament, but that the voice of the apostles forms a tradition and catholicity that is more than just the texts themselves. D. F. Wright remarks, 'The apostolic tradition is embodied in the Rule of Faith and transmitted by successions of teachers in churches of apostolic foundation.' It is on these forces, and against gnostic traditions, that Irenaeus 'erects the apostolic pillars of catholic orthodoxy'.[48]

For Irenaeus, Rome held a place of privilege regarding ecclesiastical authority because of the past presence and influence of two leading apostles there: 'The church that is the greatest, most ancient, and known to all, founded and set up by the two most glorious apostles Peter and Paul at Rome, while showing that the tradition and the faith it proclaims to men comes down through the successions of bishops even to us.'[49] Lest someone claim that at least one of these glorious apostles, Paul, having received a revelation from Christ on the Damascus road, was a Gnostic himself, Irenaeus points out that Paul did not receive a revelation any different from that of the apostles who knew Christ in his earthly ministry, as claimed in 1 Corinthians 15:8–9. Even Paul went to the other apostles to confirm his message and to be tutored by them, as he reports in Galatians 2:1–2.

The influence and even prestige that comes with Peter and Paul's influence in Rome is extremely important for this church father, especially in the principle of apostolic tradition. Although Irenaeus' list of successive Roman bishops offered future justification for elevation for that line of authority – Roman Catholic 'evidence' of patristic support of the papacy – he never distinguishes an exclusively Petrine figurehead. This leads to a historical interpretation of theological *influence* of the apostles rather than establishing of a universal *office* there.

47. For the rule of faith as found in the apostolic tradition handed down to elders, see 1.10.1–2, 2.25.1, 3.1.pref., 3.2.2, 3.3.2–4, 3.4.1, 4.26.2, 4.33.6, 5.20.1. For the rule of faith as found in the Scriptures, see 1.22, 2.13.3, 3.1.1, 3.12.6, 4.33.6, 4.35.4. For the rule of faith as characterizing all the true churches everywhere, see 1.9.5, 1.10.2, 2.27.1, 3.3.2–4, 4.1–3, 4.33.6.

48. D. F. Wright, 'Irenaeus', in *The New International Dictionary of the Christian Church*, ed. J. D. Douglas (Grand Rapids: Zondervan, 1978), pp. 516–517.

49. *Against Heresies* 3.3.2.

The apostolic tradition naturally leads to a consideration of the nature of Scripture in the thought of Irenaeus. Historical theology must recognize that the apostolic tradition has both a corollary and overlapping relationship with Scripture. On one hand, the notion of apostolic tradition is *evidenced* in Scripture with Paul and Peter exhorting readers to stay true to their teaching. On the other hand, the apostolic tradition *is* Scripture, as the very message of the apostles is recorded in the writings collected to become the New Testament. Irenaeus has this overlap in mind when he posits the priority of Scripture over other claims to revelation. Rowan Greer says it this way: 'Text and interpretation are like twin brothers; one can scarcely tell the one from the other. What emerges is an unbroken dialogue between Scripture and tradition, between the letter and the spirit, and between the word and the experience of those hearing it.'[50]

Scripture and exegesis

Irenaeus helps the early church to realize both the internal nature of Scripture and the ecclesiological authority of Scripture. Internally, Scripture is seen as true and a measure of truth, and the Old and New Testaments cohere and evidence each other. This view of Scripture translates to an exegesis that is constant and includes both testaments. Externally, his use of the writing of the apostles evidences a notion of canonicity and helps to delineate the use of particular texts in the early Christian West.

Scripture as truth. Perhaps the most impressive feature about Irenaeus is his employment of the teaching of Jesus and the church as a standard for belief for all churches throughout the world. With the esoteric gnostic claims in view, Irenaeus declares that merely claiming divine insights does not validate them: 'The fact that some people know more or less by insight does not result in changing the subject and falsely imagining a God other than the Creator, Maker, and Sustainer of this universe.'[51] Knowledge lies instead in these things, components of Scripture, which Irenaeus then places in a curious list:

- completing, investigating and adapting truths
- explaining the divine plan for humanity
- positing divine patience against rebellious angels and humanity
- positing divine creation of something eternal and something earthly

---

50. Rowan A. Greer, 'The Christian Bible', in James L. Kugel and Rowan A. Greer (eds.), *Early Biblical Interpretation* (Philadelphia: Westminster, 1986), p. 157.

51. *Against Heresies* 1.10.3.

- explaining why divine theophanies vary
- explaining covenants as divine relationships
- pondering divine mercy
- fostering thanks for the incarnation and passion
- framing the 'last days' as the theatre for divine activity
- exploring the 'last days' events
- contemplating the divine inclusion of the Gentiles
- contemplating the resurrection
- considering the irony that the chosen would reject but the rejected would be chosen

This peculiar inventory of items seems to be a smattering of doctrinal values associated with God's interaction with creation and humanity. The God of biblical history is not the god of gnostic mythology. God personally created the world and ordained the things that are, rather than being tricked by less heavenly beings:

> God did not imagine or blaspheme that above the Creator and Demiurge there is a 'Mother' of him and of them, the Desire of an Aeon that went astray . . . these masters, truly destitute of divine understanding, express themselves, while the whole church has one and the same faith in all the world.[52]

Meanwhile, the truth quality of the biblical text necessitates reliability and uniformity like that of beautiful music. He declares,

> All Scripture, given to us by God (2 Tim. 3:16), will be found consistent. The parables will agree with the clear statements and the clear passages will explain the parables. Through the polyphony of the texts a single harmonious melody will sound in us, praising in hymns the God who made everything.[53]

It is 'unadulterated truth', 'true knowledge' and 'confers on the suppliant more than he can ask from it'.[54] If mysteries remain in the Scriptures even after our reading and thinking, then such is the nature of faith: 'If we leave certain questions to God, we shall preserve our faith and remain free from peril.'[55]

---

52. Ibid. 1.10.3
53. Ibid. 2.28.3.
54. Ibid. 3.2.2, 4.33.6, 3.pref. (*ANF*).
55. Ibid. 2.28.3.

Maurice Jourjon says that for Irenaeus, Scripture is 'spiritual throughout'.[56] It is clear that Irenaeus did not merely select biblical passages and employ them without regard to context or meaning. It is clear to him that the Spirit inspired them through human agency. Finally, it is clear that they possess a righteousness of their own – the kind found in the law of God. Thus Jourjon can declare for Irenaeus, 'Since all of Scripture is spiritual, it is necessary to take precise account of it in order to read it in the manner of Christ and to proclaim, teach, and transmit the faith just as the apostles do so, namely, in conformity with the Scriptures.'[57]

Canonical principles. His biblical theology in Book 3 is one of the most important testimonies to the credibility and progress of canonicity. First, his understanding of the use of the Old Testament in the New Testament is a strong apologetic for the continuity of the Scriptures and a Christological reading of the Old Testament. Secondly, his use of the combination of scriptural writings evidences the late-second-century popularity of a collection of writings that matched the codified canon.

The relationship between the Old and New Testament finds special continuity. Throughout the Old Testament, the same Holy Spirit inspired the prophets and narrative writers to craft in a way allowing the church to now recognize Christ in the Old Covenant. The Son of God is referenced in the Psalms, seen in the Abrahamic narrative and prophesied about by Isaiah, for example.[58] For him, the Scriptures are internally consistent, and against the gnostic myths of a demiurge's creation and providence in the Old Testament, he spells out how the Old Testament points to Christ in a way that offers continuity between the Testaments and disqualifies the gnostic systems.[59] The Ethiopian eunuch in Acts 8 who read from Isaiah before his conversion was 'one precathechized by the prophets'.[60]

Against the adoptionist heresy which claimed that the man Jesus was adopted by God and endowed with divinity at his baptism, Irenaeus argues that Jesus was not merely human before then, but incarnational through the

---

56. Maurice Jourjon, 'Irenaeus's Reading of the Bible', in Paul M. Blowers (ed. and tr.), *The Bible in Greek Christian Antiquity* (Notre Dame: University of Notre Dame Press, 1997), pp. 106–107.
57. Ibid. p. 110.
58. *Against Heresies* 3.6.1–5.
59. Ibid. 4.22–4.26.
60. Ibid. 4.23.2.

virgin birth. The Old Testament points to both the humanity and the divinity of Christ, as prophecies ranging from 'the brilliant birth from the Virgin (Is. 7:14)' and 'coming on the clouds as the universal Judge (Dan. 7:13, 26)' to a man 'without beauty and capable of suffering (Is. 53:2–3) . . . the scripture predicted all this of him'.[61] Meanwhile, when Irenaeus accuses the Gnostics of twisting Scripture to establish their doctrine, he says they cite and adjust the prophetic sayings, the parables of the Lord, and the apostolic words.[62]

References to such a combination of sources of authority reveal that this church father had a notion of certain books as authoritative for church doctrine, aiding our understanding of the development of the canon. Perhaps the most important passage towards New Testament canonicity in *Against Heresies* is his case for the present four Gospels: 'There cannot be either more or fewer gospels than there are.'[63] The Ebionites used only Matthew's Gospel, those who maintained the separation of Christ's two natures used only Mark, the Marcionites used only Luke, and the Valentinians used only John. 'Those people are vain, ignorant, and especially audacious when they reject the form of the Gospel and introduce a number of gospels either greater or smaller than those we have mentioned.'[64] Unfortunately, the Lyons exegete uses analogies to justify his four Gospels in an allegorical way rejected by many contemporary readers and criticized by contemporary scholars. There are four regions of the world, four principal winds, four heads and wings of the cherubim, an image of four 'columns' to support the world, and four covenants given to humans.[65] In one passage, Irenaeus explains how each of the qualities of the animals represented in the cherubim corresponds to each of the Gospels. This is evidenced by certain qualities inherent in the Gospels, which are actually weak references by this father. They are listed in the table below for their influence on church history.

From four Gospels, Irenaeus proceeds to argue that the apostles agree with these four and with each other. Peter accompanies John in ministry, Luke agrees with Paul, Stephen was chosen by the apostles and Philip preached the

---

61. Ibid. 3.19.1–2.
62. Ibid. 1.8.1.
63. Ibid. 3.11.8.
64. Ibid. 3.11.9.
65. Ibid. 3.11.8. For a good defence of Irenaeus' seeming simplistic analogies as more advanced than understood, see Nicholas Perrin, 'Irenaeus and Lyotard Against Heresies, Ancient and Modern', in Mark Husbands and Jeffrey P. Greenman (eds.), *Ancient Faith for the Church's Future* (Downers Grove: IVP, 2008), pp. 126–140.

Animal	*Natural quality*	*Gospel*	*Literary quality*
Lion	power, primacy, royalty	John	eternality, creativity
Bull	sacrifice and priestly	Luke	Zechariah, incense, fatted calf
Man	human in nature	Matthew	genealogy, humility
Eagle	anticipatory of gift of Spirit	Mark	heavenly origin and rapidity of gospel

message of salvation.[66] Likewise, in an episode such as Paul's calling together the elders from Ephesus to Miletus, he offers continuity between the integrity of the apostle's preaching with the preaching required of them. From those like them, the gospel was transmitted from the apostles to all people, confirming what Luke declares to begin his Gospel: 'As those transmitted it to us, who from the beginning were eyewitnesses and servants of the Word.'[67] This obvious effect of catholicity makes Kurt Aland recognize that general unanimity on what was scriptural functioned like a canon. He states, 'When we follow the process of the formation of the canon in detail, we can hardly avoid the impression that the second century really had no need of a canon.'[68]

Exegetical method. On the matter of exegetical method Irenaeus is like many other early Western fathers. Typology is well developed, as the Old Testament prefigures the New Testament, especially Christ's person and work. Like Justin, he distinguishes between formal Jewish prophecies and visions of Christ and *typoi* that depict him.[69] Typology extends beyond Christ to include events like the Egyptian plagues as types of apocalyptic suffering, and the

66. *Against Heresies* 3.12.3–10.

67. Ibid. 3.14.2; Luke 1:2.

68. Kurt Aland, *A History of Christianity*, tr. James L. Schaaf (Philadelphia: Fortress, 1985), vol. 1, p. 114. The notion of a closed canon of biblical books does not find firm evidence in the earliest couple of centuries after the apostles. However, there is extremely impressive substantiation that churches recognized certain authoritative books and used them as Scripture, while rejecting other books as unauthoritative. Aland argues that the lack of canonical activities evidences that churches generally agreed on books as Scripture, so that formal lists were not necessary and came as a later development.

69. *Against Heresies* 4.20.8.

tabernacle and temple as types of heavenly realities.[70] Beyond this, Irenaeus is not above allegorical typology. This can be seen in his exposition of Mark 12:11, in which the details of the parable of the vineyard find correlation with key events in biblical history along the theme of God's economy of salvation and Jewish rejection of his provisions.[71] Thus, in the traditional categories of literal versus allegorical, he is a literal interpreter who is not above sometimes allegorizing the text to explain the mysteries of God.

When considering parables, for example, he insists that our reading must start from 'what lies before our eyes and what is set forth openly and unambiguously word for word in the Scriptures. Hence the parables ought to be adapted to what is not ambiguous.'[72] This special concern against ambiguity characterizes his lessons on interpretation. 'For then the interpreter explains them without risk, and the parables are explained by all in the same sense, and the body of the truth remains unharmed.'[73] The consistency between parables and other texts offers an important principle: the nature of Scripture is that more clear parts should be used to interpret less immediately clear parts. However, those who begin by misreading parables 'will therefore ever seek, but never find, because he has rejected the method which makes it possible for him to find anything'.[74]

Although Irenaeus keeps his interpretation within the realm of the created order and the boundaries of his Christian world view, his own allegorical practice can be seen easily enough. The two daughters of Lot represent the Jews and the Gentiles, the father who gave them birth is the Word of God, and his sleeping in the tent is the condition of humanity before the Spirit gives new life. Additionally, Lot's wife's departure from Sodom to become a pillar of salt parallels how the church leaves behind the earthly world and becomes the salt of the earth.[75]

Norbert Brox points out how 'allegory is in many cases an instrument for typology' in Irenaeus. In a fair criticism, he cannot help but point out a biased judging of exegesis by this church father:

---

70. Ibid. 4.30.4, 4.19.1.
71. Ibid. 4.36.2.
72. Ibid. 2.27.1, tr. Norbert Brox, 'Irenaeus and the Bible: A Special Contribution', in Charles Kannengiesser (ed.), *Handbook of Patristic Exegesis: The Bible in Ancient Christianity* (Boston: Brill, 2004), vol. 1, p. 488.
73. Ibid. 2.27.1, tr. Brox, 'Irenaeus', vol. 1, p. 489.
74. Ibid. 2.27.2.
75. *Against Heresies* 4.31.1–3 (*ANF*).

> One may ask whether this is still the Irenaeus of the hermeneutical counsel we have seen so far, and must answer in the affirmative. For Irenaeus, it makes a difference who is allegorizing. If the Gnostics do it, they are doing what is forbidden. If Irenaeus does, he is expounding the Bible. If simple Christians (exposed to the Gnostics) do so, they are running an irresponsible risk for their faith. What determines legitimacy is the (orthodox) result . . . Irenaeus accepts allegorizing when it is devised within the church, or stems from his own hand, for then the correct meaning is assured through the proper surroundings.[76]

Here Irenaeus anchors his exegesis in catholicity, and can at least be credited with checking his interpretation with the tradition of the churches that he perpetually holds as a balance to any scriptural activities. 'If some question of minor importance should arise, would it not be best to turn to the most ancient churches, those in which the apostles lived, to receive from them the exact teaching on the question involved?'[77]

Most importantly, he is against a practice of allegory that ignores the historical and thus literal reading of prophecy, which endorses a doctrine contrary to the perceived orthodoxy of their day and our day. In a section on the literalness of the new Jerusalem on earth, he declares, 'Such events cannot be understood as occurring in the supercelestial regions . . . none of this can be taken allegorically, but everything is solid and true and substantial.'[78] Thus he is against a level of interpretation that rejects a basic level of the text so much that it lands in the realm of speculation. He accuses the Gnostics of twisting the Scriptures for their own causes: 'They try to adjust, in agreement with their statements, sometimes parables of the Lord, sometimes prophetic sayings, and sometimes apostolic words, so that their friction may not seem without witness.'[79]

Two other theological principles surrounding interpretation deserve attention in Irenaeus. First, this church father sees the whole economy of salvation laid out in the Word of God. Interpretation of the Word is unequivocally linked to the all-important economy of God in providence and salvation (below). Brox notes how this can be seen clearly in the parable of the vineyard, whose details represent key events in salvation history:

---

76. Brox, 'Irenaeus', vol. 1, p. 490.

77. *Against Heresies* 3.4.1.

78. Ibid. 5.35.2.

79. Ibid. 1.8.1.

> Step by step the details of the text are in the narrow sense allegorically interpreted and drawn into the story as a whole, in that they are all assigned meaning as parts of this whole. That is why Irenaeus' allegorical paraphrase matches so edifyingly with the biblical text.[80]

Secondly, this church father sees the Scriptures as being provided for spiritual health and growth: 'We should exercise ourselves in the investigation of the mystery and administration of the living God, and should increase in the love of Him who has done, and still does.'[81] The pastor Irenaeus finds the very purpose of writing *Against Heresies* to be the protection of those who might be destroyed by error. 'My feeling of affection prompts me to make known to you and all your companions those doctrines which have been kept in concealment until now, but which are at last, through the goodness of God, brought to light.'[82]

Such qualities prompt scholars like Mary Ann Donovan to speak of a 'sophisticated unity' of Irenaeus' writing that the contemporary church can appreciate.[83] Polemics, Scripture, exegesis, doctrine and faith weave together in a consistent and comprehensive theology that earns him credit for being the first to write as a theologian for the church, but who also is typical of any shepherd of the church.

Catholicity

Irenaeus provides a clear and important principle of catholicity for the true church in the ancient world. This notion has already found expression in his case for the apostolic tradition:

> The Church, having received this preaching and this faith, although scattered throughout the whole world, yet, as if occupying but one house, carefully preserves it. She also believes these points [of doctrine] just as if she had but one soul, and one and the same heart, and she proclaims them, and teaches them, and hands them down, with perfect harmony, as if she possessed only one mouth. For, although the languages of the world are dissimilar, yet the import of the tradition is one and the same.[84]

Irenaeus argues that true doctrine naturally occurs throughout the churches on the basis of the truth of the doctrine: 'As the sun, that creature of God, is

80. Translation from Brox, 'Irenaeus', vol. 1, p. 501.
81. *Against Heresies* 2.28.1 (*ANF*).
82. Ibid. 1.pref.2 (*ANF*).
83. Donovan, *One Right Reading*, p. 7.
84. *Against Heresies* 1.10.2 (*ANF*).

one and the same throughout the whole world, so also the preaching of the truth shineth everywhere, and enlightens all men that are willing to come to a knowledge of the truth.'[85] In fact, anything else is impossible:

> Nor will any one of the rulers in the Churches, however highly gifted he may be in point of eloquence, teach doctrines different from these (for no one is greater than the Master); nor, on the other hand, will he who is deficient in power of expression inflict injury on the tradition. For the faith being ever one and the same, neither does one who is able at great length to discourse regarding it, make any addition to it, nor does one who can say but little diminish it.[86]

He reiterates by imagining specific geographical examples:

> For the Churches which have been planted in Germany do not believe or hand down anything different, nor do those in Spain, nor those in Gaul, nor those in the East, nor those in Egypt, nor those in Libya, nor those which have been established in the central regions of the world.[87]

Flowing into this united reservoir of belief, as we have seen, is a source of inherited apostolic authority from the apostles to Polycarp and other sub-apostolic church leaders throughout Asia:

> But Polycarp also was not only instructed by apostles, and conversed with many who had seen Christ, but was also, by apostles in Asia, appointed bishop of the Church in Smyrna, whom I also saw in my early youth, for he tarried [on earth] a very long time, and, when a very old man, gloriously and most nobly suffering martyrdom, departed this life, having always taught the things which he had learned from the apostles, and which the Church has handed down, and which alone are true. To these things all the Asiatic Churches testify, as do also those men who have succeeded Polycarp down to the present time,– a man who was of much greater weight, and a more steadfast witness of truth, than Valentinus, and Marcion, and the rest of the heretics. He it was who, coming to Rome in the time of Anicetus caused many to turn away from the aforesaid heretics to the Church of God, proclaiming that he had received this one and sole truth from the apostles,– that, namely, which is handed down by the Church

---

85. Ibid. 1.10.2. Cf. 3.3.1, as well as 5.20.1: 'The path of those belonging to the church circumscribes the whole world . . . the same.'
86. Ibid. 1.10.2 (*ANF*).
87. Ibid. (*ANF*).

> . . . Then, again, the Church in Ephesus, founded by Paul, and having John remaining among them permanently until the times of Trajan, is a true witness of the tradition of the apostles.[88]

This authority–extension relationship again evidences the inescapable overlap between tradition, Scripture and catholicity. Notice that Irenaeus sees himself as a link in the chain of the apostolic tradition that offers credibility to his accusations against heresy, as well as justification for catholicity and orthodoxy.

Irenaeus has the essential beliefs of the Christian faith in view when he speaks of this standard doctrinal belief system, or this 'rule of faith'. If one were to list the scriptural features that embody true knowledge, it would sound like the Apostles' Creed. He acknowledges God as the Father Almighty and as creator, Jesus Christ as the Son of God who became incarnate for our salvation, and the Holy Spirit as inspiration to prophets. The foretold events include the incarnation, virgin birth, crucifixion, resurrection, ascension, future resurrection and judgment.[89] Concerning these truths, the church 'diligently guards them as living in one house, believes them as having one soul and heart, and consistently preaches, teaches, and hands them down as having one mouth'.[90]

The notion of catholicity captures the influence of numerous voices of church throughout the empire, and in turn offers credibility to the essentials of the faith that are lacking among the Gnostic churches. In the end, catholicity accompanies the apostolic tradition, the rule of faith and the use of Scripture in a powerful revelation of God that functions convincingly regarding the sincerity of what becomes – and even already is – orthodoxy. This is his most effective theological tool and the cornerstone of his legacy, especially given his location as first chapter in this volume.

God, creation and providence

Irenaeus declares, 'God being all Mind and all Logos says what he thinks and thinks what he says; for his Reasoning is Logos and Logos is Mind and all-containing Mind is the Father himself.'[91] Such remarks depict an author insistent upon the independence, aseity and sovereignty of the one, true God. While Justin and Polycarp seemed to reference and reverence God in their writings, Irenaeus seems to speak *about* God at a new level, stopping to imagine and

---

88. Ibid. 3.3.2–4 (*ANF*).
89. Ibid. 1.10.1.
90. Ibid. 1.10.2 (*ANF*).
91. Ibid. 2.28.5 (*ANF*).

dwell on the glory, majesty and sovereignty that surround him. While other apologists defended God, Irenaeus seems to introduce God personally. This mood in *Against Heresies* should not be missed, as this church father contrasts the all-glorious God with the artificial glory of the gnostic gods.

Doctrine of God

Irenaeus' God is not duped by the demiurge and does not overlook the creation of the world. Nor is he partial, sharing his glory with any demiurge, aeons or *plērōma*: 'How could there be above this God . . . another God, when it is necessary for the God of all things to contain everything in his immensity and be contained by none?'[92] Thus Eric Osborn speaks of God's opulence in Irenaeus: 'God's opulence exceeds our grasp . . . gnostic error expands human psychological distinctions into divisions and applies them to God. But the undivided is simple and is all good things at once.'[93] Qualities like unity, immediacy, universality, goodness, beauty and love construct this opulence, and Osborn points out that Irenaeus' rationale is as philosophical as it is biblical, and finds an anchor in a long-standing tradition of the cosmic, divine Intellect.[94] Irenaeus says God is 'rightly called all-embracing Mind . . . he is all Mind, all Spirit, all Mentality, all Thought, all Word, all Hearing, all Eye, all Light, and entirely the source of every good thing'.[95] Such treatments of God's attributes are regularly found in the work. In the episode below, Irenaeus provides an extensive list of all the major activities of God's hands, from creation through revelation to his people to salvation:

> He is the Former, He the Builder, He the Discoverer, He the Creator, He the Lord of all . . . He is the Father, He is God, He the Founder, He the Maker, He the Creator . . . He is just, He is good, He it is who formed man . . . He is the God of Abraham . . . He it is whom the law proclaims, whom the prophets preach, whom Christ reveals, whom the apostles make known to us, and in whom the Church believes. He is the Father of our Lord Jesus Christ.[96]

His systematic theology of God is always contrasted with the gnostic system, usually through *reductio ad absurdum* exercises that he seems to enjoy.[97]

---

92. Ibid. 2.1.2.
93. Osborn, *Irenaeus*, p. 30.
94. Ibid., pp. 31–33.
95. *Against Heresies* 2.13.3–4.
96. Ibid. 2.30.9 (*ANF*). Cf. 1.10.3, 1.22.1, 2.9.1, 3.25.1.
97. Lawson, *Biblical Theology*, p. 121.

He thinks it ridiculous that a lesser being could create the world against the divine will, when that would deny the omnipotence Irenaeus has established. It is ridiculous that the heavens would have various parts that comprise the divine: that would deny the simplicity Irenaeus established. Instead, almost devotional at times in his doctrine of God, Irenaeus insists:

> For faith in our Master will always remain firm, assuring us that he is the only true God, and that we should always love him, since he is the only Father, and that we should hope to receive and learn yet more from God, for he is good and has unlimited riches and a kingdom without end and immeasurable knowledge.[98]

Trinity

Irenaeus offers an extremely advanced doctrine of Christology when he explains the relationship between Jesus and God, the work of the Son in redemption, and the Spirit in the application of redemption. He asserts that 'the Son of God pre-existed, from the fact that the Father spake with Him, and before He was born revealed Him to men . . . this Christ who was with the Father, being the Word of the Father, was thereafter to be made flesh and became man'.[99] He explains how the Gnostics wrongly say that 'Jesus is different from Christ, another is Only-Begotten, still another is Word, and another is Savior, treating this last as "the emission of the Aeons fallen into the decline".'[100] Instead, 'the Father is Lord and the Son is Lord, and the Father is God and the Son is God; for that which is begotten of God is God'.[101] Additionally, he writes, 'There is shown forth One God, the Father, not made, invisible, creator of all things . . . through all is the Son, for through Him all things were made by the Father'.[102]

Irenaeus also offers an advanced trinitarian economic description when he explains how God works in relationship to the world and even within himself. The *Demonstration* alone explicitly states numerous activities of the members of the Trinity: in the Christian baptismal formula (3, 7), in the creation (5), in redemptive history (6–7, 30, 41, 89, 97), in glorifying himself alongside the angels (10), in the incarnation act (32–33), in the resurrection (42, 56), in the covenant with David (49–50), in divine approval of Christ's ministry (53), in

98. *Against Heresies* 2.28.3.
99. *Demonstration* 51, 53.
100. *Against Heresies* 3.16.8.
101. *Demonstration* 47.
102. Ibid. 5.

renewal of the world (89), and a core belief of orthodox doctrine (100). The Gnostics lack a recognition of the Trinity and thus lack a recognition of the true God: 'They reject the Father, or they accept not the Son and speak against the dispensation of His incarnation; or else they receive not the Spirit, that is, they reject prophecy.'[103]

The strength of Irenaeus' trinitarianism lies in his recognition that among the many individual activities of the Godhead, the economy of the Trinity does not contradict monotheism. The Father, Son and Spirit are distinct, but there is only one God. In *Demonstration* 5, Irenaeus explains, 'There is shown forth One God, the Father . . . above whom there is no other God, and after whom there is no other God.' Meanwhile, 'By the Word He created the things that were made . . . rightly and fittingly the Word is called the Son.' Finally, 'God is Spirit . . . the Spirit gives order and form to the diversity of the powers . . . rightly and fittingly the Spirit [is called] the Wisdom of God.'[104] Such an understanding of God cannot be modalistic. For Irenaeus, when God takes on flesh, he becomes present in creation alongside humanity. God's activity in the creation 'refers to the relation through the Word made flesh or the Spirit outpoured, of humanity in its integrity as creature, with God in His divine integrity'.[105]

Many passages in *Against Heresies* display a formula of 'The Two Hands of God' as an expression of the Trinity. Here, the two hands are metaphors for the activities of the Son and the Spirit, whom Irenaeus believes to be divine. John Lawson explains that Irenaeus uses the formula 'simply as a method of emphasizing that it is the Supreme God and none other who is the God of Creation'.[106] For example, Irenaeus writes:

> For always with him are his Word and Wisdom, the Son and the Spirit, through whom and in whom he made everything freely and independently, to whom he also speaks when he says, 'Let Us make man after our image and likeness' (1:26), taking the substance of the creatures from himself as well as the pattern of the things he adorned.[107]

God himself is represented in creation, and God as Trinity was present and active in the event. In the doctrine of creation. 'The Two Hands of God'

---

103. Ibid. 100.
104. Ibid. 5.
105. Ibid. 97; MacKenzie, *Irenaeus's* Demonstration, p. 230.
106. Lawson, *Biblical Theology*, p. 122.
107. *Against Heresies* 4.20.1.

expression sets an orthodox doctrine of creation over against the gnostic myth of a God oblivious to a demiurge who created. Lawson declares, 'It is itself the expression of the doctrine of an immediately present and active God . . . [and] consequentially denotes "direct action" as opposed to the intermediary angels of the Gnostic systems.'[108]

Creation

This church father affirmed both creation and redemption absolutely as acts of God. 'He it is who is creator of heaven and earth and all the world, and maker of angels and men, and Lord of all, through whom all things exist and by whom all things are sustained.'[109] The one true God 'by himself created and adorned and contains everything. This "everything" includes us and our world'.[110] In fact, Irenaeus' insistence that God is the sole creator seems like overkill in his writings. Hundreds of times he affirms divine creative activities in passing, over against the gnostic belief that another heavenly being created the world. For Irenaeus to reinforce this repeatedly is to bombard the very foundation of gnostic myth itself. If the Father created through the Son, then it deflates the gnostic myth seen in Basilides that authority over the universe lies with Archons because creation was outside the knowledge of God. Likewise, if God created the world good, then it undermines negative views of the human body and physical world seen in Marcion. Only Valentinus among Gnostics seems to maintain creation as the work of the Father. The belief is an essential one, Irenaeus declares: 'If a man be once moved away from the Creator of all things, and if he grant that this creation to which we belong was formed by any others or through any other, he must of necessity fall into much inconsistency, and many contradictions of sort.'[111] One Creator God worked through his two hands, the Son and Spirit, without intermediary angels or any other heavenly being: 'For always with him are his Word and Wisdom, the Son and the Spirit, through whom and in whom he made everything freely and independently.'[112]

---

108. Lawson, *Biblical Theology*, p. 122. Cf. *Demonstration* 11, which annunciates that the 'angels were stewards' only at creation. Lawson offers an important biblical justification for the imagery in Irenaeus, such as Isa. 48:13, 'My hand has laid the foundations of the earth,' and Luke 11:20, 'If by the finger of God I cast out demons, no doubt the Kingdom of God is come upon you.'
109. *Demonstration* 8.
110. *Against Heresies* 4.20.1.
111. Ibid. 4.32.1 (*ANF*).
112. Ibid. 4.20.1.

Economy

In Irenaeus one finds a very special component to the patristic view of the providence of God. This church father employs the notion of 'economy', *oikonomia,* to describe the perfect and intricate execution of salvation history from the fall to the eschaton, all in its own time.[113] All things are ordered by God. The Lord has always been with humanity, whom he created 'by means of various dispensations, and has wrought out many things', including his plan of salvation.[114]

Beginning with creation, 'Everything has been made with a profound harmony and a sublime art.'[115] Creation includes angelic beings, which are dependent beings in the larger ordering of God. Next, in providence, only God 'can enumerate one by one all the remaining objects which have been constituted by the power of God, and are governed by his wisdom'.[116] The miraculous is included in the divine actions on earth, 'the power of God in truth to benefit humanity', including spiritual gifts in the life of the church.[117] The patriarchs and Israel were chosen by God as instruments to receive salvation.[118] The prophets are strategically gifted to communicate the message of God, and Irenaeus argues that the work of the Lord, as in the election of the apostles, is not a 'meaningless and accidental thing', but 'with great wisdom and diligence, all things have clearly been made by God, fitted and prepared . . . for all things originate from one and the same God'.[119]

At the centre of his work of providence in the divine economy is the work of salvation in biblical history, 'Sketching out like an architect, the plan of salvation.'[120] The Fall is the first major milestone, the incarnation is the halfway point, and the resurrection and millennium are the end point. Grillmeier suggests that 'only through such a universal view could he be a match for the Gnostics'. Whereas gnostic *oikonomia* excluded flesh, Irenaeus' *oikonomia* includes the incarnation of Christ and his true historical redemption, enabling

113. For a thorough explanation of the breadth and complexity of the notion of 'economy' in Irenaeus' systematic theology, see Osborn, *Irenaeus*, pp. 49–94.
114. *Against Heresies* 4.28.2 (*ANF*).
115. Ibid. 2.26.3.
116. Ibid. 2.30.3 (*ANF*).
117. Ibid. 2.31.2, 2.32.4.
118. Ibid. 4.14.2–3.
119. Ibid. 2.25.1 (*ANF*).
120. Ibid. 4.14.2 (*ANF*).

him to outmanoeuvre gnostic rejection of the Old Testament, falsified eschatology, and docetic interpretation of the incarnation.[121]

The Spirit continues the work of Christ in redemption through dwelling among the people of God: 'Where the church is, there is the Spirit of God, and where the Spirit of God is, there is the church, and all kind of grace, and the Spirit is truth (1 John 5:6).'[122] This economy is not only maintenance but eschatological. John Behr notices that for Irenaeus, 'Human death plays a pedagogical role within the divine economy, enabling man to experience to the uttermost his weakness and mortality in apostasy from God, the only source of life.'[123]

In fact, every mention of the creation, the prophets, the Law, the apostles, biblical history, the Fall and the incarnation are part of a larger economy that is positive for Irenaeus, all part of what John Lawson calls 'the self-communicating love of God' at the very heart of Irenaean theology. 'This note rings out again and again throughout the work. Here is a mark that Irenaeus was a Christian indeed.'[124]

Recapitulation

Atonement in Irenaeus is larger in scope than generally came to be inherited by Western Christianity. Using the parallel of Adam and Christ in Romans 5, the church father explains that Christ obeyed where Adam failed, and the consequences of new life extend to the same degree and the same areas that sin extends: to all of creation, which will ultimately be redeemed at the eschaton. Irenaeus writes, 'On one hand, as a man he fought for the fathers and redeemed their disobedience by his obedience, on the other hand, he has bound the strong man, set free the weak and poured out salvation on the works of his hands, destroying sin.'[125] For him, atonement not only offers a legal solution to sin through redemption, the traditional Western emphasis, but actually extends to all of creation through the victorious work of Christ.

This correction comes not only to the sin of humanity, but functions further to inaugurate a humanity free of sin and spiralling into conformity to the perfect image of Christ. It is a 'recapitulation', a summing up in solution all the effects

121. Aloys Grillmeier, *Christ in the Christian Tradition*. Vol. 1: *From the Apostolic Age to Chalcedon (451)*, tr. John Bowden (London: Mowbrays, 1975), p. 98.

122. *Against Heresies* 3.24.1.

123. John Behr, *Asceticism and Anthropology in Irenaeus and Clement* (Oxford: Oxford University Press, 2000), p. 51; cf. *Against Heresies* 3.23.6.

124. Lawson, *Biblical Theology*, p. 129.

125. *Against Heresies* 3.18.6; tr. Osborn, *Irenaeus*, p. 95.

of the great problem of sin. Eric Osborn sees at least eleven ideas combining to construct the doctrine: unification, repetition, redemption, perfection, inauguration and consummation, totality, soteriology, ontology, epistemology and ethics. Matching the overview of 'economy' above, recapitulation finds need in a first phase, initialized at creation and justified by the Fall. A second phase is the incarnation, death and resurrection, in which the image of Adam finds restoration for all generations in sin. Finally, a third phase completes the equation when all creation, particularly redeemed humanity, will be recapitulated in judgment and perfection. All of these combine to depict the complete and all-encompassing love of God for humanity. This is the divine solution for sin: overturn its effects in renewed final glory. John Behr remarks,

> This is perhaps the most profound and beautiful reflection of Irenaeus: the vibrant unity between the glory of God and the living man, the life-giving manifestation of God and the vision of God by his creatures . . . for Irenaeus it is God who seeks to glorify man, bringing him to share ever more fully in his own glory.[126]

However, this is not really an independent doctrine or concept in Irenaeus, but a way of expressing the very beliefs of creation, hamartiology, soteriology, sanctification and eschatology he articulates in his works. The notion of recapitulation harmonizes with Eastern Christianity, which speaks more freely about the redemptive effects on the created order and more confidentially about individual sanctification. In the case of the latter, the Eastern doctrine of *theōsis* demonstrates how believers hope for radical transformation as they 'become like God' in this life in a way that goes beyond most Protestant doctrines of sanctification. This radical notion seems extreme for many evangelicals, who emphasize the reality of individual depravity and a fallen world, rather than individual perfection and a recapitulated creation. Concerning the millennial aspect of Irenaeus' doctrine of recapitulation, Eric Osborn explains:

> Many interpreters of Irenaeus have been embarrassed by his millenarianism. Surely evil has been overthrown in Christ, they say, and such fantasy is inappropriate. Yet Irenaeus and his readers today are part of a world where evil is alive and well. They need an apocalypse of the consummation, when God shall dwell with his people, when death, sorrow and evil shall be no more. The recapitulation of all things in Christ is the pledge of their hope.[127]

---

126. Behr, *Asceticism and Anthropology*, pp. 56–57.
127. Osborn, *Irenaeus*, p. 140.

For Irenaeus, recapitulation naturally extends all the way to the eschaton, making the millennium a more important point and eschatology a more important doctrine than it had been for prior church fathers. John Carroll remarks, 'For Irenaeus the second coming of Christ is simply the logical and graceful end of the whole of salvation history that God began in creation.'[128]

To complicate the doctrine even further, this recapitulation involves Mary with a key role. He insists that the Adamic parallel of Romans 5 necessitates Mary as a virgin and, in a way that makes Protestants uncomfortable, asserts that Mary's obedience parallels Eve's disobedience just as Christ's obedience parallels Adam's disobedience. God fashioned the first Adam 'from earth uncultivated and still virgin', pre-empting Christ to be born of a virgin.[129] Eve was disobedient while still a virgin, but Mary is found to be obedient. Eve's action led to death for the human race, while Mary's faithful action led to salvation for it. The betrothal between man and woman functions as 'signifying the recycling that Mary effected for Eve'. Irenaeus thus declares, 'The knot of Eve's disobedience was loosed by Mary's obedience, for what the virgin Eve had bound by her unfaith, the virgin Mary loosed by her faith.'[130] Jaroslav Pelikan recognizes that this is an important component to the case for the humanity and divinity of Jesus for Irenaeus. 'Mary had served as proof for the reality of the humanity of Jesus: he had truly been born of a human mother and therefore was a man.'[131] For Irenaeus, the Virgin Mary is the obedient Eve just as Christ is the obedient Adam.

Eschatology

All of his systematizing of Scripture, and all his doctrinal construction against the gnostic system, enables Irenaeus to work through a basic eschatology. He is among the first church fathers to do so. Just as it was essential to offer an explanation of the reason and accomplishment for the incarnation, so it was also to explain the second advent of Christ: 'All the prophets announced his two advents . . . the second in which He will come on the clouds, bringing on the day which burns as a furnace, and smiting the earth with the word of His

---

128. John T. Carroll, *The Return of Jesus in Early Christianity* (Peabody: Hendrickson, 2000), p. 158.

129. *Against Heresies* 3.21.10.

130. Ibid. 3.22.4.

131. Jaroslav Pelikan, *The Christian Tradition: A History of the Development of Doctrine.* Vol. 1: *The Emergence of the Catholic Tradition (100–600)* (Chicago: University of Chicago Press, 1971), p. 241; cf. *Against Heresies* 5.1.2.

mouth.'[132] This event is important in the larger orthodox scheme of salvation history, as here Christians get a further taste of glory. 'The [earthly] kingdom is the commencement of incorruption, by means of which kingdom those who shall be worthy are accustomed gradually to partake of the divine nature.'[133]

This church father is popularly noted for maintaining a literal, earthly, thousand-year reign of Christ following his second return. Charles Hill's work on patristic eschatology shows Irenaean influence by having two categories of Christian chiliasts: Irenaeus and other Ante-Nicene Christians. He calls the former 'by far the most extensive and best reasoned in Christian literature to [that] date, on the millennium'.[134] In fact, the new earth recreated in its eternal state is blurred with the thousand years of Revelation 20 – chiliastic but perhaps eternal.

Irenaeus offers a theology of the Antichrist and tribulation that is familiar to all who read Revelation in a futurist paradigm: the Antichrist will arise as in Revelation 13, associated with the man of lawlessness in 2 Thessalonians 2:3–7, the little horn of Daniel 8, and the tribe of Dan in Revelation 7, initiating a severe tribulation of three and one-half years in Daniel 7 and 9. Irenaeus speculates about the number 666 in Revelation 13, offering three names that represent its possibilities – all associated with the Roman Empire. This is a sample of his speculation:

> The word Euanthas has the required number but we cannot say anything about it. Also Lateinos has the number 666, and it is very likely because the last kingdom has this name, the Latins ruling at this time, but we make no boast about this. Also Teitan, with the two vowels epsilon and iota in the first syllable is of all those found among us, the most worthy of credit. It contains the number mentioned and consists of six letters, each syllable with three letters.[135]

Irenaeus maintains a sabbatarian theory that sees the creation week as a type for all of human history, the last 'day' or thousand years will be the millennial

132. Ibid. 4.33.1 (*ANF*).
133. Ibid. 5.32.1 (*ANF*).
134. Charles E. Hill, *Regnum Caelorum: Patterns of Millennial Thought in Early Christianity* (Grand Rapids: Eerdmans, 2001), p. 12. See pp. 11–20 for a thorough analysis of the Irenaean millennial passages. For a good treatment of Irenaeus' synthetic view of biblical eschatology, see Brian Daley, *The Hope of the Early Church: A Handbook of Patristic Eschatology* (Cambridge: Cambridge University Press, 1991), pp. 28–32.
135. *Against Heresies* 5.30.3.

era of rest. 'The world will come to an end in as many millennia as the days in which it was made . . . if the creation was finished in six days, it is clear that the end of the things will be in the 6,000th year.'[136] This millennial hope is part of a larger understanding and defence of creation for Irenaeus, not surprisely against the gnostic view of no future earthly hope or even resurrection. God's original creation will be restored without sin, and he uses the important passage of Romans 8:18–25 as evidence.[137] Interestingly, in Irenaeus the Eucharist also foreshadows the resurrection and thus gives us hope of our own bodily resurrection.[138]

Appropriating Irenaeus

The second century of Christianity was a crucial one. Looking back and trying to understand the conflict between the church and a religiously pluralistic society, as well as the conflict between the church and rising heresy, we see what would have been a radical paradigm shift in belief from the tradition of the apostles recorded in Scripture to the gnostic system of esoteric experience. A different shift could have altered the faith completely: no need for Christ's resurrection (1 Cor. 15:12–14), no hope in our own resurrection (1 Thess. 4:13), a radical altering of our view of the physical world resulting in extreme indulgence or extreme abstinence (1 Cor. 10:31), a discarding of the permanence and reliability of a written Scripture (Deut. 29:29), and a loss of unity and respect between Christian churches (Eph. 1:4–7). Although Gnostics probably did not number so high a percentage in antiquity as would Arians in the controversy to come, Gnosticism was no mere trend but an entire paradigm shift that could so have changed the nature of the faith that it would no longer have been true. Irenaeus stands alongside writers like Hippolytus, Tertullian and Epiphanius as second-century champions for the soul of orthodoxy, to help defeat the threat of united heresy.

This very struggle is the defining characteristic of Irenaeus' legacy in church history and the centrepiece to his presence in a volume on orthodoxy's foundation. His contribution to Christian thought is forever foiled against the heresies that nuance or reject the truth. Before the archaeological discovery of the Nag Hammadi manuscripts in 1945, Irenaeus was history's primary

136. Ibid. 5.28.3.

137. Ibid. 5.32.1, 5.36.1.

138. Ibid. 4.18.5; cf. Osborn, *Irenaeus*, p. 54.

source of gnostic writings and doctrine. Now he is the second most important source. His influence can be seen in works like Hippolytus' *Refutation of All Heresies* and Epiphanius' similar *Refutation of All Heresies*. Although many later church fathers do not embellish or even mention Irenaeus' influence on them or on the early church, the evidence is there. John Behr remarks, 'What Irenaeus achieved through his struggles with the Gnostics and others cannot be gainsaid, and there is perhaps no greater testimony to his theological legacy than that it passed unobserved.'[139] It is important to note that his opposition to Gnosticism was almost entirely doctrinal in nature, given the contemporary trend to view the gnostic controversy as political and centring on centralization of power in the early church. Eric Osborn remarks, 'His irenic approach shows that his objection to heresies on matters of faith had little to do with a struggle for power.'[140]

Contribution to orthodoxy

Even though his thoughts on numerous theological issues come to us in a context of a polemical struggle, we can filter the conflict and find extremely important clues to the mystery of the development of doctrine in the first few centuries. Perhaps most important is his treatment of Scripture, which was not yet in canonical form throughout Christian communities. Irenaeus successfully appeals to a notion of catholicity, that most churches everywhere in the late second century see a certain collection of writings to be Scripture.[141] He helps to prove that churches were not in disarray, uncertain of authoritative texts of the faith, but generally united in agreeing on most books and especially not agreeing on an entirely different and threatening genre of books: gnostic writings. Thus the voice of Irenaeus still disallows even contemporary gnostic fans like Elaine Pagels, critical historians like Bart Ehrman and popular

---

139. John Behr, *St. Irenaeus of Lyons On the Apostolic Preaching* (Crestwood, NY: St Vladimir's Seminary Press, 1997), p. 5.

140. Osborn, *Irenaeus*, p. 5.

141. Allert argues fairly that the clear notion of canonicity in the second century cannot be forced into finality, but that a definite 'leveling out occurs' then. This is how charitable a historian ought to be. Given the still imperfections of canon throughout the empire, he argues, 'There is no simple "canonical" versus "noncanonical" disctinction yet' (Craig D. Allert, *A High View of Scripture? The Authority of the Bible and the Formation of the New Testament Canon* [Grand Rapids: Baker Academic, 2007], p. 50). For a discussion of the formation of the canon in a need to suppress heresy, a phenomenon of which Irenaeus is typical, see pp. 93–103.

authors like Dan Brown. He is the first to refer to a four-Gospel canon, to defend most thoroughly the apostolic authority of the Gospel writers and Paul, and among the earliest defenders of the book of Revelation while still disputed among some churches.[142]

Thus he becomes a key figure in defending canonicity today. Robert Valshoz provides a definition of canonicity that does not insist on an actual single corpus or codex of a book – this is the final product for the people of faith:

> The concept or theory of canonicity pertains to the fundamental idea that a deity communicated a message in some form with man and that he in turn accurately recorded it . . . the idea of separate books as a sacred whole preceded [the compilation] process and should be separate from it.[143]

About the year 190, Irenaeus cites 2 Peter, arguably the most questionable New Testament book among contemporary critical scholars, as authoritative.[144] His canonical perspective seems to extend to the Apocrypha, but such a perspective is common among the early church fathers and the Roman and Eastern branches today, and it does not detract from his seemingly perpetual references and allusions to the New Testament Scriptures. In the end, Irenaeus does not necessarily provide the exact parameters of canon. Craig Allert offers an important balance: 'Clearly in Irenaeus, proper interpretation of the text is more important than the issues of the selection of the text. We must keep this in mind to avoid reading a twenty-first-century closed canon perspective into Irenaeus' argument for the four-fold Gospel.'[145]

Alongside his use of the Scriptures, the apostolic tradition is an important standard Irenaeus employs. By appealing to a 'rule of faith' among churches based on the teaching of the apostles, especially that recorded in the writings of Scripture, he preserves for the church a legitimate connection between the historical Jesus and the faith of the early church. A gnostic individual cannot simply claim a subjective vision from Christ, disconnected from the witness of the apostles and from the churches (2 Cor. 11:14). The phenomenon of the

---

142. *Against Heresies* 3.11.7–8, four-Gospel canon; 3.13.3–14.1, Luke and Paul; and 5.26–35, Revelation.

143. Robert Valshoz, *The Old Testament Canon in the Old Testament Church: The Internal Rationale for Old Testament Canonicity* (Lewiston, NY: Edwin Mellin, 1990), p. 1.

144. *Against Heresies* 5.23.2, 5.28.3.

145. Allert, *High View*, p. 124.

authority of the apostolic tradition would come to be made a principle for the church in the age to come by Vincent of Lérins in the fifth century: *quod ubique, quod semper, quod ab omnibus*. These are beliefs and practices known 'everywhere, always, by all'.[146]

Irenaeus' use of the apostolic tradition has been employed by Roman Catholicism for an additional aspect, however, that Protestants reject. The Protestant branch of the faith sees Irenaeus as an advocate of Roman papal supremacy, that the tradition of Peter in Rome alongside the principle of apostolic tradition handed down to churches applies in an ecclesiastical fashion to the authority of the bishop of Rome as the head of the church on earth. After all, Irenaeus declares, 'For it is necessary for every church – that is, the believers from everywhere – to agree with this church, in which the tradition from the apostles has always been preserved.'[147] Likewise, 'The church that is the greatest, most ancient, and known to all, founded and set up by the two most glorious apostles Peter and Paul at Rome, while showing that the tradition and the faith it proclaims to men comes down through the successions of bishops even to us.'[148] However, apostolic tradition in the notion of a rule of faith does not necessitate a doctrine of ecclesiological or apostolic succession stemming from Peter to the bishop of Rome today.

The context of gnostic controversy is important in the debate – Irenaeus appeals to tradition over against esoteric visions from Christ, not to the Roman see over the rest of the worldwide church. Bruce Shelley points out, 'Up to the time of Constantine history offers no conclusive evidence that the bishop of Rome exercised jurisdiction outside of Rome. Honor, yes; jurisdiction, no.'[149] However, Protestants should beware of reducing apostolic tradition to scriptural texts alone; it is impossible to separate tradition and Scripture in Irenaeus. John Lawson insists, 'To inquire whether tradition or Scripture is the primary authority is to obscure the mind of Irenaeus.'[150] Many Protestants

---

146. Vincent of Lérins, *A Commonitory*, in Philip Schaff and Henry Wace (eds.), *A Select Library of the Nicene and Post-Nicene Fathers of the Christian Church* [*NPNF*], 2nd series (Grand Rapids: Eerdmans, repr. 1998), vol. 11, 2.6.
147. *Against Heresies* 3.3.2.
148. Ibid. Emmanuel Lanne rightly argues that 'most glorious' centres on the apostles' martyrdom, not their ecclesiastical legacy in Rome (Emmanuel Lanne, 'Église de Rome "a gloriosissimis duobus apostolis Petro et Paulo romae fundatae et constitutae ecclesiae" (Adv Haer III 3:2)', *Irénikon* 49 [1976], pp. 275–322).
149. Bruce L. Shelley, *Church History in Plain Language* (Dallas: Word, 1995), p. 134.
150. Lawson, *Biblical Theology*, p. 103. Cf. Rowan Greer quote, n. 150, above.

are too suspicious of tradition, and too many lack an understanding of the development of doctrine and canon.

Irenaeus helps contemporary Christianity to recognize the genuinely developmental aspects of Scripture and canon alongside the divine providence over it. In particular, Christians need to recognize how a historical and natural process within the church was necessary to find agreement on the authority of certain apostolic-era books considered Scripture. To neglect this process at best presumes a miraculous appearance of Scripture, and at worst sits unaware while scholarly advocates of the Bauer thesis control history.[151] For the early church, the litmus test was the apostolic credibility of the book – is this book widely accepted as linked to an apostolic figure, and does it represent the teachings of Christ through that apostle? This natural sifting is no different than so many other ways that God worked mysteriously in the seemingly natural aspects of the lives of biblical men and women, and for the early church the early recognition of Scripture was undeniably blurred with a sense of tradition.[152]

Meanwhile, the church should caution against the semi-gnostic tendency to dichotomize this world and our actions from our faith beliefs. Nick Perrin suggests that Western Christians who radically separate what they believe or practice on Sunday from the rest of the week 'betray their having succumbed unwittingly to a Gnostic script'.[153]

Along the theme of tradition, the writings of Irenaeus contain other theological elements that come to contribute to larger leanings in the early church, as well as the Roman Catholic and Eastern Orthodox branches. His use of Mary as an obedient Eve alongside the work of Christ is an early reference to a later trend to reverencing Mary and recognizing her as a key plan of God's plan of redemption. Without necessarily making her co-Redeemer, Irenaeus parallels her to Christ in obedience and offers a more symmetrical view of a redemption that is biblically unnecessary. Additionally, for him, an association is made between Mary and Christ's humanity that is influential in Christianity.[154]

---

151. The Bauer thesis was introduced in n. 2 above, whose advocates minimize the theological dimension of rejecting heresies and canonical books and exaggerate the political and polemical in the early church.

152. For a good explanation of the relationship between Scripture and tradition in the early church from an evangelical perspective, see D. H. Williams, *Retrieving the Tradition and Renewing Evangelicalism: A Primer for Suspicious Protestants* (Grand Rapids: Eerdmans, 1999), pp. 41–132.

153. Perrin,'Irenaeus and Lyotard', p. 138.

154. Pelikan, *Christian Tradition*, vol. 1, p. 241. Cf. *Against Heresies* 5.1.2; *Demonstration* 33.

Still, this is used in various ways. Catholic apologist Scott Hahn argues that Irenaeus serves in an important place in the development of Mary in the current Roman Catholic sense.[155] M. C. Steenberg posits a reading of Irenaeus that finds in Mary's person an integral and essential component of a theologically coherent system of personal and social recapitulation.[156] Mary veneration is only minor in Irenaeus, but it is still appropriate to associate such elevation of her with him.

Another high-church tradition that finds sypmpathy in this church father is the doctrine of transubstantiated communion. Irenaeus speaks as if the eucharistic elements are physically changed into the body and blood of Christ:

> Just as the bread which is from the earth, receiving the invocation of God, is now not common bread but Eucharist, constituted from two things, earthly and heavenly, so our bodies receiving the Eucharist are no longer corruptible, having the hope of resurrection.[157]

Such a position was popular in early-church sacramental theology through Augustine and into medieval Christianity, although we cannot be sure how influential the individual Irenaeus was to that process. In fact, one should beware of appropriating metaphorical language into literal reality among the fathers, but in the case of later eucharistic beliefs in the West, it seems appropriate to recognize a hope of transubstantiation in Irenaeus.

Likewise, perhaps the earliest justification for infant baptism can be found in Irenaeus:

> He came to save all men through himself: all, I mean, who through him are reborn into God, infants and children and boys and you men and elders. Therefore he passed through every age, and among infants was an infant, sanctifying infants.[158]

Everett Ferguson cautions against presuming infant baptism here, as Christ's sanctification of every age of life is part of the larger Irenaean recapitulation. Additionally, elsewhere Irenaeus speaks of infant naivety to sin and thus perhaps

---

155. Scott Hahn, *Hail, Holy Queen: The Mother of God in the Word of God* (New York: Random House, 2006), pp. 71–73.

156. M. C. Steenberg, 'The Role of Mary as Co-recapitulator in St Irenaeus of Lyons', *Vigiliae christianae* 58.2 (2004), pp. 117–137. The author argues against the possibility that Irenaeus is driven primarily by aesthetic concerns.

157. *Against Heresies* 4.18.5, tr. Donovan, *One Right Reading*, p. 743.

158. *Against Heresies* 2.22.4.

not needing a baptism that expects a forgiveness of inherited guilt from Adam.[159] He is certainly appropriated by paedobaptist advocates, though. Irenaeus' greatest contribution to the doctrine of baptism is the rich merging of imagery that comes with connecting forgiveness, cleansing, faith and the Holy Spirit.

The doctrines of God, Trinity, creation, providence, salvation and pneumatology find hall-of-fame-calibre articulation and defence in Irenaeus. He clearly argues for one God in three persons, in an age well before the trinitarian and Christological controversies of the fourth and fifth centuries. The fifth-century church historian Socrates names Irenaeus among four who represent ecclesiastical tradition influencing Nicaea on the person of Christ.[160] Iain MacKenzie remarks, 'There is little, if anything, in the Nicene formula which is not present in embryonic or directional form in the works of Irenaeus.' He further remarks that although the great champion of orthodoxy at Nicaea does not mention his predecessor in his writings, 'It is impossible to claim without question that he was beholden directly to the works of Irenaeus.'[161] To have Athanasius beholden to a predecessor is a great historical and theological honour to that predecessor, indeed.

Irenaeus argues for divine creation and providence in a way that contemporary Christianity takes for granted. Although the church today asks questions of theodicy like 'Where is God in a world of suffering?', Irenaeus had to defend God at an even more basic level: 'Did God create the world or did some demiurge when God was oblivious?' and 'If God did not control creation and Old Testament activities, can he really control his creation and our civilizations today?' An important doctrine of providence is at work in Irenaeus that finds explicit application in his protégé Hippolytus. Besides influencing him on anti-heretical apologetics, exegesis and eschatology, principles of Irenaean theodicy can be seen in Hippolytus' justification for martyrdom – a phenomenon that could have devastated the church.[162]

Irenaeus reinforces the essential Christian doctrine of gracious salvation, especially over against humanist and Pelagian theories in later generations. For

---

159. Everett Ferguson, *Baptism in the Early Church: History, Theology, and Liturgy in the First Five Centuries* (Grand Rapids: Eerdmans, 2009), p. 308; *Against Heresies* 4.28.3.

160. Socrates, *Ecclesiastical History* (*NPNF*, 2nd series , vol. 2, 3.7; cf. 5.22).

161. MacKenzie, *Irenaeus's* Demonstration, pp. 29–30. See pp. 29–34 for a summary of Irenaean influence on later church fathers.

162. W. Brian Shelton, *Martyrdom from Exegesis in Hippolytus: An Early Church Presbyter's Commentary on Daniel* (Milton Keynes: Paternoster, 2008), pp. 22–24, 43–44, 103–108, 123–126, and applied in theodicy, 96–101.

him, salvation is by the grace of God: 'Whereby receiving salvation, we continually give thanks to God who by his great, inscrutable and unsearchable wisdom delivered us . . . which we by ourselves could not attain.'[163] However, his legacy lies not in the cause of salvation as much as in its effects. The comprehensive reach of God in salvation, and the extent of optimism of its effects in his doctrine of recapitulation stand unmatched in the early church. Perrin remarks, 'For Irenaeus, the formation of a thoroughgoing Christian worldview was not an option; it followed logically and necessarily on the heels of the Incarnation.'[164]

His notion of the extent of sanctification that lies in the potential for an already active recapitulation in the world has lent itself to two doctrinal ideas popular in Eastern Christianity: *apokatastasis* and *theosis*. Both deserve consideration in the larger influence of Irenaeus on the Christian faith, and an important lesson in how to appropriate the fathers. The Greek term *apokatastasis* means 'restoration' and finds biblical precedence in Acts 3:21, '[Jesus] whom heaven must receive until the period of restoration of all things about which God spoke by the mouth of His holy prophets from ancient time' (NASB). The term describes the final effects of salvation, without insisting on universalism, and characterizes the hope of many Eastern writers, especially Origen and Gregory of Nyssa. Alongside it, the Greek term *theosis* describes the end result of the salvation process for the individual – one's sanctification – but anticipates it more highly than Western Christianity. Irenaeus merges the two ideas: 'The [earthly] kingdom is the commencement of incorruption, by means of which kingdom those who shall be worthy are accustomed gradually to partake of the divine nature.'[165]

Sanctification's effect on an individual's life is a particularly optimistic concept in Irenaeus, who declares, 'Jesus Christ our Lord, who because of his immeasurable love became what we are in order to make us what he is.'[166] Both of these ideas resonate throughout early and contemporary Eastern Christianity, and their strong incarnational basis is essential for liturgy, iconography and sacramentology.[167] In an interesting assessment on patristic

---

163. *Demonstration* 97. See MacKenzie, *Irenaeus's* Demonstration, p. 230.

164. Perrin, 'Irenaeus and Lyotard', p. 138.

165. *Against Heresies* 5.32.1 (*ANF*).

166. Ibid. 5.pref.; cf. 3.18.7.

167. For a case for a perfect union with God made possible by grace, see Christoforos Stavropoulos, 'Partakers of Divine Nature', in Daniel B. Clendenin (ed.), *Eastern Orthodox Theology: A Contemporary Reader* (Grand Rapids: Baker Academic, 2003), pp. 183–192. This book contains several essays offering the incarnational foundationalism of Orthodoxy.

soteriology, Donald Fairbairn suggests that Irenaeus' exegesis plotted a 'personal trajectory' centring on personhood in Christ.[168] Emphasizing 'corruption' followed by 'adoption', Irenaeus anticipated sanctification not in mystical participation but in an individual unity, sharing Jesus' eternal life and incorruption. Fairbairn offers this as a healthy correction to evangelicals who prize relationship with God with insufficient understanding of it.[169]

The unity and precision of God's comprehensive plan finds a special advancement in Irenaeus' writings. Based on the divine attributes of grace and love, a premeditated and seamless plan to restore humanity was at work. Biblical history for Irenaeus is not only a scriptural record but a worldview of understanding God's beginning, ongoing and salvific relationship with the world and his creatures. The organization of Irenaeus' systematic theology is first and foremost biblical in a way that is certainly influential in the church, and celebrated by all believers who recognize the place of the Word of God as the supreme revelation. James Dupuis views Irenaeus as 'organizing systematically the theology for which Justin had laid the foundation, in his theology of the Logos-revelation'.[170] Irenaeus does not absolutely replace the Old Testament with the New, but appropriates it in Christ in a way that recognizes unity with the plan of God. Terry Tiessen sees that 'Irenaeus celebrated the superiority of Christian doctrine and life to all of the law';[171] the church father recognized that, in a way essential for the early church to understand, its augmentation in Christ did not mean cancellation of the Law. For him, the Old Testament points both to the humanity and the divinity of Christ, as prophecies evidence. Not only is this Irenaeus' theology, but his very style of reading Scripture and understanding of revelation and of salvation history. From creation flows providence, from providence flows permission for Adamic sin, which leads to divine solution in covenants, ultimately in Christ's incarnation and redemption, that will be finalized at the eschaton. Like the apologists alongside him, he is philosophical and rhetorical in approach, but these skills are quickly eclipsed by his biblical approach. His philosophical skills are as basic as his biblical theology is advanced.

Since Irenaeus is the earliest advanced chiliast in the early church, many scholars and laypeople lay claim to him as an advocate of their view. However, such

---

168. Donald Fairbairn, 'Patristic Soteriology: Three Trajectories', *Journal of the Evangelical Theological Society* 50 (2007), pp. 289–310.

169. Ibid., p. 309.

170. Terrance L. Tiessen, *Irenaeus on the Salvation of the Unevangelized* (Metuchen, NJ: Scarecrow, 1993), p. 6.

171. Ibid., p. 17.

a reading can be naive. For example, Mark Hitchcock and Thomas Ice claim Irenaeus as part of an orthodox premillennialism in church history that was 'suppressed by the Catholic Church'.[172] Bock and Blaising recognize that Irenaeus 'periodizes history according to covenants', and thus conclude 'this shows the natural way in which dispensation can be extended in the periodization of biblical history'.[173] Unfortunately, progressive dispensational 'periodization' involves many elements to which Irenaeus did not subscribe, and such claims are misleading. DeMar and Gumerlock have argued that one can no longer simply marshal Irenaeus into a dispensational, premillennial system simply because he uses a principle of periodization and anticipates an earthly reign of Christ. For example, Irenaeus offers a 'late' dating of Revelation under Domitian, which is one of four possible theories of dating among the church fathers themselves.[174]

Conclusion

In a pivotal era that some contemporary scholars frame to be a struggle for various Christianities, and either imply or insist on the legitimacy of all voices that claim any version of Jesus, Irenaeus is the distinct figure viewed as shaping orthodoxy – with congratulation or condemnation. In fact, his success and association with controversial doctrines easily allow critics to charge Irenaeus with exploitation. A proponent of keeping unity with celebrants of a different dating of Easter (quartodeciminians) but an enemy of gnostic churches, he could be charged with picking and choosing his strain of truth. A constructor of theology who buttresses his Adam–Christ parallel with Eve–Mary, he could be charged with Catholic Mariology. A promoter of the profound unity between Christian and Christ, he could be charged with mysticism and perfection. However, he stands for truth preserved in the Scriptures, a belief that translates to real life, and the doctrines that helped shape orthodoxy in its formative years. From his masterful treatise *Against Heresies* and his smaller summative work *Demonstration of the Apostolic Teaching* his theological principles were used by the church to frame doctrine for almost its whole history: God,

172. Mark Hitchcock and Thomas Ice, *The Truth Behind Left Behind: A Bibilical View of the End Times* (Multnomah, OR: Multnomah, 2004), p. 197.

173. Craig A. Blaising and Darrell L. Bock, *Progressive Dispensationalism* (Grand Rapids: Baker, 1993), p. 116.

174. Gary DeMar and Francis Gumerlock, *The Early Church and the End of the World* (Powder Springs, Ga.: American Vision, 2006), pp. 127–135.

creation, providence, history, economy, salvation, resurrection, church and basic pneumatology. His presence in this volume is to be expected.

Irenaeus displays a doctrinal solidity and accuracy that does not seem so different from that of historic and contemporary Christianity. This is because Irenaeus is both typical and influential, descriptive and prescriptive. He is representative of an already established tradition that comes to be called orthodoxy. He also helps to solidify the tradition in offensive and defensive ways. Still, we cannot always distinguish between the doctrines Irenaeus already knows and accepts, and those he helps to develop. At the very least, we must grant him systematic pioneering of theology leading us to hail him 'genius'. John Lawson applauds the talent behind his legacy even more: 'Irenaeus is a man of many-sided genius.'[175]

Bibliography

Primary sources: original languages

Adversus Haereses, Patrologiae cursus completus: Series graeca [PG], ed. J.-P. Migne, 162 vols. (Paris: Cerf, 1857–86), vol. 7. Although the PG database contains a good portion of the Greek texts, it is not exhaustive.

Contre les heresies: dénonciation et réfutation de la gnose au nom menteur, livre 1, Sources chrétiennes [SC] 263–264, tr. Adelin Rousseau (Paris: Cerf, 1979). The SC series provides the text in the original language of the primary manuscripts with a French translation on the opposite page. In the case of Irenaeus' *Against Heresies*, the original text is in Greek in all five volumes listed here.

Contre les heresies: dénonciation et réfutation de la gnose au nom menteur, livre 2, Sources chrétiennes 293–294, 2nd ed., tr. Adelin Rousseau (Paris: Cerf, 1982).

Contre les heresies: dénonciation et réfutation de la gnose au nom menteur, livre 3. Sources chrétiennes 210–211, tr. Adelin Rousseau (Paris: Cerf, 1974).

Contre les heresies: dénonciation et réfutation de la gnose au nom menteur, livre 4, Sources chrétiennes 100, tr. Adelin Rousseau (Paris: Cerf, 1965).

Contre les heresies: dénonciation et réfutation de la gnose au nom menteur, livre 5, Sources chrétiennes 152–153, tr. Adelin Rousseau (Paris: Cerf, 1969).

Démonstration de la prédication apostolique, Sources chrétiennes 406, tr. L. M. Froidevaux (Paris: Cerf, 1995). The *Demonstration* comes to us only in Armenian and is not included in PG databases, but this volume is a Greek version with a French translation on opposite pages.

---

175. Lawson, *Biblical Theology*, p. 133.

Primary sources: English translations

Against Heresies, in Alexander Roberts and James Donaldson (eds.), *The Ante-Nicene Fathers* [*ANF*], vol. 1 (Grand Rapids: Eerdmans, 1953). The most popular set of early Christian writings, this series has a corresponding Nicene and Post-Nicene Fathers dual series and is available free online at <http://www.ccel.org/fathers.html>, accessed 4 Dec. 2009.

Against the Heresies, vol. 1, tr. D. J. Unger and J. J. Dillon, Ancient Christian Writers 55 (New York: Paulist, 1992). An excellent, more recent translation of the work – recommended over the *ANF* (above), if available.

Demonstration of the Apostolic Preaching: *A Theological Commentary and Translation*, ed. Iain M. MacKenzie, tr. J. Armitage Robinson (Burlington, Vt.: Ashgate, 2002).

Fragments from the Lost Writings of Irenaeus, in *ANF*, vol. 1. Fragments attributed to Irenaeus in secondary patristic and medieval literature, such as citations in Eusebius' *Ecclesiastical History*.

On the Apostolic Preaching, tr. John Behr (Crestwood, NY: St Vladimir's Seminary Press, 1997).

Proof of the Apostolic Preaching, Ancient Christian Writers 16, tr. Joseph P. Smith (Westminster, Md.: Newman, 1952).

Translation against Heresies: On the Detection and Refutation of the Knowledge Falsely So Called, tr. Robert M. Grant, *Irenaeus of Lyons*, The Early Church Fathers (New York: Routledge, 1997). Numerous select passages are translated here, not the entire work.

Secondary sources (1st tier)

Donovan, Mary Ann, *One Right Reading? A Guide to Irenaeus* (Collegeville, MN: Liturgical, 1997). Claiming to treat Irenaeus' argument for one right reading of Scripture against gnostic claims, Donovan's work is insightful, thorough and very helpful for understanding this church father. It contains biographical material and commentary on larger sections of *Against Heresies*, grouping the work's parts into treatments on heresy, Christ, salvation and eschatology.

Grant, Robert M., *Irenaeus of Lyons*, The Early Church Fathers (New York: Routledge, 1997). Perhaps the best introduction to Irenaeus' thought and theology, this work combines biography and a new translation of key passages from every section of *Against Heresies*.

MacKenzie, Iain M., *Irenaeus's* Demonstration of the Apostolic Preaching: *A Theological Commentary and Translation*, tr. J. Armitage Robinson (Burlington, VT: Ashgate, 2002). A well-written treatment on the background and content of the *Demonstration*, it also contains an excellent introduction to the church father.

Minns, Denis, *Irenaeus: An Introduction* (New York: T. & T. Clark, 2009). Only slightly modified since its original version in 1952, it offers a general explanation to Irenaean theology, particularly the most important and unique aspects of his contribution to Christian history.

OSBORN, ERIC, *Irenaeus of Lyons* (New York: Cambridge University Press, 2001). The single most thorough book on Irenaeus, it analyses Irenaean thinking, theology and style while acknowledging the difficulties in reading Irenaeus.

Secondary sources (2nd tier)

BEHR, JOHN, *St. Irenaeus of Lyons On the Apostolic Preaching* (Crestwood, NY: St Vladimir's Seminary Press, 1997).

BROX, NORBERT, 'Irenaeus and the Bible: A Special Contribution', in Charles Kannengiesser (ed.), *Handbook of Patristic Exegesis: The Bible in Ancient Christianity*, vol. 1 (Boston: Brill, 2004), pp. 483–506. An in-depth treatment of the key principles and interests of Irenaean exegesis.

DONOVAN, MARY ANN, 'Irenaeus in Recent Scholarship', *Second Century* 4.4 (1984), pp. 219–241. This article identifies issues still key in Irenaean scholarship.

FAIRBAIRN, DONALD, 'Patristic Soteriology: Three Trajectories', *Journal of the Evangelical Theological Society* 50 (2007), pp. 289–310. An assessment of Irenaean exegesis on salvation contrasted to other methodologies in the early church.

HOFFMAN, DANIEL, *The Status of Women and Gnosticism in Irenaeus and Tertullian*, Studies in Women and Religion 36 (Lewiston, NY: Edwin Mellen, 1995). Through analysis of key passages in Irenaean literature, this work challenges Elaine Pagels' claim that women in early orthodox Christian communities had a lower status compared to women in gnostic communities.

JOURJON, MAURICE, 'Irenaeus's Reading of the Bible', in Paul M. Blowers (ed. and tr.), *The Bible in Greek Christian Antiquity* (Notre Dame: University of Notre Dame Press, 1997), pp. 105–111.

LAWSON, JOHN, *The Biblical Theology of Saint Irenaeus* (London: Epworth, 1948). This older work offers a good treatment of Irenaeus' use of Scripture and important theological features.

OSBORN, ERIC, 'Irenaeus: Rocks in the Road', *Expository Times* 14 (2003), pp. 255–258. A helpful introduction to the difficulties of reading Irenaeus, and a brief overview of Osborne's larger work *Irenaeus of Lyons.*

TIESSEN, TERRANCE L., 'Gnosticism as Heresy: The Response of Irenaeus', *Didaskalia* (2007), pp. 31–48. A good summary of the difficulties of Gnosticism combined with the rationale and methodology for Irenaeus to reject this dualistic system on both philosophical and theological grounds.

—, *Irenaeus on the Salvation of the Unevangelized* (Metuchen, NJ: Scarecrow, 1993). Tiessen unpacks Irenaeus' use of Logos in his description of salvation to posit a universal self-revelation of God that draws the non-Christian to Christ.

Unger, Dominic J., 'Introduction', *St. Irenaeus of Lyons: Against the Heresies*, Ancient Christian Writers 55 (Mahwah, NJ: Paulist, 1992). An excellent overview prefacing this important historical work.

Vallée, Gérard, *A Study in Anti-Gnostic Polemics: Irenaeus, Hippolytus, and Epiphanius*, Studies in Christianity and Judaism 1 (Ontario: Wilfrid Laurier University Press, 1981).

Vogel, Jeff, 'The Haste of Sin, the Slowness of Salvation: An Interpretation of Irenaeus on the Fall and Redemption', *Anglican Theological Review* 89 (2007), pp. 443–459. An important overview of two crucial doctrines in Irenaeus.

2. TERTULLIAN

Gerald Bray

Life and writings

Quintus Septimius Florens Tertullianus, the man we know as Tertullian, was born to a pagan family in Carthage (North Africa) sometime around the middle of the second Christian century. He was converted to Christianity as an adult, sometime before the year 196, though the details of this event have not come down to us. He must have come from a well-to-do family which could afford to give him an excellent classical education, and given his vast literary output, it seems likely that he never had to work for a living. He was still alive in 212, but had probably died by the time that Cyprian embarked on his career in the Carthaginian church (sometime after 220). There is no indication that he was a martyr for his faith, or that he was ever molested by the authorities. Traditions that he was a lawyer, or that he was a presbyter in the church are unsubstantiated and must be regarded as unproved. So too is the widespread belief that in mid-career he joined the Montanist sect, which preached the approaching end of the world and advocated a rigorous ascetical discipline. There is no doubt that Tertullian sympathized with the Montanists and defended them against attack because he shared their basic moral beliefs, but to say that he broke with the mainline church at Carthage and joined the sect is taking the evidence we have too far. Though he was never declared a saint of the church, he was never branded a schismatic either, and his works were widely read in North Africa at least until the time of Augustine. This would not have happened if there had been any serious doubt about his attachment to the church, and so we ought to assume that he remained within it, even though he became ever more fiercely critical of it as time went on.

Virtually everything we know about Tertullian has to be inferred from his writings, which are voluminous. He was not the most prolific Christian author from the time of persecution (an honour that belongs to Origen), but it seems that almost everything he wrote has survived, which means that we have a more complete picture of his thought than we have from any other writer before the fourth century. There are thirty-one extant treatises that are regarded as authentic, which take up about 1,500 pages in the most recent critical edition. Perhaps the most important thing about his writings is that they cover a wide range of subjects and give us a more detailed picture of everyday Christian life than anything else before the fourth century. However unusual a person he may have been himself, in his works we get the feel of life as it really was at the time, and can see the challenges and dilemmas confronting ordinary Christians more clearly than in any other ancient author. The fact that Tertullian was a prominent member of the church without being one of its official leaders is an additional plus in this respect. He was clearly not bound to toe the party line and felt entirely free to criticize the church and its leaders whenever he wished to. This gives his books a freshness and authenticity unique in the ancient world, even if we have to be careful about drawing too many conclusions from his frequently unguarded statements.

Tertullian was the first significant Christian writer to use Latin as his medium, and was always widely read in the Western church. His style is caustic and highly memorable, though unfortunately his words have often been distorted or taken out of context by readers unable to appreciate his deep sense of irony. For example, he never said, 'I believe because it is absurd,' and his famous 'What has Athens to do with Jerusalem?' was not meant to be read as an anti-philosophical remark. On the contrary, Tertullian was deeply engaged with philosophical issues and offers us a virtually unique portrait of a Christian Stoic. What he was concerned to show was that Christian faith went far beyond the limitations of pagan philosophy, and offered solutions to problems that the non-Christian world could not come to on its own. Reason was always the handmaid of Tertullian's faith, but it remained a very active servant, and his genius for stating complex philosophical and theological issues in a clear and compelling way ensured that the Latin-speaking church was spared much of the turmoil that disturbed the Greek-speaking world in the fourth and fifth centuries.

Tertullian had an encyclopedic knowledge of the Christian Scriptures, which he must have read in Greek, since there was no Latin translation available in his day, and he had a thorough knowledge of Roman history and literature. Many of his pastoral examples were taken from Roman legends, rather than from the Bible, perhaps because both he and his readers would have been more immediately familiar with their own national history. It is interesting to note that although he referred to every New Testament book except two (2 and 3 John) as Scripture, he never wrote a commentary on any of them, nor has he left us any sermons. He believed that the Bible was the Word of God in written form and was perfectly capable of using it responsibly in debate with both heretics and unbelievers, but the closest he seems to have got in terms of systematic interpretation of it was a short statement of beliefs that we now accept as belonging to one of the traditions behind our own Apostles' Creed.

Tertullian had a good grasp of Stoic philosophy, particularly in the form in which it had appealed to the great Roman educator Seneca, whom he regarded as a kind of anonymous Christian. Stoicism made Tertullian a 'materialist', in the sense that he believed that spirit was a highly refined form of matter, and this belief was sufficient to mark him out from the Christian writers of later generations, who virtually all rejected this position. However, it is a remarkable tribute to Tertullian's sense of the inner coherence of Christian theology that his materialism was not sufficient to discount the value of his writings, even to those who no longer accepted his fundamental philosophical principles, and they have survived to the present day as one of the most important sources of early Christian doctrine.

Tertullian's legal knowledge was good though not particularly extensive, and he drew freely on Roman legal terms and concepts when formulating his own theology. To a remarkable extent, the terms he chose have remained current in Western Christianity to the present day, and continue to influence our way of thinking. For example, he was the first writer to use the Latin words *persona* and *substantia* to describe the three and one in God, and was responsible for introducing the word *sacramentum* (oath) as a description for the rite of baptism.

Tertullian was a master of Latin rhetorical style, which he used in a highly effective and individual way. It is impossible to read him without being struck by his form of expression, and he is easily the most quotable of all the early Christian writers. His knowledge of Greek is uncertain, though he presumably read the language well enough to understand the Bible, but he had the traditional Roman dislike of Greeks as people and seems to have preferred the Jews – an unusual position for any Gentile of the time to have adopted. What is certain is that his works were never translated into Greek, and although his name was known to the fourth-century Greek historian Eusebius, little or nothing of his thought ever penetrated the Greek-speaking world.

Dating his works is not easy, although several attempts have been made to do so. He may have produced an average of two books a year, though some of his writings are very long and probably took more time to complete. It is generally assumed that the treatises in which he mentions Montanists date from the later part of his career, and this has also led many scholars to assume that he grew more acerbic in his criticisms of the mainline church as he grew older. On that basis, some have tried to arrange his writings in a chronological order, but it has to be admitted that much of the argument is circular and unsatisfactory. Only occasionally, when he mentions outside events, is it possible to say that a particular work must have been written after that time, and it is this that gives us the parameters of 196–212 for the period of his known literary activity. Given the insecure basis of our knowledge, it is probably best therefore to arrange his writings thematically, rather than attempt a chronological order that may be incorrect. As we have them, his surviving treatises may be listed as follows:

1. *Philosophical.* Foremost among these is his great treatise *On the Soul*, which can stand its own with any philosophical work of antiquity. In it Tertullian argues that both the Platonic doctrine of the transmigration of souls and the Stoic belief that all human souls would be destroyed in the final conflagration at the end of the world must be rejected by Christians. A shorter work, *On the Witness of the Soul*, argues that left to itself, the natural human soul would confess Christ because it would recognize itself as having been created in the image and likeness of God. In a third treatise, addressed mainly to heretics who accepted the resurrection of the soul but denied that of the flesh, Tertullian explains that the Christian view of the afterlife includes the entire human body, in direct contradiction to the majority opinion in Greek philosophical circles.

2. *Evangelistic.* Under this heading are four works purportedly addressed to contemporary pagans. The most important of these is the famous *Apology* in which Tertullian makes the case for Christianity as a historically verifiable religion. Among other things, he claims that the records sent by Pontius Pilate to Rome in which he reported the death and apparent resurrection of Jesus still survived in the imperial archives. He also criticizes the Roman authorities for persecuting their best citizens without any rational basis for doing so. A shorter treatise, *To the Nations*, makes some of the same points, and appeals to the heroes of ancient Rome as models of virtue whom the Christians equal or surpass by their devotion to the one true God. To these should be added a satirical work, *On the Cloak*, in which he explains his abandonment of the Roman toga for the philosopher's cloak (*pallium*) as a sign of the seriousness of

his conversion to Christ, and another short letter written to the Roman governor Scapula, challenging him to reconsider the logic behind the persecution of the church, which Scapula was expected to supervise.

3. *Doctrinal and polemical.* These categories are difficult to separate, since most of Tertullian's writings against heretics involve him in a detailed exposition of some aspect of Christian doctrine. In *Against the Jews* Tertullian argues that their ancient status as God's chosen people has now passed to Christians, so that Judaism has lost its purpose in the plan of God for salvation. On the other hand, he devoted no fewer than five books to writing *Against Marcion*, the early second-century heretic who denied the Jewish roots of Christianity and tried to excise all trace of them from the New Testament. In the course of this great work, Tertullian argues that God is both the one supreme good and also the creator of the material world, that Christ is the Messiah promised to Israel and that there are no contradictions between the Old and New Testaments.

In his *Against Praxeas* Tertullian tackles the heresy of modalism, which in his words would 'crucify the Father', and demonstrates how the doctrine of the Trinity is necessary to explain the outworking of the divine plan of salvation. It is the oldest Christian work on the subject of the Trinity, and much of its vocabulary and line of argument has been standard in Western tradition ever since his time. Tertullian also wrote two anti-Gnostic treatises; one against Hermogenes, in which he argues against a dualistic view of the universe, and the other against the Valentinians, whose cosmogonic theories he holds up to ridicule without bothering to refute them in detail. Another work, *On the Prescription of Heretics*, is addressed to heretical tendencies in general. Tertullian argues that heretics have no right to appeal to the Scriptures, which belong to the orthodox believers in the church, and that all heresies are in fact parasitic on true doctrine, of which they are corruptions. Lastly, his work *On the Flesh of Christ* was written to counter the widespread belief that Christ's humanity was not fully authentic. He demonstrates how it was essential that the Son of God should become a man, since otherwise he would not have been able to pay the price for our sins in his death on the cross.

4. *Pastoral.* This is by far the largest category of works and in some ways the most interesting, because it is here that we see most clearly what the everyday life of the early church was like and how Tertullian thought it ought to be directed towards greater sanctification. The surviving treatises can be subdivided into four different types as follows:

A. *Those dealing with sex and marriage.* There are six of these, which cover everything from female dress to the obligation of widowhood. Tertullian believed that women were a chief source of temptation to men, and therefore prescribed that they should dress modestly at all times. This applied even to unmarried women, who were told to cover their heads in church even though the New Testament mentions this only with respect to the married. It is a good example of his famous rigorism – what applied in one specific instance ought to be extended and made into a general principle, because it made no sense to say that only married women had to be modest in their dress and behaviour. As far as marriage was concerned, Tertullian believed it was a gift of God, but that it must be practised only within certain well-defined limits. A widow must not remarry, but rather dedicate herself entirely to the service of God. Sexual intercourse within marriage was also to be avoided as was pregnancy, since a woman who was pregnant at Christ's second coming would be condemned to remain that way in eternity!

B. *Those dealing with martyrdom.* Four treatises come into this category, one of which deals with the problem of those who took flight in times of persecution, and another (*Scorpiace*) attacks those who tried to argue that it was not necessary to confess Christ to the point of matryrdom. A third is addressed to the martyrs themselves, encouraging them to bear their sufferings with patience, knowing that a heavenly crown awaited them, and the fourth returns to this theme, using the life of Christ as the supreme example of the patience a Christian ought to manifest under suffering.

C. *Those addressing life in a pagan environment.* There are three works specifically dealing with this question, of which the most general is his treatise *On Idolatry.* As one would expect, Tertullian points out how idolatry is not only unbiblical but also nonsensical in itself. Another treatise deals with the question of public spectacles, of which the Romans were very fond, but which Christians ought to avoid because of their idolatrous associations. Finally, there is a short treatise written in support of a soldier who refused to perform the honours due to the crown on the accession of Caracalla and Geta to the imperial throne (AD 211). Tertullian praises the soldier for refusing to participate in this pagan ceremony, and in passing hints that a military career is incompatible with the Christian life.

D. *Those dealing with Christian worship and practice.* Here there are four treatises that deal respectively with repentance, the Lord's Prayer, baptism and fasting. Tertullian rejected infant baptism, not because he thought it was meaningless but because he thought it was unfair on the child. In his eyes, a baptized person was cleansed from sin, but if that person sinned after baptism, only martyrdom could bring him back to a state of purity. Thus a child who was baptized ran the risk of sinning afterwards, probably without realizing it, and thereby of losing his salvation. The treatise on fasting is one of the most virulently pro-Montanist, so much so that its authenticity has been questioned by some. Not surprisingly, it is in these pastoral works that Tertullian's attraction to Montanism comes out most clearly, though it must be said that his rigorist views are present in all of them, whether they reflect Montanist influences or not.

Theological analysis

Tertullian's theology is noted for the remarkable degree to which it resembles later fourth- and fifth-century orthodoxy. Unaware as he was of the quarrels that would be triggered by Arius and Nestorius, it is most interesting to see how he formulated his understanding of both the Trinity and the incarnation in ways that almost seem to have anticipated their objections. It seems highly probable, in fact, that the Western church was spared much of the agony of those debates, and was able to intervene effectively to put a stop to them, largely because Westerners were schooled in the teaching of Tertullian on these matters, either directly or else through intermediate teachers who did little more than copy his ideas and draw out some of their consequences. In the controversies of his own time, against various Gnostics and Marcion, Tertullian revealed a similar disposition towards orthodoxy, and his writings were long regarded as the standard refutations of these errors. It was only in the pastoral realm, where Tertullian's rigorism was often regarded as excessive, that later generations had hesitations about accepting his teaching, though it must be remembered that the North African church, from which he sprang and within which he was especially revered, preserved a strictness of approach that was still very much alive in the time of Augustine and that was one of the chief motivations behind the Donatist schism, whose adherents thought they could create and maintain a perfect church by imposing a rigorous discipline on its members.

Theology and philosophy

Tertullian believed that the Christian faith possessed all true knowledge, and that pagan philosophy could only corrupt it with its absurdities. He was particularly critical of pseudo-Christians who tried to blend paganism and Christianity, and ended up creating a meaningless jargon, which they defended by saying that only the initiated could understand it! He expressed his views in the following eloquent passage:

> Philosophy is the substance of the world's wisdom, the rash interpreter of the nature and dispensation of God. Heresies are themselves instigated by philosophy. From

that source there came the 'eons' of the Platonist Valentinus, and goodness knows how many other forms, not to mention the trinity of man in his system. From the same source came Marcion's superior god, with all his tranquillity – a Stoic idea. The opinion that the soul is mortal comes from the Epicureans, while all of these philosophers taken together deny the resurrection of the body. Make matter equal to God and you have the teaching of Zeno, and any doctrine of a god of fire goes back to Heraclitus. The same subject matter is discussed over and over again by heretics and philosophers, and the same arguments keep coming back. Where does evil come from? Why is it permitted? What is the origin of man? How does he come into the world? And then there is the latest question brought up by Valentinus – where does God come from? He solves this by saying that he comes from *euthymesis* and *ectroma* [whatever they are].

Poor Aristotle! Who invented dialectics for these men, the art of building up and pulling down, an art so elusive in its propositions, so far-fetched in its conjectures, so crude in its arguments, so productive of contentions, embarrassing even to itself, retracting everything and really saying nothing! Where do those 'fables and endless genealogies' (1 Timothy 1:4), 'unprofitable questions' (Titus 3:9) and 'words which spread like a cancer' (2 Timothy 2:17) come from? When the Apostle [Paul] wants to protect us from all these things, he actually tells us that it is philosophy that we should be on our guard against! Writing to the Colossians he says: 'See that no-one beguiles you through philosophy and vain deceit, after the tradition of men and contrary to the wisdom of the Holy Spirit' (Colossians 2:8). He had been at Athens and had in his interviews (with its philosophers) become acquainted with that human wisdom which pretends to know the truth, while in fact it only corrupts it and is itself divided into its several heresies by the variety of its mutually antagonistic sects.

What has Athens to do with Jerusalem? What harmony is there between the academy and the church? What [common ground is there] between heretics and Christians? Our instruction comes from the porch of Solomon (Acts 3:5) who had taught that the Lord should be sought in simplicity of heart (Wisdom of Solomon 1:1). Away with all attempts to produce a hybrid Christianity out of Stoic, Platonic and dialectic components! We want no strange disputation once we possess Christ Jesus, no inquisition once we enjoy the Gospel. With our faith, we desire no further belief. For this is our glorious faith, that there is nothing which we ought to believe in addition to it.[1]

---

1. *On Prescription against Heretics* 7. All quotations are from Alexander Roberts and James Donaldson (eds.), *The Ante-Nicene Fathers*, 24 vols. (Edinburgh: T. & T. Clark, 1866–72).

At the same time, however, Tertullian also recognized that the best pagan philosophers had reached conclusions that tied in remarkably well with the fulness of the revelation given to humanity in Jesus Christ. The following passage gives us a flavour of this:

> We have already asserted that God created the world and all it contains by his Word and reason and Power. It is abundantly plain that your philosophers too, regard the Logos – that is, the Word and Reason – as the creator of the universe. For Zeno lays it down that he is the creator, having made all things according to a predetermined plan, and says that his name is fate and God and the soul of Jupiter and the necessity of all things. Cleanthes ascribes all this to spirit, which he says pervades the universe. Similarly, we also hold that the Word and reason and Power, by which God made all things, all have spirit as their proper and essential foundation. The Word speaks, Reason disposes and arranges, and Power executes, all from within this one spiritual reality. We have been taught that the Word proceeds forth from God, and in that procession he is generated, so that he is the Son of God and is called God because his substance is one with God's.[2]

Perhaps the best expression of his general attitude comes from the following passage. In it he points out how the philosophers strove for the truth but failed to find it, and when they came across something of it, they preferred to dispute among themselves, rather than submit to its authority.

> The authority of the natural philosophers is maintained among you as the special property of wisdom. You mean, of course, that pure and simple wisdom of the philosophers which attests its own weakness mainly by that variety of opinion which proceeds from an ignorance of the truth. Now what wise man is so devoid of truth as not to know that God is the father and Lord of wisdom itself and truth? Besides, there is that divine oracle uttered by Solomon: 'The fear of the Lord is the beginning of wisdom' (Proverbs 9:10). But fear has its origin in knowledge, for how will a man fear something if he knows nothing about it? So the one who has the fear of God will possess full and perfect wisdom if he has attained to the knowledge and truth of God, even if he knows nothing else. But philosophy has not clearly realized this. It may appear that in their search for wisdom, the philosophers have looked into the Scriptures because of their great antiquity, and to have got some of their opinions from that source, the fact that they have interpolated their own deductions proves that either they have despised the teaching of the Bible completely or have not fully

2. *Apology* 21.

believed it. Thus even what they discovered degenerated into uncertainty, and from one or two drops of truth a whole river of speculation emerged. Having found God, they did not leave it at that, but instead argued about his quality, his nature and his dwelling-place. The Platonists said that he cares about worldly things, because he rules over them and passes judgement on them. The Epicureans regarded him as apathetic and inert, and in their eyes a non-entity. The Stoics thought he lived outside the world and the Platonists said he lived inside it. The God whom they had so imperfectly confessed they could neither know nor fear, and therefore they could not be wise, since they wandered away from wisdom, which is the fear of God.[3]

Divine revelation

Tertullian explained to pagans what divine revelation was and how it could be perceived. He mentioned both the written word of Scripture, explaining its origin, and also the testimony of nature:

In order that we might acquire a fuller and more authoritative knowledge both of himself and of his counsels and will, God has added a written revelation for the benefit of everyone whose heart is set on seeking him, so that by seeking he may find and by finding believe, and by believing obey. From the first, he sent messengers into the world – men whose stainless righteousness made them worthy to know the Most High, and to reveal him – men abundantly endowed with the Holy Spirit, that they might proclaim that there is only one God, who made all things, who formed man from the dust of the ground – for he is the true Prometheus who put order into the world by arranging the seasons and their course. These have further set before us the proofs he has given of his majesty in his judgements by floods and fires, the rules appointed by him for securing his favour, as well as the retribution in store. We too, used to laugh at these things. We are of your stock and nature, for men are made, not born, Christians. The preachers of whom we have spoken are called prophets, from the office which belongs to them of predicting the future. Their words, along with the miracles which they performed in order for men to have faith in their divine authority, are recorded in the literary treasures which they have left us, and which are open to all.

The Jews too read them publicly and are in the habit of going to hear them every Sabbath. Whoever pays attention to them will find God in them; whoever takes the trouble to understand will be compelled to believe. Their great antiquity, first of all, claims authority for these writings. You too make it almost a religious

---

3. *To the Nations* 2.2.

> requirement that things should be very old. Well, I tell you that all your sacred books and objects put together are not as ancient as even one of our prophets. If you have heard of Moses, let me tell you that he is five hundred years older than Homer. The other prophets came later, but every one of them is older than the first of your philosophers, legislators and historians.
>
> There is another thing of even greater importance – the majesty of our Scriptures. If you doubt that they are as old as we say, we offer proof of their divine character. You can persuade yourselves of this right here, without bothering to do any research into the matter. Your instructors – the world, the times we live in and the events described – are all before you. Everything now taking place around you was announced beforehand – the swallowing up of cities by the earth, the theft of islands by the sea, wars which cause both internal and external convulsions, the collision of kingdom with kingdom, famines, pestilence, local massacres and widespread genocides, the exaltation of the lowly and the humbling of the proud, the decline of righteousness, the growth of sin, the fall-off of interest in all good things, the disorder of the seasons, the appearance of monsters – all this was foreseen and predicted before it happened. When we suffer calamities, we read of them in the Scriptures. As we examine them, they are proved to be right. The truth of a prophecy, in my opinion, is the evidence that it has come from above. We have an assured faith with regard to future events because they have already been prophesied to us. They have been uttered by the same voices and are written in the same books – all inspired by one and the same Spirit.[4]

Tertullian believed in the absolute perfection and clarity of the Scriptures. In his opinion, where there was a difference of doctrine, it was because somebody had tampered with the sacred text. Those who did this regularly were heretics, whose aim was to distort the truth. But those who stuck to the Word of God proclaimed a coherent message, expressed most clearly in the rule of faith:

> Where diversity of doctrine is found there must be corruption both of the Scriptures and the expositions of it. Those who wanted to teach something different had to arrange the texts of doctrine in a different way. They could not possibly have achieved their diversity of teaching by any other means. Corruption in doctrine could not have succeeded unless the texts which convey it were also corrupted, just as we could not have maintained the integrity of our doctrine without maintaining the integrity of our texts. What is there in our Scriptures which goes against what we teach? What have we introduced which comes from us and not from them? We are what the

4. *Apology* 18–20.

Scriptures are, and have been since the beginning. We came into being as a result of them, before any other way had appeared, and before they were interpolated by you heretics. All interpolation is a later process because it derives from rivalry which can never precede what it emulates. It is obvious that we, who have existed from the beginning, cannot have interpolated anything into the Scriptures, since those interpolations came later. One man perverts the Scriptures by altering the text, and another does it by changing the interpretation. Valentinus for example, seems to make use of the entire volume, but has laid violent hands on the truth by using his cunning mind and skill even more than Marcion. Marcion used the knife, not the pen, in that he abbreviated the Scriptures to suit his teaching. Valentinus avoided such excision. He did not invent Scriptures to fit his doctrine but adapted his doctrine to the existing texts. Yet he managed to take away more from them than Marcion did, and he added more too, because he removed the proper meaning of every particular word and added fantastic constructions of things which have no real existence.[5]

The rule of faith

Tertullian interpreted the Christian message according to what he knew as the 'rule of faith', which in many respects may be regarded as a primitive type of creed. The rule of faith contained the basic teachings of the New Testament, particularly those which were most liable to be misunderstood or rejected by a pagan society. Versions of the rule appear three times in his writings, in contexts sufficiently different from one another to make us realize that here we have a form of teaching which must have been inculcated in young believers as a way of protecting them from error. What he says is this:

The rule of faith is altogether one, alone immutable and irreformable. It is the rule of believing in only one Almighty God, the Creator of the universe, and in his Son Jesus Christ, born of the Virgin Mary, crucified under Pontius Pilate, raised again the third day from the dead, received in the heavens, sitting now at the right hand of the Father, destined to come to judge the living and the dead through the resurrection of the flesh as well [as of the soul]. This law of faith is constant, but other points of discipline and behaviour are open to correction as the grace of God operates and progresses to the [perfect] end.[6]

The rule of faith prescribes the belief that there is only one God, and that he is none other than the Creator of the world, who produced all things out of nothing by his

5. *On Prescription against Heretics* 28.
6. *On the Veiling of Virgins* 1.

> Word which he sent forth. This Word is called his Son, and under the name of God he was seen in different ways by the patriarchs, heard at all times in the prophets, and was at last brought down by the Spirit and power of the Father into the Virgin Mary, was made flesh in her womb, and being born of her, came out as Jesus Christ. He preaches this new law and the new promise of the kingdom of heaven. He worked miracles. Having been crucified, he rose again on the third day and having ascended into heaven, he sat at the right hand of the Father. In his place he then sent the power of the Holy Spirit to lead those who believe. He will come again with glory to take the saints into the enjoyment of everlasting life and of the heavenly promises. He will condemn the wicked to everlasting fire after both these classes (*i.e.* the good and the evil) have been resurrected and given back their flesh. We shall prove that this rule was taught by Christ, and the only questions it raises among us are those which are provoked by heretics.[7]

> We believe that there is only one God, but under the dispensation, as it is called, this one God has a Son, his Word, who proceeded from him, by whom all things were made and without whom nothing was made (John 1:3). We believe that he was sent by the Father into the Virgin [Mary], and that he was born of her, being both man and God, the Son of Man and the Son of God, and that he was called by the name of Jesus Christ. We believe that he suffered, died and was buried, according to the Scriptures, and after being raised again by the Father and taken back into heaven, he is now seated at the right hand of the Father, and will come to judge the living and the dead. He also sent from heaven, from the Father, as he promised, the Holy Spirit the Paraclete, the sanctifier of the faith of those who believe in the father, the Son and the Holy Spirit.[8]

Unwritten traditions

Tertullian was well aware of the problem created by the use of traditions in worship that had no express Scriptural authority. Tertullian defended these traditions as long as they were customary and could be defended on rational grounds. In doing this, he claimed to be following the use of the Roman law courts, which also granted unwritten traditions a validity equivalent to statute law if it could be shown that custom and reason supported them.

> If no passage of Scripture has prescribed a certain practice, surely custom, which flows from tradition, confirms it. For how can anything come into general use if it has not been handed down? You claim that traditions must be based on written

---

7. *On Prescription against Heretics* 13.
8. *Against Praxeas* 2.

authority to be valid. Let us inquire, therefore, to see whether this is so or not. We shall certainly agree that a given practice should not be accepted if there are no similar cases of unwritten traditions relying on the sanction of custom alone which might offer us a precedent. To deal with this matter briefly, I shall begin with baptism. Just before we go into the water, we make a solemn profession in front of the congregation and at the direction of the president, that we renounce the devil, his pomp and his angels. Then we are immersed three times and we make a somewhat fuller pledge, which the Lord has appointed in the gospel. Then when we come up out of the water as new-born children, we taste a mixture of milk and honey first of all, and we give up bathing for a week. We also take the sacrament of the eucharist before dawn, and from the hands of no-one but the presidents, which the Lord commanded us to do at meal times and enjoined on all alike. Every year we commemorate the anniversary of this event by making offerings for the dead. We think it is unlawful to fast or to kneel in worship on the Lord's day. We rejoice in the same privilege from Easter to Pentecost. We get upset if any of the bread or wine should fall to the ground, even if it is our own. We make the sign [of the cross] on our foreheads every time we go in or out, when we get dressed, when we bathe, when we sit at table, when we light the lamps and when we go to bed.

If for these, and other such rules, you demand a Scriptural injunction, you will find none. Tradition will be offered to you as their origin, custom as their confirmation and faith as their observer. That reason will support tradition, custom and faith, you will either perceive for yourself or learn from someone else who has perceived it. In the meantime, accept at least that there is some reason to which we ought to submit. Among the Jews for instance, it is usual for the women to be veiled, in order that they may not be recognized. There is no law governing this, nor has the Apostle spoken. If Rebecca drew down her veil when she saw her betrothed approaching her in the distance, this modesty of a private individual could not have made a law, or perhaps it would have done so only for those who find themselves in the same position as she did. Let virgins alone be veiled, and this when they are coming to be married, and not until they have recognized their appointed husband! There is no official dress code prescribed in the law. It was a matter of tradition, sanctified by custom, which later found its authorization in the Apostle's sanction, which he based on the true interpretation of reason. This will make it sufficiently clear to you that you can justify the keeping of unwritten traditions established by custom. Even in civil matters custom is accepted as law when positive legal enactment is wanting, and it makes no difference whether it is based on writing or on reason, since reason is the true basis of law.[9]

---

9. *On the Crown* 3–4.

Christianity and Judaism

Tertullian was greatly preoccupied with the need to establish precisely how Christianity was related to its parent religion, Judaism. There was strong prejudice against the Jews among both the Greeks and the Romans, and many pagans found it hard to know quite how Christianity was different. Tertullian realized that disagreement over the divinity of Christ was the heart of the matter, and expressed this to his pagan audiences as follows:

> We are not ashamed of Christ, for we rejoice to be counted his disciples and to suffer in his name – nor do we differ from the Jews on the question of God. We must therefore say something about Christ's divinity. In former times, the Jews enjoyed much of God's favour, when the fathers of their race were noted for their righteousness and faith. So it was that as a people they flourished greatly, and their kingdom attained great heights. So blessed were they that God spoke to them in special revelations, for their instruction, pointing out to them beforehand how they could merit his favour and avoid his displeasure. But how deeply they have sinned, puffed up to their fall with a false trust in their noble ancestors, turning from God's way into a way of sheer impiety, is clear from their present national ruin, even though they themselves would deny it. Scattered abroad, a nation of wanderers, exiles from their own land and clime, they roam over the whole world without either a human or a heavenly king, not possessing even a foreigner's right to set foot in their native country. The sacred writers gave warning of these things, and with equal clarity declared that in the last days of the world, God would choose for himself more faithful worshippers out of every nation, people and country. On them he would bestow his grace, and bestow it in fuller measure, in line with the greater extent of the higher dispensation. Thus he appeared among us as Christ, the Son of God, to renew and illuminate man's nature in ways which had been announced beforehand by God.[10]

God

Tertullian gave an eloquent explanation of the being and nature of God to the pagans he was trying to win over, and explained to them how the human soul, once it was delivered from its limitations, naturally bore witness to God:

> The object of our worship is the One God, he who by his commanding Word, his arranging wisdom, and his mighty power, brought forth out of nothing the entire mass of our world, with all its array of elements, bodies and spirits for the glory of his

10. *Apology* 21.

majesty. The Greeks recognize this and for that reason have called it the *cosmos*. The eye cannot see God, although he is spiritually visible. He is incomprehensible, though he is manifested by grace. He is beyond our utmost thought, though our human faculties conceive of him. He is therefore equally real and great. Things which can be seen, handled and conceived are by nature inferior to the eyes which see them, the hands which touch them and the minds which discover them, but the infinite is known only to itself. Paradoxically, it is this which gives us some idea of who God really is. He is beyond our conceptions, but the very fact that we cannot grasp him gives us some idea of what he really is. He is presented to our minds in his transcendent greatness, at once both known and unknown. The crowning guilt of mankind is found right here, in that they will not acknowledge the One of whom they cannot possibly be ignorant. Do you prefer the works of his hands, so numerous and so great, which both contain you and sustain you, which both minister to your enjoyment and strike you with awe, or would you rather have it from the witness of the soul itself? Though it is under the oppressive bondage of the body, led astray by depraving customs, enervated by lusts and passions, in slavery to false gods, whenever it comes to itself, as if out of a sleep or sickness, it speaks of God. 'God is great and good'; 'may God grant it' are words on every lip. It bears witness to the fact that God is judge, exclaiming: 'God sees' and 'I commend myself to God' and 'God will repay me'. O noble testimony of the soul which is Christian by nature! By using expressions such as these, the soul looks not to the seat of earthly government but to the heavens. It knows that it is there that the throne of the living God is found, because it came down from there itself.[11]

This is what he wrote on the same subject to Scapula, the Roman governor of Africa:

We are worshippers of one God, of whose existence and character nature teaches all men, at whose lightnings and thunders you tremble, whose benefits minister to your happiness. You think that others are also gods, but we know that they are devils. Nevertheless, it is a fundamental human right, a privilege of nature, that every man should worship according to his own convictions. One man's religion neither harms nor helps another man's. It is certainly no part of religion to compel religious observance. Free will and not force should lead us to that, for the sacrificial victims are demanded from a willing mind. You will render no real service to your gods by forcing us to sacrifice to them. They can have no desire to receive offerings from the unwilling, unless they are moved by a spirit of contention which is altogether undivine. The true God bestows his blessings on wicked people just as much as on

11. Ibid. 17.

> his chosen ones, which is why he has appointed an eternal judgement, when both the grateful and the ungrateful will have to stand before his bar.[12]

Tertullian also defended the biblical doctrine of God against pseudo-Christian heretics like Marcion, who apparently believed that there were two gods – a creator and a (superior) redeemer. In arguing against this, Tertullian demonstrated why it was essential to believe in only one God:

> The main, indeed the entire, contention lies in the question of number – can we admit the existence of two gods, by poetic licence if necessary, or pictorial fantasy, or by a third process which we have to call heretical depravity. Christianity has emphatically declared this principle: 'If God is not one, he does not exist,' because we correctly believe that a thing has no existence if it is not what it is supposed to be. In order for you to know that God is one, ask where God is, and then you will see that that must be the case. In so far as a human being can form a definition of God, let me present one which the conscience of all men will acknowledge. God is the great Supreme, existing in eternity, unbegotten, not made, without beginning, without end. For such a condition as this must be ascribed to that eternity which makes God to be the great Supreme, because this very attribute exists in God for that purpose. So it is also with his other qualities, so that God is the great Supreme in form and reason, in might and power. Now since everyone agrees on this point, because nobody will deny that God is the great Supreme unless he wants to state the opposite, that God is just some inferior being, in order to deny his divinity by robbing him of one of his divine attributes, what must his condition be? Surely it must be that there is nothing equal to him, because if he had an equal he would no longer be the great Supreme. The great Supreme must by definition be unique. He will not exist otherwise than by the condition which gives him his being, which is his absolute uniqueness. Since God is the great Supreme, our Christian faith has rightly declared that if he is not one, he does not exist. We have never doubted his existence, but rather have defined it in the way that makes him necessarily who he is – by calling him the great Supreme. Moreover, this great Supreme must be unique. This unique being will therefore be God. Any other god you may introduce cannot be held to be divine in this way, since two great Supremes cannot co-exist.[13]

Tertullian goes on to refute Marcion's contention that there is a division between divine goodness and divine justice. In fact, these two are and must be one and the same:

---

12. *To Scapula* 2.
13. *Against Marcion* 1.3.

> There is union and agreement between goodness and justice, so that you cannot separate them. How can you separate out two gods, one of whom is good and the other just? Where the just is, there the good is also. From the very beginning the creator was both good and just. Both his attributes advanced together. His goodness created and his justice arranged the world. In this process his justice even decreed that the world should be made of good materials, because it took counsel with goodness. The work of justice is apparent in the separation which was pronounced between light and darkness, between day and night, between heaven and earth, between the water above and the water below, between the gathering together of the sea and the appearance of dry land, between the greater lights and the lesser, between the luminaries of the day and those of the night, between male and female, between the tree of the knowledge of death and of life, between the world and paradise, between the sea and the land animals. As goodness conceived all things, so justice discriminated between them. By its determination, everything was arranged and set in order. Every position and quality of the elements, their effect, motion and state, the rise and setting of each, are the judicial determinations of the creator. Do not suppose that his function as a judge must be defined as beginning when evil began, and so tarnish his justice with the cause of evil. By such considerations then, we can show that this attribute of justice advanced in company with goodness, the author of all things. Justice too was deemed worthy of being considered innate and natural and not as accidentally accruing to God, since she was found to be in him, her Lord, as the arbiter of his works.[14]

The Trinity

Tertullian believed that the Trinity was a necessary belief, based on what the Bible teaches us about God. Nor did he draw this conclusion from the New Testament only. He purported to find trinitarian teaching right at the very beginning of the Bible, and argued for it as follows:

> If the number of the Trinity offends you because it does not appear to fit into the divine unity, I ask you how it is possible for a being who is merely and absolutely one and singular to speak in the plural phrase and say: 'Let us make man in our own image and after our likeness' (Genesis 1:26). Surely he ought to have said: 'Let me make man in my image, after my likeness,' if he were really just a unique and singular being. In the following passage however: 'Behold the man has become like one of us' (Genesis 3:22) he is either deceiving or amusing us in speaking plurally, if he is really only one and singular. Or was it to the angels that he spoke, as the Jews interpret the passage,

14. Ibid. 2.12.

because they do not recognize the Son either? Or was it because he was the Father, Son and Holy Spirit all at the same time that he spoke to himself in plural terms, thereby making himself plural as it were? No, it was because he already had his Son next to him as a second person – his own Word – and a third person also, the Spirit in the Word, that he purposely adopted the plural phrase: 'Let us make . . .' and 'in our image', and 'become as one of us'. For with whom did he make man? Who did he make man like? The Son, on the one hand, of course, who would one day take on human nature, and the Spirit on the other hand, who would one day sanctify man. It was with them that he spoke in the unity of the Trinity, using them as his servants and witnesses.[15]

Tertullian also based his trinitarian teaching on the witness of the New Testament, and especially of the Gospel of John, as the following passage indicates:

The Son alone knows the Father and has himself unfolded the Father's bosom (John 1:18). He has also heard and seen all things with the Father, and what he has been commanded by the Father, that also does he speak (John 8:26). And it is not his own will, but the Father's, that he has accomplished (John 6:38) which he had known most intimately from the beginning. 'For what man knows the things which are in God, but the Spirit which is in him?' (1 Corinthians 2:11). But the Word was formed by the Spirit, and if I may express myself like this, the Spirit is the body of the Word. The Word therefore is always in the Father, as he says: 'I am in the Father' (John 14:11) and is always with God, as it is written: 'And the Word was with God' (John 1:1). He is never separate from the Father or different from him, since: 'I and the Father are one' (John 10:30).[16]

Jesus Christ

Tertullian developed his doctrine of Christ as an extension of his teaching on the Trinity. He was particularly puzzled by those heretics whom he supposed must be Valentinians, or related to them, who divided the two natures of Christ into the 'Father', Christ's divine nature, and the 'Son', his human nature. He addresses this nonsense as follows:

The heretics divide up one person into two – Father and Son. They interpret the Son as being the flesh, that is to say, the man, or Jesus, and they interpret the Father

15. *Against Praxeas* 12.
16. Ibid. 8.

as being the spirit, that is to say, God, or Christ. Thus it transpires that at the same time as they insist that there is no distinction between the Father and the Son [in the Trinity], they go about dividing them! For if Jesus is one and Christ is someone else, then the Son must be different from the Father, because the Son is Jesus and the Father is Christ. I suppose they learned this interpretation of the divine monarchy in the school of Valentinus, but this conception of theirs has already been refuted in what we said earlier, because the Word of God or the Spirit of God is also called 'the power of the Highest', whom they identify as the Father, whereas these relations are not identical with the one whose relations they are said to be, but rather proceed from him and belong to him. But there is another refutation of their heresy. It was announced by the angel: 'Therefore that holy thing which will be born of you will be called the Son of God' (Luke 1:35). The heretics argue that as it was the flesh that was born, it must be the flesh which is the Son of God. But I say that this is spoken about the Spirit of God. For it was certainly of the Spirit that the Virgin [Mary] conceived, and what he conceived, she brought forth. What he conceived had to be born and thus had to be brought forth, which means that it was the Spirit whose 'name should be called Emmanuel, God with us' (Matthew 1:23). The flesh is not God, so the words: 'That holy thing shall be called the Son of God' could not have been said concerning it. They could only have been said about the divine being who was born in the flesh, of whom the psalm also says: 'Since God became man in the midst of it, and established it by the will of the Father' (cf. Psalm 87:5). But what divine person was born in it? The Word, and the Spirit which became incarnate with the Word by the will of the Father. The Word therefore is incarnate, and this must be the point of our inquiry. How did the Word become flesh? Was it by having been transfigured, as it were, in the flesh, or by having really clothed himself in flesh? Of course, it was by a real clothing of himself in flesh!

If the Word had become flesh by some transfiguration and change of substance, it would follow that Jesus must be a substance compounded out of two other substances – a kind of mixture of flesh and spirit which is neither one of them, but a third substance altogether. Jesus could not then have been God, for he would have ceased to be the Word made flesh, nor could he have been an incarnate man, for he would not be purely flesh, and it was flesh which the Word became. Being compounded of both he would in fact have been neither, but rather some third substance very different from either of the others. But the truth is that he is expressly set forth as both God and man, differing no doubt according to each substance in its own special properties, inasmuch as the Word is nothing but God and the flesh is nothing but man. The Apostle [Paul] also teaches this, saying: 'who was made of the seed of David' (Romans 1:3), which means that he is both man and the Son of Man. Also: 'Who was declared to be the Son of God, according to the Spirit' (Romans 1:4), in which words Jesus will be God and the Word – the Son of God. We see plainly his twofold state, which is not confounded but conjoined in one person – Jesus, God and man.

The property of each nature is so wholly preserved that the Spirit did everything in Jesus which was suitable to himself (*e.g.*, miracles, mighty deeds and wonders), and the flesh exhibited the characteristics appropriate to it. It was hungry under the devil's temptation, thirsty with the Samaritan woman, wept over Lazarus, was troubled to the point of death and in the end actually died. But if Jesus were some third substance, there would be no distinct proofs of either nature. By a transfer of functions, the Spirit would have done things belonging to the flesh and the flesh would have done what belongs to the Spirit, or else the third substance would have done things which belong neither to the flesh nor to the Spirit. On this premiss, if the Word became flesh, either it underwent death or the flesh did not die, because either the flesh became immortal or the Word became mortal. But because the two substances acted distinctly, according to their own nature, they each did what was appropriate to them. The flesh did not become Spirit, nor did the Spirit become flesh, but they co-existed in one person. Jesus is man in his flesh and God in his Spirit. The angel called him 'Son of God' (Luke 1:35) because of his Spirit, and the term 'Son of Man' was reserved for him in the flesh. The Apostle Paul called him the 'mediator between God and men' (1 Timothy 2:5) thereby affirming that he shared in both substances.[17]

Tertullian argued that it was impossible to come to a coherent understanding of Jesus Christ without confessing that he is God. He explained this from the standpoint of the Jews, who had to come to terms with this strange man in their midst:

The Jews were well aware that Christ was coming, because the prophets had told them so. Even now they are still expecting him to come, and the only real difference between them and us is over whether that coming has already occurred or not. For two comings of Christ have been revealed to us. There is a first, which has been fulfilled in the lowliness of a human life, and a second which is still imminent, when he will return in all the majesty of his deity. By misunderstanding the first, the Jews have concluded that the second, which they set their hopes on because it is more clearly predicted, is the only one there is. It was the just punishment of their sins that they did not understand the Lord's first coming, because if they had, they would have believed, and if they had believed, they would have obtained salvation. They themselves read how it is written of them that they are deprived of wisdom

17. Ibid. 27.

and understanding (Isaiah 6:10). Therefore, since they have convinced themselves, under the power of their prejudices, that Christ was no more than a man, because he appeared in such a lowly estate, it followed necessarily from that that they should regard him as a magician from the powers which he displayed – expelling devils from men by a word, restoring vision to the blind, cleansing the leprous, reinvigorating the paralytic, summoning the dead to life again, making the very elements of nature obey him, stilling the storms and walking on the sea, proving that he was the Logos of God, that primordial, first-begotten Word, accompanied by power and reason and based on Spirit, that the one who was now doing all things by his word, and the one who had done that of old, were one and the same being.

But the Jews were so exasperated by his teaching, by which their rulers were convicted of the truth and so many of them turned to him, that they brought him before Pontius Pilate, who was then governor of Syria, and by the violence of their outcries against him, extorted a sentence giving him up to them to be crucified. He himself had predicted this, though that would have meant little if the prophets of old had not done it as well. And yet, nailed upon the cross, he exhibited many noble signs, by which his death was distinguished from all others. By his own free will he dismissed the Spirit from him, in anticipation of the executioner's work. At the same time, the light of the sun was withdrawn, even though it was high noon. Those who did not know that this had been predicted about Christ probably thought it was an eclipse. Your own archives still contain a record of this event. When his body was taken down from the cross and placed in a sepulchre, the ever-watchful Jews surrounded it with a large military guard, so that his disciples would not steal the body and start proclaiming to a gullible public that the resurrection had indeed occurred on the third day, as Jesus had predicted. But on the third day there was a sudden earthquake and the stone which sealed the sepulchre was rolled away, and the guard fled in terror. Without a single disciple nearby, the grave was found empty of everything except the clothes of the man they had buried. Yet the leaders of the Jews, who had a vested interest in spreading lies and in keeping the people deceived and cut off from the faith, let it be known that the body of Christ had been stolen by his followers. For the Lord did not reveal himself publicly, lest the wicked should be delivered from their error, and also so that faith, which was destined to receive a great reward, should not be nullified. Rather, he spent forty days with some of his disciples down in Galilee, a region of Judaea, instructing them in the doctrines which they were to teach to others. Then, after giving them a commission to preach the gospel throughout the world, he was surrounded by a cloud and taken up to heaven.[18]

---

18. *Apology* 21.

Tertullian believed that God could become a man if he chose to do so, and that in that case he could not cease to be God. The result was a doctrine of Christ remarkably similar to that which was later worked out at the council of Chalcedon (AD 451):

> With God nothing is impossible, apart from what he does not will. Let us consider then whether he willed himself to be born. I put the argument very briefly. If God had not willed to be born, he would not have presented himself in the likeness of a man. Who, when he sees a man, would deny that he had been born? If God had not willed that of himself, he would certainly not have willed an illusion of birth instead. It is of the greatest importance that nothing false or pretended should be ascribed to something which in reality does not exist. You retort that his own self-consciousness was enough for him, and that if anyone thought he had been born because they saw him as a man, that was their problem, not his. Yet with how much more dignity and consistency would he have maintained the human character of the assumption that he had been born, because if he had not been, he could have undertaken the character of humanity without harming that consciousness which you claim would enable him to give the illusion of having been born even when it was not the truth!
>
> Why was it so important for Christ to exhibit himself as someone highly conscious of who he was? You cannot express any apprehension that if he had been born and had truly clothed himself with a man's nature, he would have ceased to be God, losing what he was while becoming what he was not. For God is in no danger of losing his own state and condition. You claim that I deny that God was truly changed to man in such a way as to be born and clothed with a body of flesh, for the reason that a being who is without end is necessarily incapable of change. Being changed into something else puts an end to the former state. Change therefore is impossible for a being without end. Without a doubt, the nature of things which are subject to change is regulated by this law, that they have no permanence in the state which is undergoing change in them, and that they come to an end because they lack this permanence, while in the process of change they lose what they previously were.[19]

Christ's human flesh was fully human, yet without sin. This was an especially controversial point, because most intellectuals in the ancient world believed that matter was intrinsically evil, and therefore found the Christian doctrine of the incarnation of the Son of God a logical absurdity. If God was who the Christians said he was, he must be perfectly good. But if he also became a

---

19. *On the Flesh of Christ* 3.

human being, this goodness would have been corrupted by association with evil, and so he would no longer have been God in the true sense of the word. Tertullian defended the Christian position as follows:

> The infamous heretic Alexander, driven by his love of disputation in the true spirit of a heretical temper, has risen up against us. He thinks we have said that Christ put on flesh of an earthy origin in order that he might abolish sinful flesh in his own person. Now, even if we did assert this as our opinion, we should be able to defend it in such a way as completely to avoid the extravagant folly which he ascribes to us in making us suppose that the very flesh of Christ was in himself abolished as being sinful, because we mention our belief in public, that it is sitting at the right hand of the Father in heaven, and we further declare that it will come back again in all the pomp of the Father's glory. It is therefore just as impossible for us to say that it is abolished as it is for us to maintain that it is sinful, and so made void, since there has been no fault in it. We maintain moreover, that what has been abolished in Christ is not 'sinful flesh' but 'sin in the flesh', not the material thing but its condition, not the substance but the flaw. We hold this on the authority of the Apostle who says: 'He abolished sin in the flesh' (Romans 8:3). In another sentence he says that Christ was 'in the likeness of sinful flesh', but not in the sense of a semblance of a body instead of its reality. He means us to understand likeness to the flesh which sinned, because the flesh of Christ, which committed no sin itself, resembled that which had sinned – resembled it in its nature, but not in the corruption which it received from Adam. This is why we affirm that Christ had the same flesh as that which in man is sinful. In the flesh we say that sin has been abolished, because in Christ that same flesh is maintained without sin, which in man was not maintained without sin. It would not contribute to Christ's abolishing sin in the flesh if he did not abolish it in that flesh in which the nature of sin existed, nor would that have conduced to his glory. For surely it would have been no strange thing if he had removed the stain of sin in some better flesh, and one which should possess a different, even a sinless, nature. Then, you say, if he took our flesh, Christ's was sinful once. Do not however, fetter with mystery a sense which is quite intelligible. For in putting on our flesh he made it his own; in making it his own, he made it sinless. A word of caution however, must be addressed to all who refuse to believe that our flesh was in Christ on the ground that it came not of the seed of a human father, let them remember that Adam himself received this flesh of ours without the seed of a human father, so also was it quite possible for the Son of God to take to himself the substance of the self-same flesh, without a human father's agency.[20]

20. Ibid. 16.

The Holy Spirit

There are many references to the Holy Spirit throughout Tertullian's writings, and the third person of the Trinity is pictured at work in all the main activities of God on earth. Especially characteristic of Tertullian's treatment of him is his use of the word 'Paraclete', which has Montanist associations but is clearly drawn from John's Gospel, which is an important witness for Tertullian's trinitarian doctrine. This is what he says:

> There is also the Paraclete or Comforter, whom Jesus promises to pray for to the Father, and to send from heaven after his ascension to the Father. He is called 'another Comforter' indeed, but we have already shown in what sense he is 'another': 'He shall receive of mine,' says Christ (John 16:14), just as Christ himself received of the Father's. Thus the connection of the Father in the Son and of the Son in the Paraclete produces three coherent persons, who are nevertheless distinct from one another. The three are one essence, not one person, as it is said: 'I and my Father are one' (John 10:30) in respect of unity of substance, not singularity of number.[21]

Evil spirits

Like most people in ancient times, Tertullian had a great interest in spiritual beings, particularly in evil powers that could prey on the souls and bodies of human beings. He was quite happy to endorse pagan beliefs in such powers because he believed that they were still in thrall to them, whereas Christ had broken their spell and delivered his people from their grasp:

> We agree that there are certain spiritual essences, and their name is quite familiar to us. The philosophers acknowledge that there are demons; Socrates himself waited on a demon's will. Why not, since it is said that an evil spirit attached itself especially to him even from his childhood, turning his mind away from what was good. The poets are all acquainted with demons too; even the ignorant common people often curse by them. In fact, they call upon Satan, the demon chief, in their execrations, as though from some instinctive soul-knowledge of him. Plato also admits the existence of angels. The magicians, no less, come forward as witnesses to the existence of both kinds of spirits. We are instructed moreover by our sacred books how from certain angels, who fell of their own free will, there sprang a more wicked demon brood, condemned of God along with the authors of their race, and that chief we have referred to. It will be enough for the present to give some account of their work. Their great business is the ruin of mankind. From the very first, spiritual wickedness sought

21. *Against Praxeas* 25.

our destruction. They inflict on our bodies diseases and other grievous calamities, while by violent assaults they hurry the soul into sudden and extraordinary excesses. Their marvellous subtleness and tenuity give them access to both parts of our nature. As spiritual beings they can do no harm, because we are not aware of their actions except by their effects, as for example when some inexplicable, unseen poison in the breeze blights the apples and the grain at blossom time, or kills them in the bud, or destroys them when they have reached maturity. Similarly, demons and angels breathe into the soul and rouse up its corruptions with furious passions and vile excesses, or with cruel lusts accompanied by various errors, of which the worst is the one by which these deities are commended to the favour of deceived and deluded human beings, that they may get the proper food of flesh fumes and blood when that is offered up to idol images. What is daintier food to the spirit of evil than turning men's minds away from the true God by the illusions of a false divination? Let me explain how these delusions are managed. Every spirit, angelic or demonic, is possessed of wings. Thus there can be everywhere in a single moment – the whole world is as one place to them, and they can know whatever is going on in the world without needing to have it reported to them. Their swiftness of motion is mistaken for divinity, because their true nature is unknown. Sometimes they want people to think that they are the cause of what they proclaim, and no doubt it is true that the bad things sometimes are their doing – but never the good ones. They have learned the purposes of God from the lips of the prophets and they pick them up every time they hear their works being read aloud. In this way they can set themselves up as rivals to the true God, by stealing his words. Because they live in the air and the clouds, they can know when it is going to rain and tell people that it is on the way. They are also very kind to us in the way they heal diseases. Having caused them in the first place, they fake miracles by proposing some new and untried remedy, which seems to work because in fact they withdraw their malign influence, and can thus claim to have brought about a cure! What further need do I have to speak of their deceptive power as spirits?[22]

Creation

Tertullian defended the goodness of creation against those who believed that all matter was evil by nature. In the following passage he explains how God made us with our senses, which were designed to appreciate and enjoy the beauties of the created order:

Ours is the God of nature, who fashioned man in such a way that he might desire, appreciate and partake of the pleasures afforded by his creatures. He endowed man

---

22. *Apology* 22.

> with certain senses, which act through particular parts of the body, which may be called their instruments. The sense of hearing he has planted in the ears, that of sight he lighted up in the eyes, that of taste he shut up in the mouth, that of smell he wafted into the nose and that of touch he fixed in the tips of our fingers. By means of these organs of the outer man, which do duty for the inner man, the enjoyment of the divine gifts is conveyed by the senses to the soul. What is it about flowers that you particularly enjoy? Either the smell, you say, or the colour, or perhaps both. What parts of the body have these senses allotted to them? The eyes and the nose, I presume. With sight and smell then, make use of flowers, for these are the senses by means of which they are supposed to be enjoyed. The desire for enjoyment comes from God, though the means by which you enjoy the flowers comes from the material world. Never mind – the use of material means does not preclude the enjoyment of the thing desired. Let flowers be what they are – things to be looked at and smelled.[23]

The human soul and flesh

Tertullian believed that the human soul was material, not purely spiritual, and argued his case from the evidence of the New Testament as follows:

> The Gospels contain the clearest evidence for the corporeality of the soul. In hell the soul of a certain man is in torment, punished in flames, suffering excruciating thirst, and imploring from the finger of a happier soul, for his tongue, the solace of a drop of water (Luke 16:23–24). Do you suppose that this end of the blessed poor man and the miserable rich man is only imaginary? Then why the name of Lazarus in this narrative, if it was not a real occurrence? But even if it is to be regarded as imaginary, it will still be a witness to truth and reality. For unless the soul possessed corporeality, the image of a soul could not possibly contain a finger of a bodily substance, nor would the Scripture feign a statement about the limbs of a body if these had no existence. What is it that is taken away to hell after the separation from the body? What is detained there, which is reserved to the day of judgement? What did Christ descend to after he died? I imagine that it is the souls of the patriarchs. But why say all this if the soul is nothing in its subterranean abode? For nothing is exactly what it is if it is not a bodily substance. Whatever is incorporeal cannot be kept or guarded in any way; it is also exempt from either punishment or refreshment. There has to be a body, since otherwise neither punishment nor refreshment could be experienced. Therefore, whatever amount of punishment or refreshment the soul tastes in hell, in its prison or lodging, in the fire or in Abraham's bosom, it gives proof thereby of its

23. *On the Crown* 5.

> own corporeality. An incorporeal thing suffers nothing, since it has nothing which is capable of suffering. If it has such a capacity, it must be a bodily substance. For just as every corporeal thing is capable of suffering, so everything capable of suffering must be corporeal.[24]

Tertullian knew the arguments for the creation of individual souls at birth, but preferred to understand the soul's origin as coinciding with conception in the womb. Not only that, but it was at the same time that the sex of the future human being was decided:

> The soul is seminally placed in man by human agency, and from the very beginning its seed is uniform. We must now look in order at the points which proceed from this assertion. The soul, being sown in the womb at the same time as the body, receives its sex along with it. Indeed, this happens so simultaneously that neither the flesh nor the soul can be regarded as the cause of the sex. If the semination of these two substances allowed for any interval between the conception of the flesh and that of the soul, it might be possible to think that one or the other possessed sexuality and that the one which appeared first would be able to impress its sex on the other. Apelles the heretic said that the souls of men and women take priority over their bodies, a teaching which he had received from Philomena, and therefore he makes the flesh receive its sex from the soul. Those who think that the soul comes into the flesh after birth also believe that its sex is predetermined by whether the flesh which it will enter is male or female. But the truth is that the seminations of the two substances are inseparable in time, and their effusion is also one and the same, which guarantees that they will have the same sex. On this view we have an attestation of the method of the first two formations, when the male was moulded and tempered in a completer way. For the male was formed first, in a completer way, and the woman came far behind him. For a long time her flesh lacked specific form, such as she afterwards assumed when she was taken out of Adam's side, but even so she was still then a living being, because at that time her soul was part of Adam's. besides, if Adam had not transmitted his soul to her as well as his flesh, God would surely have breathed his breath into her.[25]

Tertullian believed that humanity fell into sin because of the temptation of Adam and Eve by Satan. This sin lived in the human body, and principally in the soul. When the Bible speaks of the flesh as the seat of sin, it is saying that

24. *On the Soul* 7.
25. Ibid. 36.

the flesh acts as the soul's agent, not that it is responsible for sin apart from the soul. He explains this as follows:

> Every soul has its nature in Adam until it is born again in Christ. It is unclean as long as it remains without this regeneration, and because it is unclean it is actively sinful, and covers the flesh with its own shame. Although the flesh is sinful and we are forbidden to walk according to it (Galatians 5:16) and its works are condemned because they lust against the spirit (Galatians 5:17), and on its account men are censured for being carnal (Romans 8:5), yet the flesh does not get this bad reputation on its own account. It is not of itself that it thinks or feels anything for the purpose of advising or commanding sin. How indeed should it? It is only a servant, and its service is not like that of a human servant or friend who are animated human beings, but rather like that of a vessel. It is a body, not a soul. A cup may be of service to a thirsty man, but if the man does not take the cup to his lips, it will be of no use to him. Therefore the distinguishing property of a man does not lie in is earthly element, nor is the flesh to be equated with the human person, as if it were some faculty of the soul and a personal quality. It is something of quite a different substance and condition, although it is annexed to the soul as a chattel or instrument for the necessities of life. Thus it is that the flesh is blamed in the Scriptures, because nothing is done by the soul without the flesh. Concupiscence, appetite, drunkenness, cruelty, idolatry and other works of the flesh are operations which are not confined to sensations, but result in effects. When the emotions of sin do not result in effects, they are usually blamed on the soul: 'Whoever looks on a woman to lust after her, has already committed adultery with her in his heart' (Matthew 5:28). But what has the flesh ever done by way of virtue, righteousness, endurance or chastity, without the co-operation of the soul? What an absurdity it is then, to attribute sin and crime to that substance to which you do not assign any good actions or character of its own. The ancillary party to a crime may be brought to trial, but only the principal offender can bear the weight of the penalty. Greater is the odium which falls on the main offender when his subordinates are punished because of him! The one who orders and instigates the crime is beaten with more stripes, while at the same time the one who obeys such commands is not acquitted.[26]

The church

Tertullian was deeply attached to the Christian church, despite its faults and indiscipline, and gives the following picture of it to his pagan audiences:

---

26. Ibid. 40.

Let me explain the characteristics of the Christian society, so that just as I have refuted evil attacks against it, I may also point out its positive aspects. We are a body knit together by a common religious profession, by unity of discipline and by the bond of a common hope. We meet together as an assembly and congregation, so that by offering up prayer to God with a united force, we might wrestle with him in our supplications. This is the kind of violence which God delights in. We pray for the emperors, for their ministers and for all in authority, for the welfare of the world, for the spread of peace and for the delay of the last judgement. We assemble in order to read our sacred writings whenever special circumstances make advance warning or reminders necessary. But regardless of that, we nourish our faith with the sacred words, we animate our hope and we make our confidence more steadfast. By studying God's precepts we inculcate good habits. In the same place, exhortations are made, rebukes and sacred censures are administered. For the work of judging is carried on with great seriousness among us, as befits those who feel assured that they are in the sight of God. You have the most remarkable example of the judgement to come when someone has sinned so grievously that he must be cut off from us in prayer, in the congregation and in all sacred fellowship. The experienced men among our elders preside over us, obtaining that honour not by purchase but by establishing their good character. There is no buying or selling of any sort where the things of God are concerned. We have our treasure chest, but it does not contain purchase money, as if we put a price tag on our religion. People make a monthly donation if they wish, but it is entirely voluntary. These gifts might be called devotion's deposit fund. They are not taken out and spent on feasts, bouts of drinking or restaurants, but are used to support and bury poor people, to supply the wants of boys and girls destitute of means and parents, and of old people who are now house-bound. They are also used to help the shipwrecked, and if there happen to be any in the mines, or banished to the islands, or shut up in the prisons on account of their loyalty to God's church, then they become the dependants of their confession as well.

It is mainly the deeds of such noble love which make us so hated. 'See how they love one another' they say, for they are moved by mutual hatred; 'how they will die for one another', because they would rather kill than be killed. They are angry with us too, because we call one another brothers. The only reason for this, I think, is that among them such names are a mere pretence of affection. We are your brothers too, of course, because of our common mother nature, though you are hardly men because of your unkindness. At the same time, how much more fitting it is for those who have been led to the knowledge of God as their common father, who have come out of the same struggle in the womb of ignorance into the light of a common truth, to be called brothers. Perhaps we are regarded as being less than true brothers because no mishap gets in the way of our fellowship, and our family possessions, which so often provoke division among you, create fraternal bonds among us. We are one in mind and soul, and so we do not hesitate to share our earthly goods with one another. We have everything in common except our wives.[27]

Tertullian was deeply concerned with the imperfections he saw in the church, and became increasingly critical of lax believers as he grew older. However, he was also capable of keeping this in perspective, particularly when it came to dealing with the taunts of pagans, as the following passage demonstrates:

You say of us that we are a most shameful group of people, utterly steeped in luxury, avarice and depravity, and we will not deny that this is indeed true of some. But it is a sufficient witness to our name that this cannot be said of all, or even of most of us. Even in the healthiest and purest body there are bound to be moles, warts or freckles to disfigure it. Not even the sky itself is so perfectly calm and clear as not to be troubled by the occasional passing cloud. A slight spot on the face is obvious because it occurs in such a prominent part of the body, but in reality it only serves to show the purity of the complexion. The goodness of the greater part is well attested by the slender flaw. You may prove that some of our people are evil, but that does not mean that they are Christians. Look and see whether there is any sect to which a partial shortcoming is imputed as a general stain. You yourselves criticize us by saying things like: 'Why is so-and-so deceitful, when Christians are normally so self-denying? Why is he ruthless, when Christians are normally so merciful?' Thus you yourselves bear witness to the fact that these blemishes are not characteristic of Christians.[28]

Unlike most ancient philosophers, Christians believed in the resurrection of the flesh as an integral part of God's saving work. Tertullian expounds this as follows:

Let us consider the special relationship between the flesh and Christianity, and see what a great privilege God has conferred on this poor and worthless substance. It would be enough to say, in fact, that there is not a soul which can procure salvation unless it believes while it is still in the flesh. So true is it that the flesh is the very condition on which salvation hinges. And since the soul is chosen to the service of God because of its salvation, it is the flesh which actually renders it capable of such service. The flesh is washed so that the soul might be cleansed. The flesh is anointed

27. *Apology* 39.
28. *To the Nations* 1.5.

> so that the soul might be consecrated. The flesh is signed with the cross so that the soul too may be fortified. The flesh is covered by the laying on of hands, so that the soul may be illuminated by the Spirit. The flesh feeds on the body and blood of Christ so that the soul may fatten on God. They cannot therefore be given different rewards when they have laboured together in service. Moreover it is the flesh which performs those sacrifices which are acceptable to God – spiritual struggles, fasting, abstinences and the related humiliations – and which suffers as a consequence. Virginity, widowhood and chaste behaviour within marriage are fragrant offerings to God paid by the good offices of the flesh. Come then, give me your opinion of the flesh, when it has to contend for the name of Christ by dying for him. Most blessed and most glorious must be the flesh which can repay its master Christ so vast a debt, and so completely that the only obligation remaining is that by death it should cease to owe him more, but be all the more bound to him in gratitude because it has been set free for ever.[29]

Baptism

Tertullian held a high doctrine of baptism, though it was not quite the teaching of baptismal regeneration that became the standard view in later times. Instead, he thought of the sacrament as a preparation for the coming of the Holy Spirit, a cleansing of the flesh rather than a rebirth of the soul. He expressed this view as follows:

> We do not obtain the Holy Spirit in the water of baptism, but in that water, under the witness of an angel, we are cleansed and prepared for the Holy Spirit. There was a type of this in John's baptism, who prepared the way of the Lord in that way (Luke 1:76). Similarly, the angel who bears witness to baptism 'makes the paths straight' (Matthew 3:3) for the Holy Spirit who is about to come upon us, by the washing away of sins, which faith, sealed in the name of the Father, the Son and the Holy Spirit, obtains. For if it is true that 'in the mouth of three witnesses every word shall stand' (Deuteronomy 19:15; Matthew 18:16; 2 Corinthians 13:1), how much more does the number of the divine names suffice to give us assurance of our hope![30]

Church and state

Tertullian argued passionately against the persecution of Christians by the Roman authorities, and never tired of pointing out how false Roman official religion was. Yet at the same time he recognized the importance of the state

---

29. *On the Resurrection of the Flesh* 8.
30. *On Baptism* 6.

and its role in protecting people from chaos and disorder. This is what he says about the Christian's attitude to the secular authorities of his day:

> We must by all means offer prayers for the emperor, for the complete stability of the empire and for Roman interests in general. We know that a great disaster is hovering over the whole earth – the very end of things, no less, threatening dreadful woes – and that this is only retarded by the continued existence of the Roman empire. We have no desire to be overtaken by these dreadful events, and by praying that their coming may be delayed, we are lending our support to Rome's duration. We do not swear by the genius of the emperors, but rather by their safety, which is worth more than any genius. Do you not know that these genii are demons? We respect the fact that the emperors have been set over us by God and we know that they possess the power which God wanted them to have. We therefore pray for the safety of whatever it is that God has willed, and we take our allegiance to it with the utmost seriousness. But as for demons, that is your genii, we are in the habit of exorcizing them, not of swearing by them, and thereby conferring some divine honour on them.[31]

Like many early Christians, Tertullian was very doubtful about the lawfulness of military service, because of its vocation to defend and extend secular power. He argued as follows:

> Can a believer dedicate himself to military service, and can a soldier be admitted to the faith, even if he is a private or one of the lower ranks, and is not personally involved in sacrifices [to idols] or capital punishments? There is no connection between the divine and the human sacrament, the standard of Christ and the standard of the devil, the camp of light and the camp of darkness. One soul cannot serve two masters, God and Caesar. And yet Moses carried a rod and Aaron wore a buckle and John [the Baptist] was clothed in leather, and Joshua the son of Nun led a line of marchers, and the people of God went to war – if you want to debate the subject. But how can a Christian man go to war, or even serve in peace, for that matter, without a sword, which the Lord has taken away (Matthew 26:52). For even if soldiers had come to John and had received the formula of their rule (Luke 3:12–13), and although a centurion had believed (Matthew 8:5), when the Lord later disarmed Peter, he unbelted every soldier. No dress is lawful among us if it is related to any unlawful action.[32]

---

31. *Apology* 32.
32. *On Idolatry* 19.

On the same subject:

> Is warfare a proper profession for Christians? Do we believe that it is all right for a human oath to be added to a divine one, for a man to have a master other than Christ? Is it lawful to make an occupation of the sword when the Lord says that he who lives by the sword shall die by the sword?
>
> Shall a man of peace take part in a battle when he abstains from lawsuits in court? Can a man who refuses to avenge the wrongs done to him use the chain, the prison and torture? Can he stand on guard for others even more than for Christ? Can he do this even on the Lord's Day, when he cannot do it for his own Lord? Can he guard the temples of gods which he has renounced? The list of offences which a solider must commit in the line of duty goes on and on!
>
> Of course it is different in the case of soldiers who become Christians later. Look for instance at those faithful centurions whom John received for baptism, the centurion whom Jesus approved of and the one whom Peter instructed in the faith. Yet at the same time, when a man has become a believer and his faith has been sealed, he must either abandon his profession immediately (as many have done), or else there will be endless prevarication and making of excuses in an effort to avoid offending God, and such behaviour would not be tolerated among civilians. Nor is a military man protected from the fate which the faith of civilians must endure. Military service is not an escape from the punishment of sins, nor does it grant any exemption from martyrdom.[33]

Persecution

Tertullian argued that persecution was illogical and against the interests of the state itself. He realized that the battle was a spiritual one, and insisted that the proper attitude of Christians towards their persecutors was one of love, since only that was likely to persuade them to change their minds.

The following passage is the introduction to his letter to the Roman governor of Africa, outlining his position:

> We are not particularly bothered about the persecutions which we suffer because of the ignorance of others, for we have become Christians by accepting the terms of its covenant. Thus, as people whose lives are not our own, we engage in these conflicts, desiring to obtain God's promised rewards and afraid that if we fail, the woes which he threatens to inflict on an unchristian life will overtake us too. We do not shrink from getting to grips with your deepest rage, and we come to battle of our own

---

33. *On the Crown* 11.

accord. To be condemned by you gives us more pleasure than to be acquitted. It is for this reason that we have written to you. We are not worried about ourselves, but are concerned for you and for all our enemies, to say nothing of our friends. For our religion commands us to love our enemies also, and to pray for those who persecute us. It aims at a perfection all its own, and seeks in its disciples something of a higher type than the commonplace goodness of the world. Everybody loves those who love them, but only Christians love those who hate them. And so, mourning over your ignorance, sympathizing with human error and looking towards that future of which every day offers threatening signs, necessity is laid upon us to come forward in this way also, that we may set out the truth which you will not listen to publicly.[34]

Eschatology

Tertullian tackled the vexed question of what happens to the soul after death, particularly in the interval that precedes its reunion with the body at the resurrection. He believed that the soul in hell received either punishment or reward according to its good deeds on earth, before being raised with the flesh for the final judgement. He developed this unusual idea as follows:

All souls are confined to hell [after death], where punishments and consolations are already being experienced, as the story of the rich man and Lazarus makes clear. Why can you not accept this? You answer that it is impossible because in justice there should be no inkling of the punishment or reward before the final sentence is pronounced, and this should not happen until the flesh is restored to the soul, since it was a partner in the soul's actions and therefore ought to share in the judgement passed upon it. What then takes place in that interval? Will we sleep? But souls do not sleep even when people are alive – it is the business of bodies to sleep and to die, since sleep is but the counterfeit of death. Are you going to say that nothing happens in the place where the whole human race is drawn to, and where everyone's future expectation is postponed for safe keeping? Do you think this state is a foretaste of judgement, or the start of judgement itself? Is it a premature encroachment on it, or the first instalment of it? Would it not be the greatest possible injustice, even in hell, if the guilty were still doing well there but the righteous had not yet received their reward? Would you make our hope even more confused after death? Would you have it mock us still more with uncertain expectation? Or will it now become a review of past life, and an arranging of judgement, with the inevitable feeling of trembling fear?

34. *To Scapula* 1.

Must the soul always wait for the body in order to experience sorrow or joy? Is it incapable of suffering either or both of these sensations on its own?

Even in hell the soul knows how to joy or sorrow even without the body. In the flesh, it feels pain when it chooses to do so, even when the body is unhurt, and it can feel joy even when the body is in pain. If such sensations occur at will during life, why can they not happen after death by God's own judicial appointment? The soul does not need the flesh in order to act, and the judgement of God pursues its inmost thoughts and desires. 'Whoever looks on a woman to lust after her has committed adultery with her already in his heart' (Matthew 5:28). So you see that it is quite right for the soul to be punished for what it has done independently of the flesh, without having to wait for the flesh to catch up with it. In the same way, it will receive the reward for its pious thoughts, which it had without the aid of the flesh, without the flesh's participation in it. Even in matters done through the flesh, it is the soul which is the first to conceive them, the first to arrange them, the first to authorize them, the first to precipitate them into acts. Even if it is sometimes unwilling to act, it is still the first to treat the object which it means to effect by help of the body. There is no case in which an event can take place before it has been conceived in the mind. It is therefore quite in keeping with the order of things that that part of our nature should be the first to have the recompense and reward which it deserves on account of its priority. Since we understand the prison mentioned in the Gospel to be hell (Matthew 5:25), and interpret 'the uttermost farthing' (Matthew 5:26) to mean the very smallest offence which has to be paid for there before the resurrection, no-one will hesitate to believe that the soul undergoes some remedial discipline in hell without prejudice to the full process of the resurrection, when the reward will be administered through the flesh as well.[35]

But Tertullian did not believe that the soul would be punished without the flesh. He believed in the resurrection of the body for this purpose, which he explained as follows:

The reason why the soul is restored to the body is the appointed judgement. Everyone has to come back just as he was before so as to receive judgement at God's hands, whether for good or for evil. This is why the body will appear as well, because the soul cannot suffer without the solid substance (the flesh), nor is it right for the soul to bear all the wrath of God by itself. Souls did not sin without their bodies, and everything they did was done in them.[36]

---

35. *On the Soul* 58.
36. *Apology* 48.

Like most early Christians, Tertullian believed in the imminent return of Christ and the final consummation of all things. He had heard reports that a city, presumably the new Jerusalem, had been seen in the sky over Judea, and interpreted this as the beginning of the coming end:

> It is clear from the testimony of even pagan witnesses that there was a city suspended in the sky over Judaea early every morning for forty days. As the day wore on, its walls would gradually fade away, and sometimes it would vanish instantly. We believe that this city was provided by God for receiving the saints at their resurrection and refreshing them with the abundance of every true spiritual blessing as a recompense for the things which we have either despised or lost in this world, since it is both just and worthy of God that his servants should have their joy in the place where they have also suffered affliction for his name's sake. This is the way it will all work out. After its thousand years are over, within which period the resurrection of the saints will be completed (for they will rise sooner or later, according to what they deserve), there will ensue the destruction of the world and the conflagration of all things at the judgement. We shall then be changed in a moment into the substance of angels, even by putting on an incorruptible nature, and so be taken up to that kingdom in heaven which we have just been talking about.[37]

Tertullian developed his picture of the final consummation of all things at the end of his treatise *On Spectacles*, in which he severely criticized the theatre and other amusements as nothing more than vanity and occasions for sin. In contrast, Christians were waiting for the greatest show of all – the return of Jesus Christ and the last judgement:

> What a spectacle the fast-approaching return of our Lord will be, when everyone will acknowledge him, highly exalted and triumphant as he will be. How great the exultation of the angelic hosts will be! How spectacular the glory of the saints rising from the dead! How great the kingdom of the righteous from that moment on! What a city the New Jerusalem will be! Yes, and there are other sights galore – the last day of judgement with its eternal decisions, that day unlooked for by the nations, the subject of their contempt, when the world, weighed down with old age and all its fruits, will be consumed in one great flame. What an enormous spectacle will then burst forth upon the eye. What will there excite my admiration? My contempt? My joy? My exultation? As I see so many illustrious monarchs, whose entry into heaven was publicly announced, groaning now in the lowest darkness with great

37. *Against Marcion* 3.24.

Jupiter himself, along with those who were witnesses of their exultation. There are provincial governors there too, who persecuted the name of Christ, now burning in fires fiercer than those with which, in the days of their pride, they raged against the Christians. And look at the wise men of this world, the philosophers themselves, who taught their followers that God had no interest in anything which happened under the sun, and were in the habit of assuring them either that they had no souls, or that they would never return to the bodies which they left when they died. Now they are covered with shame in the presence of the poor deluded ones, as one fire consumes them both. There are poets there too, trembling not before the judgement seat of Rhadamanthus or Minos, but before Christ, which was the last thing they expected!

I shall have a better opportunity then to hear the tragedians, louder voiced than ever as they face their own calamity. I shall get a better view of the play-actors, who will be much more 'dissolute' in the flame which dissolves them. I shall see the charioteer, glowing in his chariot of fire, and the wrestlers, not in their gymnasia, but tossing in the fiery billows. Perhaps though, when the time comes, I shall not be too bothered about such servants of sin, and shall be much more intent on focussing my gaze on those whose fury vented itself against the Lord. I shall say: 'This is the carpenter's or hireling's son, that Sabbath-breaker, that Samaritan and devil-possessed man! This is the one you purchased from Judas! This is the one whom you struck with reed and fist, whom you contemptuously spat upon, to whom you gave gall and vinegar to drink. This is the one whose disciples secretly stole away, that it might be said that he had risen again, or that the gardener had removed him so that his lettuce would not be trampled on by the hordes of pilgrims coming to the tomb.' What civic official or priest in his generosity will grant you the favour of seeing and rejoicing in such things as these? Yet even now we can do so in some measure by our faith, in the pictures of our imagination. What are the things which eye has not seen, nor ear heard, and which have not so much as dimly dawned upon the human heart? Whatever they are, they are far nobler, in my opinion, than any circus, theatre or racecourse.[38]

Sexual continence

One of the ways in which Tertullian's rigorist approach to Christian self-discipline manifested itself was in his attitude towards sexual relations. Unlike many others in the early church, he did not advocate total abstinence at all times. He believed that matrimony was a biblical institution and was himself married, though he thought that married couples should abstain from sexual

---

38. *On Spectacles* 30.

intercourse as much as possible. Likewise, those who were widowed should not marry again, but devote themselves to a life of prayer and the service of God. His attitude is expressed most clearly in the following passage, written to a man who had recently lost his wife:

> I doubt not, brother, that after your wife's untimely passing, you are concentrating on putting your life back together and contemplating the loneliness of old age. You obviously need some guidance in this, even though in cases of this kind, each individual ought to consult his own faith and test its strength. But in this particular matter, the necessity of the flesh (which is faith's great enemy) sets people thinking, which is why faith needs outside support in order to oppose that very necessity. It can in fact be dealt with quite easily, as long as we focus on what God wants for us and not merely on what he is prepared to tolerate. There is no merit in taking advantage of God's tolerance, but only in prompt obedience to his will. The will of God is our sanctification (1 Thessalonians 4:3), because he wants his image in us to become his likeness so that we may be holy just as he is holy (1 Peter 1:16). Sanctification comes in many different forms, and we must be found in one of them. The first of these is virginity from birth, and the second is virginity from second birth (*i.e.* after baptism). This second type of virginity keeps itself pure, either within the bond of marriage or else in freely chosen widowhood. There is also a third kind of sanctification, monogamy, which means renouncing sexual intercourse after the death of a spouse. The first virginity is the virginity of happiness, because it consists of total ignorance of the thing which you want to be free from. The second virginity is that of virtue, because it consists in renouncing what you know full well. The third is both the glory of virtue and also of moderation, for moderation is not regretting something which has been taken away, particularly when it has been taken away by God, without whose will a leaf does not fall from a tree nor does a sparrow fall to the ground (Matthew 10:29).[39]

Fasting

Another area in which Tertullian's rigorism comes to the fore is that of fasting. He believed it was a principle that could be traced back to the creation of man in the Garden of Eden, and even blamed the Fall on Adam's failure to observe it:

> Adam had received from God the law of not tasting 'of the tree of the knowledge of good and evil', with the punishment of death decreed for failure to observe it

39. *On Exhortation to Chastity* 1.

(Genesis 2:16–17). But even Adam reverted to the state of an unspiritual man, and that after the spiritual ecstasy in which he had prophetically interpreted that 'great sacrament' (Ephesians 5:32; cf. Genesis 2:23–24) of Christ and the church. No longer capable of doing the things which belong to the Holy Spirit (cf. 1 Corinthians 2:14), he surrendered to his stomach rather than to God, heeding the meat rather than the mandate, and sold his salvation in order to satisfy his gullet! To be blunt about it, Adam ate the fruit and perished, when he would have been saved if he had only fasted from one little tree! Thus we see that even at that early date, unregenerate faith can recognize its own progeny, seeing in Adam the source of its desire for carnal things and its rejection of spiritual ones. It seems to me therefore that from the beginning, God intended that the appetite should be punished with the torments and penalties of hunger.[40]

Church services

In Tertullian's day, holding church services was illegal and could easily lead to persecution. Many Christians seemed to think that the way around this was to bribe the authorities to leave them alone. Tertullian rejected this solution, and recommended a more spiritual course of action:

How shall we assemble together? How shall we observe the ordinances of the Lord? Just as the Apostles did, of course – protected by faith, not by money. If faith can remove a mountain, it can certainly remove a soldier as well! Let wisdom be your safeguard, not bribery. Even if you buy off the interference of soldiers, that will still not give you protection against other people. All you need for your safety is faith and wisdom. If you do not make use of these, you may lose even the deliverance which you have purchased for yourself, and if you do use them, then you will have no need of ransom money. If you cannot assemble by day, then there is always the night, when the light of Christ will brighten up the darkness. Be content with a church of threes. It is better not to have big crowds than to subject yourselves to the yoke of bribery. Keep Christ's betrothed virgin pure for him, and do not let anyone make money off her. These things may seem harsh and unbearable, but remember that God has said: 'He who receives it, let him receive it' (Matthew 19:12). Anyone who is afraid to suffer cannot belong to the One who suffered [for us]. The man who is not afraid to suffer will be perfect in love, the love of God that is, because 'perfect love casts out fear' (1 John 4:18). 'Many are called but few are chosen' (Matthew 22:14). God does not ask who is prepared to follow the broad way, but who will endure the narrow one. This is why we need the Comforter, who guides us

40. *On Fasting* 3.

into all truth and strengthens us to all endurance. Those who have received him will neither flee from persecution nor buy it off, for they have the Lord himself, who will stand by us to aid us in our suffering and be our mouthpiece when we are put on trial.[41]

Tertullian's spiritual legacy

What lessons are there to be learned today from a man like Tertullian? There is no doubt that much of what he said and did seems strange to us, and even in his own day he was regarded as an extremist in many quarters. Changed circumstances make much of what he had to say seem outdated or inapplicable now, even if it is still true that Christians may be called to suffer persecution for the name of Christ. But having said that, Tertullian's legacy remains with us and there are still a number of things we can learn from him and the example he set.

First of all, Tertullian teaches us that to be a Christian is to live a new life, baptized in the faith of Christ and separate, without being separated, from the world. As Christians we live in the midst of unbelievers, but are called to be witnesses to them, even to the point of death, if necessary. Today we read that statistics for divorce (to take but one common example) are just as high among churchgoers as in the general population. For Tertullian, this would have been scandalous because he would have seen it as evidence that the people concerned were not truly born again. We may not want to go that far, but it is certainly true that modern Christians do not pay enough attention to what ought to make them distinctive in the world. Yet unless we are different, and seen to be happier and more fulfilled as a result, how can we expect others to believe the claims we make about salvation in Christ?

Secondly, Tertullian teaches us to see that the principles of our faith have implications for every aspect of our life and thought. If we believe that God is the creator of the universe, we cannot call anything useless or unclean, nor can we preach a gospel that speaks only to a part of our reality. In his day, the danger was that people would talk about saving souls but ignore the resurrection of the flesh, and something similar is still a problem today. It is too easy to speak of spiritual experiences without grounding them in physical reality, which is equally part of the created order and cannot be ignored or despised. Modern Christians desperately need to anchor their spirituality in everyday life, without succumbing to the temptation to do social work instead of preach the gospel. There is

41. *On Flight in Persecution* 14.

a balance of body and spirit that we are called to maintain, and Tertullian's was one of the loudest voices proclaiming that truth in the early church.

Thirdly, Tertullian teaches us never to be complacent about our spiritual life. We may not follow him in his attraction to Montanism, but his belief that the church is always in need of improvement is surely one we can accept without quibble. Growth in grace and in the Holy Spirit is what the Christian life is all about, and if it is not happening then something is seriously wrong. Tertullian knew that, and stirred up the Christians of his day to get them to pursue the life of holiness that is God's will for us. It is all too easy for us to put family, friends and fellowship ahead of holiness and purity in the life of the church. Often we fail (or refuse) to denounce sin because to do so might provoke division, and fail to recognize that such complacency weakens the church. Tertullian helps us to get our priorities right and to remember that we are called to be one in the Spirit above all else.

Fourthly, Tertullian teaches us the importance of doctrinal orthodoxy. If we go astray in our doctrine, then our practice will be unsound and we shall be liable to fall into heresy and sin. Modern Christians are perhaps too ready to excuse doctrinal faults if they do not seem to compromise personal behaviour, but Tertullian sees that this dichotomy is ultimately untenable. The mind is the governing part of the soul, which means that belief is the determining part of life. Consistency here is the mark of the Christian and must be sought after by all who sincerely want to follow Christ in their lives. Modern Christians tend to discount the importance of doctrine, or regard it as the concern of a few somewhat eccentric specialists, but it is the foundation of our common life and witness. Orthodoxy is not just one opinion among many; it is the cornerstone of the church which must not be shifted or weakened. We have seen how theological liberalism in one generation leads to indiscipline and sexual immorality in the next. Tertullian knew this, and in his writings constantly reminds us not to be fooled by preachers who try to attract followers by diluting the content of the gospel message.

Lastly, Tertullian teaches us to expect that the end may come at any time and that we must prepare for it in the way we think and act. To be ready for God's call is the challenge that faces every Christian – then as well as now. None of us can say when our time will come, but come it surely will – and often at a time quite unexpected by us. The readiness is all, and obedience is better than sacrifice. Times have changed, but the reality of death remains the same. Tertullian hoped that he would live to see the second coming of Christ, and so do we; but whether we do or not, we must be just as prepared to give our lives for the sake of the kingdom of heaven as the martyrs celebrated by Tertullian were. As we read his words, let us be prepared to hear the voice of the Lord Jesus Christ calling us too, to follow in the footsteps of his faithful servant Tertullian and earn with him a crown of everlasting glory among the saints in heaven.

Bibliography

Primary sources

The standard critical edition of Tertullian's works is *Opera omnia*, ed. A. Reifferscheid, G. Wissowa, A. Kroymann, H. Hoppe, V. Bulhart and P. Borleffs, and published in Corpus scriptorum ecclesiasticorum latinorum 20, 47, 69, 70, 76 (Vienna: 1890–1957); repr. in Corpus scriptorum ecclesiasticorum latinorum 1–2 (Turnhout: Brepols, 1954).

Translations

The only complete translation of Tertullian's works into English is by P. Holmes and S. Thelwall, *Ante-Nicene Fathers*, vols. 3–4 (Buffalo, NY: Christian Literature, 1885–96; repr. Peabody, MA; Hendrickson, 1994).

Translations of some individual treatises have been made by E. Evans, of which the most significant are *On the Incarnation* (London: SPCK, 1956) and *Adversus Marcionem*, 2 vols. (Oxford: Oxford University Press, 1972).

General introductions

BARNES, T. D., *Tertullian: A Historical and Literary Study* (Oxford: Oxford University Press, 1971). Mainly concerned with reconstructing a biography and within the North African context.

DUNN, GEOFFREY D., *Tertullian* (London: Routledge, 2004). Contains significant extracts from Tertullian's writings.

OSBORN, ERIC, *Tertullian, First Theologian of the West* (Cambridge: Cambridge University Press, 1997). The best recent study of Tertullian.

QUASTEN, J., *Patrology*, 3 vols. (Utrecht: Spectrum, 1950–60), vol. 2, pp. 246–340. Probably the most useful study for beginners and those who want information about certain aspects of Tertullian's thought. It is helpfully subdivided according to theological themes and individual treatises, with an extensive bibliography for each section.

WRIGHT, D., 'Tertullian', in P. F. Esler (ed.), *The Early Christian World*, (London: Routledge, 2000), vol. 2, pp. 1027–1047.

Studies

BRAY, G. L., *Holiness and the Will of God* (London: Marshall, Morgan & Scott, 1979).

DALY, C., *Tertullian the Puritan and his Influence* (Dublin: Four Courts, 1994).

KEARSLEY, R., *Tertullian's Theology of Divine Power* (Carlisle: Paternoster, 1998).

O'MALLEY, T., *Tertullian and the Bible: Language, Imagery, Exegesis* (Nijmegen: Dekker, 1967).

Rankin, D. I., *Tertullian and the Church* (Cambridge: Cambridge University Press, 1995).
Sider, R. D., *Ancient Rhetoric and the Art of Tertullian* (Oxford: Oxford University Press, 1971).
Trevett, C., *Montanism: Gender, Authority and the New Prophecy* (Cambridge: Cambridge University Press, 1996).

The best studies of Tertullian's theology are in French:

Braun, R., *Approches de Tertullien* (Paris: Etudes Augustiniennes, 1992).
—, *Recherches sur le vocabulaire doctrinal de Tertullien*, 2nd ed. (Paris: Etudes Augustiniennes, 1977).
Moingt, J., *Théologie trinitaire de Tertullien*, 4 vols. (Paris: Aubier, 1966–9).

3. ORIGEN

Bryan Litfin

A diamond with a traditional 'brilliant cut' sparkles with astonishing beauty because its fifty-seven facets disperse white light into the colours of the spectrum. As light enters the gem, it is reflected and refracted and returned to the viewer's eye from many angles. Words like *fire*, *brilliance* and *scintillation* describe how a diamond gleams as if a living flame were inside. The light's journey through the gem's many facets contributes to the beauty of the whole.

Origen of Alexandria (186–254) was known in his day as Adamantius.[1] The nickname derives from a Greek word meaning 'untamed' or 'undefeated'. By implication, the word came to refer to the hardest of gems, the diamond. It is an apt name for one of the greatest figures the Christian church has ever known. Like a diamond, Origen was *hard*: impervious to the pleasures of the flesh during his lifetime, and unbroken by Roman torture in his death. Origen was also *multifaceted*: he comes down to us in the sources as an instructor, a theologian, a philosopher, a preacher, a Bible scholar, an ascetic and especially an exegete. Yet in the end Origen was most like a diamond in that he was *beautiful*. His heart was enraptured by the utter transcendence of the one true God. Every aspect of Origen's thought celebrated the cosmic mystery that the Word became flesh to lead the souls of the faithful back to the divine. Origen's

1. Eusebius, *Ecclesiastical History* 6.14.10; Jerome, *Epistle* 33.3.

writings sparkle with the light of heaven. Just as we would never throw away a diamond – even one with flaws in it – so let us not cast Origen aside as a piece of historical debris. He is far too valuable for such waste.

The warning not to disregard Origen is by no means superfluous; evangelicals are often tempted to do just that.[2] Athanasius, Augustine, Anselm – such names can be trusted when evangelicals take the time to borrow from the Christian past. But Origen? Is he not that notorious Bible-corrupter who cut off his testicles? For some reason, these two slurs have found a welcoming home in the evangelical mind: that Origen used the allegorical method to undercut the Bible's meaning, and that he committed the vaguely titillating atrocity of self-castration. It is true that Origen used allegory, and he may well have castrated himself. Yet it is fair to ask, should we remain content with a superficial awareness of these historical facts? Or should we dig deeper into the enigmatic life of this ancient Christian? In seeking to unravel the conundrum of Origen, perhaps a more profound understanding will reveal itself to those willing to pursue the labour of investigation.

Origen's life and setting

Times were tough for Christians in Origen's day. He lived in an age when Christianity could no longer be ignored as a marginal Jewish sect within the Roman Empire. It was a vibrant force, an aggressive and growing religion. As such, the imperial authorities were bound to respond to it as a threat to the old, unifying force of paganism. But the third century AD was not an era of irenic tolerance of every man's faith. The emperors and provincial bureaucrats recognized the signs of decay within their domain. Barbarians were pressing from the outside, and the machinery of Roman governance was crumbling from overextension and decay. Though it would be fifteen centuries before Edward Gibbon would famously describe the period of Origen's life as the beginning of the 'decline and fall of the Roman Empire', plenty of evidence existed at the time to tell the emperors something needed to be done about the influx of strange, new religions. Along these lines, Emperor Septimius Severus initiated a persecution against the Christians in 202. The specific decree forbade

2. On the popular scepticism with which some view Origen, see John R. Franke, 'Origen: Friend or Foe? He Has Been Called the Father of Christian Biblical Exegesis, the First Systematic Theologian . . . and a Heretic. How Should we Assess his Legacy Today?', *Christian History* 80 (2003), pp. 18–23.

conversion to both Judaism and Christianity.[3] Although Origen himself was not arrested at the time, the repercussions were nonetheless severe: his father was imprisoned and beheaded, and the family's property stripped away.[4]

Like so many noteworthy figures in church history, Origen came from a solid Christian home. His father Leonides did Origen the dual service of providing a fine education, and loving his son with tender affection. Leonides drilled Origen in Greek literature, but emphasized the study of God's Word as even more important. Origen took to these lessons readily, showing remarkable aptitude and zeal. In fact, Origen's questions about sacred Scripture were so profound and inquisitive that his father sometimes had to rebuke him for inordinate curiosity. Yet in his heart, Leonides 'rejoiced greatly, and gave profound thanks to God, the Author of all good things, that He had deemed him worthy to be the father of such a boy'.[5] In fact, Leonides would often slip to Origen's bedside at night and kiss his son's bosom, overcome with delight in the holy spirit he saw developing in the boy, and counting himself very blessed to be his father.

It was no small blow to Origen, then, when at the age of sixteen he lost his father to martyrdom. Origen was initially caught up in a burning desire to join his father in prison and follow him to death. But God – and Origen's mother – had other plans. After pleading to no avail for Origen to abandon

---

3. *Historia Augusta* 17.1. The authenticity of the assertion that Christians were specifically persecuted by Septimius Severus is debated, although W. H. C. Frend, a leading authority on Christianity in Africa, considers it valid ('A Severan Persecution? Evidence of the *Historia Augusta*', *Forma futuri* [Turin: Bottega d'Erasmo, 1975], pp. 470–480).
4. The facts of Origen's life are recorded in two main sources: Eusebius' *Ecclesiastical History*, Book 6, and an oration attributed to Gregory the Wonderworker (Thaumaturgus), one of Origen's students, usually called *Address to Origen*. For English editions, see Eusebius, *The Ecclesiastical History*, vol. 2, tr. J. E. L. Oulton, Loeb Classical Library (Cambridge, MA: Harvard University Press, 1932); and Alexander Roberts and James Donaldson, *The Ante-Nicene Fathers* [*ANF*], vol. 6 (Buffalo: Christian Literature, 1886), pp. 21–39. The letters of Jerome also provide some background information. Excellent full-length biographies of Origen can be had in Henri Crouzel, *Origen: The Life and Thought of the First Great Theologian*, tr. A. S. Worrall (San Francisco: Harper & Row, 1989); Joseph W. Trigg, *Origen* (New York: Routledge, 1998); and John Anthony McGuckin (ed.), *The Westminster Handbook to Origen* (Louisville: Westminster John Knox, 2004).
5. Eusebius, *Ecclesiastical History* 6.2.10 (Oulton, p. 13).

such a rash course of action, his mother finally hid his clothes so he could not go outside, thereby preventing his death. In this way (at least as Eusebius interprets it in his biographical sketch of Origen) God's providence worked toward the greater good through Origen's mother. With nothing else to do, Origen could only write a letter to his father in prison, urging him not to waver in his steadfastness or change his mind on account of his family. Leonides remained firm in his intent to bear the ultimate witness; and so Origen's family was left penniless upon his death. The martyrdom would have a profound impact on Origen, not only in his immediate financial situation, but in his high regard for the Christian duty to die to the world and its attractions.

With a mother and six younger brothers, Origen realized he needed to find gainful employment right away. For a time, a wealthy lady in Alexandria provided for his needs, but Origen soon grew uncomfortable with this godly woman's lack of discernment: she had taken under her wing a young man named Paul who taught heresy. Although Origen had to interact with Paul, he never prayed with him, because Paul did not hold to the church's correct rule of doctrine. Though we do not know the precise nature of Paul's heresy, the story illustrates Origen's concern for doctrinal purity. As Origen himself said, 'We must watch out for ourselves lest we be caught up by the specious arguments of heretical doctrine and fall away from the mystery of the church.'[6] It is ironic that, long after he died, Origen was widely accused of heresy.

Origen began to support his impoverished family as a schoolteacher, but it wasn't long before the bishop in the city, Demetrius, took note of this brilliant and fervent young believer. In addition to his duties teaching Greek literature, Origen was given the responsibility for all Christian catechesis in Alexandria. In Eusebius' account, it appears at first glance that Origen presided over a formal 'catechetical school', perhaps even approaching the status of what might be called a university, founded by Pantaenus and supervised by Clement of Alexandria before being handed over to Origen.[7] However, this approach reads too much into the evidence. While Alexandria with its famous library was indeed a magnet for intellectuals, and while Origen's educational efforts ranged into philosophical discussions that went far beyond the scope of the church's traditional catechesis, we should not picture Origen as a kind of academic dean or provost presiding over a Christian college. Instead, we should view him as

---

6. Origen, *Homily on Job* 20.15, in Hans Urs von Balthasar, *Origen: Spirit and Fire: A Thematic Anthology of His Writings*, tr. Robert J. Daly (Washington, DC: Catholic University of America Press, 1984), p. 172.
7. Eusebius, *Ecclesiastical History* 6.6.1 (Oulton, p. 27).

a spiritual director teaching his disciples the rudiments of the Christian faith – and eventually the deeper principles of the Christian life.[8]

We can see Origen's master–disciple relationships lived out in that age of persecution by the way he followed his students into prison, fearlessly walking the road to martyrdom with them until the very end, even at great danger to himself.[9] We also gain a window into Origen's very personal discipleship ministry when we consider the praise heaped upon him in an oration by one of his former students, Gregory the Wonderworker. Describing the impact Origen had on him and his brother as they considered their life's calling, Gregory says:

> He did not aim merely at getting round us by any kind of reasoning; but his desire was, with a benign and affectionate and most benevolent mind, to save us, and make us partakers in the blessings that flow from philosophy . . . And thus, like some spark lighting on our inmost soul, love was kindled and burst into flame within us – a love at once to the Holy Word, the most lovely object of all, who attracts all irresistibly toward Himself by His unutterable beauty, and to this man, His friend and advocate.[10]

Clearly, Origen had the kind of spiritual magnetism that drew disciples to his side. He was no ivory-tower academic teaching a scientific theology in a classroom setting, but a lifelong mentor to those who wished to progress deeper in their walk with Christ. The students who followed Origen were drawn to the power of his spiritual life. We should be careful to locate Origen in the context of service to the church, rather than define him as a kind of parachurch intellectual.[11]

---

8. Robert L. Wilken, 'Alexandria: A School for Training in Virtue', in Patrick Henry (ed.), *Schools of Thought in the Christian Tradition* (Philadelphia: Fortress, 1984), pp. 15–30.
9. Eusebius, *Ecclesiastical History* 6.3.3–7 (Oulton, pp. 17–19). We may wonder why Origen himself was not martyred in the course of these activities. Crouzel (*Origen*, p. 6) and McGuckin (*Westminster Handbook*, p. 3) follow the opinion of Aline Rousselle that Septimius Severus' persecution was directed against the upper classes, to which Leonides belonged, but to which Origen, whose mother was of lower social status, did not (A. Rousselle, 'The Persecution of Christians at Alexandria in the 3rd Century', *Revue historique de Droit français et étranger* 2 [1974], pp. 222–251).
10. Gregory the Wonderworker, *Address to Origen* (*ANF*, vol. 6, 28; slightly adapted).
11. Alister Stewart-Sykes argues that Origen's social role in Alexandria was that of the 'intellectual', defined in sociological terms as 'an expert whose expertise is

Over the next three decades, Origen's life as a Christian teacher at Alexandria involved the highest level of scholarship, and at the same time, the highest level of spiritual devotion. To some, it may seem those two purposes are at odds with each other. Today we often contrast the 'head' and the 'heart' – the head being cold and sterile, the heart being warm and pious. Nothing could be further from how Origen viewed things. For him, the use of the mind to investigate spiritual truth was the highest form of devotion, and the task could not be pursued except by one whose heart was pure. Origen achieved great notoriety as a brilliant intellect in Alexandria, even studying under the foremost philosopher of the day, Ammonius Saccas, the ostensible founder of the Neoplatonist movement. Non-Christian scholars, drawn to Alexandria by the intellectual beacon of its great library, made a point of meeting the renowned Christian apologist – and some were won to his faith.[12] Yet, for all his brilliance, Origen maintained a profound piety that in no way detracted from his intellectual work. He recognized that ascending to the mountaintop

---

unwanted by society' ('Origen, Demetrius, and the Alexandrian Presbyters', *St. Vladimir's Theological Quarterly* 48.4 [2004], pp. 415–429). Though Bishop Demetrius took over Origen's independent school and turned it into a vehicle for catechesis, Origen continued to play the outsider's role of the intellectual whose views could be considered dangerous or deviant, as opposed to the acceptable 'recognized expert', who employs his expertise on behalf of society. In response to Stewart-Sykes, it must be admitted that there was tension between the brilliant but edgy Origen and the older, more conservative, episcopal hierarchy in Alexandria. Nevertheless, Origen always viewed his intellectual work as service *to* the church, from *within* the church – even if it meant opposing his bishop on certain matters.

Joseph Trigg points out that Origen, in attempting to reconcile the social roles of 'intellectual' and 'churchman', appealed to his charismatic leadership ('The Charismatic Intellectual: Origen's Understanding of Religious Leadership', *Church History* 50.1 [1981], pp. 5–19). To explain why Origen consistently remained an ecclesiastical outsider, Trigg shows how Origen's model of leadership centred on a personal divine charism that demanded to be exercised even if it meant opposing the growing clerical authority in Alexandria. Origen had many negative things to say about unworthy, grasping bishops (Trigg, *Origen*, p. 14), but that does not mean he conceived of himself as being outside the church. For Origen, 'the bishop at the front of the church may well be bogus while the real bishop is lost in the congregation' (p. 15). In other words, Origen often served the church as loyal opposition within the ranks.

12. Eusebius, *Ecclesiastical History* 6.3.13 (Oulton, p. 23).

requires diligent preparation and hard labour. In this recognition, Origen became one of the first Christian ascetics.

Though he was a teacher, Origen did not lead the cushy life of a man of leisure. He was no tenured professor with a light teaching load and his summers off. Eusebius describes how Origen sold his entire library of literature books in exchange for a meagre pension on which he could barely scrape by. It was a substantial sacrifice for a learned man like Origen. From then on 'he continued to live like a philosopher in this wise, putting aside everything that might lead to youthful lusts; all day long his discipline was to perform labours of no light character, and the greater part of the night he devoted himself to studying the divine Scriptures'.[13] Origen's spiritual disciplines included fasting, limiting his sleep to short periods on a hard floor, minimizing his personal possessions (to the point of never wearing shoes!), and refraining from wine or superfluous food. These were not the acts of a man seeking to earn merit with God in some legalistic sense. They were the acts of a man who believed 'God is loved with the whole soul by those who through their great longing for fellowship with God draw their soul away and separate it, not only from their earthly body, but also from every corporeal thing'.[14] That is to say, Origen believed he could not know the spiritual God above unless he had purged himself of unworthy attraction to the things below. Such asceticism would be one of the hallmarks of Origen's thought. It contributed a great deal to the new Christian monasticism that had begun to take shape in the third century, and which blossomed mightily in the fourth.

Of course, not everything Origen did in his zeal for God deserves to be emulated. According to Eusebius, Origen literally obeyed Matthew 19:12, which speaks about men who made themselves eunuchs for the sake of the kingdom of heaven, and had himself castrated.[15] Bishop Demetrius initially approved of the act; but later, when he had a falling out with Origen, used the deed to tarnish Origen's reputation. Because Demetrius provides the only contemporaneous testimony to the castration, and his motives in repeating the slander were less than pure, some modern scholars deny the validity of the report, though others do not doubt it. Origen himself, commenting on Matthew 19:12 at a more mature stage of his life, attributes such behaviour

13. Ibid. 6.3.9–12 (p. 21).

14. Origen, *Exhortation to Martyrdom* 3 (Rowan Greer, *Origen* [New York: Paulist, 1979], p. 42).

15. Crouzel refers to it as 'the only thing the general public usually knows about Origen' (*Origen*, p. 9).

to 'fanciful fear of God and unmeasured desire for self-control'.[16] He goes on to describe the physiological problems resulting from castration, and adds that anyone who does so will 'subject themselves to reproach', not only from unbelievers, but from Christians as well.[17] It seems clear Origen is speaking from personal experience here.

What do we make of a man who took such extreme steps in his battle against the flesh? Was it an act of pathological self-hatred? Or was it, as Eusebius would have us believe, an act of youthful indiscretion – but one that nonetheless proves Origen's 'faith and self-control'?[18] In assessing the matter, we should keep in mind that human castration, though considered a freakish act in today's society, was quite common in ancient times, particularly among slaves imported from outside the empire.[19] The physical methodology of castration was well understood from the practice of animal husbandry, and eunuchs served a valid social purpose as slaves whose occupations necessarily brought them into close association with women. Religious castration was also practised (*e.g.* by the devotees of Cybele, or the Magna Mater). Even among the early Christians, the practice is attested.[20] In the second and third centuries it sometimes received admiration as a dramatic commitment to chastity, but it had become subject to widespread criticism and reproach by the fourth century. In fact, the very first canon of the Council of Nicaea (325) prohibits castrated men from serving as clergy, unless the castration was carried out for medical reasons or was performed forcibly on a slave.[21] The need to address the matter in canon law speaks to the frequency of its occurrence in the early

---

16. Origen, *Commentary on Matthew* 15.1, tr. Daniel F. Caner, 'The Practice and Prohibition of Self-Castration in Early Christianity', *Vigiliae christianae* 51 (1997), p. 401.
17. Ibid. In his comprehensive and learned article Caner accepts the validity of Origen's castration, as do Crouzel (*Origen*, p. 9) and Trigg (*Origen*, p. 14), while McGuckin rejects it as 'hardly credible' (*Westminster Handbook*, p. 6).
18. Eusebius, *Ecclesiastical History* 6.8.1 (Oulton, p. 29).
19. On this subject, in addition to Caner's study, see Piotr O. Scholz, *Eunuchs and Castrati: A Cultural History*, tr. John A. Broadwin and Shelley L. Frisch (Princeton: Wiener, 2001), pp. 159–191.
20. R. P. C. Hanson, 'A Note on Origen's Self-Mutilation', *Vigiliae christianae* 20.2 (June 1966), pp. 81–82.
21. Philip Schaff *et al.* (eds.), *A Select Library of Nicene and Post-Nicene Fathers of the Christian Church* [*NPNF*], 2nd series, vol. 14 (New York: Christian Literature, 1900), p. 8.

church. We also note that the council fathers did not see fit to issue a general prohibition of the practice, but only an injunction against the ordination of castrated men.

Therefore, we should not regard Origen's action as gravely out of step with the culture of his day. Sexual sin was considered a grievous matter, and the ancient Christians were willing to resort to extreme measures to gain victory over it. Jesus taught that lust was tantamount to adultery, and the church fathers took him seriously. Theirs was an age of profound commitment to *askēsis*, bodily self-discipline. They valued absolute bodily mastery for a number of reasons, not the least of which was because they knew it might be demanded of them, not only in daily life, but in a Roman torture chamber. Though cooler heads eventually prevailed, and castration came to be viewed as an inappropriate solution for the cravings of the flesh, it was not unheard of in the ancient church. Origen's action becomes understandable when set in historical context.

As Origen's fame as a scholar and ascetic grew, he undertook some travels abroad, visiting prominent church leaders in Rome, Athens and Palestine. He was even summoned to discuss theology at Antioch with Julia Mamaea, the virtuous mother of Emperor Alexander Severus, who had initiated a temporary hiatus to Christian persecution. Meanwhile, back home in Egypt, Bishop Demetrius was growing resentful of Origen's international acclaim. The silent tug of war between the two men finally broke into the open. A candid assessment of their dispute would admit that Origen at times pushed the theological envelope too far. To complicate matters, he was supremely confident that his intellectual capacities gave him the right to explore all matters theological, no matter what his bishop might think about his opinions. Demetrius, for his part, no doubt envied the young Origen, and his conservative instincts were aroused when Origen started travelling around teaching less-than-traditional ideas with no intent to submit to his local bishop. Things came to a head when, during a trip to Caesarea on the Palestinian coast, the bishop there ordained Origen and allowed him to preach. Demetrius was incensed, for Origen was under his pastoral oversight, not the bishop of Caesarea's. It was at this heated juncture that Demetrius began accusing Origen of rashness in the matter of his castration, as well as certain unorthodox teachings. The dispute resolved itself when Demetrius died and Origen moved in AD 233 to greener pastures in Caesarea, where the local Palestinian clergy were happy to have him. After thirty years of teaching in Egypt, Origen took up residence in the Holy Land for the final two decades of his life.

Living there afforded Origen the opportunity to delve even more deeply into the text of Scripture. Of course, in one sense, this was nothing new for him. Origen had already gained a reputation as an exegete, and was well known for his immense output of biblical commentaries and theological treatises. At times he had as many as seven stenographers taking turns as they transcribed his learned dictation.[22] Nevertheless, the congenial environment at Caesarea offered Origen new avenues of scriptural investigation. He was able to expand and complete his famous *Hexapla*, a comparison of the Hebrew text of the Old Testament and various versions of the Greek text in six parallel columns. Such a massive project testifies to Origen's great love for God's Word. Living in Palestine also allowed Origen to visit the lands of the Bible, and he made use of the research from his travels in his many biblical commentaries. Origen now came into contact with Jewish rabbis, which resulted in fruitful exegetical discussions. Furthermore, we must remember that as a newly ordained pastor, Origen was called upon to preach regularly in the gathered assembly. In all these ways, he expanded his already-considerable knowledge of Scripture while at Caesarea.

Because of Origen's lifelong commitment to biblical studies, his total literary output was astonishing. When we consider the sum of his writings (most of which are now lost), he may well have been the most prolific author in all of antiquity.[23] The church father Jerome summarized Origen's work by saying,

> He knew the scriptures by heart and labored hard day and night to explain their meaning. He delivered in church more than a thousand sermons, and published innumerable commentaries . . . Which of us can read all that he has written? And who can fail to admire his enthusiasm for the scriptures?[24]

Keep in mind, this remark comes from one of Origen's most hostile opponents!

In the year 249, a new emperor, Decius, came to the imperial throne. Conservative by nature, Decius sought to restore the glory of ancient Rome through a policy of religious uniformity. That is to say, Decius wanted every subject of the empire to be a loyal adherent of the traditional pagan religion. To enforce this policy, he required all citizens to swear allegiance to the ancient gods through a token sacrifice, and then to obtain a legal certificate indicating the sacrifice had been performed. Obviously, this created havoc in the church, and many Christians across the empire refused to obey. Decius also made a

---

22. Eusebius, *Ecclesiastical History* 6.23.1–2 (Oulton, p. 69).
23. Crouzel, *Origen*, p. 37.
24. Jerome, *Letter* 84.8 (*NPNF*, vol. 6, pp. 179–180).

point of singling out the church's leaders, and this turned the elderly Origen into a marked man. He was arrested and brought to the torture chamber, where constant and horrific torments were inflicted on him in an attempt to force the famous Christian to deny his faith. Origen was not allowed to die in prison, but was tortured for a prolonged period with burning implements and the extreme stretching of his legs. He was left in the stocks for days at a time with his legs extended to the most excruciating degree. In the oppressive darkness and chains of his cell, perhaps Origen recalled the words he had written several years earlier to some friends facing martyrdom (see below): 'When [the martyr] sees that he has been delivered from the body of death by his confession, he will make the holy proclamation, "Thanks be to God through Jesus Christ our Lord!"'[25]

At last Emperor Decius died and the persecution abated. Origen was released from prison without having denied his faith, but was maimed by the agony he had endured. No doubt crippled and in constant pain, he spent his last few years writing letters of encouragement, offering 'sayings full of help for those who needed uplifting'.[26] And then, quietly, this giant of the Christian church slipped off the stage of history.

Theological analysis

The staggering scope of Origen's theology would be difficult to circumscribe in a single book, much less a single chapter within a book. The preceding survey of his life has begun to offer some perspective on the patterns of his thought. Yet as we have seen, his literary output and intellectual power do not lend themselves to easy summarization. Our task now will be to examine some representative selections of Origen's writings, while at the same time accessing the broad sweep of his life's work.

Origen is famous for transmitting to posterity three 'senses of Scripture', corresponding to the text's body, soul and spirit.[27] Although a page of Scripture contained a single text, the capable interpreter who combed over it would find

25. Origen, *Exhortation to Martyrdom* 3 (Greer, *Origen*, p. 42).

26. Eusebius, *Ecclesiastical History* 6.39.5 (Oulton, p. 95).

27. Origen, *On First Principles* 4.2.4. In reality, Origen's practice with respect to the 'senses' of Scripture could employ a twofold, threefold or fourfold scheme. The medieval world drank deeply from Origen's exegesis, to the point that Henri de Lubac could speak of the 'Latin Origen'. For an important study of this matter, see

multiple layers of truth springing to the imagination. Origen was like that too: a single man, but one susceptible to many characterizations. Playing with this metaphor, perhaps we can examine the 'three senses of Origen' by investigating his thought under three key rubrics: Asceticism, Exegesis and Theology.

Origen the ascetic

Emphasis on bodily self-discipline for the attainment of higher spiritual purposes is known as 'asceticism'. The notion of ascetic preparation is very important for Origen, though the term itself is not always easy to grasp.[28] The Greek word *askēsis* refers to exercise, practice or training.[29] Somewhat surprisingly, the word is absent from the New Testament, though the concept is there.[30] For example, in 1 Corinthians 9:24–27 Paul describes the laborious exercise he undertakes so that he might win a prize at the conclusion of the games. At its root, *askēsis* cannot be separated from the arena of Greek athletic competition. It refers to the advance training undertaken in preparation for the day of the contest. Applied to the spiritual life, asceticism was the practice of mortifying the flesh so that the Christian might be victorious in the day of temptation, receiving the prize of intimacy with God.

Origen addresses the subject of temptation in his treatise *On Prayer*. It is one of only two 'occasional' works; that is to say, works written to address a specific need at a given time.[31] He wrote it just after his arrival in Caesarea around 233 or 234, when his friend Ambrose asked him if prayer is futile

---

Henri de Lubac, *Medieval Exegesis: The Four Senses of Scripture*, vol. 1, tr. Mark Sebanc (Grand Rapids: Eerdmans, 1998), p. 161.

28. Everyone agrees Origen was an ascetic, yet defining 'asceticism' is a difficult task. Elizabeth Clark, one of the foremost experts on the subject, struggled to define the very topic to which she has devoted much of her scholarly career. After intense debate, the study group on Greco-Roman asceticism in the Society of Biblical Literature could agree only to define 'ascetic behaviour', not asceticism per se. Elizabeth A. Clark, *Reading Renunciation: Asceticism and Scripture in Early Christianity* (Princeton: Princeton University Press, 1999), p. 14.
29. Liddell and Scott, *An Intermediate Greek-English Lexicon* (Oxford: Clarendon, 1997), p. 124.
30. It does appear as a verb in Acts 24:16 ('I exert myself'), but the term has no unique or significant meaning, other than 'I endeavour'.
31. The other is his *Exhortation to Martyrdom* (J. E. L. Oulton and H. Chadwick, *Alexandrian Christianity*, Library of Christian Classics [Philadelphia: Westminster, 1954], vol. 2, p. 180).

because God already knows the outcome. Origen replies theologically, yet also develops the moral ramifications of his views. Human beings face a world full of moral choices. Temptations assail us constantly, but as we encounter them, we do not have to stand unprepared. Discipline can make us ready in advance. Origen writes:

> Now the use of temptation is something like this. What our soul has received escapes everyone's knowledge but God's – even our own. But it becomes evident through temptations, so that we no longer escape the knowledge of what we are like. And in knowing ourselves, we are also conscious, if we are willing, of our own evils; and we give thanks for the good things that have been made evident to us through temptations . . . Therefore, in the times of relief between temptations let us stand firm for their onset, and let us be prepared for everything that can happen, so that whatever comes to pass, we may not be tested as though unready, but may be revealed as those who have disciplined themselves with extreme care. For when we have accomplished all we can by ourselves, God will fulfill what is lacking because of human weakness. In everything He works for good with those who love Him, those who are foreseen for whatever they will be by themselves, according to His foreknowledge, which cannot be false.[32]

Clearly, Origen envisioned a large role for human effort and self-discipline in the Christian life. Yet if we suppose Origen's moral outlook only has to do with grudging obedience to a demanding deity, we miss his point. Origen cites Romans 8:28 to show that God, with sovereign foreknowledge of all things, works to aid the moral efforts of those who know him personally, and in fact *love* him. It is utter delight in the Lord, not teeth-gritting endurance, that drives the Christian's disciplined spiritual life.

Origen believed the Christian must learn to cultivate the skill of moral excellence – a skill God stands ready to aid, but humans nonetheless must labour to acquire. Origen says Christians can

> quench all the fiery arrows sent against them by the Evil One, whenever they have in themselves rivers of water welling up to eternal life that do not allow the arrow of the Evil One to prevail, but easily destroy it by the flood of divine and saving thoughts impressed from contemplations of the truth upon the soul of the one who trains himself to be spiritual.[33]

---

32. Origen, *On Prayer* 29.17, 19 (Greer, *Origen*, pp. 161–162).
33. Ibid. 30.3 (p. 163).

Notice the twofold action here: God must supply the rivers of living water, yet Christians must train themselves to be spiritual through holy contemplations in advance of the trial. Righteous living is a skill that can be learned, though, of course, grace is needed throughout the growth process.

The ascetic as martyr

In Origen's setting, a disciplined life was especially necessary because of the possibility of martyrdom. We cannot underestimate the shaping influence persecution played in Origen's life.[34] As already mentioned, his father, Leonides, was martyred, and according to Eusebius, 'Origen's soul was possessed with such a passion for martyrdom, while he was still quite a boy, that he was all eagerness to come to close quarters with danger, and to leap forward and rush into conflict.'[35] Eusebius would have us believe this was just boyish enthusiasm, yet the evidence suggests martyrdom remained a fundamental expression of Origen's asceticism. The Christian ascetic was as good as dead already. He or she had died to the world, and lived only for Christ, just like a martyr. This is why Origen could so fearlessly associate with the martyrs in prison at Alexandria, even offering them the kiss of fellowship on their way to death. His willingness to die to the present world made Origen impervious to the threat of danger.

During the Caesarean period of Origen's life, another imperial persecution arose and two of his friends faced death. Origen wrote them a letter called *Exhortation to Martyrdom* that provides us insight into his perspective on dying to the world. 'The martyr who does not refuse the "affliction upon affliction," but welcomes it like a noble athlete, immediately welcomes the "hope upon hope" as well, which he will enjoy shortly after the "affliction upon affliction."'[36] In other words, because of his hope in the next world, the martyr can contend like a 'noble athlete' in the here and now. The martyr has died to self, and longs only for God. Origen writes:

> God is loved with the whole soul by those who through their great longing for fellowship with God draw their soul away and separate it, not only from their earthly

---

34. Rowan Williams, the present Archbishop of Canterbury, notes that 'Without this background [of persecution and martyrdom] it is impossible to understand Origen'. In fact, 'Origen's abiding conviction [was] that Christian baptism was a pretty direct calling to one or another sort of martyrdom' (Rowan Williams, 'Ascetic Enthusiasm: Origen and the Early Church', *History Today* [Dec. 1989], p. 32).
35. Eusebius, *Ecclesiastical History* 6.2.3 (Oulton, p. 11).
36. Origen, *Exhortation to Martyrdom* 1 (Greer, *Origen*, p. 41; slightly adapted).

> body, but also from every corporeal thing. For them no pulling or dragging takes place even in putting off their lowly body, when the time allows them to take off the body of death . . . And when he sees that he has been delivered from the body of death by his confession, he will make the holy proclamation, 'Thanks be to God through Jesus Christ our Lord!' If such a view seems hard to anyone, then he has not thirsted for God, the Mighty One, the living God.[37]

We see in this text that anyone who truly thirsts for God must possess a longing to overcome the physical body, to detach the soul from lowly things, to escape the body of death. For Origen, the Christian life is always the martyr's life.[38]

Of course, not every person will actually face persecution, imprisonment, torture or martyrdom. Even so, the ascetic life is required of every Christian, for it achieves more than just the preparation of the body. The soul too is prepared for the vision of God by being purged of earthly attachments. Origen asks:

> Why do we hang back and hesitate to put off the perishable body, the earthly tent that hinders us, weighs down the soul, and burdens the thoughtful mind? Why do we hesitate to burst our bonds and depart from the stormy billows of a life with flesh and blood? Let our purpose be to enjoy with Christ Jesus the rest proper to blessedness, contemplating Him, the Word, wholly living. By Him we shall be nourished; in Him we shall receive the manifold wisdom and be modeled by the Truth Himself. By the true and unceasing Light of knowledge our minds will be enlightened to gaze upon what is by nature to be seen in that Light with eyes illuminated by the Lord's commandment.[39]

The souls of humankind are burdened by flesh, but asceticism or martyrdom enables the physical body to be transcended so that God might be grasped more perfectly. This idea is fundamental to Origen's thought, and it derives – at least in part – from his Platonic conception of the world.

---

37. Ibid. 3 (p. 42).
38. Pamela Bright, 'Origenian Understanding of Martyrdom and its Biblical Framework', in Charles Kannengiesser and William L. Petersen (eds.), *Origen of Alexandria: His World and His Legacy* (Notre Dame: University of Notre Dame Press, 1988), pp. 180–199.
39. *On Prayer* 47 (Greer, *Origen*, p. 76).

The Platonic assumptions of Origen's asceticism

Plato was born more than six hundred years before Origen. Nevertheless, outside Scripture, there was no more influential source for Origen's thought than the Platonic training he received in Alexandria.[40] The subject of Greek philosophy's influence on Origen has been studied in great detail, so that today, to say Origen was a Christian Platonist is axiomatic.[41] What is usually meant by 'Platonism' is a sharp distinction between the higher world of eternal and unchanging Ideas or Forms, and the world of physical matter, which is inherently flawed and mutable. Therefore, according to Platonist philosophy, the wise man's goal is to be freed of attachment to corporeality, ascending by means of inner meditation to contemplate ultimate reality as it truly exists. The philosopher is aided in this task by the fact that his eternal soul – unlike the body in which it is trapped – retains an affinity for the world above, and so naturally gravitates in that direction.

It was not just the individual soul whose task it was to escape the corporeal world and contemplate higher realities. In the Christian Platonism to which Origen adhered, the history of the world is in fact a great cosmic drama of fall and return. The goal of human life is oneness with the divine. For Origen, God is unapproachable in his utter goodness, existing as a divine Mind far removed from the world. The rational principle (*Logos* in Greek) inherent within this Mind served as the agent through whom the world was made. Human beings consist of rational souls in physical bodies. Given moral freedom by God so that they might freely choose to love him, humans instead capitulated to laziness and neglect, withdrawing from the goodness of God to contemplate the base and the lowly. Therefore, the Logos (or Word) became flesh to enter the world and lead the souls of men back to the contemplation of God himself. Such radical self-giving warms the believer's heart to Christ the Bridegroom,

---

40. Properly speaking, what Origen knew was not Plato in his original context, but the school of thought called Middle Platonism, especially as mediated by the first-century AD Jewish philosopher Philo of Alexandria. We should also recall that Origen was trained under the eminent Platonist, Ammonius Saccas. A foundational study in this context is Charles Bigg, *The Christian Platonists of Alexandria* (Oxford: Clarendon, 1886).
41. Mark Edwards remarks with wry humour that 'among theologians Alexandria stands for Platonism, as London stands for smog' (Mark Julian Edwards, *Origen against Plato* [Aldershot: Ashgate, 2002], p. 1). Edwards offers an excellent contrarian view of the ways in which Origen went against the Platonic tradition or modified it according to Christian revelation.

who tenderly loves his Bride enough to wash and purify her in salvation. In Origen's vision of the Christian life, the believer must long for Christ as a deer pants for water, embarking on an intense, lifelong pursuit after the heavenly Logos. Salvation, then, is the descent of God into our fallen estate through Jesus Christ, and the ascent of our souls back to God through participation in his Son.

However, because earthly people are not yet perfect, we must always guard against the possibility that we might turn our eyes away from God. Origen warns:

> We should also realize that just as illicit and unlawful love can come upon the outer man, for example, that he should love not his bride or wife, but a harlot or adulteress, so also there can come upon the inner man, that is, the soul, a love not for its legitimate bridegroom, who we have said is the Word of God, but for some adulterer and seducer . . . And so the spiritual love of the soul blazes up, as we have taught, sometimes toward certain spirits of wickedness, but sometimes toward the Holy Spirit and the Word of God, who is called the faithful bridegroom and husband of the well-trained soul.[42]

Just as a husband must not allow adulterous thoughts to drag him away from his true beloved, so to love God, to see him face to face in the most intimate way, requires purification from all competing attractions. For Origen, that meant victory over anything the natural man craves, such as sex, food, sleep, the extravagances of wealth and comfort, human acclaim, and much more. The vision of God is granted only to the pure. As Jesus clearly said, and Origen believed, 'Blessed are the pure in heart, for they shall see God' (Matt. 5:8 ESV).

How is this holy vision achieved? Where do humans see God? Receiving a direct mystical vision was not out of the question in Origen's understanding of the Christian life. God can also be seen in 'the beauty of his works and the comeliness of his creatures'.[43] However, the most sublime place for the believer to encounter the face of God is in the pages of Scripture.[44] For Origen, exegesis

---

42. Origen, *Prologue to the Commentary on the Song of Songs* (Greer, *Origen*, p. 223).
43. Origen, *On First Principles* 1.1.6 (G. W. Butterworth, *Origen: On First Principles* [Gloucester, MA: Smith, 1973], p. 10).
44. 'To dig into the Scriptures, [Origen] insisted, it is necessary to dig into our hearts, ridding them of darkness, purging them of vices, maintaining our minds in purity. Reading the Bible, therefore, involved a strenuous asceticism, because the

was a means of ascent, a road to holiness available to anyone able and willing to undertake the labours of the journey.[45] The most sacred Christian task of all is to be enlightened by the Word of God, Christ himself, into the meaning of the Bible, which is his body. 'You are therefore to understand the scriptures in this way: as the one, perfect body of the Word.'[46] It is no wonder that Origen considered exegesis such a holy task. As Bernard and Patricia McGinn put it:

> We have only a portion of Origen's vast literary output, but these works show him to combine the roles of exegete, theologian, and mystic with great creativity and intellectual power. While these three modes of thought are intimately related in his work, Origen remains first and foremost an exegete, perhaps the greatest Christianity has ever known.[47]

High praise, indeed. And so, we now turn to the subject of exegesis.

Origen the exegete

Origen's greatest work was his theological tome *On First Principles*. In it he describes the elemental or foundational truths by which Christian doctrine must be pursued. Written between 220 and 230 while Origen was in his prime at Alexandria, the work starkly reveals the cosmic scope of his thought. The following selection from the preface is critical for understanding Origen's interpretative method, for it highlights the Christocentric nature of scriptural exegesis:

> All who believe and are convinced that grace and truth came by Jesus Christ, and who know Christ to be the truth (in accordance with his own saying, 'I am the truth') derive the knowledge which calls men to lead a good and blessed life from no other source but the very words and teaching of Christ. By the words of Christ we do not mean only those which formed his teaching when he was made man and dwelt in the flesh, since

---

understanding of God's word would certainly be distorted in a dark heart' (Patrick Henry Reardon, 'Scripture Saturation: To Achieve Holiness, Believed the Early Monks, You Must Soak in the "Moral Sense" of the Word', *Christian History* 80 [2003], p. 33).

45. P. W. Martens, 'Interpreting Attentively: The Ascetic Character of Biblical Exegesis according to Origen and Basil of Caesarea', in *Origeniana octava: Origen and the Alexandrian Tradition* (Leuven: Leuven University Press, 2003), pp. 1115–1121.
46. Origen, *Homily on Jeremiah, Fragment* (von Balthasar, *Origen*, p. 88).
47. Bernard and Patricia McGinn, *Early Christian Mystics: The Divine Vision of the Spiritual Masters* (New York: Crossroad, 2003), p. 23.

> even before that Christ the Word of God was in Moses and the prophets. For without the Word of God how could they have prophesied about Christ? In proof of which we should not find it difficult to show from the divine scriptures how Moses or the prophets were filled with the spirit of Christ in all their words and deeds, were we not anxious to confine the present work within the briefest possible limits. I count it sufficient, therefore, to quote this one testimony of Paul, taken from the epistle he writes to the Hebrews, where he speaks as follows: 'By faith Moses, when he was grown up, refused to be called the son of Pharaoh's daughter, choosing rather to suffer affliction with the people of God than to enjoy the pleasures of sin for a season, accounting the reproach of Christ greater riches than the treasures of Egypt.' And as for the fact that Christ spoke in the apostles after his ascension into heaven, this is shown by Paul in the following passage: 'Or do ye seek a proof of him that speaketh in me, that is, Christ?'[48]

The central premise of Origen's biblical interpretation is that Christ, the Logos of God, speaks through every verse of Scripture, whether in the Old or New Testament. Obviously, Christ's words are found in the Gospels, but Origen begins his central work of theology by showing that Christ spoke through Moses and the prophets as well. Of the many biblical proofs Origen could cite, he chooses Hebrews 11:24–26, where Moses is said to have borne 'the reproach of Christ'.[49] In other words, Moses testified to Jesus, even though Moses lived a millennium and a half before the Saviour's birth. Likewise, those who lived after the earthly sojourn of the Lord still proclaimed his very words. The apostle Paul proved this in 2 Corinthians 13:3 when he asserted that Christ spoke through him. Origen believed the written word of God – the Law, the prophets, the writings, the Gospels, the apostles – reverberates on every page with the voice of Jesus Christ, the only-begotten Word of God. This is the most important pillar of Origen's exegesis.

Book 4 of *On First Principles* lays out Origen's exegetical method in detail. Origen begins with the fundamental premise of Scripture's divine inspiration. After showing how various Old Testament passages speak prophetically of Christ, he goes on to say that

> he who approaches the prophetic words with care and attention will feel from his very reading a trace of their divine inspiration, and will be convinced by his

48. Origen, *On First Principles* pref.1 (Butterworth, *Origen*, p. 1).
49. It was common among many Eastern church fathers to attribute authorship of the letter to the Hebrews to the apostle Paul. Modern scholars, including most evangelicals, do not consider Hebrews to be Pauline.

> own feelings that the words which are believed by us to be from God are not the compositions of men. Now the light which was contained within the law of Moses, but was hidden under a veil, shone forth at the advent of Jesus, when the veil was taken away and there came at once to men's knowledge those 'good things' of which the letter of the law held a 'shadow.'[50]

Origen's understanding of inspiration meant that Christology was latent in the Old Testament, veiled in shadows for a long time, until Christ came at last to reveal the fullness of the truth. Origen appeals to what is for him a key biblical passage, 2 Corinthians 3, in which the apostle Paul claims that a veil lies over the minds of Jewish interpreters. The veil is only removed when a person turns to the Lord for wisdom. Origen often cited the Pauline dictum 'the letter kills, but the Spirit gives life' (2 Cor. 3:6 ESV) In other words, the literal sense of the text will 'kill' if it is not allowed to speak beyond its initial context to incorporate the cosmic fact of the incarnation. The inspired Scriptures have much more to give us than a summary of Jewish history.

Spiritual exegesis

Because Holy Scripture is inspired and therefore pregnant with meaning, it must be read spiritually. According to Origen, many interpreters have failed to do so. For example, the Jews, in their literalism, 'think that they are keeping close to the language of the prophecies', but in fact they are missing the point.[51] Heretics, on the other hand, who read certain Old Testament texts and do not like what they find, attribute the writings to a false god. A third group of erroneous interpreters is the simple, uninstructed Christians. They are the sort of people you can still find in churches today: believers with very little biblical education, but with hearts entirely devoted to God. Origen treats these 'simple believers' with genuine pastoral concern, though perhaps with unwitting elitism as well. When the simple Christians discover difficult Old Testament passages, such as when God repents (1 Sam. 15:11) or when evil is said to come from God (Isa. 45:7; Mic. 1:12), they take it at face value, and lapse into unworthy beliefs about the Almighty. Origen responds:

> Now the reason why all those we have mentioned hold false opinions and make impious or ignorant assertions about God appears to be nothing else but this, that scripture is not understood in its spiritual sense, but is interpreted according to the

---

50. Origen, *On First Principles* 4.1.6 (Butterworth, *Origen*, p. 265).
51. Ibid. 4.2.1 (p. 269).

> bare letter . . . That there are certain mystical revelations made known through the divine scriptures is believed by all, even by the simplest of those who are adherents of the word; but what these revelations are, fair-minded and humble men confess that they do not know . . . And they declare that all narratives that are supposed to speak about marriage or the begetting of children or wars or any other stories whatever that may be accepted among the multitudes are types; but when we ask, of what, then sometimes owing to the lack of thorough training, sometimes owing to rashness, and occasionally, even when one is well-trained and of sound judgment, owing to man's exceedingly great difficulty in discovering these things, the interpretation of every detail is not altogether clear.[52]

In the light of such widespread exegetical uncertainty, Origen promises to lay out the correct method of biblical interpretation. The spiritual methodology he uses to decipher the Old Testament applies also to the New, so that Origen can claim the Bible contains 'thousands of passages that provide, as if through a window, a narrow opening leading to multitudes of the deepest thoughts'.[53] The riches of God's Word can scarcely be exhausted.

The senses of Scripture

The proper method for expounding the Scriptures, Origen says, is grounded in the threefold division of a human being. In a very important text he writes:

> The right way, therefore, as it appears to us, of approaching the scriptures and gathering their meaning, is the following, which is extracted from the writings themselves. We find some such rule as this laid down by Solomon in the Proverbs concerning the divine doctrines written therein: 'Do thou portray them threefold in counsel and knowledge, that thou mayest answer words of truth to those who question thee.'[54] One must therefore portray the meaning of the sacred writings

52. Ibid. 4.2.2 (pp. 271–273).
53. Ibid. 4.2.3 (p. 274).
54. Origen here cites as support for his method the injunction of Prov. 22:20 to 'portray them threefold' (his Greek Septuagint version differed from the Hebrew text). However, Prov. 22:20 is not the primary verse to which Origen appeals in defence of allegory. He looks more often to the example provided by New Testament exegesis of the Old Testament. In addition, Origen appears to have picked up certain aspects of his threefold interpretative method from the Jewish philosopher Philo. See David Dawson, 'Plato's Soul and the Body of the Text in Philo and Origen', in *Interpretation and Allegory* (Leiden: Brill, 2000), pp. 89–107.

> in a threefold way upon one's own soul, so that the simple man may be edified by what we may call the flesh of the scripture, this name being given to the obvious interpretation; while the man who has made some progress may be edified by its soul, as it were; and the man who is perfect and like those mentioned by the apostle, 'We speak wisdom among the perfect; yet a wisdom not of this world, nor of the rulers of this world, which are coming to nought; but we speak God's wisdom in a mystery, even the wisdom that hath been hidden, which God foreordained before the worlds unto our glory' – this man may be edified by the spiritual law, which has 'a shadow of the good things to come.' For just as a man consists of a body, soul, and spirit, so in the same way does scripture, which has been prepared by God to be given for man's salvation.[55]

The 'body' of Scripture for Origen is the literal sense – the historical–grammatical meaning of the text that is obvious on an initial reading. This level is appropriate for edifying the simple Christians. Yet the text also has a 'soul' and a 'spirit'. Origen's second and third senses are sometimes connected with the moral meaning (the application of the biblical passage to one's own soul) and the Christological meaning (the relationship of Christ and the church).[56] In addition, the Origenist tradition of interpretation often included a fourth division, the anagogic, which referred to the final destiny of the world.[57]

Though this approach may sound strange to our ears, Origen takes the Bible itself as the authority for his method. One of his primary supports, to which he often appeals, is Galatians 4:22–26. The apostle Paul speaks of Hagar and Sarah as standing for two covenants, then remarks that this matter is to be understood 'allegorically'.[58] Another key passage is 1 Corinthians 10:1–4, where the apostle describes the rock that gave water to the Israelites in the

---

55. Origen, *On First Principles* 4.2.4 (Butterworth, *Origen*, p. 276).
56. Although Origen lays out this threefold scheme in *On First Principles*, he sometimes inverts the order of the second and third elements, and also fails to apply it in a consistent manner when doing exegesis. In reality, his scheme is twofold: there is the literal sense, and then a spiritual application of some sort. Whether the interpretation has two, three or four elements depends on the verse in question. Henri de Lubac, *History and Spirit: The Understanding of Scripture According to Origen*, tr. Anne Englund Nash (San Francisco: Ignatius, 2007), pp. 159–171.
57. See de Lubac, *Medieval Exegesis*, for a history of the Origenist tradition in the Latin Middle Ages.
58. Origen, *On First Principles* 4.2.6 (Butterworth, *Origen*, pp. 279–280).

wilderness, noting, 'the rock was Christ' (ESV).[59] Or again, in 1 Corinthians 9:9–10, Paul says the Jewish law allowing the ox to eat while treading grain applies to the church leader who rightfully receives support from his people. It is for our sake the Law was written, Paul insists. Whose sake? Not just the miller in ancient Israel who wanted to know whether he could put a muzzle on his beast, but the preacher living 1,500 years later in the Roman Empire who wanted to know whether the minister of the gospel is worthy of his wage. For Paul, there were two levels of meaning in Deuteronomy 25:4 – the original, literal one, and the subsequent spiritual application. This multilayered approach became a fundamental principle of hermeneutics for Origen. He assumed all the precepts of the Law were written 'for our sake' so Christians might uncover symbolic meaning in them. Abraham's two wives, or a desert rock gushing with water, or an ox labouring on the threshing floor – each carried significance for the original writer and his Jewish audience. At the same time, Paul states that these incidents offer timeless Christian truth as well. Because this was how Paul interpreted Scripture, Origen felt justified in pursuing a layered approach to the Bible in which the literal meaning was not the only one.

Among the books of the Bible, the one considered best suited to allegorization was the Song of Songs. In Origen's way of thinking, this book about love reached its most sublime heights when it addressed the love of Christ for his church, or the longing of the soul to be united with the glorious God. Of course, Origen recognized that at the literal level, the book was about a bride and bridegroom. He interpreted it as a dramatic play written by Solomon to describe the experiences of two lovers.[60] Those who are less advanced in their Christian faith may understand the story on this level, and so be nourished by it the same way a baby is nourished by milk (Heb. 5:12–14). Yet Origen urges his readers to progress to a higher level, partaking of the 'solid food' available to more mature believers.

For example, consider how Origen interprets Song of Songs 1:2, 'Let him kiss me with the kisses of his mouth; / for your breasts are better than wine.'[61] Origen begins with the literal interpretation in which the text describes the

59. Ibid.

60. Origen, *Prologue to the Commentary on the Song of Songs* (p. 217).

61. Modern versions read 'your *love* is better than wine', but the Hebrew consonantal noun is ambiguous, and could mean 'love' or 'breasts', depending on the vowels used. The translators of the Greek Septuagint read it (quite legitimately) as *mastoi* (breasts), which is what Origen saw in his Bible.

Shulamite's longing for her lover. She is overjoyed when her prayer in the third person ('let him kiss me') is answered by his arrival, so that she may address him directly ('for your breasts . . .'). After Origen discusses the literal meaning, he moves to the more profound interpretation. The 'breast' of the bridegroom leads Origen to consider the scene in the upper room when the beloved disciple reclined on the breast of Jesus. The true follower of Christ will drink the delightful wine that comes from him, leaning against his bosom to partake of his wisdom. Origen explains:

> Now this is certainly what the text means: John is said to have reposed on the seat of Jesus' heart, that is, on the inner meaning of his teachings. There he sought and investigated 'the treasures of wisdom and knowledge that are hidden in Christ Jesus' [Col. 2:3]. And so I don't think it is inappropriate to refer to the place of his holy teachings as 'the bosom of Christ'. . . . In this present passage [from the Song] which describes the behaviour and conversation of lovers, I think it is entirely fitting that the same inner seat of the heart should be described as 'breasts'. Therefore the breasts of the Bridegroom are good, because in them 'are hidden the treasures of wisdom and knowledge'. The Bride, moreover, compares these breasts to wine. In fact she says the breasts are better than wine. Now the 'wine' is intended to refer to the ordinances and teachings which the Bride had become accustomed to partake of through the Law and the Prophets, before the advent of the Bridegroom. But now when she considers the teaching that flows from the breasts of the Bridegroom, she is amazed and struck with awe. She can see it is far superior to the wine that was served to her by the holy fathers and prophets – the 'spiritual' wine, so to speak, that used to gladden her heart before the advent of the Bridegroom.[62]

In this way, a text originally written as erotic Hebrew poetry becomes, for Origen, an exhortation to mystical union with Christ. The modern exegete is not used to making interpretative moves like this. Whether or not we are willing to question the assumption that modern standards should be the only criteria for evaluating exegesis, at the very least let us appreciate that for Origen, allegory was in no way intended to circumvent Scripture.[63] Rather, it was a way to reveal fully the Saviour of whom Scripture speaks on every page.

---

62. Origen, *Commentary on the Song of Songs* 1.2.4, 7–8 (tr. mine).
63. On the history of criticism of Origen's allegory, beginning with Martin Luther and continuing from there to become a staple of modern assessments of Origen, see Karen Jo Torjesen, *Hermeneutical Procedure and Theological Method in Origen's Exegesis* (Berlin: de Gruyter, 1986), pp. 1–3.

In theory, such an approach could work. We must now investigate Origen's actual theology to determine whether he did, in fact, stay within the bounds of biblical doctrine.

Origen the theologian

We begin our investigation of Origen's theology with a selection from his preface to *On First Principles* where we find one of the most concise statements of his thought in all his writings:

> The kind of doctrines which are believed in plain terms through the apostolic teaching are the following: **First**, that God is one, who created and set in order all things, and who, when nothing existed, caused the universe to be. He is God from the first creation and foundation of the world . . . This just and good God, the Father of our Lord Jesus Christ, himself gave the law, the prophets, and the gospels, and he is God both of the apostles and also of the Old and New Testaments. **Then again:** Christ Jesus, he who came to earth, was begotten of the Father before every created thing. And after he had ministered to the Father in the foundation of all things, for 'all things were made through him,' in these last times he emptied himself and was made man, was made flesh, although he was God; and being made man, he still remained what he was, namely, God. He took to himself a body like our body, differing in this alone, that it was born of a virgin and of the Holy Spirit. And this Jesus Christ was born and suffered in truth and not merely in appearance, and truly died our common death. Moreover he truly rose from the dead, and after the resurrection companied with his disciples and was then taken up into heaven. **Then again:** the apostles delivered this doctrine, that the Holy Spirit is united in honor and dignity with the Father and the Son . . . It is, however, certainly taught with the utmost clearness in the Church, that this Spirit inspired each one of the saints, both the prophets and the apostles, and that there was not one Spirit in the men of old and another in those who were inspired at the coming of Christ. **Next after this** the apostles taught that the soul, having a substance and life of its own, will be rewarded according to its deserts after its departure from this world; for it will either obtain an inheritance of eternal life and blessedness, if its deeds shall warrant this, or it must be given over to eternal fire and torments, if the guilt of its crimes shall so determine. Further, there will be a time of resurrection of the dead . . . **This also is laid down** in the Church's teaching, that every rational soul is possessed of free will and choice; and also, that it is engaged in a struggle against the devil and his angels and the opposing powers.[64]

---

64. Origen, *On First Principles* pref.4–5 (Butterworth, *Origen*, pp. 3–4).

Origen is here summarizing the church's rule of faith, the basic instructional material taught to those who had offered themselves for Christian baptism. As a catechist, Origen would have expounded these doctrines many times to new converts in Alexandria. We notice first of all his emphasis on the creator God from whom all things derive: the universe itself, and the Scriptures of the Old and New Testaments. Origen then teaches the role of God's only-begotten Son in creation (John 1:3; Col. 1:16), followed by the historical life, death and resurrection of the incarnate Jesus. Next, the addition of an article on the Holy Spirit turns the formula into a trinitarian one. Origen goes on to address Christian eschatology in his description of bodily resurrection for final judgments and rewards at the end of time. The importance of free will and the existence of angels and demons are further important doctrines featured here. This brief selection epitomizes the main contours of Origen's systematic theology, inviting us to a more detailed examination.

Epistemology

Any investigation of Origen's theology should begin with the overarching methodology by which he conducted the theologian's task. Therefore, we must begin with epistemology, since everything else flows from this. For Origen, true knowledge is grounded in God himself, and as such, it is a gift – but only to those who make themselves worthy of it. 'Worthiness' is a concept Origen mentions often. In his monumental apologetic work against the pagan critic Celsus, Origen writes:

> it is probable that the knowledge of God is beyond the capacity of human nature (that is why there are such great errors about God among men), but by God's kindness and love to man, and by a miraculous divine grace, the knowledge of God extends to those who by God's foreknowledge have been previously determined, because they would live lives worthy of Him after he was made known to them.[65]

The notion of being worthy of God's illumination may sound strange to a grace-oriented Protestant, but remember, Origen was not living in the age when 'merit' and 'works righteousness' were being debated. His view that illumination comes only to those who follow hard after Christ was nothing more than the natural implication of the saying 'seek, and you will find' (Matt. 7:7 ESV). Knowing God takes effort; wisdom does not just fall into one's lap.

---

65. Origen, *Against Celsus* 7.44. Henry Chadwick, *Origen: Contra Celsum* (Cambridge: Cambridge University Press, 1953), p. 432.

Apprehension of the highest truths will come only to those who choose to value it and to strive after it. Origen had no time for intellectual laziness.

We should take note of the rationalistic aspect here. Although divine illumination did have a mystical element for Origen, he certainly did not sit around Alexandria gazing at his navel to work himself into a trance. Illumination came by means of the *intellect*, and that meant study was required. First and foremost, the seeker who wished to know God should study the Scriptures. We have already observed how devoted Origen was to the Bible. But wisdom could be gained from other sources as well. Another excellent vehicle for training the mind was philosophy, especially that of Plato. There is no doubt Origen had drunk deeply at the Platonic wellspring, yet he was no slavish follower of the Greeks. Origen was one of the first Christian thinkers to develop the metaphor of 'plundering the Egyptians', in which the Israelites recast the gold and silver of their Egyptian slave masters to make holy things for the tabernacle during their wilderness sojourn.[66] Using this remarkable Exodus event as an illustration, Origen exhorts his student Gregory the Wonderworker to

> accept effectively those things from the philosophy of the Greeks that can serve as a general education or introduction for Christianity and those things from geometry and astronomy that are useful for the interpretation of the Holy Scriptures. For just as the servants of philosophers say concerning geometry, music, grammar, rhetoric, and [astronomy] that they are adjuncts to philosophy, we say this very thing about philosophy itself with regard to Christianity.[67]

In this way, the metaphorical 'gold' of the pagans can be reused in the service of God. But it is significant that Origen goes on to urge his admiring disciple to 'seek correctly and with unshakable faith in God the sense of the divine Scriptures hidden from the many. Do not be content with knocking and seeking, for prayer is most necessary for understanding divine matters.'[68] For Origen, philosophy provided some useful raw materials to be refashioned for holy purposes, but prayerful contemplation of the Scriptures provided the

---

66. Irenaeus had already mentioned the concept of plundering the Egyptians around AD 180, but applied the metaphor to the general benefits of the wider culture, not Greek philosophy per se (*Against Heresies* 4.30 [*ANF*, vol. 1, pp. 502–504]).
67. Origen, *Letter to Gregory* 1 (Trigg, *Origen*, p. 211). Gregory the Wonderworker delivered an oration in his master's honour, as noted above.
68. Ibid. 4 (p. 212).

very sustenance of the Christian's soul. Both avenues of knowledge required a rational or intellectual approach.

Doctrine of God

The God that Origen believed in was the Creator described in the Old Testament and the Father of Jesus in the New – one and the same God. Though Origen was in touch with heretical streams of thought, he had no interest in the divine *plērōma* of the Gnostic sects, or the alien deity of the Marcionites. For Origen (as also for Middle Platonism) God was one, eternal, immutable, incorporeal, indivisible and utterly good. In fact, God is Goodness itself – the ground of all other goods. Unlike everything in the created order, God is not derived from a source. God simply *is*. Therefore, he is qualitatively different from human beings, who are temporally and spatially limited. This raises a genuine problem: How can God be known by people? Following the Platonic maxim that 'to find the maker and father of this universe is hard enough, and even if I succeeded, to declare him to everyone is impossible',[69] Origen believed God's transcendent splendour and humanity's finite capacities made God, at least in his divine essence, very difficult to know:

> Having then refuted, to the best of our ability, every interpretation which suggests that we should attribute to God any material characteristics, we assert that in truth he is incomprehensible and immeasurable. For whatever may be the knowledge which we have been able to obtain about God, whether by perception or by reflection, we must of necessity believe that he is far and away better than our thoughts about him. For if we see a man who can scarcely look at a glimmer or the light of the smallest lamp, and if we wish to teach such a one, whose eyesight is not strong enough to receive more light than we have said, about the brightness and splendor of the sun, shall we not have to tell him that the splendor of the sun is unspeakably and immeasurably better and more glorious than all this light he can see? In the same way our mind is shut up within bars of flesh and blood and rendered duller and feebler by reason of its association with such material substances; and although it is regarded as far more excellent when compared with the natural body, yet when it strains after incorporeal things and seeks to gain a sight of them it has scarcely the power of a glimmer of light or a tiny lamp.[70]

---

69. *Timaeus* 28c (John M. Cooper and D. S. Hutchinson, *Plato: Complete Works* [Indianapolis: Hackett, 1997], p. 1235).
70. *On First Principles* 1.1.5 (Butterworth, *Origen*, pp. 9–10).

God is beyond the grasp of the human mind, just as the brilliance of the sun exceeds the flame of an oil lamp. And yet, despite our difficulty in approaching God, Christianity promises we can know him. How can this be?

As perfect and eternal Goodness, God is characterized by, among other things, rationality. Therefore, God can be described as a Divine Mind that possesses its own Reason. He is a 'simple intellectual existence' and 'the mind and fount from which originates all intellectual existence or mind'.[71] We have already seen that the Greek word *logos*, which can be translated 'reason' or 'word', is an important term for Origen. It describes the Son of God who became incarnate as Jesus Christ. As the Logos sent from heaven, Jesus bridges the gap between the Divine Mind of the Father and the created order. Consider as an analogy the way the human mind works. In a certain sense, a person's mind is one thing, and its rational thought is something else. They are at once separate and united. In the act of thinking, a kind of inner dialogue takes place, so that the thinker's thoughts reveal the contents of his mind. In the same way, the Logos mediates the thoughts of the Divine Mind to the world. 'For as the word in us is the messenger of what the mind perceives,' Origen writes, 'so the Word of God, since he has known the Father, reveals the Father whom he has known, because no creature can come into contact with him without a guide.'[72] In this passage from Origen's commentary on John 1:1, we see how the Logos played an intermediary role between the unapproachable creator God and a world separate from him by nature. The great dilemma of how God can be known is now answered: God is revealed to us through Christ, who works especially through Scripture.

Origen has indicated that the Father and Son are united, yet are separate beings, which is considered good trinitarian theology today. Even in his era, Origen knew the Trinity was a tricky doctrine to get right. In a dialogue with a bishop whose theological credentials had been called into question, Origen cautioned, 'we must formulate the doctrine carefully, and show in what sense [the Father and Son] are two and in what sense the two are one God'.[73] Some of

---

71. *On First Principles* 1.1.6 (Butterworth, *Origen*, p. 10).
72. Origen, *Commentary on John* 1.277 (Ronald E. Heine, *Origen: Commentary on the Gospel According to John Books 1–10* [Washington, DC: Catholic University of America Press, 1989], p. 91).
73. *Dialogue with Heraclides* 124 (Oulton and Chadwick, *Alexandrian Christianity*, p. 438). It may seem strange for Origen to be discussing 'twoness' and 'oneness', when trinitarian language normally speaks of 'three' and 'one'. However, as the actual historical debate unfolded, it was the initial question of the Son's relationship to

Origen's ideas about the Trinity were precisely followed by the fourth-century defenders of orthodoxy. Origen insisted on a balance of unity and plurality in the Godhead, and also articulated the notion of 'eternal generation', the timeless and continual act by which the Father begets the Son.[74] However, some notions Origen offered about the Trinity are today considered inaccurate. He tended to make the Son subordinate to the Father, not just as an obedient Son carrying out his Father's will, but by actually ranking the Son at a lower level.[75] Origen also believed the Holy Spirit is a created being. He said that 'the Holy Spirit is the most honored of all things made through the Word' and is '[first] in rank of all the things which have been made by the Father through Christ'.[76] As we consider this doctrinal inaccuracy, we must remember Origen began his ministry more than a hundred years before the Council of Nicaea defined orthodox trinitarianism. The correct view of the Trinity was somewhat fuzzy among the ante-Nicene church fathers. Origen should not be held to the theological standards of a later generation, or be expected to have foreseen how the ancient trinitarian debates would shake out a century after his time. Though he made some serious mistakes, his ruminations about the Trinity nonetheless became a starting point for the early church's reflection on the Three and One.

The ascent of the human soul

We have observed how, in Origen's theological understanding, the trinitarian God is mediated to the world through the Logos. The Holy Spirit also plays an important revelatory role through the work of inspiration. But does this mean every person knows the true God, or serves him in obedience? The answer is obviously no. Yet every person has the capacity to do so. Origen taught that God, prior to the creation of the physical cosmos, had created a large number of rational natures, or celestial intelligent beings without bodies. Endowed with free will, these beings chose to gaze upon God; but eventually some turned away from the contemplation of God and cooled off in their ardour for him. These fallen intelligences became the souls of humanity, housed in

---

the Father that occupied the minds of those who began to investigate the Trinity. Only later was the doctrine of the Holy Spirit worked into the equation.

74. Origen calls it 'an eternal and everlasting begetting, as brightness is begotten by light' (*On First Principles* 1.2.4 [Butterworth, *Origen*, p. 18]).

75. *E.g.* Christ is said to be 'worthy of the second place of honour, after the God of the universe' (*Against Celsus* 7.57 [Chadwick, *Origen*, p. 443]).

76. *Commentary on John* 2.75 (Heine, *Origen*, p. 114).

physical bodies that God created for them because of their fall. Therefore, Origen believed a person's soul pre-existed his or her earthly life – a remarkable doctrine that has more to do with Platonic cosmology than biblical theology. The Christian tradition has not seen fit to agree with Origen on this point.

The fallen souls of humanity, according to Origen, continue to have free will. This means they can choose to begin the journey back to God.[77] Of course, human beings can also choose to decline further away from him. Origen taught that

> every being which is endowed with reason and yet fails to adhere to the ends and ordinances laid down by reason, is undoubtedly involved in sin by this departure from what is just and right. Every rational creature is therefore susceptible of praise and of blame; of praise, if in accordance with the reason which he has in him he advances to better things; of blame, if he departs from the rule and course of what is right, in which case he is also rightly subject to pains and penalties.[78]

Most human beings choose to fall away from God, and so incur his judgment. Enmeshed in the physical pleasures of the body, the souls of the wicked become mired in sin and fascinated with ignorance. We should note that for Origen, sin is not so much a legal verdict of guilt inherited from Adam, as a corruption that imitates Adam's pattern by making sinners turn away from the God who first loved them. Adam simply acted as a conduit for sin's entry into the world. Commenting on Romans 5:12, where Paul writes that 'sin came into the world through one man' (ESV), Origen interprets the world as 'either the place in which men dwell, or the earthly and bodily life in which sin has a place'.[79] Adam's notorious accomplishment, then, was to open the world to

---

77. Origen was emphatically on the 'free will' side of the age-old debate between determinism and libertarianism, which is usually framed in evangelical circles as a debate between 'Calvinism' and 'Arminianism'. If the Calvinists can count Augustine among their pantheon of historical supporters, the Arminians have every right to claim Origen for theirs.
78. *On First Principles* 1.5.2 (Butterworth, *Origen*, p. 44).
79. Origen, *Commentary on Romans* 5.1.17–18 (Thomas P. Scheck, *Origen: Commentary on the Epistle to the Romans Books 1–5* [Washington, DC: Catholic University of America Press, 2001], pp. 312–313). Scheck observes, 'nowhere does Origen develop the concept of guilt inherited or imputed from Adam, as taught by Augustine and Ambrosiaster in the subsequent doctrine of original sin' (p. 303).

sin; yet he did not pass actual unrighteousness to his posterity. Each individual is responsible for his or her freely chosen sin.

Despite the presence of sin in the world with all its tempting attractions, a few souls will decide to embark upon a return to divine contemplation. Their avenue for achieving this ascent is the orthodox Christian faith. Salvation cannot be accomplished through heresies or pagan philosophy. Only Christ the Logos can offer restoration. However, the precise means by which Jesus saves a person is by training the soul and leading it towards virtue. In other words, Origen taught an 'educational' model of the atonement. Of course, he did not deny the concept of a substitutionary sin sacrifice. In his commentary on the 'Lamb that is slain' in Revelation 5:6, Origen writes, 'In accordance with the Father's love for man, [the Lamb] also submitted to slaughter on behalf of the world, purchasing us with his own blood from him who bought us when we had sold ourselves to sin.'[80] Or again, Christ 'is he who "blotted out the handwriting against us" with his own blood and removed it from our midst, that no traces even of the sins which have been expunged may be found, "having fastened it to the cross."'[81] While the language of blood sacrifice and debt payment can be found in Origen, his primary lens for understanding the atonement is intimate participation in Jesus Christ by which the soul is restored to godliness through training in the Lord's ways.[82]

The final goal of the soul's ascent is perfect union with God. This great movement of fall and return is entirely consistent with a Platonic cosmology. At the same time, an eschatological outlook in which Christ reigns triumphant at the end of time, and the cosmos is restored to final obedience, finds resonance with scriptural patterns. For example, the apostle Paul proclaims in 1 Corinthians 15:24–28 that everything will be put in subjection to Jesus,

---

80. *Commentary on John* 6.274 (Heine, *Origen*, p. 242).

81. Ibid. 6.285 (p. 245). The Scripture reference Origen cites here is Col. 2:14–15.

82. Peter Gorday surveys various interpreters of Origen (such as von Balthasar, de Lubac and Crouzel), and ultimately concludes that Origen did have 'a real theology of redemption in his theology of the cross'. However, for Gorday the cross of Jesus in Origen is the martyr's cross, whose powerful testimony is a spur to improved ethics (Peter J. Gorday, 'The Martyr's Cross: Origen and Redemption', in Elizabeth A. Dryer [ed.], *The Cross in Christian Tradition: From Paul to Bonaventure* [New York: Paulist, 2000], p. 142). No doubt there is some truth in Gorday's assessment. But, for the propitiatory and substitutionary aspects of the atonement in Origen, see Joseph O'Leary, 'Atonement', in McGuckin, *Westminster Handbook*, pp. 67–68.

and Acts 3:21 promises the 'restoration' (*apokatastasis*) of all things. While eschatological restoration and final triumph are biblical themes, some of the details of Origen's theology deserve critique. In his own day, and especially in the subsequent centuries, Origen was accused of teaching universal salvation, to the point that even the devil and his demons would eventually be saved.[83] The accusations levelled against Origen for such radical *apokatastasis* served as a major impetus for his condemnation (implicitly, if not explicitly) by later generations.[84] Even if theologians today are not inclined to follow Origen on matters of angelology and eschatology, we should nonetheless recognize

83. Origen's angelology is connected to his theory of fallen intelligences. Some intelligences fell to a middle ground and became human souls, while others fell to a lesser degree (becoming the good angels) or a greater degree (Satan and the demons). All of these intelligences in their various gradations have the opportunity to move back towards God in a cosmic fluctuation of fall and return. See *On First Principles* 1.5.1–5 and 1.6.1–3 (Butterworth, *Origen*, pp. 44–58). Depending on whether the surviving Greek text or Rufinus' Latin translation is considered valid, Origen either suggested the possibility, or directly posited, that 'there are some [demons] who will one day in the ages to come succeed in turning to goodness' (Butterworth, *Origen*, p. 56). Yet in other places Origen considers hell to be the final destination of Satan: 'For that one who is said to have fallen from heaven, there will not be any conversion at the end of the age' (*Commentary on Romans* 8.9.4 [Scheck, *Origen*, p. 168]). When Origen was accused during his lifetime of teaching the salvation of the devil, he explicitly denied it, claiming that his recorded statements on the matter had been interpolated with assertions he never made. 'They declare that I hold . . . the devil is to be saved, a thing which no man can say even if he has taken leave of his senses and is manifestly insane' (Rufinus, *Concerning the Adulteration of the Works of Origen* [*NPNF*, 2nd series, vol. 3, p. 423]).
84. The present chapter excludes an extended discussion of the complex Origenist Controversy because it occurred well after Origen's lifetime. In a nutshell, Origen was severely criticized in the 390s, and again in the mid-500s, for his views on the Trinity, the nature of resurrection bodies and the universal restoration of fallen souls (including Satan and the demons). Surrounding these matters were the patristic disputes about allegorical versus literal exegesis, as well as a debate about the value of the human body and reproduction in an ascetic context. At the Fifth Ecumenical Council under Emperor Justinian in 553, certain Origenistic ideas were condemned. See Elizabeth A. Clark, *The Origenist Controversy: The Cultural Construction of an Early Christian Debate* (Princeton: Princeton University Press, 1992).

and appreciate the underlying rationale for Origen's theology of hope: the awesome goodness of God. 'Providence will never abandon the universe,' Origen insisted. 'For even if some part of it becomes very bad because the rational being sins, God arranges to purify it, and after a time to turn the whole world back to Himself.'[85] Origen's theological project centres on the steadfast faithfulness of the God who saves.

Evaluation of Origen

Though the jeweller's microscope has revealed some flaws, the diamond that is Origen still shines brightly today. His life is revealed as one of those powerful lives that inevitably reverberates through the centuries. Origen's student Gregory the Wonderworker claimed that the day he began to study with his master was 'the first day to me, and the most precious of all days, if I may so speak, since then for the first time the true Sun began to rise upon me'.[86] Any teacher who could inspire such devoted followers – as well as equally vehement enemies – must have been dealing with great themes of fundamental importance. Yet in the end, Origen's goal was simple: 'I want to be a *man of the church*,' he said. 'I do not want to be called by the name of some founder of a heresy, but by the name of Christ, and to bear that name which is blessed on the earth. It is my desire, in deed as in Spirit, both to be and to be called a Christian.'[87] Perhaps Christians today will be more willing than earlier generations to let Origen attain his desire.

Origen's contributions to historical theology can be a useful part of the evangelical ressourcement of the ancient fathers. As an *ascetic*, Origen reminds us that the goal of moral purity is not to be taken lightly. Mastery of the body is not a concern only for hair-shirted monks of yesteryear with shaven heads and sour expressions. The life of chastity and self-control cannot be passed off as a Victorian obsession, one that is no longer relevant in our enlightened times. In his book *Seven Faith Tribes*, social science researcher George Barna suggests that 66% of the adult population in the United States belongs to a group he calls 'Casual Christians' who practice an insipid faith-lifestyle with no real attempt to uphold the strenuous morality of the Bible. In an age of relativistic ethics and dubious morals, Origen offers a welcome reminder that the Christian life

---

85. Origen, *Against Celsus* 6.99 (Chadwick, *Origen*, p. 263).
86. Gregory the Wonderworker, *Oration* 6.73 (*ANF*, vol. 6, p. 27).
87. *Homily on Luke* 16.6 (von Balthasar, *Origen*, p. 155).

is about good works after all. Sanctification is every Christian's call, so that the face of God may be seen without obscurity.

The ancient understanding of asceticism stands in sharp contrast to the modern way of viewing it as puritanical prudishness or legalistic abstinence. While self-discipline and rigorous training for the sake of athletic achievement is widely appreciated in contemporary Western culture, spiritual asceticism is hardly in vogue today. The 'ascetic' is either a finger-pointing moralist with a repressed libido, or a guilt-ridden works-salvationist trying to earn his way into God's favour. In both cases, the ascetic tendency is distinctly negative. It can be viewed only as something to transcend or shed in order to reach a more enlightened state. It is not a path to maturity, but a hindrance.

For Origen, however, *askēsis* was the pathway to a higher life. One does not find in Origen the sorts of diatribes against the lascivious and sexy ways of women, or the pedantic exhortations to chastity, that one can find in his fellow-African and contemporary Tertullian. Origen did not urge asceticism by means of the Judeo-Christian prohibition 'Thou shalt not . . .' Instead, he issued a call. Peter Brown characterizes Origen's asceticism as a mandate for transformation: 'I beseech you, therefore, be transformed,' Origen urged. 'Resolve to know that in you there is a capacity to be transformed.'[88] This transformation is, at its heart, *preparatory*. That is to say, through practice and diligence, the soul is made ready for the vision of God.

Evangelicals have been quick to point out that Origen's understanding of asceticism was coloured with a Platonic brush. When Origen remarks, 'For all material and corporeal things, whatever they are, are reckoned as a fleeting and feeble shadow,'[89] the statement could have been Plato's. Nevertheless, Origen finishes the thought in an eminently Christian way. Corporeal things are considered shadows, he says, 'since they can in no way be compared to the saving and holy gifts of the God of all'.[90] What Christian, Origen asks, would prefer earthly wealth to the wealth of divine knowledge? Who would be so insane as to prefer physical health to the health of the mind and the soul? 'If all these things are put in harmony by the Word of God, they make bodily sufferings nothing but an insignificant scratch, indeed less than a scratch.'[91] Whenever

88. Origen, *Dialogue with Heraclides* 150, quoted in Peter Brown, *The Body and Society: Men, Women, and Sexual Renunciation in Early Christianity* (New York: Columbia University Press, 1988), p. 162.

89. Origen, *On Prayer* 17.1 (Greer, *Origen*, p. 116).

90. Ibid.

91. Ibid.

Origen woke up in the middle of the night hungry, tired and stiff from sleeping on the floor, he probably reminded himself that his meditative hours of Bible study were far preferable to the meagre gains that the sleeping citizens of Alexandria could obtain in their quiet beds.

We may find it hard to understand how the extreme bodily rigour practised by the ancient ascetics can be so easily disregarded as 'less than a scratch', but that is because we do not understand what Origen meant when he said he was deriving something supremely worthy from his bodily mortification. What exactly did he receive? The answer is, a vision of God, a direct encounter with the divine; for Origen's asceticism had a decidedly mystical bent.[92] In other words, the Christian life offered much more than 'rules to live by' or 'good moral principles'. It offered the chance to ascend towards the living God. Even though Origen's asceticism was couched in the language of Plato, his desire for intimacy with God and his abhorrence of the sins of the flesh should ring true in evangelical ears.

As an *exegete*, Origen towers over the Christian past like Alexandria's famous lighthouse – and like a lighthouse, if the beacon is ignored, it is to our own peril. Whatever else we might say about Origen of Alexandria, we must recognize he was a man who loved the Bible. He immersed himself in the text of Scripture more than anyone else of his day. The sheer quantity of his literary oeuvre demonstrates this, as does the kind of sustained effort it took to publish a philological work like the *Hexapla*. Anyone who believes Origen was somehow 'against the Bible' or that he tried to 'undercut its meaning' is working from a caricature of him, and has not come face to face with Origen's exegesis. His scriptural commentaries overflow with a desire to uncover the truth of God from the sacred page. 'Devote yourself above all to knowledge of the holy scripture,' he wrote, 'with faith and God-pleasing readiness.'[93] How does one do this, according to Origen? He advises, 'it is not enough to knock and seek, for what is most necessary for understanding the things of God is prayer'.[94]

Why, then, does a man with such affection for God's word have the reputation as a Bible corrupter? The answer is because he used *allegory*. In some circles of evangelicalism, allegorical interpretation is akin to ripping pages

92. For the Platonic roots of Origen's mysticism, see ch. 4 in John Macquarrie, *Two Worlds Are Ours: An Introduction to Christian Mysticism* (Minneapolis: Fortress, 2005).

93. Origen, *Letter to Gregory Thaumaturgus* (von Balthasar, *Origen*, p. 94).

94. Ibid.

out of the Bible and scattering them on the floor.[95] But is such an assessment fair? Before Origen is consigned to the ash heap of history, a genuine attempt should be made to appreciate his allegorical interpretative method in its historical context. Only then will we be in a position to appreciate the true beauty of the multifaceted Origen. This is not to say his exegesis was always sound, or that he can never be critiqued. However, critique is a right earned by giving someone a true hearing. It should only come on the other side of sympathetic understanding.

It is fair to say Origen produced innumerable interpretations that, from a historical point of view, could not have been in the consciousness of the human author when he penned a verse of Scripture. If we evaluate Origen according to the hermeneutical standard of 'authorial intent' – defined as the content of the inspired author's mind at the moment of writing – then Origen fails the test.[96] Yet consider two points. First, as mentioned earlier, Origen did not regard human beings to be the ultimate authors of Scripture. The Bible was authored by the Logos himself.[97] Because of Scripture's divine authorship, hidden layers of meaning are lodged in the pages of the biblical text that the original authors did not perceive, or perceived only through spiritual illumination. It is the interpreter's task to discover this divine content. Thus Origen did believe in 'authorial intent', but what mattered was the intent of Scripture's true Author, God himself.[98]

---

95. A brief anecdote illustrates how allegorization is often poorly received in evangelical circles. A colleague of mine once turned to me after we had both listened to a sermon and said, 'Al really showed up today.' The preacher's name was not Al, so I glanced at my friend with a quizzical expression. 'Who's Al?' I asked. 'You know', he answered, 'Al E. Gory.' The remark was not intended as a compliment.
96. On this subject, see Jeremy M. Bergen, 'Origen on the Authorial Intention of Scripture', *Conrad Grebel Review* 23.3 (autumn 2005), pp. 85–96.
97. Though he often attributes authorship to the Logos, Origen can just as easily describe the Bible as being inspired by the Holy Spirit. 'In Origen's view, the entire purpose of theology is to understand the Spirit's words in their proper spiritual sense and to convey them to others in a way appropriate to their needs. The theologian, beginning from the Spirit-filled Scriptures, thus continues and participates in the pedagogical work of the Spirit' (Maureen Beyer Moser, *Teacher of Holiness: The Holy Spirit in Origen's Commentary on the Epistle to the Romans* [Piscataway, NJ: Gorgias, 2005], p. 172).
98. Michael Holmes asks whether Origen believed in 'inerrancy', and concludes that he did – but only for the spiritual sense of the text. The literal text contains errors that

Secondly, Origen believed reliance on authorial intent (defined in a strict sense) would reduce the Bible to a book of curious antiquities and historical trivia. This is particularly true of the Old Testament. How can a book of Israelite history, laws, poetry and oracles be made to convey theological wisdom that transcends the ages? If the significance of a given verse is limited to the kind of thing a Hebrew shepherd like Moses from the late Bronze Age could have known, or if the ancient Near Eastern world view is the only acceptable ground of meaning for a text, then it becomes very difficult to make the Bible speak with timeless truth to the Christian church, whether in Origen's day or our own.[99] We may ask, for example, whether the prophet Hosea, writing in the eighth century BC, was thinking about the incarnate Son of God, or about Israel and the exodus, when he wrote, 'out of Egypt I called my son' (Hos. 11:1 ESV). The only plausible historical answer is that Hosea was looking back to Israel's greatest moment of deliverance; yet Matthew's Gospel tells us it was simultaneously a reference to Jesus Christ (Matt. 2:15). This sort of multilayered and prophetic approach to Scripture is viewed as completely legitimate when pursued by a biblical author. Is it really much of a stretch to imagine that if the New Testament writers interpreted the Old Testament this way, it must be God's own way of doing exegesis? Origen believed it to be exactly that: the God-ordained means of interpreting his written word. Of course, we may want to argue with Origen on this point, but at least we should recognize that he had what he believed to be a very good rationale for moving ahead in the way he did.

It is true that Origen sometimes abandoned the literal sense in order to make the text speak about Christ. In fact, Origen believed the Holy Spirit

---

God purposely implanted so the true divine meaning would be sought (Michael W. Holmes, 'Origen and the Inerrancy of Scripture', *Journal of the Evangelical Theological Society* 24.3 [Sept. 1981], p. 221).

99. This problem, and Origen's response to it, is examined very thoroughly and with great insight by Joseph T. Lienhard, 'Origen and the Crisis of the Old Testament in the Early Church', *Pro ecclesia* 9.3 (summer 2000), pp. 355–366. Lienhard writes, 'Origen assured the Old Testament a permanent place in the Christian church not by an abstract theory but by working his way through the entire Old Testament, book by book, sentence by sentence, and word by word. Origen provided the church with the first Christian commentary on virtually the entire Old Testament . . . Someone might say that Lewis and Clark should have followed a better way across this continent; but the fact remains that they were the first to chart *a* way; and so it is with Origen' (p. 362).

inserted intentional errors or impossibilities into the literal text of Scripture so the interpreter would be prompted to look for a hidden Christological meaning.[100] To our modern ears, this sounds like licence for absolute subjectivism. The exegete would have free rein to introduce whatever interpretations he or she could imagine, and so the sacred task of understanding God's Word would be corrupted by human whims.[101] However, Origen did not view things this way. For him, the danger of fanciful or erroneous conclusions being introduced through allegory would be counteracted by several factors. For one, the orthodox Christian exegete would be limited by the church's rule of faith (the summary of theology taught to new converts). Interpretations that did not square with sound doctrine would be excluded. Furthermore, the good exegete was not some stranger off the street. He was a mature and upright Christian of proven character, led by the Holy Spirit down the path of righteousness, and approved by the acclaim of the church. Such a person would not be inclined to make radical mistakes when interpreting the biblical text. But most important of all, Origen was confident allegory would not lead him astray because he knew what the Bible was fundamentally about: the Lord Jesus Christ. Origen often referred to John 5:39, where Jesus proclaims that all Scripture testifies about him. The books of the Bible are, in reality, a single Christocentric book. 'Christ is written about even in the Pentateuch,' Origen insists. 'He is spoken of in each of the Prophets, and in the Psalms, and in a word, as the Savior himself says, in all the Scriptures.'[102]

Without a doubt, Origen got many interpretations flat-out wrong; yet the stimulus behind his spiritual exegesis ought not to be forgotten by today's interpreter. To retrieve Origen critically in modern times does not mean the pastor should begin waxing eloquent about the delightful kisses and luxuri-

---

100. Origen, *On First Principles* 4.2.9 (Butterworth, *Origen*, pp. 285–287; see esp. the Latin paraphrase of the text by Rufinus).

101. One critic of Origen (though an appreciative one) in modern times is R. P. C. Hanson, who observes, 'Where the Bible did not obviously mean what [Origen] thought it ought to mean, or even where it obviously did not mean what he thought it ought to mean, he had only to turn the magic ring of allegory, and – Hey Presto! – the desired meaning appeared. Allegory, in short, instead of ensuring that he would in his exegesis maintain close contact with biblical thought, rendered him deplorably independent of the Bible' (R. P. C. Hanson, *Allegory and Event: A Study of the Sources and Significance of Origen's Interpretation of Scripture* [Richmond, VA: John Knox, 1959], p. 371).

102. Origen, *Commentary on John* 5.6 (*ANF*, vol. 9, p. 347).

ant bosom of Jesus. Allegorical interpretation as the ancients understood it – whether of the Song of Songs or any other biblical book – is hardly feasible today. Instead, what Origen offers is the boldness to free our minds from a rationalistic hermeneutic that scarcely escapes the 'original setting' of the biblical text. Origen frequently warned that 'the letter kills'. Much to our surprise, we discover he was right. Interpretation can too easily become a dead exercise in Bible backgrounds or ancient Near Eastern or Greco-Roman world views. Many biblical scholars (especially those who are not practitioners in the pulpit) have got stuck in the time period of their academic discipline, so that their conclusions about the meaning of the text have very little timeless significance. In an attempt to control the sacred page, interpreters are taught to pursue a pseudo-science of computer word counts and sentence diagramming. Some academic commentators seem to care more about what the ancient audience would have heard than what the people of God need to hear today. Genuine bridging of the two worlds does not always take place, and pastors are tempted to function as historians of antiquity rather than prophetic heralds. Is there room in today's churches for pastors to pursue a more imaginative exegesis? Dare we turn the Spirit-filled preacher loose to paint a biblical picture with deftness and artistry, relying on his intuition as much as his concordance?

Although we can no longer pursue the kind of interpretative moves Origen made, the underlying assumptions of his spiritual exegesis remind us that Scripture is a cohesive book authored by God to proclaim a fundamental truth: Jesus is Lord. A single, overarching narrative runs through the canon. There are no wasted pages in the storybook of the Bible. Moses spoke of Jesus just as truly as Matthew did. According to Origen, the revelation that comes by means of the Logos has now invested every verse – indeed, every word in every verse – with new interpretative potential. Origen states, 'Believing in the words of my Lord Jesus Christ, I think that even an "iota or dot" is full of mystery, and do not think that any of these "will pass away until all is accomplished."'[103] Perhaps today's interpreter should be more aggressive in using his sanctified imagination to elucidate – and even construct – the fuller sense of the text. Let the Logos be heard once again in the church.

As a *theologian*, Origen stands as one of the high points of the ancient church, rivalled only by Augustine in the scope of his influence. In fact, Origen might be called the Greek Augustine. That is to say, the kind of seminal influence Augustine exercised on the Latin West could be claimed for Origen on the Greek East. Yet even this would be an underestimate of Origen's impact,

103. Origen, *Homily on Exodus* 1.4 (von Balthasar, *Origen*, p. 89; slightly adapted).

because he heavily influenced (though not always with direct acknowledgment) such Western writers as Jerome, Rufinus, Ambrose and indeed Augustine himself.

Unfortunately, while Origen got some doctrines exquisitely right, he got others dreadfully wrong. We ought not to follow him down his more speculative paths, hoping to see the devil in the by and by, or thinking of the Son as a kind of second-tier being within the Trinity. We must resist Origen on certain points, even as we grant that some of his errors can be overlooked in an age when orthodoxy was still being worked out.

On a more serious note, we must admit that Origen did not give adequate space in his theological framework to Christ's substitutionary atonement. His understanding of salvation as educational progress, though not incorrect in itself, remains unbalanced by a robust theology of the sacrificial death on the cross. Thus a lesser facet of the atonement has become the main one in Origen. We must look to other historical theologians to offset Origen on this point.

Even so, Origen's educational view of the atonement, in which Christ offers an example of perfect righteousness and calls us to imitate him, can teach us something important about the Christian life. Despite the tacky marketing of 'What would Jesus do?' products, the question itself is entirely valid. Evangelicals often need to be reminded that moral progress is experienced as a series of yeses and noes to the options before us. In such moments, there is no better model than Christ himself.

At the same time, while the life of virtue is a path freely chosen by the Christian, it is not achieved through human effort alone. Some theologians have argued Origen's radical view of freedom undercuts the doctrines of sin and grace. While it is true Origen did not teach the Augustinian doctrine of utter human inability to choose the good, he did hold the majority view in Christian history, which is that man's nature is not so vitiated by sin that he is unable to make a move towards God.[104] Taking the many biblical exhortations to moral excellence at face value (on the assumption that it would be unworthy of God to require a course of action unless it were possible to achieve it), Origen finds no warrant for the view that humans cannot make free choices

104. Groups that adhere to this general view would include many Eastern Orthodox, the 'Semi-Pelagian' medieval Roman Catholics as well as contemporary Roman Catholicism, most Anglicans and Episcopalians, Arminians, Wesleyans and Methodists, the Holiness and Stone-Campbellite denominations, many Baptists and Pentecostals, and revivalist evangelicals.

for good or evil. In fact, it was the Gnostics in his day who claimed people are 'predestined' to one fate or another. Origen's soteriology undoubtedly possessed a strong libertarian bent. He emphasized human cooperation with the grace of God – a grace offered in Christ, but one to which we must say *yes* as well. Even a 'Calvinist' like the author of this chapter can benefit from the reminder that the Christian walk requires moral choices, and Jesus shows us how to make them wisely.

Where Origen excels theologically is his insistence on the grandeur of God and the glory of the eternal Logos. The pattern of Origen's life, no less than the precepts of his writings, testify to what was once called 'the fear of the Lord'. In an age of studied familiarity, when God is our 'co-pilot' and Jesus is the 'boy next door', Origen reminds us not to approach the Holy One with our shoes on. God is distant for Origen, a faraway deity who is difficult for fallen human beings to know. Does this premise shock us? Do we resent the idea that God is not near to hand? If so, perhaps we do not fully appreciate the magnitude of his divine glory. Of course, Origen did not believe God was impossible to know, or that intimacy with him could not be achieved. Rather, Origen insisted that knowing God was the fruit of a laborious search. Those who want to see the face of God must embark on a holy pilgrimage in which Jesus Christ, the abiding Logos, will serve as the soul's mediator and guide. Whether preaching a sermon, commenting on Scripture, mentoring disciples or enduring the torturer's flames, Origen lived out a theology of reverent awe right to the end. For that reason, if for no other, he is a shaper of orthodoxy whose ancient voice deserves to be heard today.

In 1950 the French Jesuit scholar Henri de Lubac wrote a book in which he faced head-on the modern person's utter estrangement from Origen. De Lubac remarks:

> I find the distance to be as great as anyone else does, that distance which separates us irremediably from this Alexandrian of the third century and from his intellectual universe. The river does not flow back to its source . . . The wells once dug by Origen have long been covered over with sand. But the same deep layer of water is still there, which he can help us find once again in order to quench the same thirst.[105]

Fitting words of hope from one 'man of the church' to another.

---

105. De Lubac, *History and Spirit*, p. 14.

Bibliography

Primary sources, original languages

Origen's writings may be obtained in the Patrologiae cursus completus: Series graeca, ed. J.-P. Migne, 162 vols. [Paris: Cerf, 1857–86], vols. 11–17; and in Die griechische christliche Schriftsteller der ersten [drei] Jahrhunderte, subtitled *Origenes Werke*, 1–12.2 (Leipzig: Akademie, n.d.). The best critical editions of Origen are those in Sources chrétiennes. Several of Origen's most important works are enumerated below. For a complete list of texts in the original languages and English translations, see McGuckin, *Westminster Handbook*, pp. 41–44.

Brésard, Luc, *et al. Commentaire sur le Cantique des Cantiques*, Sources chrétiennes 375–376 (Paris: Cerf, 1991–2).

Crouzel, Henri, and Manlio Simonetti, *Traité des Principes*, Sources chrétiennes 252–253, 268–269, 312 (Paris: Cerf, 1978–84).

Koetschau, Paul, *Die Schrift vom Martyrium, Buch 1–IV gegen Celsus* and *Buch V–VIII gegen Celsus, Die Schrift vom Gebet*, Die griechische christliche Schriftsteller der ersten [drei] Jahrhunderte 1–2 (Leipzig: Akademie, 1899).

Primary sources, English translations

Balthasar, Hans Urs von, *Origen: Spirit and Fire: A Thematic Anthology of His Writings*, tr. Robert J. Daly (Washington, DC: Catholic University of America Press, 1984).

Butterworth, G. W., *Origen: On First Principles* (Gloucester, MA: Smith, 1973).

Chadwick, Henry, *Origen: Contra Celsum* (Cambridge: Cambridge University Press, 1953).

Daly, Robert J., *Origen: Treatise on the Passover and Dialogues or Origen with Heraclides and His Fellow Bishops, on the Father, the Son, and the Soul*, Ancient Christian Writers 54 (New York: Paulist, 1992).

Greer, Rowan, *Origen: An Exhortation to Martyrdom, Prayer, First Principles: Book IV, Prologue to the Commentary on the Song of Songs, Homily XXVII On Numbers* (New York: Paulist, 1979).

Heine, Ronald E., *Origen: Commentary on the Gospel According to John, Books 1–10*, and *Commentary on the Gospel According to John, Books 13–32*, Fathers of the Church 80, 89 (Washington, DC: Catholic University of America Press, 1989, 1993).

Lawson, R. P., *The Song of Songs: Commentaries and Homilies*, Ancient Christian Writers 26 (New York: Newman, 1957).

Oulton, J. E. L., and Henry Chadwick, *Alexandrian Christianity*, Library of Christian Classics 2 (Philadelphia: Westminster, 1954).

Roberts, Alexander, and James Donaldson (eds.), *The Ante-Nicene Fathers*, vols. 4, 9 (Buffalo: Christian Literature, 1885, 1896).

SCHECK, THOMAS P., *Origen: Commentary on the Epistle to the Romans Books 1–5* and *Commentary on the Epistle to the Romans Books 6–10*, Fathers of the Church 103, 104 (Washington, DC: Catholic University of America Press, 2001, 2002).

—, *Origen: Homilies on Numbers*, Ancient Christian Texts (Downers Grove: IVP, 2009).

Best secondary sources

CROUZEL, HENRI, *Origen: The Life and Thought of the First Great Theologian*, tr. A. S. Worrall (San Francisco: Harper & Row, 1989).

DE LUBAC, HENRI, *History and Spirit: The Understanding of Scripture According to Origen*, tr. Anne Englund Nash (San Francisco: Ignatius, 2007).

KANNENGIESSER, CHARLES, and William L. Petersen, *Origen of Alexandria: His World and His Legacy* (Notre Dame: University of Notre Dame Press, 1988).

MCGUCKIN, JOHN ANTHONY (ed.), *The Westminster Handbook to Origen* (Louisville: Westminster John Knox, 2004; repr. *The SCM Press A–Z of Origen*, London: SCM, 2007).

TRIGG, JOSEPH W., *Origen* (New York: Routledge, 1998).

Other important studies

BIGG, CHARLES, *The Christian Platonists of Alexandria* (Oxford: Clarendon, 1866; repr. Chestnut Hill, MA: Adamant Media, 2005).

CHADWICK, HENRY, *Early Christian Thought and the Classical Tradition: A Study in Justin Martyr, Irenaeus, Tertullian, and Origen* (Oxford: Oxford University Press, 1966).

CLARK, ELIZABETH A., *The Origenist Controversy: The Cultural Construction of an Early Christian Debate* (Princeton: Princeton University Press, 1992).

DANIELOU, JEAN, *Origen*, tr. Walter Mitchell (New York: Sheed & Ward, 1955).

DREWERY, BENJAMIN, *Origen and the Doctrine of Grace* (London: Epworth, 1960).

EDWARDS, MARK J., *Origen Against Plato* (Aldershot: Ashgate, 2002).

FAIRWEATHER, WILLIAM, *Origen and Greek Patristic Theology* (New York: Charles Scribner's Sons, 1901; repr. BiblioLife, 2009).

HANSON, R. P. C., *Allegory and Event: A Study of the Sources and Significance of Origen's Interpretation of Scripture* (Richmond, VA: John Knox, 1959).

HEIDL, GYÖRGY, *Origen's Influence on the Young Augustine: A Chapter in the History of Origenism* (Piscataway, NJ: Gorgias, 2003).

KING, J. CHRISTOPHER, *Origen on the Song of Songs as the Spirit of Scripture: The Bridegroom's Perfect Marriage-Song* (Oxford: Oxford University Press, 2005).

LAURO, ELIZABETH Ann Dively, *The Soul and Spirit of Scripture within Origen's Exegesis* (Leiden: Brill, 2005).

LEDEGANG, F., *Mysterium Ecclesiae: Images of the Church and its Members in Origen* (Leuven: Peeters, 2001).

MOSER, MAUREEN BEYER, *Teacher of Holiness: The Holy Spirit in Origen's Commentary on the Epistle to the Romans* (Piscataway, NJ: Gorgias, 2005).

RANKIN, DAVID, *From Clement to Origen: The Social and Historical Context of the Church Fathers* (Aldershot: Ashgate, 2006).
ROWE, J. NIGEL, *Origen's Doctrine of Subordination: A Study of Origen's Christology* (Bern: Lang, 1987).
SCHECK, THOMAS P., *Origen and the History of Justification: The Legacy of Origen's Commentary on Romans* (Notre Dame: University of Notre Dame Press, 2008).
TORJESEN, KAREN JO, *Hermeneutical Procedure and Theological Method in Origen's Exegesis* (Berlin: de Gruyter, 1986).
TRIGG, JOSEPH W., *Origen: The Bible and Philosophy in the Third-Century Church* (Atlanta: John Knox, 1983).
TRIPOLITIS, ANTONIA, *Origen: A Critical Reading* (Frankfurt: Lang, 1985).
TZAMALIKOS, PANAYIOTIS, *Origen: Cosmology and Ontology of Time* (Leiden: Brill, 2007).
—, *Origen: Philosophy of History and Eschatology* (Leiden: Brill, 2006).
WIDDICOMBE, PETER, *The Fatherhood of God from Origen to Athanasius* (Oxford: Clarendon, 1994).

In addition to these resources, scholarly papers on various subjects related to Origen have been delivered at the International Origen Congress held every four years since 1973, published in the *Origeniana* volumes. The most recent to appear is G. Heidl and R. Somos, *Origeniana Nona: Origen and the Religious Practice of His Time* (Leuven: Peeters, 2009).

4. ATHANASIUS

Carl Beckwith

Athanasius lived a long and tumultuous life. He was born in Egypt around the year 298 and died in 373. Although we know very little about his parents or anything specific about his early years, we do know that he was familiar with Christianity and its sacred rites at a young age.[1] He lived through and witnessed as a young child the horrors of the Great Persecution under the emperor Diocletian. He was taken into the bishop of Alexandria's residence as a teenager in order to prepare for a life of service to the church. In his late twenties, he attended the Council of Nicaea (325) as the bishop's secretary and soon thereafter became bishop of Alexandria in 328 on the eve of his thirtieth birthday. Athanasius spent the next forty-five years of his life defending the gospel and the doctrine of the Trinity. He was exiled five times from his

---

1. This description of Athanasius' childhood accepts the broad outline of Rufinus of Aquileia's well-known account of the young Athanasius' playing bishop and baptizing his friends along the seashore. See Rufinus of Aquileia, *Church History* 10.15; *The Church History of Rufinus of Aquileia: Books 10 and 11*, tr. Philip R. Amidon (Oxford: Oxford University Press, 1997), pp. 26–27. For a very different view on Athanasius' childhood, suggesting that he was not raised as a Christian, see the tenth-century *History of the Patriarchs of Alexandria*, Patrologia orientalis, vol. 1, 4 (408), quoted and discussed in Khaled Anatolios, *Athanasius* (London: Routledge, 2004), pp. 3–4.

episcopal see of Alexandria, spending around seventeen of his forty-five years as bishop in exile.[2] On 2 May 373, around the age of seventy-five, the patriarch of Egypt, bishop of Alexandria, and resilient confessor of Christ, died.

In this chapter we will look at the world in which Athanasius grew up, the historical situation of the church during his lifetime, his theological contribution to the fourth-century discussions on the Trinity and Christ, and his impact, as bishop and patron, on the urban landscape and people of Alexandria. The theological theme that runs throughout this chapter is one that characterizes all of Athanasius' efforts: the victory of the cross. Athanasius begins and ends with Jesus Christ, the eternal Word of God, who assumed flesh, conquered sin, death and the devil, and rose again, opening the gates of paradise to us. For Athanasius the victory of the cross signals not only our reconciliation with the Father through the saving work of the Son but also our renewal in this life and our transformation from lives of darkness to light, from corruption to incorruption, from sinners to sons and daughters of God. The Word who created and redeemed us is the same Word who becomes our co-worker in the life of sanctification and by his grace through the Holy Spirit renders us holy. Our transformation – our deification, as Athanasius prefers to put it – and our lives of holiness serve as a testimony and witness to the world of Christ's victory. For Athanasius, you need not involve yourself in the high-level theological debates of the fourth century on the doctrine of the Trinity to know the truth of the creed from Nicaea. Rather, you need only look at the world around you and marvel at the courage of the martyrs, the deeds of the monks and the steadfastness of ordinary Christians to know that the Christ who conquered on the cross continues to live and conquer in the lives of his followers. The world itself is a new creation with the blessings of God everywhere to be seen.

Historical context: from persecution to prosperity

Athanasius grew up during a time of intense anti-Christian sentiment. When he was around five years old, Christianity came under attack and endured such a horrendous persecution by the order of the emperor Diocletian that historians have since labelled this the Great Persecution. Men, women and children were

---

2. Athanasius' five exiles are as follows: 335–7 to Trier; 338–45 to Rome; 356–62 to the Egyptian desert; 362–3 and 365–6 both to the desert. Athanasius' golden decade of relative peace was from 346 to 356. During this time in Alexandria, he composed such works as the *Orations against the Arians* and *Defence of the Nicene Council* (*De decretis*).

sought out by the Roman authorities, tortured and threatened with death if they did not renounce their faith in Jesus Christ. This persecution was particularly violent in the eastern part of the Roman Empire where Athanasius lived. During this decade of horror, the imperial authorities issued edict after edict, intensifying their efforts against the Christians, with the goal of 'terminating' Christianity, as we are told by a church historian of the day.[3] Churches were looted and destroyed. The Scriptures were publicly burned. In the early stages of persecution, Diocletian ordered the execution of 268 Christians – men, women and children – by all sorts of unimaginable violence in the town of Nicomedia.[4] In 308, 227 Christians were arrested in Egypt and severely tortured before being released; many of them would die as a result of that torture.[5] Such horrific scenes of violence were seen throughout the eastern provinces.

The Roman authorities eventually began to focus their cruel efforts on the higher clergy, the bishops and priests, favouring torture over persecution. Years later, in 325 at the Council of Nicaea, many of these bishops and priests would gather for what is now known as the first ecumenical council of the Christian church. Although he did not participate in the council, Athanasius saw, for the first time, the great extent of the persecution and the remnants of its violence in the scars, mutilations and other horrific marks of torture. Despite the events of the fourth century, the imperial patronage of Christianity, and indeed the birth of Christendom itself, this awareness of the church as a church of martyrs, a church of witnesses, who traded life on earth for eternal life in heaven, would remain a lasting and defining image in the minds of the fourth-century Christians.[6]

---

3. Lactantius, *Of the Manner in Which the Persecutors Died* (*De mortibus persecutorum*) 12 (A. Roberts and J. Donaldson [eds.], *Ante-Nicene Fathers* [*ANF*] [T. & T. Clark: Edinburgh, 1871; repr. Grand Rapids: Eerdmans, 1993–4], vol. 7, p. 305).
4. Eusebius of Caesarea, *Ecclesiastical History* 8.6.6–7 (P. Schaff, *A Select Library of the Nicene and Post-Nicene Fathers of the Christian Church* [*NPNF*], 2nd series [Edinburgh: T. & T. Clark, 1989], vol. 1, pp. 327–328; cf. E. Ferguson [ed.], *Encyclopedia of Early Christianity*, 2nd ed. [New York: Garland, 1998], pp. 898–899).
5. Eusebius of Caesarea, *Martyrs of Palestine* 8.1, 13 (*NPNF*, 2nd series, vol. 1, pp. 349–350). Cf. Eusebius, *Ecclesiastical History* 8.8–9 (*NPNF*, 2nd series, vol. 1, pp. 329–330).
6. For an example of how the suffering of the martyrs affected theological reflection on Christ during the fourth century, see Carl L. Beckwith, 'Suffering Without Pain: The Scandal of Hilary of Poitiers' Christology', in Peter Martens (ed.), *In the Shadow of the Incarnation: Essays in Honor of Brian E. Daley* (Notre Dame: University of Notre Dame Press, 2008), pp. 86–89.

In the year 313 the Edict of Milan, that great edict of religious toleration, was issued by Constantine in the West and Licinius in the East. This edict brought an end to the brutal persecution enacted under Diocletian and ushered in a new beginning for the church. As Athanasius moved from adolescence to adulthood, to the world stage of ecclesiastical politics, the church itself underwent a dramatic and almost indescribable transformation. If we use Constantine and the Edict of Milan as our historical marker, we can draw a general picture of the transformation witnessed by Athanasius of the church and Christianity. Before Constantine, Christianity was a persecuted minority; after Constantine, and almost overnight it seemed, Christianity had become the protected and favoured majority. To worship as a Christian before Constantine was to gather privately, often in secret, at the break of dawn, in a simple structure like a house church. After Constantine, worship became public, held in magnificent, indeed extravagant, churches and basilicas.

Constantine and his mother, Helena, undertook a massive building programme in the first half of the fourth century, transforming the Roman landscape by Christianizing the art and architecture of cities. These old Roman towns, once littered with pagan temples to various deities and filled with the foul smoke of their temple sacrifices, were now defined by magnificent Christian basilicas and the sweet-smelling incense of prayers rising to heaven. Egeria, a Spanish nun from the early fifth century, went on a pilgrimage to Jerusalem and recorded her travels in a diary. She offers the following description of one of these great basilicas built by Constantine and notes especially its decoration during the festival of Pentecost. She writes:

> You see nothing there but gold and gems and silk. If you look at the hangings, they are made of silk with gold stripes; if you look at the curtains, they are also made of silk with gold stripes. Every kind of sacred vessel brought out on that day is of gold inlaid with precious stones. How could the number and weight of the candle holders, the candelabra, the lamps, and the various sacred vessels be in any way estimated and noted down? And what can I say about the decoration of this building which Constantine, with his mother on hand, had embellished with as much gold, mosaics, and marble as the resources of his empire permitted . . .[7]

The awe expressed by Egeria tells us a great deal about the visual impression and stimulation of the senses that Constantine's Christianity must have

7. *Egeria: Diary of a Pilgrimage* 25, tr. George E. Gingras, *Ancient Christian Writers* (New York: Newman, 1970), p. 95.

made on many in the fourth century. What we encounter in Egeria's description is what we might call a theology of space or the story we tell about ourselves and, in this case our faith, through art and architecture. In the fourth century this was a story of triumphalism. That triumph, that victory, could only have come about, Athanasius argues, through Jesus Christ our Saviour, the eternal Son of the Father, revealed to us by the Holy Spirit, who has renewed all of creation through his incarnation and cleansed the air and the space around us of demons. Thus, for Athanasius, it was Jesus who emptied the temples, vanquished the evil spirits, and transformed these pagan cities.[8]

The victory of the church in the fourth century was a great blessing for many reasons. Christians were able to proclaim their faith publicly and witness to the world around them without fear of torture or persecution. At the same time, a public Christianity also provided an opportunity for all the different voices within the church to be heard. As these many voices emerged, it soon became apparent that a serious misunderstanding of Christianity had been embraced by some. Athanasius found himself at the centre of this theological storm and rightly or wrongly became the symbol of Nicaea and the most visible exponent of Nicene Christianity.

The Council of Nicaea and rise of Arianism

A few years before the Council of Nicaea in 325, Alexander, bishop of Alexandria and predecessor to Athanasius, delivered a sermon on the mystery of the Holy Trinity. Arius, a senior presbyter from the outskirts of Alexandria, found Alexander's teaching unreasonable. He asked, 'If the Father begat the Son, he that was begotten had a beginning of existence and from this it is evident that there was a time when the Son was not. It therefore necessarily follows that he had his subsistence from nothing.' The fifth-century church historian relating this episode continues, 'having drawn this inference from his novel train of reasoning, he [Arius] excited many to a consideration of the question; and thus from a little spark a large fire was kindled.'[9] Alexander

---

8. Athanasius, *On the Incarnation* 25 (Crestwood, NY: St. Vladimir's Seminary Press, 1998). All quotations of *On the Incarnation* are from the St. Vladimir's Seminary Press edition.

9. Socrates, *Ecclesiastical History* 1.5–6. All quotations of Socrates are from *NPNF*, 2nd series, vol. 2.

excommunicated Arius, and the great dispute over the Trinity and Christ would occupy the church well into the fifth century.[10]

Arius was a popular preacher and spiritual director. His charismatic and ascetic personality appealed to both the common person and desert hermit.[11] He was the senior presbyter at a small church in the region of Boukolia, located east of Alexandria and at the opposite end of the city from the bishop's headquarters at the western gate. This region, as the name suggests, was full of herdsman and shepherds.[12] This hardworking and rough lot would prove quite loyal to Arius and his theological heirs as the controversy over the Trinity escalated. Indeed, years later, Athanasius would complain of 'a multitude of herdsman and shepherds' who armed themselves with 'swords and clubs' and attacked those loyal to Athanasius and the theology of Nicaea.[13] Arius also seems to have appealed to a large number of ascetics; many of whom found the region of Boukolia conducive to their spiritual pursuits.[14]

Arius was trained in philosophy and acquainted with the theological and liturgical history of the Alexandrian church. His eccentric personality and wide appeal is perhaps seen in no better place than the manner in which he recorded his own confession of faith. He presented his theological views and the disputed points of the debate between Alexander and himself not in a detailed exegetical and theological treatise nor in a precisely worded creedal statement but in a work of verse. This writing has been dubbed the *Thalia* by Arius' opponents,

---

10. For a detailed analysis of the early pre-Nicene documents surrounding this controversy and a proposed revision to H. G. Opitz's chronology, see Rowan Williams, *Arius: Heresy and Tradition*, 2nd ed. (Grand Rapids: Eerdmans, 2001), pp. 48–66. For example, Opitz's chronology of events begins in 318 and Williams suggests 321. For a convenient chart of their respective chronologies, see pp. 58–59 of Williams. For his response to criticisms of his proposed chronology, see pp. 251–256.
11. Rowan Williams, 'Athanasius and the Arian Crisis', in G. R. Evans (ed.), *The First Christian Theologians: An Introduction to Theology in the Early Church* (Oxford: Blackwell, 2004), p. 159.
12. Christopher Haas, *Alexandria in Late Antiquity: Topography and Social Conflict* (Baltimore: Johns Hopkins University Press, 1997), p. 270; Epiphanius, *Panarion* 69.1.1–2.
13. Athanasius, *History of the Arians* 10. Unless otherwise stated, all quotations of Athanasius are from the *NPNF*, 2nd series, vol. 4.
14. Even St Antony considered settling in the Boukolia before retreating to the desert. See Athanasius, *Life of Antony* 49.

which Rowan Williams translates as 'dinner party songs'.[15] Arius' choice of genre to address such an important and sublime subject was quite intentional. Indeed, it seems to have been his preferred approach to theological exchange and catechesis. Philostorgius, an ancient church historian, tells us that Arius 'wrote songs for sailing, grinding, travelling, and so on, set them to the music he thought suitable to each, and through the pleasure given by the music stole away the simpler folk for his own heresy'.[16] These songs show Arius' unique personality and commitment to teaching the people of his church.[17] Given the loyalty shown Arius and the success of his teachings among a great number of individuals throughout the fourth and fifth centuries, it also shows the insidiousness of false teaching and how easily the charisma of the teacher and the trendiness of the delivery can lead people away from orthodoxy and the scriptural witness of who Christ is and what he has done for us.[18]

Efforts by Eusebius of Caesarea and Eusebius of Nicomedia, among others, to persuade Alexander that Arius' teachings were acceptable proved unsuccessful and only further revealed the deep division in the fourth-century church on the doctrine of the Trinity.[19] After his victory over Licinius, Constantine, now emperor of both East and West, learned of the 'insignificant matter', as he described it, between Arius and Alexander and convened a council at Nicaea during the summer of 325 to discuss the issue.[20] At this council, three significant theological declarations were made regarding the Greek word *ousia*,

15. Williams, 'Athanasius', p. 161.

16. Philostorgius, *Ecclesiastical History* 2.2. The ecclesiastical history of Philostorgius is no longer extant. We do, however, possess an epitome of the history by the ninth-century patriarch of Constantinople, Photius. For a recent English translation, see *Philostorgius: Church History*, tr. R. Amidon Philip (Atlanta, GA: Society of Biblical Literature, 2007), p. 16.

17. For Athanasius' various comments on Arius' songs, see *Defence of the Nicene Council* 16, *Defence of Dionysius* (*De sententia Dionysii*) 6 and *On the Councils of Ariminum and Seleucia* (*De synodis*) 15.

18. For an orthodox use of songs and hymns in the early church, see the hymns and catechetical works of Nicetas of Remesianus, Ambrose of Milan and Venantius Fortunatus. See also the anonymous fourth-century hymn of praise, *Te Deum laudamus*.

19. The following material is a condensed and simplified version of my summary of these debates in *Hilary of Poitiers on the Trinity: From 'De Fide' to 'De Trinitate'*, Early Christian Studies (Oxford: Oxford University Press, 2008), pp. 15–21.

20. See Constantine's letter written in 324 to Alexander of Alexandria, in Socrates, *Ecclesiastical History* 1.7.

which means 'being' or 'essence' and represents 'that-which-a-thing-is'.[21] The bishops gathered at Nicaea confessed that the Son was 'from the *ousia*' of the Father, the Son possessed the same being or essence (*homoousios*) as the Father, and, in the anathemas attached to the creed, condemned anyone who taught that the Son was 'of a different *hypostasis* or *ousia* from the Father'.[22]

The theological commitment of the Council is often summarized with the word *homoousios*; namely, to say that the Father and Son are of the same essence or substance is to assert that whatever the Father is as God so too the Son is as God. To put this more formally, whatever we predicate of the Father's being or essence, so too we predicate of the Son. This means that when we say the Father is almighty, we also say the Son is almighty. When we say the Father is all-powerful, good, wise and holy, we also say the Son is all-powerful, good, wise and holy. Moreover, to be *homo-ousios* is to be the 'same' or 'identical' in being or essence. Therefore, when we say the Father and the Son are 'of the *same* being' and that whatever we predicate of the Father we predicate of the

---

21. Although our concern in this chapter is only with the trinitarian pronouncements made at the Council of Nicaea, the bishops assembled dealt with a number of other issues, which, from Constantine's perspective, were of greater importance. For example, the Council addressed the complex question of the dating of Easter, the marriage of priests, and questions regarding penance. The bishops also recognized the Petrine church and not the Melitian church as the legitimate ecclesial body in Alexandria, vindicating the position and authority of Alexander, Athanasius' mentor and predecessor.
22. The correlation of *hypostasis* and *ousia* in this anathema from Nicaea show how these words were understood synonymously in 325. Through the theological efforts of the Cappadocian fathers, these words would be distinguished from one another. By 381 and the Council of Constantinople, theological exchange and reflection permitted the fathers to designate the Trinity as one in *ousia* (essence) and three in *hypostasis* (person). The first term designates their unity or oneness and the second, their diversity or threeness.

    For the Greek of the creed from Nicaea and a good discussion of its terms, see T. Herbert Bindley, *The Oecumenical Documents of the Faith*, 4th ed., rev. F. W. Green (Oxford: Oxford University Press, 1950), pp. 26–49. Bindley also provides the Greek and Latin for a number of the creeds issued between Nicaea and Constantinople. See also J. N. D. Kelly, *Early Christian Creeds* (London: Longman, 1960), pp. 231–262; Christopher Stead, *Divine Substance* (Oxford: Oxford University Press, 1977), pp. 233–242; and R. P. C. Hanson, *The Search for the Christian Doctrine of God: The Arian Controversy, 318–381* (Grand Rapids: Baker Academic, 2005), pp. 181–207.

Son, we mean further that they are not two almighties, two all-powerfuls and so on, but that they are 'one' almighty, all-powerful, good, wise and holy God, who is Father, Son and Holy Spirit. This is what it means to call the Father 'God' and the Son 'God'. And, as the Council of Constantinople in 381 would further clarify, this is what it means to call the Holy Spirit the Lord and Giver of life. As Athanasius himself puts it, the Holy Spirit is 'glorified together with the Father and the Son, in the one faith of the Holy Trinity because there is in the Holy Trinity one Godhead'.[23] Put simply, the Holy Spirit is also *homoousios* with the Father and the Son.[24]

Here we begin to see the great mystery of the Christian faith and what it means to confess the Holy Trinity and the scriptural witness concerning our God who is three Persons and yet one essence. Although it would take decades of theological reflection and polemical exchange, the church would confess with the Nicene Creed that the Lord our God is one indivisible being (Deut. 6:4; 1 Cor. 8:6) who exists as three eternally distinct and consubstantial Persons: Father, Son and Holy Spirit (Matt. 28:19). They are not three gods but one God who in a sublime and ineffable way share totally and completely in who they are as God and yet subsist as three eternally distinct *hypostases* or Persons.[25] They differ only in their relationship to one another. The Father is unbegotten, the Son begotten (Matt. 16:16; John 3:16), and the Holy Spirit proceeds (John 15:26; 16:7). This, the mystery of the Holy Trinity, reflected most clearly in St Matthew's baptismal formula, is what Alexander preached and to what Arius objected as being unreasonable. On this point, Arius is right. The Trinity offends our human reason but so too does the crucifixion of the Lord of Glory (1 Cor. 1:18–25; 2:1–10). Just as these latter events transcend the limits of human reason and demand faith (Isa. 55:8–9) so too does our profession and proclamation of the Holy and Blessed Trinity (1 Cor. 12:3; John 14:16; 1 John 4:15).[26]

---

23. Cf. Athanasius, *Epistle* 56.4; here slightly altered.
24. Athanasius, *Letters to Serapion on the Holy Spirit* 27 (Patrologiae cursus completus: Series graeca [PG], ed. J.-P. Migne, 162 vols. [Paris: Cerf, 1857–86], vol. 26), in Anatolios, *Athanasius* (2004), p. 227.
25. Cf. Athanasius, *Orations Against the Arians* (*Contra Arianos*) 1.18, 'the Triad is not originated, but there is an eternal and single Godhead in a Triad, and there is one glory of the Holy Triad'.
26. On the relationship between faith and reason in grasping the mystery of the Holy Trinity, see Carl L. Beckwith, 'A Theological Reading of Hilary of Poitiers' "Autobiographical" Narrative in De Trinitate I.1–19', *Scottish Journal of Theology* 59.3 (2006), pp. 249–262; and *Hilary of Poitiers*, pp. 151–185.

There was one further problem raised with this word *homoousios* by those gathered at Nicaea and during the subsequent debates about its meaning. The term was not found in the Scriptures. Although it was employed to express the relationship between the Father and the Son in a way that was faithful to the Scriptures, many throughout the fourth century, especially those who tended to be sympathetic to Arius' position, objected to the use of non-scriptural terms. The fathers gathered at Nicaea used this word because it alone seemed able to expose Arius' subordinationist teaching about the Son.[27] Despite the acceptance of this term by nearly all of the bishops present at the council, the creed and its terms received wide interpretation among those who signed it.[28]

Eusebius of Caesarea, who signed the creed after taking a day to think it over, no doubt to the great consternation of his colleagues, interpreted the key phrases from the creed, 'begotten not made' and '*homoousios* with the Father',

27. On the evangelical use of extra-biblical words, see Martin Luther, *On the Councils and the Church*, Helmut T. Lehman (ed.), *Luther's Works* (St Louis: Concordia, 1966), vol. 41, p. 83, 'It is certainly true that one should teach nothing outside of Scripture pertaining to divine matters, as St. Hilary writes in *On the Trinity*, Book I, which means only that one should teach nothing that is at variance with Scripture. But that one should not use more or other words than those contained in Scripture – this cannot be adhered to, especially in a controversy and when heretics want to falsify things with trickery and distort the words of Scripture.' For Arius' dislike of *homoousios*, see his *Letter to Alexander of Alexandria* in Edward R. Hardy (ed.), *Christology of the Later Fathers* (Philadelphia: Westminster, 1954), pp. 332–334. Arius also rejects the term in his *Thalia*. See Athanasius, *On the Councils of Ariminum and Seleucia* 15.
28. Modern scholarship has rightly demonstrated that, following the council of Nicaea, no unified party of 'Arians' opposed an equally unified party of 'Nicenes'. See, among others, R. C. Gregg (ed.), *Arianism: Historical and Theological Reassessments: Papers from the Ninth International Conference on Patristic Studies*, Patristic Monograph Series 11 (Philadelphia: Philadelphia Patristic Foundation, 1985); R. Williams, *Arius*; Hanson, *Search*; M. R. Barnes and D. H. Williams (eds.), *Arianism after Arius: Essays on the Development of the Fourth Century Conflicts* (Edinburgh: T. & T. Clark, 1993); D. H. Williams, *Ambrose of Milan and the End of the Arian–Nicene Conflicts* (Oxford: Oxford University Press, 1995); Mark Weedman, *The Trinitarian Theology of Hilary of Poitiers* (Leiden: Brill, 2007); and Beckwith, *Hilary of Poitiers*. An especially helpful discussion on possible categories that would more accurately reflect the theological sympathies of the main participants in these debates is found in J. Lienhard, *Contra Marcellum: Marcellus of Ancyra and Fourth-Century Theology* (Washington, DC: Catholic University of America Press, 1999), pp. 28–46.

in a manner that agreed with his own subordinationist teaching on the Father and the Son.[29] For Eusebius, the Son was generated 'from the Father', made 'like' him before creation, as the firstborn of all creation (Col. 1:15). By misconstruing the intention of the council, Eusebius assented to its chief anathema against Arius and his teachings. He writes, 'Nor did I think it improper to anathematize the term, "Before he was begotten he was not," since all confess that the Son of God was before [his] generation *according to the flesh*.'[30] Eusebius interprets this anathema as addressing the Son's incarnation, which it did not intend to do, and ignores the proper context of the phrase; namely, the eternal generation of the Son from the Father. To assert, as the Scriptures do, that the Son was eternally begotten from the Father is to say that there was never a time when the Son was not. There is no time or mental concept of 'before' when talking about the generation or begotteness of the Son. As Athanasius argues, to say 'Father' always implies 'Son'. If there was a time when the Son was not, then there was a time when God was not Father. Therefore, if the Father is eternal, as all parties agree, then the Son is eternal. Moreover, the Son's begotteneness or generation is a term not used to designate temporality but relationship. How does the Father relate to the Son and the Spirit? The Father is unbegotten, the Son is begotten, and the Spirit proceeds. These are terms of relationship, not being, essence or nature.

Eusebius of Nicomedia, a close associate of Eusebius of Caesarea, signed the creed but refused to acknowledge the anathemas, determining that they misrepresented the teachings of Arius or, more likely, finding nothing in Arius' teaching that offended him.[31] Eusebius, who, like Arius, may have been

---

29. It should be noted that Eusebius' subordinationist theology is not strictly the teaching embraced by Arius and more closely resembles the Homoian theology from the late 350s. Nevertheless, Eusebius supported Arius and thought his position accorded sufficiently with his own to write on his behalf to Alexander.
30. Hardy, *Christology*, p. 339; my emphasis. For the Greek text of Eusebius' creed, see Bindley, *Oecumenical Documents*, p. 53.
31. Eusebius of Nicomedia and Theognis of Nicaea both signed the creed but not the anathemas and were, three months after the council, sent into exile by Constantine. They describe their actions at the synod in a letter to Constantine in 328 requesting readmission to their sees, which they promptly received. Eusebius would years later baptize Constantine on his deathbed. For Constantine's letter to the Nicomedians describing his reasons for banishing Eusebius and Theognis, see Theodoret of Cyrus, *Ecclesiastical History* 1.19; for the letter from Eusebius and Theognis to Constantine in 328, see Socrates, *Ecclesiastical History* 1.14, and Philostorgius, *Ecclesiastical History* 2.7.

theologically indebted to Lucian of Antioch,[32] taught that the Son was completely subordinated to the Father, possessing an entirely different nature.[33] In a letter written a few years before the council, Eusebius rejected the phrase 'from the being of the Father' as a materialistic expression, suggesting, he thought, that the Son was a portion or emanation of the Father's substance. He preferred to express their relationship as a moral union or union of will rather than using language that would suggest the Son is co-essential and co-eternal with the Father. For Eusebius of Nicomedia, this would mean that the Son is good and wise, or any other attributes we could think of, only in so far as he was in agreement with the will of the Father. Eusebius contended that the Father alone is good and wise, that he alone is almighty and all-knowing. These things could not belong to Jesus as the Son of God by being or essence but only by means of participation and union with the will of the Father. To put this more polemically as a way of seeing the real consequence of Eusebius' position, the Son is – in terms of who he is, his essence, being and power – utterly different from the Father and therefore less than the Father or subordinate to him in being and power. For Eusebius, to call Jesus the Son of God is not to identify his nature as the same as the Father (*homoousios*) but to identify his sanctified relationship with the Father in terms of a harmony of will.

Marcellus of Ancyra also signed the creed at Nicaea. In his estimation, *homoousios* implied a strict identity between the Father and Son that excluded any eternal distinction within the Godhead. Marcellus is often characterized as teaching a form of the third-century heresy known as Sabellianism. In order to make more reasonable the scriptural commitment to the oneness or unity of God and the scriptural witness to the diversity of God as Father, Son and

32. See *The Letter of Arius to Eusebius of Nicomedia* in Hardy, *Christology*, pp. 329–331. Arius ends his letter, 'So I pray that you may prosper in the Lord, remembering our afflictions, fellow Lucianist, truly Eusebius.' The word used here by Arius is *sulloukianisthē*. It is not entirely clear what Arius means by this word.

33. Eusebius describes his position in a letter to Paulinus of Tyre. See Theodoret of Cyrus, *Ecclesiastical History* 1.5. For a discussion and appraisal of Eusebius' letter and theology, see Christopher Stead, '"Eusebius" and the Council of Nicaea', *Journal of Theological Studies* 24 (1973), pp. 85–100; and Lienhard, *Contra Marcellum*, pp. 78–82. For an overly sympathetic look at Eusebius and his thought, see Colm Luibhéad, 'The Arianism of Eusebius of Nicomedia', *Irish Theological Quarterly* 43 (1976), pp. 3–23. Luibhéad's defence of Eusebius leads him to conclude, 'it has to be assumed, regardless of mere assertions to the contrary, that Eusebius was not in fact an Arian' (p. 23).

Holy Spirit, the Sabellians in the third century and Marcellus in the fourth century argued that God is truly and eternally one (a monad), who, at creation, expanded into two (a dyad), and at Pentecost, into three (a triad), but will, at the end of time, when all things are subjected to God and he is all in all (1 Cor. 15:28), return to one (a monad)! It was to refute such Sabellian notions that the phrase 'his kingdom will have no end' was inserted into the second article of the Nicene Creed at the Council of Constantinople in 381. To what extent this sort of position was fully embraced by Marcellus has been debated.[34] What is clear, however, is that Marcellus sought to preserve a strict Christian monotheism and, at this time in his theological understanding, failed to account for any eternal 'hypostatic' distinction, to use a later understanding of the word, within the Godhead.[35]

Following the Council of Nicaea, the bishops were sharply divided, condemning each other, and issuing numerous statements of faith.[36] At the centre of this ecclesiastical storm were (1) the Eusebians, who, despite their many

---

34. It has recently been argued that this description of Marcellus' theology is more indebted to his opponents than his own theological reflections and is therefore more caricature than reality. For a very thorough presentation of what we can say about Marcellus' theology, see Lienhard, *Contra Marcellum*, pp. 49–68.
35. Lienhard argues that Marcellus did eventually embrace 'the eternal coreign of the Son with the Father' in his written profession of faith to Pope Julius at the synod of Rome in 341. Not surprisingly, the Eastern bishops gathering at Serdica (Philippopolis) rejected this confession as a deception. Marcellus would a few years later become attracted to some of Photinus of Sirmium's teachings and suffer rebuke from Athanasius and a severing of communion. According to Hilary of Poitiers, however, Marcellus repented and we are left with the impression that he died an orthodox bishop. As Lienhard puts it, 'Marcellus was, perhaps, easily swayed and a little fickle, but not obstinate in his beliefs' (p. 156). See also Lienhard, *Contra Marcellum*, pp. 163–164, 174. For the account in Hilary, see *Collectanea Antiariana Parisina (fragmenta historica)* B 2.9.1–3 (Corpus scriptorum ecclesiasticorum latinorum 65.146–147); Lionel Wickham, *Hilary of Poitiers: Conflicts of Conscience and Law in the Fourth-Century Church* (Liverpool: Liverpool University Press, 1997), pp. 56–58.
36. For a detailed discussion of the debates between the Council of Nicaea in 325 and the Council of Constantinople in 381, see Hanson, *Search*; and Lewis Ayres, *Nicaea and Its Legacy: An Approach to Fourth-Century Trinitarian Theology* (Oxford: Oxford University Press, 2004).

protestations, were repeatedly associated with Arius,[37] and (2) Athanasius, who became the symbol of the *homoousion* or Nicene party, and was therefore repeatedly condemned by anti-Nicene synods influenced by the Eusebians and their associates.[38] Although I risk oversimplification in stating things this way, from Athanasius' perspective, Arius and those theologians in sympathy with him argued that Jesus was not the true Son of God, not co-eternal with the Father, but was rather *a* son of God, just as we all by grace and adoption are sons and daughters of God. Despite the numerous protestations and theological gymnastics of those sympathetic to Arius' theological position, it is correct and fair to say that they believed the Son of God was created.

The Council of Nicaea rightly excommunicated Arius, and it was to this controversy over the doctrine of the Trinity and Christ that Athanasius devoted his pastoral and theological life. Athanasius was, in this sense, something of a one-issue man. All that he wrote and all that he laboured to do focused on the Trinity and Jesus Christ. He did this, however, not by first appealing to abstract theological language like *homoousios*, which, although an important and

---

37. For example, at the Council of Antioch in 341, the Eusebian party issued the following statement: 'We have not been followers of Arius. For how could we, as bishops, follow a presbyter?' That such a statement would need to be made in 341, five years after Arius' death and sixteen years after Nicaea, shows not only the Eusebian sensitivity to any identification with Arius but also the polemical utility of Arius' name and the epitaph 'Arians' for those construed with the heresiarch's theology. For this statement, see Athanasius, *On the Councils of Ariminum and Seleucia* 22, and Socrates, *Ecclesiastical History* 2.10.
38. For example, at the synod of Arles in 353, Paulinus of Trier was asked not to condemn Nicaea or its creed but simply Athanasius himself. Just as support for Athanasius was seen as support for Nicaea, so too condemning him would show theological rejection of Nicaea. When a similar course of action was taken at the synod of Milan in 355, Eusebius of Vercelli called those sympathetic to the Eusebian position, which by this time had been fully embraced by the emperor Constantius, and agreed to condemn Athanasius if they would agree to sign the creed from Nicaea. As the story goes, one of the bishops present began to write down his profession of the creed when Valens of Mursa, a supporter of the Eusebian/Arian party, 'violently seized the pen and paper from his hands'. Chaos ensued and the bishops quickly retreated to the emperor's palace (he was in Milan at the time). The emperor condemned and exiled Eusebius and all those who agreed with the creed. See Hilary of Poitiers, *Liber I Ad Constantium* 8 (Corpus scriptorum ecclesiasticorum latinorum 65:187.12–15).

decisive word, belongs to the end of the conversation, never its beginning. Rather, Athanasius begins his refutation of Arius and his own articulation of the doctrine of the Trinity by reflecting on our salvation, on the gospel of Jesus Christ and the victory of his cross, and on our transformation by grace from darkness to light, from idolatry to co-labourers with Christ.

Christ as Saviour: the victory of the cross

As mentioned above, the Edict of Milan and Constantine's preference for Christianity dramatically changed the Roman world. Athanasius and many other church fathers saw the hand of God at work in the expansion of Christianity and its triumph or victory in the fourth century. The historical question that naturally came to mind was how this triumph could have happened. Although the answer differed among the church fathers, the answer for Athanasius was obvious: Jesus Christ. The transformation of the world began when the eternal Word of God, Jesus Christ, 'became flesh and dwelt among us' (John 1:14; my tr.).

Athanasius begins his earliest theological treatise, a two-part work, *Against the Heathen* and *On the Incarnation of the Word*, written soon after the Council of Nicaea and perhaps before he was appointed bishop, by emphasizing the relationship between creation and redemption, the very truth rejected by Arius' theology.[39] For Athanasius, our very existence, our very being, is a gift from the Father in the Son by the Holy Spirit. We are sustained in this life, we breath, we think, we move, at the mercy of our triune God. The Son through whom all things were created entered creation, becoming man, dwelling in our midst, teaching, healing and finally suffering death on a cross, becoming a sacrifice for our sins, conquering death through death, and rising again on the third day. Athanasius writes, 'by what seems [to be] his utter poverty and weakness on

39. *Against the Heathen* (*Contra gentes*) and *On the Incarnation* (*De incarnatione*) are two parts of a single treatise written by Athanasius some time after the Council of Nicaea in 325. The dating for this treatise is disputed, but I am persuaded by Khaled Anatolios that it should be dated somewhere in the late 320s or early 330s. See Khaled Anatolios, *Athanasius: The Coherence of his Thought* (London: Routledge, 1998), pp. 26–30. For an excellent introduction to these works and the theology of Athanasius, see Thomas Weinandy, *Athanasius: A Theological Introduction* (Burlington, VT: Ashgate, 2007). See also Weinandy, p. 11, n. 2, for a detailed discussion of the various dating options. Weinandy accepts 335/336.

the cross he overturns the pomp and parade of idols, and quietly and hiddenly wins over the mockers and unbelievers to recognize him as God'.[40] How did the church triumph in the fourth century? The answer for Athanasius was simple: Jesus Christ.

Athanasius asks a second question, a theological one: Why did the eternal Son of God take on flesh and dwell among us? Put simply, it was for our salvation. Athanasius explains, 'It was our sorry case that caused the Word to come down, our transgression that called out his love for us, so that he made haste to help us and to appear among us.'[41] Athanasius then pauses and reflects on the history of humanity. We were created, he explains, in the image of God and were to remain for ever in his eternal presence, in a state of incorruption. We turned from the contemplation of God to the contemplation of evil, the contemplation of that which is not God, the contemplation of nothingness. We fell into 'lust' of ourselves.[42] We turned from God to ourselves, focusing our attention inward to what pertains to ourselves and our own disordered loves and desires. We closed our eyes to the light, took up residence in a world of darkness, and acted as if that darkness were light. We saw darkness; we called it light. We contemplated evil; we thought it good. We rejected God and acted as if we were our own gods. The law of death seized us and, as Athanasius rightly puts it, we were 'in a process of becoming entirely corrupted'.[43] We had been created and given life out of nothing and, by our own sins, we were now returning, through corruption, to nothingness.[44] We were 'disappearing', writes Athanasius, we were becoming less and less human, as the work of God was being 'undone'.[45] Put another way, as we continued to sin, we drew 'near to the dead', filling ourselves with 'dead nourishment'.[46]

For Athanasius, there was only one solution to this problem: the incarnation of the very Son of God. The Word of God through whom all things were made would enter our world, become truly human, suffer for the sins of all, and surrender his body to death.[47] He did this, explains Athanasius, 'out of sheer love for us, so that in his death all might die' and through the 'grace of his res-

---

40. Athanasius, *On the Incarnation* 1.
41. Ibid. 4.
42. Athanasius, *Against the Heathen*, 3.2.
43. Athanasius, *On the Incarnation* 4.
44. Ibid.
45. Ibid. 6.
46. Athanasius, *Epistle* 7.2.
47. Athanasius, *On the Incarnation* 8.

urrection' all might rise from corruption to incorruption.[48] Athanasius refers to Christ's saving work on the cross as the 'sufficient exchange' for all; what the Reformers would later call the 'blessed exchange'. Christ died our death that we by faith might live his life. Echoing the apostle Paul (2 Cor. 5:14–15), Athanasius explains that through his death he abolished death that 'we should no longer live *unto ourselves*, but *unto him* . . . our Lord Jesus Christ'.[49]

Athanasius' theology begins with the assertion that the purpose of our creation is to know God. For this reason, we were made in the image and likeness of God that 'through this gift of God-likeness', as he calls it, we might be able to know the Word and through him the Father. This, insists Athanasius, is 'the only really happy and blessed life'.[50] But, with the fall we rejected this 'grace' and not only lost our understanding of God but also the understanding of ourselves. When we turned to idolatry and transferred the honour due to God to things of this world, we turned from Truth to nothingness; this nothingness, for which we were not created, led to the 'dehumanizing' of humankind.[51] Why did the eternal Son of God take on flesh and dwell among us? He did this 'to renew his Image in mankind' that we might once more come to know the triune God and ourselves.[52]

The One who created in the beginning came in the fullness of time to recreate us anew. Christ, the eternal Son of God, not only conquered sin and death through the cross, but reordered our hearts and 'centered [our] senses on Himself'.[53] To renew us, to centre our senses, is to free us from our dehumanizing tendencies, to free us from our bondage and slavery to sin. In what is perhaps the most famous line from Athanasius' treatise on the incarnation, and often used to summarize his teaching on salvation, he says that the purpose of the incarnation, passion and resurrection of our Lord was this: 'He was humanized that we might be deified.'[54] That is to say, *he was humanized* that we might once more become truly *human* and becoming human, centre our affections and thoughts and loves on our triune God; that we might once more enjoy by God's grace that intimate relationship and union with the

48. Ibid.
49. Ibid. 10; my emphasis.
50. Ibid. 11.
51. Ibid. 13.
52. Ibid.
53. Ibid. 16.
54. Ibid. 54. I have followed here the more familiar translation of Athanasius' statement from Hardy, *Christology*, p. 107, n. 79.

Father in the Son by the Holy Spirit. This reality, however, could happen only if Jesus Christ, true God and true man, became the perfect 'ransom for the sins of all' and 'sacrifice for the salvation of all', bearing our sins and suffering for our sakes.[55] He gave his life for our life and for our salvation so that 'we who believe in Christ no longer die'.[56] All of this hinges for Athanasius on the truth that Jesus Christ is truly the eternal Son of God who became true man for us, who suffered and died on the cross for our sins, and who is therefore the Lord and Saviour of all.[57]

Christ as Lord: the transformation of the world

Athanasius' reflections on the course of history and the triumph of the church in the fourth century form the theological backdrop and foundation of his dispute with the Arians over the doctrine of the Trinity. When Arius comes along, Athanasius understands very clearly that at stake is the gospel itself, our salvation and eternal life with the Father, Son and Holy Spirit. If Christ is not true God and true man, the eternal Son of God, who has assumed our flesh, suffered for our sins and risen again as our Lord and Saviour, then we have not been brought from death to life, from corruption to incorruption. Arius' contention, however, is clearly wrong. One need not appeal to grand theological formulae or abstract philosophical arguments to demonstrate the truth of the gospel. Towards the end of *On the Incarnation*, Athanasius sounds a theme that he will repeat in nearly all of his writings. He observes the world around him and notes the many ways in which Christ's victory over death is proclaimed, not in words, but in deeds.

As someone who grew up during the most intense period of persecution in the history of the early church, it comes as no surprise that Athanasius' attention falls on the heroism of the martyrs, the witnesses who exchanged temporal life for eternal life because of their faith in Jesus Christ. Athanasius writes that the victory of the cross is seen in that these men, women and children, these ordinary people, these unnamed saints, this cloud of witnesses, faced scorn, abuse, torture and ultimate persecution without fear because of their faith.[58] Athanasius ends his reflection on martyrdom saying, 'Doubt no longer,

---

55. Athanasius, *On the Incarnation* 40, 37, 34.
56. Ibid. 37, 21.
57. Ibid. 19.
58. This understanding of the martyrs is widespread in both Christian and Jewish circles. For example, in the *Martyrdom of Polycarp* (12.1) the fear of Polycarp's

then, when you see death mocked and scorned by those who believe in Christ, that by Christ death was destroyed.'[59] The certainty of this truth rests, insists Athanasius, on the prior truth that the Son of God, the second person of the Holy and Blessed Trinity, became true man and dwelt among us.

The transformation of ordinary people into bold defenders and witnesses of the faith all testify for Athanasius to the proper identity of Jesus Christ as Lord and Saviour. Brought to faith by the grace of the Holy Spirit, these former pagans are a 'new creation' in Christ Jesus (2 Cor. 5:17).[60] In a lengthy statement from his *Orations against the Arians*, Athanasius explains beautifully the Christological and theological implications of our new creation or deification in Christ and how our transformed lives testify as clearly as the creed from Nicaea does to the true identity of Jesus. Athanasius writes:

> But all this [new creation] would not have happened if the Word was a creature. The devil, who is himself a creature, would persist in battle forever if he was contending against a creature. Humanity, stuck in the middle of this battle, would be always intimidated by death, not having one through whom and in whom it can be joined to God so that it may become entirely free from fear. Truth shows, therefore, that the Word is not one of the things that come to be, but rather their creator. He took to himself the body that was human and had a beginning so that he who is its creator may renew it and thus divinize it in himself and lead all of us into the kingdom of heaven, in accordance with his own likeness.
>
> But humanity would not have been deified if joined to a creature, or unless the Son was true God. And humanity would not have come into the presence of the Father unless the one who put on the body was his true Word by nature. Just as we would not

---

impending death is replaced by joy (*chara*), and in the *Martyrdom of Perpetua and Felicitas* (18.1) Perpetua trembled with joy (*gaudio*) not fear (*timore*). Cf. the rabbinic martyrdom of Akiva, whose sufferings were met with joy. See also Hilary of Poitiers' similar understanding of the martyrs in *De Trinitate* 10.46.3–12. For Polycarp, see Michael W. Holmes (ed.), *The Apostolic Fathers: Greek Texts and English Translations* (Grand Rapids: Baker, 1999), p. 234; for Perpetua, see H. Musurillo (ed.), *The Acts of the Christian Martyrs* (Oxford: Clarendon, 1972), p. 127; and for Akiva, see Robert Selzer, *Jewish People, Jewish Thought: The Jewish Experience in History* (New York: Macmillan, 1980), pp. 303–304. For examples from other Christian martyrdoms, see Mark Weedman, 'Martyrdom and Docetism in Hilary's *De Trinitate*', *Augustinian Studies* 30 (1999), pp. 33–35.

59. Athanasius, *On the Incarnation* 29.
60. Athanasius, *Orations against the Arians* 2.69–70.

> have been freed from sin and the curse unless the flesh which the Word put on was human by nature – for there would be no communion for us with what is other than human – so also humanity would not have been deified unless the Word who became flesh was by nature from the Father and true and proper (*idios*) to him. Therefore the conjoining that came about was such as to join what is human by nature to what is of the nature of divinity, so that humanity's salvation and deification might be secured.[61]

For Athanasius the doctrines of the Trinity and Christology are firmly rooted in the proclamation of the gospel. Moreover, the hope we have in Christ and the salvation we proclaim to the world demands that Christ be truly and completely human and truly and completely divine. He is our Mediator who joins us for ever, by the grace of the Holy Spirit, to God the Father.

The victory of the cross that Athanasius observes in the martyrs is also found in the transformed lives of desert monks, virgins and ordinary people. The prophets and apostles proclaim that Jesus Christ is the eternal Word of God made flesh and so too do the deeds of self-sacrifice and love performed by Christians in this world. For Athanasius the victory of the cross over sin, death and the devil is an eternal victory to be enjoyed by those of faith in eternity but also a victory that bears immediate fruit in this life. The sin that deformed our nature and turned us in on ourselves has been vanquished. The same Christ, then, who was at work as creator and redeemer continues to work in our lives. This 'co-working' (*synergeia*) is the life-giving, transforming and perfecting work of the Word in this life.

Our perfecting in this life has been made possible by the incarnation and the Word's sojourn among us. Moreover, it serves as a witness, a testimony of Christ's saving work, for all the world to see. Athanasius explains this in a prayer. He writes in the voice of the Word speaking to the Father:

> their perfecting shows that your Word has sojourned among them; and the *world* seeing them perfect and full of God, will believe altogether that you have sent me, and I have sojourned there. For where does their perfecting come but that I, your Word, having borne their body, and become man, have perfected the work, which you gave me, O Father? And the work is perfected, because men, redeemed from sin, no longer remain dead; but being deified, have in each other, by looking at me, the bond of love.[62]

---

61. Ibid. 2.70, in Anatolios, *Athanasius* (2004), p. 163.

62. Ibid. 3.23.

The Christ-centred, transformed lives of ordinary people bear witness to the world of the saving work of Christ. In a real sense for Athanasius, the world itself is a visual representation of the gospel. Those outside the faith need only consider the virtue and courage of ordinary people who give their lives for the faith they proclaim, who retreat from the comforts and amusements of the world to the desert, or who reject the immoral sensibilities and selfishness of the world for chaste lives of love and service to their neighbour.

Athanasius always underscores that the transformed and virtuous lives of Christians come about only by grace and in Christ. Our deification, our perfecting, means that 'we are sons and gods because of the Word in us' and this happens 'by adoption and grace, as partaking of his Spirit'.[63] We are truly sons and daughters of God not by nature as the Son of God is but by grace. Athanasius writes, 'although there be one Son by nature, True and Only-begotten, we too become sons, not as he in nature and truth, but according to the grace of him that calleth, and though we are men from the earth, are yet called gods, not as the True God or his Word, but as has pleased God who has given us that grace'.[64] Our transformed lives by the grace of the Holy Spirit and the co-working of Christ unite us to the Father, render us truly human in his sight and make us gods, sons and daughters of the Most High (Ps. 82:6). We are, for Athanasius, missionaries to the world through our words and deeds, witnessing to the victory of life over death, incorruption over corruption by Jesus Christ, our Lord and Saviour.[65]

Christ as co-worker: the ideal monk

The Christological character of this perfecting or deification is seen in no better place than Athanasius' *Life of Antony*. Antony, an Egyptian by birth, came from a Christian family of wealth. He had little interest in education and preferred to remain at home as a 'plain man'.[66] Around the age of twenty, Antony's parents died and he was entrusted with the care of his younger sister. About six months after the death of his parents, as Athanasius relates to us, Antony was on his way to church and as he walked he thought deeply about the life of

63. Ibid. 3.25, 3.19.
64. Ibid. 3.19.
65. For comments on the missionary success of Christianity in the early part of the fourth century, see Athanasius, *On the Incarnation* 30, 52.
66. Athanasius, *Life of Antony* 1.

the apostles and how they sold all of their possessions, distributed them to the needy, and followed Christ. As he entered the church, Matthew's Gospel was being read. He heard Jesus say to the rich man, 'If you would be perfect, go, sell what you possess and give to the poor, and you will have treasure in heaven' (Matt. 19:21).[67] Antony believed that God had intended for him to hear this word on this very day. He immediately went out from the church and sold all he had. He gave most of it to the poor and set aside a certain amount for his sister. He entrusted her to a convent of faithful virgins and devoted himself to a life of discipline (*askēsis*).

Antony's programme of discipline required guidance and he began travelling around to different hermits to learn from their wisdom and imitate their piety. He subjected himself in sincerity to the hermits he visited and learned thoroughly where each surpassed him in zeal and discipline. Athanasius writes:

> He observed the graciousness of one; the unceasing prayer of another; he took knowledge of another's freedom from anger and another's loving-kindness; he gave heed to one as he watched, to another as he studied; one he admired for his endurance, another for his fasting and sleeping on the ground; the meekness of one and the long-suffering of another he watched with care, while he took note of the piety towards Christ and the mutual love which animated all.[68]

Before Antony's eyes was the classroom of Christ himself who was active by his Spirit and grace in the transformation and perfecting of these hermits; men from diverse backgrounds of affluence or poverty united by a common faith in Christ and set apart for a life of meekness, prayer and piety.

Antony applied to his own life what he had learned from these hermits and devoted himself to work (2 Thess. 3:10) and unceasing prayer (1 Thess. 5:27). Immediately, recounts Athanasius, the devil began to launch his fiery darts at Antony and whisper temptations in his ears. He tempted Antony with the memory of his wealth and the abandonment of his sister. He tempted Antony with love of money and glory, the pleasures and amusements of life, and harassed him with foul thoughts and sexual desires. Antony countered these temptations 'with faith, prayers, and fasting'.[69] His discipline and victory against the devil, however, were not by his own power but rested on the victory

---

67. Ibid. 2.
68. Ibid. 4.
69. Ibid. 5.

of the cross and the grace of God. The Word, who worked in creating and redeeming Antony, was now at work alongside him in his fight with the devil. Athanasius writes, 'For the Lord was working with Antony (*synērgei*) – the Lord who for our sake took flesh and gave the body victory over the devil, so that all who truly fight can say, "not I but the grace of God which was with me"' (1 Cor. 15:10).[70] Indeed, Antony's victory over the devil was not because of the exceptional discipline that he had embraced, a discipline that set him apart from his peers, excelling not only his brothers and sisters in Christ who remained in the world but also his fellow hermits. No, Antony's victory was because of his faith in Christ who worked in him. Athanasius emphatically states, 'this victory was the Savior's work in Antony'.[71] Antony's victory was the result of his faith in Christ, a faith claimed by those who labour in the desert like Antony, those who labour in the arena of theological dispute like Athanasius,[72] those who devote their lives to acts of service and charity to the world, and those who assume the ordinary duties of Christian life such as marriage, the rearing of children and service in the world. What unites these individuals and what conquers the devil with all his wiles and fiery darts is not the mere act of discipline but the transformative and life-giving power of faith in Jesus Christ, true God and true man, who has conquered sin, death and the devil, and who by grace continues to work in us and with us in this life.

Christ as co-worker: the married life

Although Athanasius greatly praised and cherished the monastic life above all other vocations, he also held in great esteem those who were called to the more moderate and ordinary estate of marriage. Not everyone in his day shared this opinion on the blessings of marriage. Those hermits and monks who sacrificed the pleasures and joys of the world, who committed themselves to harsh discipline and lives of unceasing prayer, and who laboured against self and the devil in taming and conquering the desires of the body, began to scorn the body itself, dangerously sailing close to the shores of dualism by despising the very creation of God. They looked with contempt on those who

70. Ibid.

71. Ibid.

72. On this theme of ecclesiastical service as yet another vocation for the Christian, in addition to the others identified and discussed in this chapter, see Athanasius, *Epistle* 49, to Dracontius, the bishop of Hermupolis Parva.

remained within the ordinary structures of life. To these individuals and their 'evil objections', Athanasius responded, 'All things made by God are beautiful and pure, for the Word of God has made nothing useless or impure.'[73] This means, continues Athanasius, all of the functions of our bodies, from the natural processes of digesting and discharging our food to the proper use of our sexual organs within marriage, are the 'work of God's hands'.[74] Although these physical necessities are good, as all things made by God are good, they can be abused and used improperly. As we can abuse our need for food by becoming gluttonous, we can also abuse God's command to 'increase and multiply' by committing adultery and other sundry acts. Not only has God said, 'increase and multiply', but also that 'marriage is honourable' and that the marriage bed should be undefiled (Gen. 1:28; Heb. 13:4).[75]

Those who pursue the 'moderate and ordinary' course of life by means of marriage are 'blessed' and called to 'beget children'.[76] These 'two ways in life' – marriage and celibacy – are both ordained by God, even if they yield different fruit. Athanasius writes:

> Now if a man choose the way of the world, namely marriage, he is not indeed to blame; yet he will not receive such great gifts as the other. For he will receive, since he too brings forth fruit, namely thirtyfold. But if a man embrace the holy and unearthly way, even though, as compared with the former, it be rugged and hard to accomplish, yet it has the more wonderful gifts; for it grows the perfect fruit, namely a hundredfold.[77]

Whatever our calling or station in life, we are to serve God with a pure heart and therefore pray, with David:

> Create in me a clean heart, O God,
> and renew a right spirit within me.
> (Ps. 51:10 ESV)[78]

The Lord is at work in the ordinary life of marriage as he was with the martyrs and is with the hermits. That is to say, the same Lord who is at work in the desert to

---

73. Athanasius, *Epistle* 48.
74. Ibid.
75. Ibid.
76. Ibid.
77. Ibid.
78. Ibid.

protect Antony from the snares of the devil works also in the home of a faithful couple struggling against the world to raise their children in a godly way. The faith is one that unites the hermit in the desert to the congregation in the world.

The spirituality of the cross

Although God appoints different vocations for his people to serve him, the faith engendered by the grace of the Holy Spirit remains the same. For Athanasius, this unity, this brotherhood, is seen in no better place than the supreme mystery celebrated by the church, the sacrament of the Lord's Supper, the feast of life, and especially at the annual celebration of Easter. The life of the church, structured around the liturgical calendar, finds its beginning and end in the paschal feast. Here rich and poor, male and female, monk and married gather together to celebrate and declare together, 'Christ, our Passover lamb, has been sacrificed' (1 Cor. 5:7 ESV).[79] When Athanasius became the bishop and patriarch of Alexandria, the responsibility fell to him to circulate each year a festal letter indicating the dates for Lent and the celebration of the paschal feast. In addition to establishing these dates, his letters offer brief pastoral reflections on the life of faith and the joy that fills Christians at Easter and should govern their entire lives. Although persecution, exile and circumstance scatter Christians, their faith and celebration of the Easter feast demonstrate their unity before the world. Athanasius writes:

> For although place separates us, yet the Lord the giver of the feast, and who is Himself our feast, who is also the bestower of the Spirit, brings us together in mind, in harmony, and in the bond of peace. For when we mind and think the same things, and offer up the same prayers on behalf of each other, no place can separate us, but the Lord gathers and unites us together.[80]

Athanasius' festal letters reveal not only his deep pastoral concerns for his people but also a life lived and shaped by the victory of the cross. It is this spirituality of the cross that further demonstrates Athanasius' commitment to the gospel, to the gifts of God bestowed on us through the Son and Holy Spirit and received by faith. It is this spirituality of the cross that forms the heart of Athanasius' faith.

---

79. Ibid. 6.2.
80. Ibid. 10.2.

When we gather at Easter to participate in that 'heavenly and eternal feast', to take in 'the food of life' and 'partake of the Word', we receive grace and anticipate that 'perfect joy which is in heaven'.[81] This feast, this Eucharist, explains Athanasius, is 'a pledge that we shall have everlasting life hereafter'.[82] This is, indeed, the reason for the feast and must ever be before our minds. Athanasius writes:

> For the Lord died in those days, that we should no longer do the deeds of the dead. He gave his life, that we might preserve our own from the snares of the devil. And, what is most wonderful, the Word became flesh, that we should no longer live in the flesh, but in the spirit should worship God, who is Spirit.[83]

And so it is, explains Athanasius, 'we are bound to celebrate this feast, not to ourselves but to the Lord; and to rejoice, not in ourselves but in the Lord, who bore our griefs'.[84]

The gifts of Christ on the cross and offered in this sacrament are far too much for us to comprehend. Indeed, we are like the thief on the cross who 'instead of death had received life, instead of bondage, freedom, and instead of the grave, the kingdom of heaven'.[85] Such blessings cannot be fully comprehended and certainly not repaid. They must, however, be acknowledged. Therefore, 'let us render him thanks while we persevere in piety'. We do this, continues Athanasius, 'when we offer ourselves to the Lord, like the saints, when we subscribe ourselves entirely as living henceforth not to ourselves, but to the Lord Who died for us'. When we do this, we rightly say with the blessed Paul, 'I am crucified with Christ, yet I live; yet not I, but Christ lives in me.'[86] Therefore, we must 'no longer live to ourselves but as servants to the Lord'.[87]

To live as a servant to the Lord and no longer to ourselves is to 'acknowledge him who died' and who now 'lives in us'.[88] As Paul boasted to the Corinthians that he always bore in his body the death of Christ (2 Cor. 4:10)

81. Ibid. 4.3, 5.1, 5.5, 6.1.
82. Ibid. 1.10.
83. Ibid. 6.1.
84. Ibid. 6.7.
85. Ibid. 5.3.
86. Ibid.
87. Ibid. 6.4.
88. Ibid. 5.4.

and as David cried out that for the sake of the Lord we die all the day (Ps. 44:22), we too should bear in ourselves the death of Christ, the Lord of glory. Athanasius explains, 'For he who is made like him in his death, is also diligent in virtuous practices, having mortified his members which are upon the earth, and crucifying the flesh with the affections and lusts, he lives in the Spirit, and is conformed to the Spirit.'[89] When 'by faith' a person embraces this 'true life', this conformity of the Spirit, he is 'always mindful of God and forgets him not'.[90] Our days are spent in virtuous conduct and our nights in repenting 'of all that we have neglected, whatever it may be, for there is no one free from defilement, though his course may have been but one hour on the earth'.[91] When we contemplate our own death and the death of Christ, when we always have before our thoughts God and his blessings, our joy and boast is 'our Lord and Savior Jesus Christ', who suffered and died for all that 'the salvation effected by the cross might be shown to be for all men everywhere'.[92]

Athanasius is careful to note that we are able to embrace such a life of joy and gladness and render our good works to the Lord only because of 'the grace given us from the Savior'.[93] That is to say, the God who created and redeemed us has also sanctified us to live a life of holiness. This life of sanctification and renewal is a gift and blessing from him who works in us and with us. When we render our good works to God, we are not offering gifts to him but more precisely returning the gifts he has bestowed upon us to him. Athanasius writes, 'when we make a return we give nothing of our own, but those things which we have before received from him, this being especially of his grace, that he should require, as from us, his own gifts'.[94] It is as if Christ were to say to us, 'those things which you give Me are yours, as having received them from Me, but they are the gifts of God'.[95] Therefore, 'let us rejoice, not in ourselves, but in the Lord, that we may be inheritors with the saints'.[96]

These works done by the saints reveal the unity of all those gathered by faith in Christ and proclaim to the world the joy and peace all have in the Word who assumed flesh and opened the gates of paradise. When we arrive at our

---

89. Ibid. 7.1.
90. Ibid. 7.1–2.
91. Ibid. 5.5.
92. Ibid. 27.1, 22.1.
93. Ibid. 4.3.
94. Ibid. 5.4.
95. Ibid.
96. Ibid. 6.12.

heavenly home, we will with all the saints cry out and rejoice with that voice of gladness and thanksgiving. It is there where 'pain and sorrow and sighing have fled, and upon our heads gladness and joy shall have come to us'.[97] In this life, however, we are 'nourished with his words' in the sermon, we 'keep the feast' of his body and blood with all those saints who have gone before us and 'with one mouth we truly give thanks to the Lord'.[98] This feast is a 'service of the soul' that occupies itself with 'prolonged prayer to God, and unceasing thanksgiving' and witnesses to the world the reconciliation and renewal brought about by Christ in the faithful.[99] Although we scatter from the cross to the world, in the feast, the Lord's Supper, God gathers all his saints into one. Indeed, writes Athanasius,

> we were scattered in time past and were lost, and are found. We were far off, and are brought nigh, we were strangers, and have become his, Who suffered for us, and was nailed on the cross, Who bore our sins, as the prophet says and was afflicted for us, that he might put away from all of us grief, and sorrow, and sighing.[100]

Whether it is the monk in the desert or the married couple in the city, they remain united in spirit by their faith in Christ and their participation in his feast. Athanasius writes, 'For this is the marvel of his loving kindness, that he should gather together in the same place those who are at a distance; and make those who appear to be far off in the body, to be near together in unity of spirit.'[101] Indeed, no matter the distance imposed by this world, by faith, the sons and daughters of God 'sit at table with the saints' and 'share in the one voice of gladness' when they gather for the feast of the Lord.[102]

Christ-centred devotion

In addition to encouraging the Christian community and preparing them for the great paschal feast, Athanasius' festal letters sought also to correct

97. Ibid. 1.10.
98. Ibid. 2.1, 2.7.
99. Ibid. 3.2.
100. Ibid. 20.1.
101. Ibid. 5.2.
102. Ibid. 7.7.

divergent devotional practices. On the one hand, we see in these letters the pastoral Athanasius offering assurance and hope to the faithful as they prepare themselves to participate in the Eucharist and to receive the true body and blood of their Lord, Jesus Christ. On the other hand, these letters also show Athanasius' concern that all the devotional practices of the Egyptians, no matter their pious intentions, remain Christ-centred.

The Egyptian Christians were attracted not only to charismatic and ascetic figures but also the remains of the martyrs. A particularly problematic practice that developed late in Athanasius' life was the desire by some in Egypt to exhume the bones of the martyrs.[103] These individuals sought to establish continuity with the church of the martyrs by claiming their remains. Athanasius denounced the practice and argued that continuity with the martyrs exists not in housing their remains but in confessing 'him whom the martyrs confessed'.[104] Once again we see the centrality of Christ and the victory of the cross in Athanasius' thought and practice.

When these bones of the martyrs were exhumed, shrines would be established and healings or exorcisms promised. Athanasius tells us that those who exhumed these bodies sought to deceive the simple, fill their churches with the curious, and, in the process, exploit the sacred bones of the martyrs for 'financial gain'.[105] Not only were the remains of the martyrs violated but also simple believers were led to place their trust in the martyr rather than the Christ whom the martyrs confessed. Athanasius writes:

> When they say that many people who had unclean spirits have been healed in the martyr shrines, these are their excuses [Luke 4:41 and Acts 16:18, which Athanasius had previously discussed]. Let them listen, and I will answer them by saying that they are not healed by the martyrs coming upon the demons, but they are healed by the Savior, the one whom the martyrs confessed.

---

103. The letters in question here are reckoned as *Festal Letter* 41 and 42. They have been preserved only in Coptic and are not found in the *NPNF* volume. For a translation of these letters, see David Brakke, '"Outside the Places, Within the Truth": Athanasius of Alexandria and the Localization of the Holy', in David Frankfurter (ed.), *Pilgrimage and Holy Space in Late Antique Egypt* (Leiden: Brill, 1998), pp. 474–481. On the practice of exhuming the bones of the martyrs, see Athanasius, *Festal Letter* 41 (Brakke, 'Outside the Places', p. 477).
104. Athanasius, *Festal Letter* 41, 42 (Brakke, 'Outside the Places', pp. 477 and 479 respectively).
105. Ibid. 41 (Brakke, 'Outside the Places', p. 478).

Indeed, these individuals have confused matters altogether, thinking that the martyrs speak through the demons. Athanasius continues:

> But the martyrs did not confess that they would speak through the demons and that the Lord, whom the martyrs confessed and who did not abandon those who confessed him, spoke through the demons. This is the humiliation of the saints and a sign of ignorance about what a martyr is. For if they understood, they would believe that the martyrs are in Christ, not in the demons, and they would call upon Christ who is in them . . .[106]

Here we see Athanasius labouring not only on behalf of the martyrs and the reverence owed to their remains, but also to keep these matters centred on Christ. The martyr shrines that filled the landscape of the Egyptian deserts and the reports of healings and exorcisms that travelled from desert to city were not allowed to develop into cult-followings of remarkable martyrs but, through Athanasius' influence, were focused on Christ and the victory of the cross.

For mine eyes have seen thy salvation: a city transformed

At the beginning of this chapter, I briefly mentioned the building programme undertaken by Constantine and his mother, Helena. They used the resources of the empire to transform the Roman landscape by Christianizing the art and, most significantly, the architecture of its cities. As we have seen, when Egeria, the Spanish nun, visited one of their churches during her pilgrimage to Jerusalem, she was at a loss to describe what her eyes encountered. The cultural message conveyed by Constantine's patronage was one of triumph. What was recently a persecuted and despised religion was now the favoured religion of the emperor and the recipient of his lavish gifts. For Athanasius, this victory was not to be misunderstood. It was not to be attributed to Constantine, his military might and patronage, but rather to Jesus Christ, who had renewed creation through his incarnation and cleansed the air and civic space of demons. It was Jesus, not Constantine, who had emptied the pagan temples, vanquished the evil spirits and transformed these pagan cities.[107]

As the patriarch of Egypt and bishop of Alexandria, Athanasius used his influence and resources to transform the art and architecture of Alexandria.

---

106. Ibid. 42 (Brakke, 'Outside the Places', pp. 479–480).

107. Athanasius, *On the Incarnation* 25.

He constructed new Christian buildings, expanded existing structures and converted old pagan temples into churches.[108] His interest in converting the civic space of Alexandria continued the efforts of his predecessor, Alexander. During Alexander's tenure as patriarch (312–28), he oversaw the enlargement of the church of St Theonas and the conversion of an important pagan temple of Kronos (Saturn) into a church dedicated to the archangel Michael.[109] St Theonas was located on the main thoroughfare through Alexandria, the Via Caponica, and next to the western gate, the Gate of the Moon. It would have been the first impressive structure encountered by travellers from the west to Alexandria. Its lavish adornment, moreover, would have conveyed clearly to all visitors the special status of Christianity in the city and the prosperity of the Christians. Athanasius would learn well from his predecessor the power of such visually impressive Christian markers at strategically located places throughout the city for travellers to Alexandria and its non-Christian citizens.

During Athanasius' tenure as bishop, he secured the Caesarion, an enormous complex of buildings located in the city centre along the Great Harbour.[110] As soon as a traveller rounded the lighthouse on the island of Pharos and entered the Great Harbour of Alexandria, his eyes would immediately be drawn, as it was in the days of Julius Caesar, to the impressive Caesarion, flanked by two obelisks, Cleopatra's Needles, as they were called, which now stood as a symbol of Christian triumphalism for all to see on their arrival into Alexandria. The structure was originally built by Cleopatra during the first century BC and had served as the centre for the imperial cult for over three hundred years.[111] Athanasius transformed this large structure into the Great Church or Patriarchal Cathedral and moved the bishop's headquarters from the periphery of the city at the western gate to the city centre. Athanasius' message to the long-time residents of Alexandria and to those

---

108. Haas, *Alexandria in Late Antiquity*, pp. 208–212. Converting pagan temples to Christian churches also had a practical reason. Haas writes, 'The topography of Alexandria was too constrained by natural barriers to permit a reconfiguration of the pronounced design system, which dated from the city's foundation by Alexander [the Great]' (pp. 207–208).

109. Ibid., pp. 209–210.

110. Ibid. The building was originally donated by the emperor Constantius to George of Alexandria (339–46), an Arian bishop who had been appointed during one of Athanasius' exiles. When Athanasius returned to the city from exile, he took over this building in the city centre and converted it into the bishop's headquarters.

111. Ibid., p. 210.

passing through was unmistakable: the pagan past was gone and the victory of Christ and his church was here to stay. Athanasius reinforced this point every time he converted strategically located pagan temples throughout the city into churches.[112]

The visual impression of the architecture and the regularized celebration of the paschal feast by Athanasius offered a powerful display of Christian unity and prosperity to the non-Christian citizens of Alexandria and the numerous travellers who would arrive by ship in the Great Harbour. The smoke of the pagan sacrifices had been replaced by the incense of Christian worship. The triumph seen throughout the empire in the courage of the martyrs was now before the eyes of the traveller and citizens of Alexandria in the ornate and impressive stone structures of the city. Christianity, which only a few short years before had been savagely persecuted, was now firmly anchored in the heart and soil of one of the oldest and richest cities of the ancient world.

Conclusion: appropriating Athanasius today

At the beginning of the second century, perhaps around the year 110, merely a decade after the death of the apostle John, a bishop from Antioch by the name of Ignatius was transported by ten soldiers to Rome to suffer martyrdom for his confession of Christ. The journey took about six weeks. As he travelled, Ignatius wrote letters to some of the Christian communities he passed by and one to Polycarp, bishop of Smyrna, who had known and been instructed by the apostle John.[113] In these letters he urges his fellow Christians to remain united in their confession of Jesus Christ, true God and

---

112. For a discussion of the individual buildings in Alexandria, see Annik Martin, 'Les premiers siècles du christianisme à Alexandrie. Essai de topographie religieuse (IIIe-IVe siècles)', *Revue des etudes augustiniennes* 30 (1984), pp. 211–225. Athanasius' final building project was the conversion of an old pagan temple that would later bear his name; *Festal Index* 41–32; Annick Martin and Micheline Albert (eds.), *Histoire 'acéphale' et index syriaque des letters festales d'Athanase d'Alexandrie* (Paris: Cerf, 1985), pp. 272–274; David Brakke, 'Athanasius', in Philip F. Ensler (ed.), *The Early Christian World*, vol. 2 (London: Routledge, 2000), p. 1115.

113. For a convenient Greek–English edition of Ignatius' letters, see Michael W. Holmes (ed. and tr.), *The Apostolic Fathers*, 3rd ed. (Grand Rapids: Baker Academic, 2007).

true man, who truly suffered, died and rose again for their salvation.[114] He also warns them to avoid all who expound the Old Testament Scriptures apart from Jesus Christ. Indeed, in their presence, you must make yourself deaf, literally closing your ears to their false teaching.[115] Athanasius read these letters by the Blessed Ignatius, as he refers to him, and sees in this bishop-martyr from the early second century the same theological concerns he seeks to defend in the fourth century. Athanasius describes Ignatius as a Christ-centred theologian who sought only to expound the truth of Scripture to the Christians of his day. For this reason, Athanasius commends Ignatius to his fellow Christians of the fourth century and encourages them to listen to and learn from this great witness of the faith.[116]

The commendation of Ignatius by Athanasius is yet another lesson we learn from the great bishop of Alexandria. The interest and enthusiasm Athanasius has for Ignatius is the same interest and enthusiasm we should have for those faithful writers from the history of the church who have preceded us in the faith. Indeed, whether it is Ignatius, Athanasius, Augustine or Anselm, we should be attentive to their theological labours, knowing that these faithful members of the body of Christ, with all their virtues and shortcomings, pursued the very thing we pursue; namely, a deeper understanding of the inspired word of God and the salvation we have in Christ Jesus alone. At the same time, as evangelical Christians, committed to *sola scriptura* as the rule and norm for all articles of faith and not to the opinions or writings of the fathers, we bear a responsibility when we read and listen to others expound the Scriptures.[117] Athanasius listened to Ignatius and received his teaching because it was Christ-centred and grounded in the Scriptures alone. Our reading of the fathers proceeds in the same way.

---

114. Ignatius of Antioch, *To the Smyrnaeans* 1.1–3.3, and *To the Trallians* 9.1–10.1, in ibid., pp. 249–251, 221 respectively.

115. Ignatius of Antioch, *To the Trallians* 9.1, and *To the Philadelphians* 6.1, in ibid., pp. 221, 241 respectively.

116. Athanasius, *On the Councils of Ariminum and Seleucia* 47 (PG 26).

117. Acts 17:11; 1 John 2:18–27; 4:1–6. Cf. Martin Luther, who warns, 'It will not do to make articles of faith out of the words or works of the holy Fathers' (*Smalcald Articles* 2, 2.15, in Theodore G. Tappert [ed.], *The Book of Concord* [Philadelphia: Fortress, 1954], p. 295). Thomas Aquinas makes the same point at the beginning of his *Summa Theologica* in the question on *sacra doctrina*. See Thomas Aquinas, *Summa Theologica* 1, Q1, a8, ad2, tr. Fathers of the English Dominican Province (New York: Christian Classics, 1981), p. 6.

When we listen to and learn from Athanasius, we are especially struck by his consistent appeal to the gospel in all theological reflection. He teaches us that the trinitarian debates of the fourth century were not academic disputes about finer points of theology, much less exercises in abstract philosophical terms, but were always about Jesus Christ as true God and true man, who lived, suffered, died and rose again for our salvation. Athanasius understood that at the heart of the dispute with Arius was our salvation. Amidst great difficulty and persecution he tirelessly defended the scriptural witness to the doctrine of the Trinity and our salvation in Christ Jesus alone. Athanasius also understood that the gospel impacts our daily lives and strove to teach all the faithful, from the desert monk to the Christian family, that every aspect of our lives is to be lived in the light of the victory of the cross. As we live, pray, suffer and approach the end of our earthly sojourn, we do so as those clinging to Christ alone and enfolded in the faith of his cross.

A few years after his death, Gregory of Nazianzus delivered an oration on the life of the 'Great Athanasius'. He began his oration by saying, 'In praising Athanasius, I shall be praising virtue. To speak of him and to praise virtue are identical, because he had, or, to speak more truly, has embraced virtue in its entirety.'[118] It is safe to say that not everyone in the fourth century would agree with this high assessment of Athanasius' character. Throughout his life he was repeatedly accused by his theological and political enemies of financial improprieties, sacrilege and even violence. Athanasius was a man of his times and there is undoubtedly some truth to these charges. He was a sinner, but, as Gregory of Nazianzus rightly insists, he was also a saint. What lies behind these charges and ultimately what so greatly provoked his opponents to send him into exile on five different occasions was Athanasius' stubborn certainty about the truth of his theological position.[119] He would not yield on any point that compromised his faith in Jesus, true God and true man, co-eternal and

---

118. Gregory of Nazianzus, *Oratio* 21.1 (*NPNF*, 2nd series, vol. 7, p. 270.)

119. Such steadfastness and uncompromising insistence on the Scriptures continues to trouble commentators in our day. Commentators today regularly assert that Athanasius deliberately misrepresented the historical record, was an unscrupulous pamphleteer, a subtle and skilful liar who regularly employed violence and intimidation against his enemies and, in short, was a Christian gangster. For a summary of the scholarly opinion of Athanasius from different points of view, see Duane W.-H. Arnold, *The Early Episcopal Career of Athanasius of Alexandria* (Notre Dame: University of Notre Dame Press, 1991), pp. 9–23; T. D. Barnes, *Athanasius and Constantius: Theology and Politics in the Constantinian Empire* (Cambridge,

co-equal with the Father, in whom alone we have salvation. It is here that we see the real character of Athanasius and his greatness. It lies in his uncompromising steadfastness to the gospel, his resolute belief in the victory of the cross, and his unwavering commitment to Jesus Christ and the doctrine of the Trinity. It is this faithfulness that makes him such a compelling figure for us today. Indeed, it is for this reason that when we read Athanasius we do so, as Søren Kierkegaard put it, 'with a throbbing heart'.[120]

Bibliography

Primary sources in the primary languages

BARTELINK, G. J. M., *Athanase d'Alexandrie: Vie d'Antoine*, Sources chrétiennes (Paris: Cerf, 1994). This is a critical edition with introduction and notes of Athanasius' *Life of Antony*.

CAMELOT, P. T., *Athanase d'Alexandrie: Contre les Païens*, Sources chrétiennes (Paris: Cerf, 1977). This is a critical edition with introduction and notes of Athanasius' *Against the Heathen* (*Contra gentes*).

KANNENGIESSER, C., *Athanase d'Alexandrie: Sur l'incarnation du Verbe*, Sources chrétiennes (Paris: Cerf, 1973). This is a critical edition with introduction and notes of Athanasius' *On the Incarnation* (*De incarnatione*).

MONTFAUCON, B., *Athanasii archiepiscopi Alexandrini opera omnia quae exstant*, in J.-P. Migne (ed.), Patrologiae cursus completus: Series graeca, 162 vols. (Paris: Cerf, 1857–86), vols. 25–26. This is a collection of Athanasius' writings in Greek and Latin.

OPITZ, H. G., *Athanasius Werke*, Herausgegeben in Auftrage der Kirchenväter-Kommission der Preußischen Akademie der Wissenschaften, 3 vols. (Berlin: de Gruyter, 1996). These volumes are recent critical editions of many of Athanasius'

MA: Harvard University Press, 1993), pp. 1–9; and James D. Ernest, *The Bible in Athanasius of Alexandria* (Leiden: Brill, 2004), pp. 1–5.

The widely quoted claim that Athanasius was a gangster comes from T. D. Barnes: 'Athanasius possessed a power independent of the emperor which he built up and perpetuated by violence. That was both the strength and the weakness of his position. Like a modern gangster, he evoked widespread mistrust, proclaimed total innocence – and usually succeeded in evading conviction on specific charges' (*Constantine and Eusebius* [Cambridge, MA: Harvard University Press, 1981], p. 230).

120. *The Journals of Søren Kierkegaard*, tr. Alexander Dru (London: Oxford, 1938), p. 58 (14 Apr. 1838).

works. These texts should be consulted first in any advanced work done on Athanasius.

Primary sources in English translation

ANATOLIOS, KHALED, *Athanasius* (London: Routledge, 2004). Collected in this book are translations of works by Athanasius against the Arians, on the Council of Nicaea and on the Holy Spirit.

ATHANASIUS, *On the Incarnation* (Crestwood, NY: St Vladimir's Seminary Press, 1998). Introduced by C. S. Lewis and translated in readable English, this is one of Athanasius' most widely read works among students today. In this work Athanasius explores the meaning of the incarnation and its significance for our salvation.

GREGG, R. C., *Athanasius: The Life of Antony and the Letter to Marcellinus* (New York: Paulist, 1980). This is an important work on monasticism and the life of St Antony. Athanasius' *Life of Antony* was one of his most popular works during early church history. Augustine makes reference to it in his *Confessions* and describes for us the impact this work had on Christian men and women who heard it and decided to embrace the monastic life. The *Letter to Marcellinus* is a short work on how to read the Psalms.

ROBERTSON, A., *St. Athanasius: Select Works and Letters*, in H. Wace and P. Schaff (eds.), *A Select Library of Nicene and Post-Nicene Fathers of the Christian Church* [*NPNF*], 2nd series, vol. 4 (Grand Rapids: Eerdmans, 1987). This single volume contains nearly all of Athanasius' writings in English.

Introductory studies

BRAKKE, DAVID, 'Athanasius', *The Early Christian World*, vol. 2, ed. Philip F. Ensler (London: Routledge, 2000), pp. 1102–1127. This short article is an excellent introduction to the life and thought of Athanasius.

WEINANDY, THOMAS, *Athanasius: A Theological Introduction* (Burlington, VT: Ashgate , 2007). For a recent bibliography of articles written on Athanasius, see Weinandy, pp. 144–146. This is a recent monograph on Athanasius that explores the major theological themes in his writings. Weinandy focuses especially on Athanasius' understanding of salvation, the Trinity and the sacraments.

WILLIAMS, ROWAN, 'Athanasius and the Arian Crisis', in G. R. Evans (ed.), *The First Christian Theologians: An Introduction to Theology in the Early Church* (Oxford: Blackwell, 2004), pp. 157–167. This is an excellent and brief introduction to the historical and theological debates on the Trinity between Athanasius and his 'Arian' opponents.

Additional key studies and resources

ANATOLIOS, KHALED, *Athanasius: The Coherence of his Thought* (London: Routledge, 1998). In this book Anatolios resists approaching Athanasius' theology in the light of the fourth-century trinitarian and Christological debates and instead argues that the coherence of Athanasius' thought is found in the distinction and simultaneous relation between God and the world. This is a difficult read but one that offers an interesting and engaging perspective on Athanasius.

Arnold, D. W. H., *The Early Episcopal Career of Athanasius of Alexandria* (Notre Dame: University of Notre Dame Press, 1991). This is a careful historical study of Athanasius' early episcopal career from his consecration as bishop in 328 to his banishment by Constantine in 335.

Ayres, Lewis, *Nicaea and its Legacy: An Approach to Fourth-Century Trinitarian Theology* (Oxford: Oxford University Press, 2004). This is a recent study of the fourth-century trinitarian debates that discusses both the history and theology of these debates and their legacy for the church today. Ayres's monograph is highly recommended for anyone exploring the Trinity in the early church and its place in our theological reflection today.

Barnes, T. D., *Athanasius and Constantius: Theology and Politics in the Constantinian Empire* (Cambridge, MA: Harvard University Press, 1993). This book offers a careful historical and political reconstruction of Athanasius' ecclesiastical career. Although Barnes's approach is critical and sees Athanasius as little more than a power-hungry bishop, the careful historical work done by Barnes should be consulted by anyone working on Athanasius.

Brakke, David, *Athanasius and Asceticism* (Baltimore: Johns Hopkins University Press, 1995). This work explores Athanasius' theological and political efforts to integrate the vast ascetic movement in Egypt and its values into the broader institutional church. Brakke also includes a few translations of Athanasius' ascetic and pastoral works at the end of this volume.

Ernest, James D., *The Bible in Athanasius of Alexandria* (Leiden: Brill, 2004). This book offers a detailed description of the rhetorical and exegetical strategies used by Athanasius in his reading of Scripture.

Hanson, R. P. C., *The Search for the Christian Doctrine of God: The Arian Controversy, 318–381* (Grand Rapids: Baker Academic, 2005). This is an exhaustive study of the fourth-century trinitarian debates and a standard work for anyone exploring the doctrine of God in the fourth century.

Williams, Rowan, *Arius: Heresy and Tradition*, 2nd ed. (Grand Rapids: Eerdmans, 2001). This is a careful and thorough study of Arius' theology.

5. THE THREE CAPPADOCIANS

Robert Letham

The three Cappadocians are so called because they lived and worked for most of their careers in Cappadocia. The leading figure of the group was Basil; Gregory of Nyssa was his younger brother and Gregory of Nazianzus, a close friend. Both of the latter were to some extent or other under Basil's patronage at important stages in their respective ministries. Moreover, while the two Gregories were brilliant intellects, and Gregory of Nazianzus one of the greatest orators and preachers in the history of the church, Basil was – besides his writings – a significant churchman in his own right, an accomplished organizer and promoter of monasticism.[1]

Basil the Great (330–79)

As Anthony Meredith points out, we know more about Basil than any other ancient writer, with the exception of Cicero and Augustine.[2] He studied rhet-

1. The biographies below are based, in varying degrees, on similar short biographical summaries in my book *Through Western Eyes: Eastern Orthodoxy: A Reformed Perspective* (Fearn: Mentor, 2007), and are used here with permission.
2. A. Meredith, *The Cappadocians* (Crestwood, NY: St Vladimir's Seminary Press, 1995), p. 20.

oric under his father, and then moved to Antioch, to study with the celebrated pagan rhetorician, Libanius, who later taught Chrysostom. Accompanied by Gregory of Nazianzus, he continued his education at Athens, which possibly included the study of science.

Basil was not baptized until 357. Influenced by his sister, Macrina, he developed an ascetic interest. In 360 he came into contact with the portentous Eunomius at a synod in Constantinople; he played a prominent part at the synod and found himself strongly opposing Eunomius, whose theology was close to that of Arius. More skilful than Arius – besides the fact that he was a bishop – and so an extremely formidable adversary, Eunomius held that the Son came into being at a particular point, was created and so of a different being than the Father. This was contrary to Athanasius who supported the Creed of Nicaea, which affirmed that the Son is of the same, identical being as the Father. Basil was at this time not prepared to go as far as Athanasius; the group with which he was connected were known as the *homoiousians*, since they taught that the Son is of a *like* being to the Father, neither identical to him nor different from him.

Basil was consecrated bishop of Caesarea in 370, and tried to remove Eunomius' followers from influence. Since the emperor Valens encouraged the promotion of Arians, this was no easy matter. Simultaneously, Basil was moving closer to an agreement with Athanasius on the Trinity. This he did by a significant semantic proposal. The fourth-century trinitarian crisis had been bedevilled by technical and philosophical terminology. Frequently antagonists spoke past each other, for they used words that had no fixed meaning. Moreover, they used them in differing ways. Athanasius paved the way for a breakthrough when, in his *Tome to the People of Antioch* (*Tomus ad Antiochenos*, 362), he argued that more important than the precise words was the meaning attached to the words. This helped the participants in the debate to ask what each other intended by their language. Basil took the matter a vital step further. The terms *ousia* and *hypostasis* were used in various ways up to this point, often as synonyms. Basil proposed that *ousia* be reserved for the one being of God, while *hypostasis* be used for the way he is three. This gave the tools needed to consider how God is one in distinction from the way he is three. Moreover, Basil freed trinitarian discussion from the straightjacket of philosophical terminology and granted it the flexibility needed for the crisis to be resolved.

Basil wrote voluminously. We have a large collection of his letters, wherein he interacts with a range of figures in the church. His treatise *On the Holy Spirit* was the first on the Holy Spirit in church history, a landmark in the development of trinitarian doctrine, although Athanasius had a few years earlier written an important series of letters to Serapion on the Holy Spirit. Basil's book emerged from worship; his liturgical formula had aroused criticism, and he defended and explained it here. Some have suggested that Basil was reluctant to call the Holy Spirit 'God'; some claim he did not regard him as God, while others consider – with far more justification – that he was cautious on the matter, preferring to preserve the unity of the church as far as possible. However, Basil writes so strongly of the Holy Spirit that it is difficult to make a case for his seeing the Spirit as anyone less than God; the terms he uses for the Spirit demand nothing less than full deity.

Basil is also important for the future development of the theology of the Eastern church. In opposing Eunomius' rationalism – he and his followers held there to be an exact correspondence between divine and human knowledge – he taught the incomprehensibility of God, distinguishing between the being of God (who God is), which is beyond our capacity to know, and the actions of God, which we can know. In this he has been accused of agnosticism.

Basil attended closely to his own diocese. Emperor Valens, the Arian sympathizer, attempting to curtail Basil's growing influence, cut the diocese into two, leaving him with the smaller part, so reducing the number of bishops Basil could appoint. However, as R. P. C. Hanson – himself at one point a bishop – remarks, parting a bishop from his diocese is like trying to tear a dog from a bone. In response, Basil simply doubled the number of episcopal positions under his jurisdiction!

Examples of Basil's preaching can be found in his *Hexaemeron*, on the six days of creation, a series of homilies on the first chapter of Genesis, in which he not only expounds the chapter but interacts with contemporary scientific knowledge. He established hospitals for the poor and promoted monasticism. His monastic rule greatly influenced the later work of St Benedict, who urged his monks to read it in addition to the Bible.[3] Basil was not a supporter of solitary monasticism, of the forms of withdrawal associated with the Egyptian monks. For him, the life of a community was essential, with manual labour an integral part, and care for the poor central to its operation. As Meredith indicates, both Gregory of Nyssa and Gregory Nazianzen wrote on love for the poor, and it is easy to trace the impact of Basil at this point.[4]

His writings include a work against Eunomius, a range of ascetic works and educational treatises. His large collection of letters is written in a fine literary style and ranges across theological, organizational and pastoral matters. He is probably the main source of the Liturgy of St Basil, still used in the Orthodox Church at various feasts.

---

3. Ibid., p. 24.
4. Ibid., p. 27.

Gregory of Nyssa (d. c. 394)

Basil's brother, Gregory, may have married, although the experience was apparently an unhappy one. Unlike Basil, he did not travel to receive a wide-ranging education but attributed his learning to Basil's own teaching. He is widely regarded as the most brilliant of the Cappadocians. However, Basil was responsible for his brother's ecclesiastical appointments, although Gregory was singularly ill suited to them. After Valens' division of his diocese, Basil appointed Gregory in 372 to one of the new jurisdictions he created – the tiny and unpretentious see of Nyssa. Three years later, due to Arian intrigues, Gregory was forced into exile, to return in 378.

Around this time, Gregory composed his vast refutation of Eunomius, *Against Eunomius* (*Contra Eunomium*). The first two books of this enormous work were probably written before the Council of Constantinople (381) and read to a select gathering before the council met, while the remainder were completed a couple of years later. He preached the funeral orations for the first moderator of the council, Meletius, who died shortly after it began, also for the emperor's wife in 383, and his younger daughter two years later.[5] He wrote a large number of treatises and homilies, and shared many of his brother's concerns.

In his criticism of Eunomius, Gregory stressed the point – also asserted by Basil – that the being of God is beyond our capacity to define. God is infinite and beyond the grasp of the human mind. By his hair-splitting rationalism, Eunomius was destroying the Christian faith. In contrast, human beings live by faith, and depend on God's revelation. In this, Gregory prepared the ground for the apophatic approach that has come to be characteristic of Eastern theology, especially in the writings of Dionysius the Areopagite. This is the idea that knowledge of God is not primarily to be found in positive affirmations about him but by way of negation, not the intellectual negation commonly used in the West, but through abandoning reliance on rational thought in prayer and contemplation.

Gregory was strongly influenced by Platonism, yet the extent to which this is so has been disputed. He had a strong grasp of the materiality of creation, and man as both body and soul, and emphatically teaches the bodily resurrection of Christ. Evil is a privation of the good, as Plotinus argued and as Augustine was famously to teach. When redemption has run its course, evil will disappear and all things will be restored. Redemption itself must display

5. Ibid., pp. 52–53.

the justice of God, and does so by tricking Satan, who had first tricked man. Thus, as Adam was deceived into eating the fruit, so the devil was deceived by the humanity of Christ as bait, his deity being concealed. The devil fell for the bait and swallowed it, and was destroyed in the process.

For Gregory, the ultimate end of redemption is our deification. This occurs by our bodies being transformed by the body of Christ, by coming into contact with the author of eternal life; this takes place in the Eucharist. There Christ unites us with himself so that we may share in incorruptibility and immortality. This is what deification means, not any absorption of humanity into God but its partaking of bodily immortality.

Additionally, Gregory wrote a number of other treatises on the Holy Spirit and in defence of trinitarian doctrine, a number of homilies and works of biblical exegesis, ascetic treatises (including an early book on virginity), and letters.

Gregory Nazianzen (c. 330–91)

Life

Gregory is called by the Eastern church 'the theologian', a title he shares with the apostle John alone. He was born at Arianzus, a country estate belonging to his father, near Nazianzus, probably around 330. His father – also Gregory – had been a member of an obscure heretical sect before becoming a Christian through the influence of his wife, Nonna. Shortly afterwards the elder Gregory was made bishop of Nazianzus. Our Gregory was born after his father's ordination, and the father frequently urged him to ordination saying, 'You have not been so long in life as I have spent in sacrifice.'

Gregory had a wide-ranging education. When thirteen, he and his brother (who became a doctor in the imperial court at Constantinople) were sent to Caesarea in Cappadocia, where he met Basil, who became a lifelong colleague. Later he went to Caesarea in Palestine, to study rhetoric, and then to the university at Alexandria, while Athanasius was bishop, although his time there probably coincided with Athanasius' second exile (340–347). Gregory was in Athens for a longer time.

At Athens from the age of eighteen to past thirty, he renewed acquaintance with Basil. They agreed to renounce the attractions of the city and devote themselves to the church. Basil returned sooner to Cappadocia and monastic seclusion. When Gregory went back, his parents were still alive, his father still a bishop. Gregory divided his time between helping his father with his episcopal duties and spending time in the mountains, at Basil's monastic base, in prayer, meditation, study and manual labour.

With the acclamation of the people of Nazianzus Gregory was probably ordained at Christmas 361, but against his will. Oppressed by what he called this 'tyranny' he fled to Pontus. He returned by the following Easter but when he preached his first sermon, many stayed away in protest. Later he wrote an apology for his flight, saying he shrank from the huge responsibilities thrust upon him against his will.

In 370 Basil was elected bishop of the metropolitan see of Caesarea. When Basil doubled the number of bishops under his jurisdiction, he found a place for Gregory too. However, it was a tiny obscure backwater called Sasima, at a road junction, without water or grass, full of dust, noise and vagabonds. Gregory was furious – but, due to military occupation of the area, very likely never took charge, for his father needed his help at Nazianzus. After his parents' death in 374 Gregory went into seclusion for the rest of his life, except for a short but unhappy spell as bishop of Constantinople, during which he presided briefly at the ecumenical council. He died in 391.

Contemporaries described Gregory as of medium height, pale, with thick hair and a short beard, and conspicuous eyebrows. He had a scar by his right eye and his knees were worn out by excessive kneeling. His asceticism was widely considered overdone. He was cut off from the world and lacked experience of human nature. His love of solitude prevented him from producing the theological output he could have done. But what he did write stands any test. He is the single most quoted author in the East, after the Bible.[6]

Thought

At Constantinople Gregory's main theme was worship of the Trinity. Between 379 and 381 he preached five sermons (the *Theological Orations*) that permanently established his reputation. As one critic put it, 'Critics have rivalled each other in the praises they have heaped upon them, but no praise is so high as that of the many theologians who have found in them their own best thoughts.'[7] Gregory's principal opponents in these sermons were the Eunomians.[8] With

---

6. J. Binns, *An Introduction to the Christian Orthodox Churches* (Cambridge: Cambridge University Press, 2002), p. 72.
7. P. Schaff, *A Select Library of the Nicene and Post-Nicene Fathers of the Christian Church* [*NPNF*], 2nd series (Edinburgh: T. & T. Clark, 1989), vol. 7, pp. 333–336; B. Studer, *Trinity and Incarnation: The Faith of the Early Church*, ed. M. Westerhoff and A. Louth (Collegeville, MN: Liturgical, 1993), pp. 143–144.
8. For what follows, see R. Letham, *The Holy Trinity: In Scripture, History, Theology, and Worship* (Phillipsburg: Presbyterian & Reformed, 2004), pp. 157–164.

a strong belief in the capacities of human logic, they maintained we are capable of comprehending God, assuming there to be a univocal relation between the divine and human mind (an identity of meaning for both God and man). For them, the Son is absolutely unlike the Father. God is absolute being, and generation cannot be predicated of him. Because of the correspondence between the mind of God and human reasoning, generation attributable to the Son is to be understood in terms of generation as we know it on the human level. Eternal generation is inconceivable; the Son's generation must have had a beginning. Therefore, there was a time when the Son did not exist. The Son was the first to be created and is the instrument by which God created the world. The Holy Spirit is even further removed from God.

In contrast, Gregory follows the stress of the other two Cappadocians on the incomprehensibility of God. It is impossible for anyone fully to grasp God's nature. We can only speak in negatives. It is difficult to conceive of God but to define him in words is an impossibility. It is one thing to be persuaded of God's existence and quite another to know what he is. On the other hand, God revealed himself, to Abraham, Manoah, Isaiah and Paul. This is true knowledge but is not direct knowledge of God's essence (from *esse*, to be) (*Theological Orations* 3.12). In the same way, our bodily existence prevents us grasping spiritual realities.

Gregory then unfolds his own teaching. He starts by affirming the monarchy (the principle of unity in God). The Cappadocians have been (wrongly) taken to task by some for making the Father the cause of the deity of the Son and the Holy Spirit, by arguing that the Father is the source of the divine essence. Nothing could be further from Gregory's mind. The monarchy is not limited to one person so that, although the persons are numerically distinct there is no severance of essence. The Father is the begetter and emitter, the Son is the begotten, and the Holy Spirit the emission, but this is so in the context of equality of nature, a union of mind, an identity of motion (3.2). The begetting of the Son and the procession of the Spirit took place beyond time and above reason, for there never was when the Father was not, nor was there such with respect to the Son and the Holy Spirit. The Son and the Spirit are from the Father but not after the Father (3.3). To be begotten and to proceed are concurrent with to be (3.9). All this is, of course, beyond our comprehension. Yet this does not negate it, any more than we reject God's existence because we cannot comprehend him (3.8). The begetting of the Son by the Father establishes their identity of nature, for the offspring is of the same nature as the parent (3.10). The thing to note, he says, is that the begetting and being begotten (and, we may add by inference, procession) is a property of the persons (the hypostases), not the one essence (3.12). In the same way, Father does not denote the essence of God but the relation in which the Father stands to the Son, which also denotes the identity of nature between the Father who begets and the Son who is begotten (3.16). Thus there was never a time when the Father was without the Son, nor the Son without the Father (3.17). Since his opponents were accustomed to cite biblical passages attributing weakness and subordination to the Son, Gregory points to the incarnation as the occasion for such descriptions: 'What is lofty you are to apply to the Godhead . . . but all that is lowly to the composite condition of him who . . . was incarnate' (3.18).[9] He remained God while adding human nature (3.19), while his humanity was united to God and became one person so that we might be made God so far as he is made man.

On the question of the Holy Spirit the *pneumatomachi* (fighters against the Holy Spirit) were the problem. They were followers of Macedonius, a deposed bishop, and were also known as Macedonians. They denied the deity of the Holy Spirit, considering him even more removed from God than the Son. For his part, Gregory makes a point from the theology of deification. In salvation we are made God. But if the Holy Spirit is not from eternity, how can he make me God, or join me with the Godhead (5.4)? Gregory points to the confusion that then existed over the status of the Spirit (5.5). His opponents were asking Gregory to make clear definitions, since they supposed human logic capable of unfolding the truth about God. He replies by saying that with respect to the procession of the Spirit, as with the begetting of the Son, human language about God is not to be understood in a univocal sense (5.7). Thus we are unable to define the procession of the Spirit and the generation of the Son (5.8).

How, then, does the Spirit differ from the Son? The difference of manifestation, or the difference in relations, gives rise to the difference of their names (5.9). Their respective properties (unbegotten, begotten, proceeding) has given them their respective names (Father, Son, Holy Spirit) 'that the distinction of the three persons may be preserved in the one nature . . . of the Godhead'.

Appropriately, Gregory turns to a consideration of worship. The Spirit is the one in whom we worship and in whom we pray. Thus prayer to the Spirit is, in effect, the Spirit offering prayer or adoration to himself. The adoration of the one is adoration of the three, because of the equality of honour and deity between the three (5.12). The questions of the deity of the Son and the Holy Spirit are connected – once the former is acknowledged, the other follows (5.13).

Gregory points to the historical and progressive outworking of revelation to explain the comparative reticence of Scripture concerning the Spirit:

---

9. Quotations of *Theological Orations* are from *NPNF*, 2nd series, vol. 7.

> The Old Testament proclaimed the Father openly, and the Son more obscurely. The New manifested the Son, and suggested the deity of the Spirit. Now the Spirit himself dwells among us, and supplies us with a clearer demonstration of himself. For it was not safe, when the Godhead of the Father was not yet acknowledged, plainly to proclaim the Son; nor when that of the Son was not yet received to burden us further . . . with the Holy Spirit . . .[10]

He also says:

> Now, worship and baptism establish the Spirit's deity for we worship God the Father, God the Son, and God the Holy Spirit, three persons, one Godhead, undivided in honour and glory . . . for if he is not to be worshipped, how can he deify me by baptism? But if he is to be worshipped, surely he is an object of adoration, and if an object of adoration he must be God.[11]

Gregory, then, has a clear grasp of the distinct persons while holding firmly to the unity of the undivided Godhead. For him, the Trinity was not an abstract puzzle but the heart of the Christian faith and the centre of true worship. 'But when I say God, I mean Father, Son, and Holy Spirit.'[12]

Basil

The trinitarian controversy

In *On the Holy Spirit* (*De Spiritu sancto*) 6.13 Basil explains the origin of the controversy in which he had become embroiled. It occurred in the context of the church's worship:

> Our opponents . . . are annoyed with us for completing the doxology to the Only-Begotten together with the Father, and for not separating the Holy Spirit from the Son.
>
> The grounds of their indignation are these: The Son, according to them, is not together with the Father, but after the Father. Hence it follows that glory should be ascribed to the Father '*through* him', but not '*with* him'; inasmuch as '*with* him' expresses equality of dignity, while '*through* him', denotes subordination. They further assert that the Spirit is not to be ranked along with the Father and the Son, but under

10. *Theological Orations* 5.26.
11. Ibid. 5.28.
12. *Oration* 38, *On the Theophany, or Birthday of Christ* 8.

> the Son and the Father; not co-ordinated but subordinated; not connumerated but subnumerated.[13]

Eunomius – whose ideas were similar to those of the heretic Arius – held that the Son was created by God and not co-eternal with the Father, nor of identical being to him. Similarly, the Holy Spirit was a creature. This represented a hierarchy, which Basil here opposes. For Basil, both the Son and the Spirit have equal dignity with the Father and so are to be worshipped with him.

Common conceptions of the Holy Spirit

At this time there was a high degree of ambiguity and uncertainty about the status of the Holy Spirit. Basil explains this in *On the Holy Spirit* 9.22. Basil himself, as mentioned above, has been considered to be reticent at ascribing full deity to the Spirit, although the evidence I will present indicates he clearly regarded him as God. However, due to the confusion that reigned, he felt a need to present the evidence for the Spirit's status indirectly:

> Let us now investigate what are our common conceptions concerning the Spirit, as well those which have been gathered by us from Holy Scripture concerning it as those which we have received from the unwritten tradition of the Fathers. First of all we ask, who on hearing the titles of the Spirit is not lifted up in soul, who does not raise his conception to the supreme nature? It is called 'Spirit of God', 'Spirit of truth which proceedeth from the Father', 'right Spirit', 'a leading Spirit.' Its proper and peculiar title is 'Holy Spirit'; which is a name specially appropriate to everything that is incorporeal, purely immaterial, and indivisible. So our Lord, when teaching the woman who thought God to be an object of local worship that the incorporeal is incomprehensible, said 'God is a spirit.' On hearing, then, of a spirit, it is impossible to form the idea of a nature circumscribed, subject to change and variation, or at all like the creature. We are compelled to advance in our conceptions to the highest, and to think of an intelligent essence, in power infinite, in magnitude unlimited, unmeasured by times or ages, generous of its good gifts, to whom turn all things needing sanctification, after whom reach all things that live in virtue, as being watered by its inspiration and helped on toward their natural and proper end; perfecting all other things, but itself in nothing lacking; living not as needing restoration, but as supplier of life; not growing by additions but straightway full, self-established, omnipresent, origin of sanctification, light perceptible to the mind, supplying, as were, through itself, illumination to every faculty in the search for truth; by nature unapproachable, apprehended by reason of

---

13. All quotations of *On the Holy Spirit* are from *NPNF*, 2nd series, vol. 8.

> goodness, filling all things with its power, but communicated only to the worthy; not shared in one measure, but distributing its energy according to 'the proportion of faith'; in essence simple, in powers various, wholly present in each and being wholly everywhere; impassively divided, shared without loss of ceasing to be entire, after the likeness of the sunbeam, whose kindly light falls on him who enjoys it as though it shone for him alone, yet illumines land and sea and mingles with the air. So, too, is the Spirit to every one who receives it, as though given to him alone, and yet it sends forth grace sufficient and full for all mankind, and is enjoyed by all who share it, according to the capacity, not of its power, but of their nature.

The Trinity, the Holy Spirit, baptism and salvation

Basil had been attacked for his doxology. It was precisely in worship and the liturgy, particularly in baptism, that he found evidence of the Spirit's deity. In *On the Holy Spirit* 10.26 he writes:

> Whence is it that we are Christians? Through our faith, would be the universal answer, And in what way are we saved? Plainly because we were regenerate through the grace given in our baptism. How else could we be? And after recognising that this salvation is established through the Father and the Son and the Holy Ghost, shall we fling away 'that form of doctrine' which we received?

This is so since faith and baptism go together. In 10.28 we read:

> Faith and baptism are two kindred and inseparable ways of salvation; faith is perfected through baptism, baptism is established through faith, and both are completed by the same names. For as we believe in the Father and the Son and the Holy Ghost, so are we also baptized in the name of the Father and the Son and the Holy Ghost: first comes the confession, introducing us to salvation, and baptism follows, setting the seal upon our assent.

However, the grace in baptism comes from the Holy Spirit. There is no power inherent in the water; baptismal efficacy comes exclusively from the Spirit. In 10.35 he writes:

> Hence it follows that the answer to our question why the water was associated with the Spirit is clear: the reason is because in baptism two ends were proposed; on the one hand, the destroying of the body of sin, that it may never bear fruit unto death; on the other hand, our living unto the Spirit, and having our fruit in holiness; the water receiving the body as in a tomb figures death, while the Spirit pours in the quickening power, renewing our souls from the deadness of sin unto their original

> life. This then is what it is to be born again of water and of the Spirit, the being made dead being effected in the water, while our life is wrought in us through the Spirit. In three immersions, then, and with three invocations, the great mystery of baptism is performed, to the end that the type of death may be fully figured, and that by the tradition of the divine knowledge the baptised may have their souls enlightened. It follows that if there is any grace in the water, it is not of the nature of the water, but of the presence of the Spirit. For baptism is 'not the putting away of the filth of the flesh, but the answer of a good conscience towards God'.

The Holy Spirit and theosis

The Holy Spirit effects salvation, which in the fullest sense results in our being made God – what the Eastern church calls *theosis* (deification), by which we are made partakers of the divine nature, as 2 Peter 1:4 states. This Basil indicates in *On the Holy Spirit* 9.23:

> Hence comes foreknowledge of the future, understanding of mysteries, apprehension of what is hidden, distribution of good gifts, the heavenly citizenship, a place in the chorus of angels, joy without end, abiding in God, the being made like to God, and, highest of all, the being made God.

In a remarkable figure of speech, in 26.62, he says that the Holy Spirit is 'the place of them that are being sanctified . . . the special and peculiar place of true worship'. Referring to John 4:21–24, he argues that the place of Christian worship is the Holy Spirit, for 'the Spirit is . . . the place of the saints and the saint is the proper place for the Spirit, offering himself as he does for the indwelling of God, and called God's Temple'. The Spirit is in the saints in different kinds of ways but in relation to the Father and the Son he is not so much in them as with them. Thus even in our own worship the Holy Spirit is inseparable from the Father and the Son.

The Holy Spirit is ranked together with God

Hence, the conclusion Basil reaches is that the Spirit must be ranked on the side of God and not the creatures:

> But the Spirit is ranked together with God, not on account of the emergency of the moment, but on account of the natural fellowship; is not dragged in by us, but invited by the Lord.[14]

---

14. *On the Holy Spirit* 10.30.

> Let us then revert to the point raised from the outset, that in all things the Holy Spirit is inseparable and wholly incapable of being parted from the Father and the Son.[15]

> Moreover, from the things created at the beginning may be learnt the fellowship of the Spirit with the Father and the Son . . . And in the creation bethink thee first, I pray thee, of the original cause of all things that are made, the Father; of the creative cause, the Son; of the perfecting cause, the Spirit; so that the ministering spirits subsist by the will of the Father, are brought into being by the operation of the Son, and perfected by the presence of the Spirit. Moreover, the perfection of angels is sanctification and continuance in it. And let no one imagine me either to affirm that there are three original hypostases or to allege the operation of the Son to be imperfect. For the first principle of existing things is One, creating through the Son and perfecting through the Spirit. The operation of the Father who worketh all in all is not imperfect, neither is the creating work of the Son incomplete if not perfected by the Spirit. The Father, who creates by His sole will, could not stand in any need of the Son, but nevertheless He wills through the Son; nor could the Son, who works according to the likeness of the Father, need co-operation, but the Son too wills to make perfect through the Spirit. 'For by the word of the Lord were the heavens made, and all the host of them by the breath [the Spirit] of his mouth.'[16]

Hypostasis *and* ousia

Basil played a leading role in resolving the trinitarian crisis of the fourth century by distinguishing between the terms *ousia* and *hypostasis*. Previously these words, borrowed from Greek philosophy, had been given a range of meanings and were often used as effective synonyms. The result was massive confusion. The church simply did not have the linguistic tools to settle the dispute over how God is both one and three. Eventually, Athanasius recognized that what was of greatest importance was not the words that were used but the meaning of the words. This paved the way for some to realize that others who employed different terminology might after all be intending the same. It was Basil, in *Letter* 214.3–4, who proposed that settled meanings be given to these two words:

> What more serious calumny could there be? What better calculated to disturb the faith of the majority than that some of us could be shewn to assert that there is one

15. Ibid. 16.37.
16. Ibid. 16.38.

hypostasis [roughly corresponding to 'person'] of Father, Son, and Holy Ghost? We distinctly lay down that there is a difference of Persons; but this statement was anticipated by Sabellius, who affirms that God is one by hypostasis, but is described by Scripture in different Persons, according to the requirements of each individual case; sometimes under the name of Father, when there is occasion for this Person; sometimes under the name of Son when there is a descent to human interests . . . ; and sometimes under the Person of Spirit . . . If, then, any among us are shewn to assert that Father, Son and Holy Ghost are one in substance, while we maintain the three perfect Persons, how shall we escape giving clear and incontrovertible proof of the truth of what is being asserted about us?

The non-identity of hypostasis and ousia is, I take it, suggested even by our western brethren. . . . If you ask me to state shortly my own view, I shall state that ousia has the same relation to hypostasis as the common has to the particular. Every one of us both shares in existence by the common term of essence (ousia) and by his own properties is such an one and such an one. In the same manner, in the matter in question, the term ousia is common, like goodness, or Godhead, or any similar attribute; while hypostasis is contemplated in the special property of Fatherhood, Sonship, or the power to sanctify. If then they describe the Persons as being without hypostasis, the statement is *per se* absurd; but if they concede that the Persons exist in real hypostasis as they acknowledge, let them so reckon them that the principle of the homoousion may be preserved in the unity of the Godhead, and that the doctrine preached may be the recognition of true religion, of Father, Son, and Holy Ghost, in the perfect and complete hypostasis of each of the Persons named.[17]

He explains this further in *Letter* 236.6:

The distinction between ousia and hypostasis is the same as that between the general and the particular; as, for instance, between the animal and the particular man. Wherefore, in the case of the Godhead, we confess one essence or substance so as not to give a variant definition of existence, but we confess a particular hypostasis, in order that our conception of Father, Son and Holy Spirit may be without confusion and clear. If we have no distinct perception of the separate characteristics, namely, fatherhood, sonship, and sanctification, but form our conception of God from the general idea of existence, we cannot possibly give a sound account of our faith. We must, therefore, confess the faith by adding the particular to the common. The Godhead is common; the fatherhood particular. We must therefore combine the two and say, 'I believe in God the Father.' The like course must be pursued in the

17. Quotations from Basil's letters are from *NPNF*, 2nd series, vol. 8.

confession of the Son; we must combine the particular with the common and say 'I believe in God the Son', so in the case of the Holy Ghost we must make our utterance conform to the appellation and say 'in God the Holy Ghost.'

Order of our knowledge and the order of relations

For Basil, there is a distinction to be drawn between the way we know God and the way the three persons relate to each other in the unity of God's being. The Holy Spirit grants us access *through* Christ the Son *to* the Father, whereas the order in the works and ways of the Trinity is *from* the Father *through* the Son *by* the Spirit. However, this must not be understood as a hierarchy of superiors and inferiors; the Eunomians used the Greek word *taxis* in that way, denoting a hierarchy of both status and being. For Basil the idea was that of a suitable disposition, a fitting arrangement, in which the three are seen as equal in status and identical in being. So, in *On the Holy Spirit* 18.47 he points out the following:

> 'No man knoweth the Father save the Son.' And so 'no man can say that Jesus is the Lord but by the Holy Ghost.' For it is not said through the Spirit, but by the Spirit, and 'God is a spirit, and they that worship Him must worship Him in spirit and in truth,' as it is written 'in thy light shall we see light', namely by the illumination of the Spirit, 'the true light which lighteth every man that cometh into the world.' It results that in Himself He shows the glory of the Only-begotten, and on true worshippers He in Himself bestows the knowledge of God. Thus the way of the knowledge of God lies from One Spirit through the One Son to the One Father, and conversely the natural Goodness and the inherent Holiness and the royal Dignity extend from the Father through the Only-begotten to the Spirit. Thus there is both acknowledgment of the hypostases and the true dogma of the Monarchy is not lost. They on the other hand who support their sub-numeration by talking of first and second and third ought to be informed that into the undefiled theology of Christians they are importing the polytheism of heathen error. No other result can be achieved by the fell device of sub-numeration than the confession of a first, a second, and a third God. For us is sufficient the order prescribed by the Lord. He who confuses this order will be no less guilty of transgressing the law than are the impious heathen.

God's essence is unknowable: we know him through his attributes (energies)

In *Letter* 234 Basil sets out what was to become an axiom of Eastern thought. We cannot know God in his essence, as he is in himself, for he infinitely transcends us. He dwells in light inapproachable. However, we can know him by means of his attributes or energies (*dynameis*, 'powers'). Our knowledge is therefore limited to his revelation of himself in his creation. This was denied by the Eunomians, who held that human knowledge of God was identical to God's knowledge of himself. This was a rationalist position, with a strong view of the capacities of the human mind but a correspondingly weak view of the supremacy of God:

> Do you worship what you know or what you do not know? If I answer, I worship what I know, they immediately reply, What is the essence of the object of worship? Then, if I confess that I am ignorant of the essence, they turn on me again and say, So you worship you know not what. I answer that the word to know has many meanings. We say that we know the greatness of God, His power, His wisdom, His goodness, His providence over us, and the justness of His judgment; but not His very essence. The question is, therefore, only put for the sake of dispute. For he who denies that he knows the essence does not confess himself to be ignorant of God, because our idea of God is gathered from all the attributes which I have enumerated. But God, he says, is simple, and whatever attribute of Him you have reckoned as knowable is of His essence. But the absurdities involved in this sophism are innumerable. When all these high attributes have been enumerated, are they all names of one essence? And is there the same mutual force in His awfulness and His loving-kindness, His justice and His creative power, His providence and His foreknowledge, and His bestowal of rewards and punishments, His majesty and His providence? In mentioning any one of these do we declare His essence ? If they say, yes, let them not ask if we know the essence of God, but let them enquire of us whether we know God to be awful, or just, or merciful. These we confess that we know. If they say that essence is something distinct, let them not put us in the wrong on the score of simplicity. For they confess themselves that there is a distinction, between the essence and each one of the attributes enumerated. The operations are various, and the essence simple, but we say that we know our God from His operations, but do not undertake to approach near to His essence. His operations come down to us, but His essence remains beyond our reach.

Unwritten traditions

Basil, in opposing the Eunomians, also has important things to say about the relationship between Scripture and unwritten traditions, which he claims were handed down from the apostles. In *On the Holy Spirit* 27.66 he writes:

> Of the beliefs and practices whether generally accepted or publicly enjoined which are preserved in the Church some we possess derived from written teaching; others we have received delivered to us 'in a mystery' by the tradition of the apostles; and both of these in relation to true religion have the same force. And these no one will

> gainsay; – no one, at all events, who is even moderately versed in the institutions of the Church. For were we to attempt to reject such customs as have no written authority, on the ground that the importance they possess is small, we should unintentionally injure the Gospel in its very vitals; or, rather, should make our public definition a mere phrase and nothing more. For instance to take the first and most general example, who is there who has taught us in writing to sign with the sign of the cross those who have trusted in the name of our Lord Jesus Christ? What writing has taught us to turn to the east at the prayer? Which of the saints has left us in writing the words of the invocation at the displaying of the bread of the Eucharist and the cup of blessing? For we are not, as is well known, content with what the apostle or the Gospel has recorded, but both in preface and conclusion we add other words as being of great importance to the validity of the ministry and these we derive from unwritten teaching.

Here Basil asserts that the sources of the church's practice are twofold. First, there are those things that are 'derived from written teaching', which is a reference to the Bible, particularly the Gospels and the writings of the apostles. However, by itself written teaching is insufficient. Unwritten traditions originating with the apostles 'have the same force'. If the church were to abandon these traditions, the gospel would be harmed and the church's profession of faith weakened. So the church is not content with the written teaching alone but 'we add other words'. For Basil, as for the Eastern church thereafter, Scripture is part of a larger whole rather than standing alone.

The interpretation of Scripture

It was common in the fourth century for the Old Testament to be interpreted in an allegorical manner. Origen (185–254) was particularly noteworthy as one who sought hidden meanings in the text. In his *On First Principles* (*Peri Archōn*) he argued that the text of the Bible was threefold, in keeping with his trichotomist view of human beings. The straightforward, historical meaning corresponded to the bodily sense, suitable for new believers. The moral significance of the text was for the more mature, while the spiritual meaning was intended for those who had made significant advance in the Christian life. Hence biblical exegesis focused increasingly in penetrating beneath the surface meaning of the text, discovering deeper, spiritual significance. Basil rejected this approach and advocated a simpler, more literal form of interpretation. In his *Hexaemeron* 9.1 he explains this:

> I know the laws of allegory, though less by myself than from the works of others. There are those truly, who do not admit the common sense of the Scriptures, for

whom water is not water, but some other nature, who see in a plant, a fish, what their fancy wishes, who change the nature of reptiles and of wild beasts to suit their allegories, like the interpreters of dreams who explain visions in sleep to make them serve their own ends. For me grass is grass; plant, fish, wild beast, domestic animal, I take all in the literal sense. 'For I am not ashamed of the gospel.' . . . giving themselves up to the distorted meaning of allegory, [they] have undertaken to give a majesty of their own invention to Scripture. It is to believe themselves wiser than the Holy Spirit, and to bring forth their own ideas under a pretext of exegesis. Let us hear Scripture as it has been written.[18]

Gregory of Nyssa

The simplicity of God

It has often been claimed that the Western church has a strong emphasis on the divine simplicity and that this has hampered its appreciation of God as Trinity. God's simplicity is his being one and indivisible; he is not composed of parts less than the whole of who he is. At times the accusation against the West sticks. Aquinas, for instance, had such a strong stress on the simplicity of God that some have claimed that he found it difficult to do justice to the three persons.[19] However, this passage from Gregory, in his vast *Against Eunomius* (1.19), demonstrates that this doctrine was not the preserve of the Latin West but was equally maintained in the East. Gregory does not yield an inch to Eunomius, whose teaching, Gregory holds, entails a view of God as composed of individual parts. We recall that, for Eunomius, the Son and the Holy Spirit are beings other than the Father, created and neither eternally co-equal nor identical in being:

But let us still scrutinize his [Eunomius'] words. He declares each of these Beings, whom he has shadowed forth in his exposition, to be single and absolutely one. We believe that the most boorish and simple-minded would not deny that the Divine Nature, blessed and transcendent as it is, was 'single.' That which is viewless, formless, and sizeless, cannot be conceived of as multiform and composite. But it will be clear, upon the very slightest reflection, that this view of the supreme Being as 'simple,' however finely they may talk of it, is quite inconsistent with the system which they have elaborated. For who does not know that, to be exact, simplicity in

18. Ibid.

19. See Letham, *Holy Trinity*, pp. 228–237, and sources cited there.

the case of the Holy Trinity admits of no degrees. In this case there is no mixture or conflux of qualities to think of; we comprehend a potency without parts and composition; how then, and on what grounds, could any one perceive there are differences of less and more.

If he had been thinking of a Being really single and absolutely one, identical with goodness rather than possessing it, he would not be able to count a greater and a less in it at all.

It is, indeed, difficult to see how a reflecting mind can conceive one infinite to be greater or less than another infinite. So that if he acknowledges the supreme Being to be 'single' and homogenous, let him grant that it is bound up with this universal attribute of simplicity and infinitude. If, on the other hand, he divides and estranges the 'Beings' from each other, conceiving that of the Only-begotten as another than the Father's, and that of the Spirit as another than the Only-begotten, with a 'more' and 'less' in each case, let him be exposed now as granting simplicity in appearance only to the Deity, but in reality proving the composite in Him.[20]

Gregory asserts here that Eunomius cannot hold to simplicity, since, in his teaching, the Son and the Holy Spirit are different beings from the Father. Rather, the doctrine of simplicity requires that all three persons be of the one identical being, indivisible and without composition into parts.

The names Father, Son, and Holy Spirit denote eternal realities and demonstrate the unity of God and the distinctions of the persons

In *Against Eunomius* 2.2 Gregory maintains that God has revealed to us the names we are to use of him. Eunomius instead adopts different names, which he co-opts in the service of his particular views on the persons of the Son and the Holy Spirit. Gregory holds that Christ gave us the names of the persons. We believe that God has one name, which is distinguished into three; these are relational names, the Father indicating a relation to the Son, and so forth. For Gregory, it is a matter of importance for orthodox theology that it be thought out on the basis of the teaching of Christ rather than something we may propose:

Since then this doctrine is put forth by the Truth itself, it follows that anything which the inventors of pestilent heresies devise besides to subvert this Divine

20. Quotations of *Against Eunomius* are from Philip Schaff and Henry Wace (eds.), *A Select Library of Nicene and Post-Nicene Fathers of the Christian* Church [*NPNF*], 2nd series (Edinburgh: T. & T. Clark, 1988), vol. 5.

utterance, – as, for example, calling the Father 'Maker' and 'Creator' of the Son instead of 'Father', and the Son a 'result', a 'creature', a 'product', instead of 'Son', and the Holy Spirit the 'creature of a creature', and the 'product of a product', instead of His proper title the 'Spirit', and whatever those who fight against God are pleased to say of Him, all such fancies we term a denial and violation of the Godhead revealed to us in this doctrine. For once for all we have learned from the Lord, through Whom comes the transformation of our nature from mortality to immortality, – from Him, I say, we have learned what we ought to look at with the eyes of our understanding, – that is, the Father, the Son, and the Holy Spirit.

For while there are many other names by which Deity is indicated in the Historical Books, in the Prophets and in the Law, our Master Christ passes by all these and commits to us these titles as better able to bring us to the faith about the Self-Existent, declaring that it suffices us to cling to the title, 'Father, Son, and Holy Ghost', in order to attain to the apprehension of him who is absolutely Existent, Who is one and yet not one. In regard to essence He is one, wherefore the Lord ordained that we should look to one Name: but in regard to the attributes indicative of the Persons, our belief in Him is distinguished into belief in the Father, the Son, and the Holy Ghost; He is divided without separation and united without confusion. For when we hear the title 'Father' we apprehend the meaning to be this, that the name is not understood with reference to itself alone, but also by its special signification indicates the relation to the Son. For the term 'Father' would have no meaning apart by itself, if 'Son' were not connoted by the utterance of the word 'Father.' When, then, we learnt the name 'Father' we were taught at the same time, by the selfsame title, faith also in the Son. Now since Deity by its very nature is permanently and immutably the same in all that pertains to its essence, nor did it at any time fail to be anything that it now is, nor will it at any future time be anything that it now is not, and since He Who is the very Father was named Father by the Word, and since in the Father the Son is implied, – since these things are so, we of necessity believe that He Who admits no change or alteration in His nature was always entirely what He is now, or, if there is anything which He was not, that He assuredly is not now. Since then He is named Father by the very Word, He assuredly always was Father, and is and will be even as He was.

These names, Gregory argues, are not only given us by Christ as the names of the three persons, but demonstrate both unity of nature and the distinct personal relations. Thus the Father is eternally the Father, and the Son is eternally the Son. The name 'the Father' entails relations and, specifically, 'the Son.' The immutability of God is the key, for he does not change and so as he has named himself so he ever is.

The ineffability of the divine essence

However, that does not mean that we can penetrate to the divine essence (being) so as to know God as he is in himself. Like Basil, Gregory is insistent that God's essence is beyond us; we are given to know what is needed for our salvation, not what we might wish to know to satisfy our curiosity. In *Against Eunomius* 2.3 he spells this out:

> And by this deliverance the Word seems to me to lay down for us this law, that we are to be persuaded that the Divine Essence is ineffable and incomprehensible: for it is plain that the title of Father does not present to us the Essence, but only indicates the relation to the Son. It follows, then, that if it were possible for human nature to be taught the essence of God, He 'who will have all men to be saved and to come to the knowledge of the truth' would not have suppressed the knowledge upon this matter. But as it is, by saying nothing concerning the Divine Essence, he showed that the knowledge thereof is beyond our power, while when we have learnt that of which we are capable, we stand in no need of the knowledge beyond our capacity, as we have in the profession of faith in the doctrine delivered to us what suffices for our salvation.

Here Gregory's theology is shaped by the gospel and salvation. There are clear bounds beyond which we cannot go and on which we must not speculate. God has provided all we need for our salvation; this should suffice us. He reaffirms this in *Against Eunomius* 3.5. This stress on the ineffability of God's essence was to become a hallmark of Eastern Christianity. Since we cannot know God in himself, rational thought is of itself limited in its capabilities. The knowledge of God is to be found, rather, by way of prayer, mystical contemplation and liturgical practice:

> Now if any one should ask for some interpretation, and description, and explanation of the Divine essence, we are not going to deny that in this kind of wisdom we are unlearned, acknowledging only so much as this, that it is not possible that that which is by nature infinite should be comprehended in any conception expressed by words. The fact that the Divine greatness has no limit is proclaimed by prophecy, which declares expressly that of His splendour, His glory, His holiness, 'there is no end': and if His surroundings have no limit, much more is He Himself in His essence, whatever it may be, comprehended by no limitation in any way.
>
> Accordingly, since the Deity is too excellent and lofty to be expressed in words, we have learnt to honour in silence what transcends speech and thought.
>
> Learning this, therefore, from Paul, we boldly declare that, not only are the

judgments of God too high for those who try to search them out, but that the ways also that lead to the knowledge of Him are even until now untrodden and impassable. For this is what we understand that the Apostle wishes to signify, when he calls the ways that lead to the incomprehensible 'past finding out', showing by the phrase that that knowledge is unattainable by human calculations, and that no one ever yet set his understanding on such a path of reasoning, or showed any trace or sign of an approach, by way of perception, to the things incomprehensible.

Learning these things, then, from the lofty words of the Apostle, we argue, by the passage quoted, in this way: – If His judgments cannot be searched out, and His ways are not traced, and the promise of His good things transcends every representation that our conjectures can frame, by how much more is His actual Godhead higher and loftier, in respect of being unspeakable and unapproachable, than those attributes which are conceived as accompanying it . . .

Generation

The relation of the Son to the Father is by generation. The Father has begotten the Son from eternity. Arius and Eunomius used this to argue that therefore the Son had a beginning. Human generation occurs at a point in time; a father begets a son but before that he is not a father, since his son does not yet exist. Therefore, so the argument went, the Son began to be when the Father begat him. Before that took place God was not the Father and, since the Son came into existence he is not of the same status or being as God. The question Gregory faces in *Against Eunomius* 2.9 is how we are to understand the idea of generation in the context of the relations between the Father and the Son:

For it would be well, I think, to consider in a somewhat careful investigation the exact meaning of the term 'generation'. That this expression conveys the meaning of existing as the result of some cause is plain to all and I suppose there is no need to contend about this point: but since there are different modes of existing as the result of a cause, this difference is what I think ought to receive thorough explanation in our discussion by means of scientific division. Of things which have come into being as the results of some cause we recognize the following differences. Some are the result of material and art, as the fabrics of houses and all other works produced by means of their respective material, where some art gives direction and conducts its purpose to its proper aim. Others are the result of material and nature; for nature orders the generation of animals one from another, effecting her own work by means of the material subsistence in the bodies of the parents; others again are by material efflux. In these the original remains as it was before, and that which flows from it is contemplated by itself, as in the case of the sun and its beam, or the lamp and its radiance, or of scents and ointments, and the quality given off from them. For these, while remaining undiminished in themselves, have each accompanying them the special and peculiar effect which they naturally produce, as the sun his ray, the lamp its brightness, and perfumes the fragrance which they engender in the air. There is also another kind of generation besides these, where the cause is immaterial and incorporeal, but the generation is sensible and takes place through the instrumentality of the body; I mean the generation of the word by the mind. For the mind being in itself incorporeal begets the word by means of sensible instruments. So many are the differences of the term generation, which we discover in a philosophic view of them, that is itself, so to speak, the result of generation.

And now that we have thus distinguished the various modes of generation, it will be time to remark how the benevolent dispensation of the Holy Spirit, in delivering to us the Divine mysteries, imparts that instruction which transcends reason by such methods as we can receive. For the inspired teaching adopts, in order to set forth the unspeakable power of God, all the forms of generation that human intelligence recognizes, yet without including the corporeal senses attaching to the words. For when it speaks of the creative power, it gives to such an energy the name of generation, because its expression must stoop to our low capacity; it does not, however, convey thereby all that we include in creative generation, as time, place, the furnishing of matter, the fitness of instruments, the design in the things that come into being, but it leaves these, and asserts of God in lofty and magnificent language the creation of all existent things, when it says, 'He spake the word and they were made, He commanded and they were created.' Again when it interprets to us the unspeakable and transcendent existence of the Only-begotten from the Father, as the poverty of human intellect is incapable of receiving doctrines which surpass all power of speech and thought, there too it borrows our language and terms Him 'Son', – a name which our usage assigns to those who are born of matter and nature. But just as Scripture, when speaking of generation by creation, does not in the case of God imply that such generation took place by means of any material, affirming that the power of God's will served for material substance, place, time and all such circumstances, even so here too, when using the term Son, it rejects both all else that human nature remarks in generation here below, – I mean affections and dispositions and the co-operation of time, and the necessity of place, – and, above all, matter, without all which natural generation here below does not take place. But when all such material, temporal and local existence is excluded from the sense of the term 'Son', community of nature alone is left, and for this reason by the title 'Son' is declared, concerning the Only-begotten, the close affinity and genuineness of relationship which mark His manifestation from the Father. And since such a kind of generation was not sufficient to implant in us an adequate notion of the ineffable

> mode of subsistence of the Only-begotten, Scripture avails itself of the third kind of generation to indicate the doctrine of the Son's Divinity, – that kind, namely, which is the result of material efflux, and speaks of him as the 'brightness of glory', the 'savour of ointment', the 'breath of God'; illustrations which in the scientific phraseology we have adopted we ordinarily designate as material efflux. But as in the cases alleged neither the birth of the creation nor force of the term 'Son' admits time, matter, place, or affection, so here too the Scripture employing only the illustration of effulgence and the others that I have mentioned, apart from all material conception, with regard to the Divine fitness of such a mode of generation, shows that we must understand by the significance of this expression, an existence at once derived from and subsisting with the Father.
>
> . . . by such a mode of generation is indicated this alone, that the Son is of the Father and is conceived of along with him, no interval intervening between the Father and his who is of the Father.
>
> . . . he therefore affirms of the Word that He essentially subsisted in the first and blessed nature itself.

Hence, Gregory argues, the primary denotation of generation or begottenness is that the Son is of the same nature as the Father. That the Father begets the Son indicates that the Son is not a creature but of the same kind as the one who begat him.

The Holy Spirit is of the same rank as the Father and the Son

As the conflict shifted in the 370s towards the deity of the Holy Spirit, Gregory joined the fray, with perhaps a more frontal attack than Basil had made:

> We confess that the Holy Spirit is of the same rank as the Father and the Son, so that there is no difference between them in anything . . . We confess that, save his being contemplated as with peculiar attributes in regard of person, the Holy Spirit is indeed from God, and of the Christ, according to Scripture, but that, while not to be confounded with the Father in being never originated, nor with the Son in being the Only-begotten, and while to be regarded separately in certain distinctive properties, he has in all else . . . an exact identity with them.[21]

Against the argument that, since the Spirit was revealed third, he is therefore not to be identified with God, Gregory asserts that it is 'unreasonable

21. *On the Holy Spirit against the Followers of Macedonius*, 2 *NPNF* 5: 315. All quotations of *On the Holy Spirit against the Followers of Macedonius* are from *NPNF*, 2nd series, vol. 5.

to suppose the numerical order to be a sign of any diminution or essential variation'.[22]

In *Against Eunomius* 2.15 he states this again:

> Accordingly from the identity of operations it results assuredly that the Spirit is not alien from the nature of the Father and the Son. And to the statement that the Spirit accomplishes the operation and teaching of the Father according to the good pleasure of the Son we assent. For the community of nature gives us warrant that the will of the Father, of the Son, and of the Holy Ghost is one, and thus, if the Holy Spirit wills that which seems good to the Son, the community of will clearly points to unity of essence.

The three persons are inseparable

Since the Spirit, together with the Father and the Son, is fully God, he is inseparable from them in the indivisibility of God's simple being :

> We are not to think of the Father as ever parted from the Son, nor to look for the Son as separate from the Holy Spirit. As it is impossible to mount to the Father, unless our thoughts are exalted hither through the Son, so it is impossible also to say that Jesus is Lord except by the Holy Spirit. Therefore Father, Son, and Holy Spirit are to be known only in a perfect Trinity, in closest consequence and union with each other, before all creation, before all the ages, before anything whatever of which we can form an idea. The Father is always Father, and in him the Son, and with the Son the Holy Spirit.[23]

In terms of the relations of the three persons, there is an order between them

> But the fountain of power is the Father, and the power of the Father is the Son, and the spirit of that power is the Holy Spirit.[24]

> There is no interval of separation between the Son and the Holy Spirit . . . so inseparable is the union of the Spirit with the Son.[25]

---

22. *On the Holy Spirit against the Followers of Macedonius*, 6; *NPNF* 5: 317.
23. Ibid., 15; *NPNF* 5: 319.
24. Ibid., 15; *NPNF* 5: 320.
25. Ibid., 18; *NPNF* 5: 321.

> You see the revolving circle of glory moving from like to like. The Son is glorified by the Spirit; the Father is glorified by the Son; again, the Son has his glory from the Father; and the Only-begotten thus becomes the glory of the Spirit.[26]

It is clear that Gregory considers this order between the trinitarian persons to be compatible with their unity and identity of being and status. The Father begets the Son, and never vice versa; this belongs to them as persons subsisting in the unity of the indivisible Trinity.

Perichoresis

Since the Son is all that the Father is except for being the Father, it follows that he and the Father indwell one another. As Gerald Bray has described it, they occupy the same infinite divine space.[27] The Son reveals the Father to us, and shares fully in all that the Father is and has. This means, among other things, that the Son is not some second-class god with lesser power than the Father – he is equal in power and glory with the Father:

> For the heir of all things, the maker of the ages, He Who shines with the Father's glory and expresses in Himself the Father's person, has all things that the Father Himself has, and is possessor of all His power, not that the right is transferred from the Father to the Son, but that it at once remains in the Father and resides in the Son. For He Who is in the Father is manifestly in the Father with all His own might, and He Who has the Father in Himself includes all the power and might of the Father. For He has in Himself all the Father, and not merely a part of Him: and He Who has Him entirely assuredly has His power as well.[28]

God reveals himself visibly in creation

In a lengthy section in *Answer to Eunomius*, Book 2, Gregory argues for the priority of visible forms over the verbal. It is worth reproducing this section in full since it is paradigmatic for the more visual form of worship of the Eastern church and raises far-reaching questions concerning the nature of God's revelation in creation and Scripture:

> But, says he, the record of Moses does not lie, and from it we learn that God spake. No! nor is great David of the number of those who lie, and he expressly says: 'The

---

26. Ibid., 24; *NPNF* 5: 324.
27. Gerald Bray, *The Doctrine of God* (Leicester: IVP, 1993), p. 158.
28. *Against Eunomius* 2.6.

heavens declare the glory of God, and the firmament showeth His handy work. Day unto day uttereth speech, and night unto night showeth knowledge'; and after saying that the heavens and the firmament declare, and that day and that night showeth knowledge and speech, he adds to what he has said, that 'there is neither speech nor language, and that their voices are not heard.' Yet how can such declaring and showing forth be other than words, and how it that no voice addresses itself to the ear? Is the prophet contradicting himself, or is he stating an impossibility, when he speaks of words without sound, and declaration without language, and announcement without voice? or, is there not rather the very perfection of truth in his teaching, which tells us, in the words which I have quoted, that the declaration of the heavens, and the word shouted forth by the day, is no articulate voice nor language of the lips, but is a revelation of the power of God to those who are capable of hearing it, even though no voice be heard?

What, then, do we think of this passage? For it may be that, if we understand we shall also understand the meaning of Moses. It often happens that Holy Scripture, to enable us more clearly to comprehend a matter to be revealed, makes use of a bodily illustration, as would seem to be the case in this passage from David, who teaches us by what he says that none of the things which are have their being from chance or accident, as some have imagined that our world and all that is therein was framed by fortuitous and undesigned combinations of first elements, and that no Providence penetrated the world. But we are taught that there is a cause of the system and government of the Universe, on whom all nature depends, to whom it owes its origin and cause, towards whom it inclines and moves, and in whom it abides. And since, as saith the Apostle, His eternal power and godhead are understood, being clearly seen through the creation of the world, therefore all creation and, before all, as saith the Scripture, the system of the heavens, declare the wisdom of the Creator in the skill displayed by His works. And this is what it seems to me that he is desirous to set forth, viz. the testimony of the things which do appear to the fact that the worlds were framed with wisdom and skill, and abide for ever by the power of Him who is the Ruler over all. The very heavens, he says, in displaying the wisdom of Him Who made them, all but shout aloud with a voice, and, though without voice, proclaim the wisdom of their Creator. For we can hear as it were words teaching us: 'O men, when ye gaze upon us and behold our beauty and magnitude, and this ceaseless revolution, with its well-ordered and harmonious motion, working in same direction and in the same manner, turn your thoughts to Him Who presides over the system, and, by aid of the beauty which you see, imagine to yourselves the beauty of the Archetype. For in us there is nothing without its Lord, nothing that moves of its own proper motion: but all that appears, or that is conceivable in respect to us, depends on a Power who is inscrutable and sublime.' This is not given in articulate speech, but by the things

> which are seen, and it instils into our minds the knowledge of Divine power more than if speech proclaimed it with a voice. As, then, the heavens declare, though they do not speak, and the firmament shows God's handy-work, yet requires no voice for the purpose, and the day uttereth speech, though there is no speaking, and no one can say that Holy Scripture is in error – in like manner, since both Moses and David have one and the same Teacher, I mean the Holy Spirit, Who says that the fiat went before the creation, we are not told that God is the Creator of words, but of things made known to us by the signification of our words. . .

Note the sentence above, 'This is not given in articulate speech, but by the things which are seen, and it instils into our minds the knowledge of Divine power more than if speech proclaimed it with a voice.' This is a claim pregnant with significance. Gregory argues that what we see is of greater moment than what we hear, that the visible creation is clearer in its articulation of the truth of God than any revelation in words. In asserting this, Gregory also allows a significant scope to the imagination. This basic assumption accounts for the priority of the visual in the worship of the Eastern church. Everywhere in the church building are icons; the worship of the church is seen as the meeting place between heaven and earth, the present worshippers and the transcendent array of saints and angels.[29]

Apostolic tradition

In *Against Eunomius* 4.6 Gregory attacks Eunomius on the grounds that his views are a novelty. In contrast, Gregory has the support of generations reaching back to the apostles. This continuous transmission of apostolic doctrine he believes to stand on its own. In contrast, Eunomius needs all the logical skill he can muster to bolster his argument:

> And let no one interrupt me, by saying that what we confess should also be confirmed by constructive reasoning: for it is enough for proof of our statement, that the tradition has come down to us from our fathers, handed on, like some inheritance, by succession from the apostles and the saints who came after them. They, on the other hand, who change their doctrines to this novelty, would need the support of arguments in abundance, if they were about to bring over to their views, not men light as dust, and unstable, but men of weight and steadiness: but so long as their statement is advanced without being established, and without being proved,

29. Letham, *Through Western Eyes*, pp. 143–152.

> who is so foolish and so brutish as to account the teaching of the evangelists and apostles, and of those who have successively shone like lights in the churches, of less force than this undemonstrated nonsense?

Christ's humanity transformed to what is divine

In *Against Eunomius* 5.3 Gregory considers the effect of the Son of God becoming incarnate on the humanity he assumed. Since this was, and is, the humanity of the Son, it is transformed by that assumption and, after the resurrection, exalted as Lord and Christ:

> We on our part assert that even the body in which He underwent His Passion, by being mingled with the Divine Nature, was made by that commixture to be that which the assuming Nature is. So far are we from entertaining any low idea concerning the Only-begotten God, that if anything belonging to our lowly nature was assumed in His dispensation of love for man, we believe that even this was transformed to what is Divine and incorruptible; but Eunomius makes the suffering of the Cross to be a sign of divergence in essence, in the sense of inferiority, considering, I know not how, the surpassing act of power, by which He was able to perform this, to be an evidence of weakness; failing to perceive the fact that, while nothing which moves according to its own nature is looked upon as surprisingly wonderful, all things that overpass the limitations of their own nature become especially the objects of admiration, and to them every ear is turned, every mind is attentive, in wonder at the marvel. And hence it is that all who preach the word point out the wonderful character of the mystery in this respect – that 'God was manifested in the flesh', that 'the Word was made flesh', that 'the Light shined in darkness', 'the Life tasted death', and all such declarations which the heralds of the faith are wont to make . . .
>
> Who then was 'exalted'? He that was lowly, or he that was the highest? and what else is the lowly, but the humanity? what else is the highest but the divinity? Surely, God needs not to be exalted, seeing that he is the highest. It follows, then, that the Apostle's meaning is that the humanity was exalted: and its exaltation was effected by its becoming Lord and Christ. And this took place after the Passion . . .

Communicatio idiomatum

This raises the question of the reality of Christ's humanity. Gregory immediately deals with the issue in *Against Eunomius* 5.5. The natures of the incarnate Christ remain distinct and retain their integrity. Deity remains deity, and humanity remains humanity; there is no confusion of the two. Yet the characteristics of both are equally attributable to the person of Christ:

But the flesh was not identical with the Godhead, till this too was transformed to the Godhead, so that of necessity one set of attributes befits God the Word, and a different set of attributes befits the 'form of the servant'.

Our contemplation, however, of the respective properties of the flesh and of the Godhead remains free from confusion, so long as each of these is contemplated by itself, as, for example, 'the Word was before the ages, but the flesh came into being in the last times': but one could not reverse this statement, and say that the latter is pretemporal, or that the Word has come into being in the last times. The flesh is of a passible, the Word of an operative nature: and neither is the flesh capable of making the things that are, nor is the power possessed by the Godhead capable of suffering.

So much as this is clear (even if one does not follow the argument into detail), that the blows belong to the servant in whom the Lord was, the honours to the Lord Whom the servant compassed about, so that by reason of contact and the union of natures the proper attributes of each belong to both, as the Lord receives the stripes of the servant, while the servant is glorified with the honour of the Lord; for this is why the Cross is said to be the Cross of the Lord of glory, and why every tongue confesses that Jesus Christ is Lord to the glory of God the Father.

The Godhead 'empties' itself that it may come within the capacity of the Human Nature, and the Human Nature is renewed by becoming Divine through its commixture with the Divine.

And as fire that lies in wood hidden below the surface is often unobserved by the senses of those who see, or even touch it, but is manifest when it blazes up, so too, at His death (which he brought about at his will, who separated his soul from his body, who said to his own Father 'Into Thy hands I commend My Spirit', who, as he says, 'had power to lay it down and had power to take it again'), he who, because he is the Lord of glory, despised that which is shame among men, having concealed, as it were, the flame of his life in his bodily nature, by the dispensation of his death, kindled and inflamed it once more by the power of his own Godhead, fostering into life that which had been brought to death, having infused with the infinity of his divine power that humble first-fruits of our nature, made it also to be that which he himself was – making the servile form to be Lord, and the man born of Mary to be Christ, and him who was crucified through weakness to be Life and power, and making all that is piously conceived to be in God the Word to be also in that which the Word assumed, so that these attributes no longer seem to be in either nature by way of division, but that the perishable nature being, by its commixture with the Divine, made anew in conformity with the nature that overwhelms it, participates in the power of the Godhead, as if one were to say that mixture makes a drop of vinegar mingled in the deep to be sea, by reason that the natural quality of this liquid does not continue in the infinity of that which overwhelms it. This is our doctrine, which does not, as

> Eunomius charges against it, preach a plurality of Christs, but the union of the man with the Divinity.

Gregory antedates the Christological crisis of the next century and so we should not judge him by developments of which he was ignorant. However, it is clear that he affirms both the unity of Christ's person and the integrity of the two natures. The natures are neither confused nor separated. Moreover, the eternal Son is the person who assumes the humanity; the latter is invested with the honour and glory of the Son who assumed it. This was to be the basis of the Christological settlement of the fifth and sixth centuries, and would underlie the Eastern doctrine of deification as the centuries progressed.

Gregory of Nazianzus

Gregory held the Trinity to be absolutely basic to the whole of theology. It is the Christian doctrine of God. He said on more than one occasion, 'But when I say God, I mean Father, Son, and Holy Ghost.'[30]

Generation concerns the relations of the persons, not the divine essence

The doctrine of the Trinity, as it was being forged in the fourth century, entailed huge questions about the relations between the three trinitarian persons. Eunomius argued that talk of the Son's being begotten, or generated, by the Father required a beginning of existence for him. If it was held that the Son is of the same being as the Father, then he must share the Father's characteristic of being unbegotten. Gregory countered this argument by pointing out that the generation of the Son by the Father is a matter involving the relations between them, and so does not impinge on the divine essence. Hence the Father is unbegotten and the Son begotten:

> But, they say, if the Son is the same as the Father in respect of essence, then if the Father is unbegotten, the Son must be so likewise. Quite so – if the essence of God consists in being unbegotten; and so he would be a strange mixture, begottenly unbegotten. If, however, the difference is outside the essence, how

---

30. *Oration 38 on the Theophany* 8 (also *Oration 45, the Second Oration on Easter* 4). Quotations of Gregory's orations are from *NPNF*, 2nd series, vol. 7.

> can you be so certain in speaking of this? . . . Is it not evident that our enquiry into the nature of the essence of God, if we make it, will have personality absolutely unaffected?[31]

In the final analysis, Gregory insisted, in contrast to Eunomius' rationalism, that generation and procession are both matters beyond us. We cannot give a description of what they respectively entail; to do this we would have to be God, and to try to do so would invite madness. He considers the ineffability of generation and procession: 'What then is procession? Do you tell me what is the unbegottenness of the Father, and I will explain to you the physiology of the generation of the Son and the procession of the Spirit, and we shall both of us be frenzy-stricken for prying into the mystery of God.'[32]

The relations of the Father and the Son

What we can say, according to Gregory, is that the personal names of the three make known their relations to one another. They are not to be understood after the manner of human relations, in which a man becomes a father and a son begins to be. Instead, they denote identity of nature and signify a certain relation between them. Thus the Son is so called because he is identical in being to the Father, of precisely the same nature. At the same time, the name denotes an order between the two in which the Son, according to his personal relations, is of the Father:

> the Father is not a name either of an essence or an action, most clever sirs. But it is the name of the relation in which the Father stands to the Son, and the Son to the Father. For as with us these names make known a genuine and intimate relation, so, in the case before us too, they denote an identity of nature between him that is begotten and him that begets.[33]
>
> In my opinion he is called Son because he is identical to the Father in essence; and not only for this reason, but also because he is of him. And he is called Only-begotten, not because he is the only Son and of the Father alone, and only a Son; but also because the manner of his Sonship is peculiar to himself and not shared by bodies.[34]

---

31. *Oration 29 on the Son* 12.
32. *Oration 31 on the Holy Spirit* 8.
33. *Oration 29 on the Son* 16.
34. *Oration 30 on the Son* 20.

The Father and the Son are eternally Father and Son

These relations are eternal. They did not begin to be at some point but always were and are. The Father is eternally the Father, and so is always with the Word: 'There never was a time when he was without the Word, or when he was not the Father, or when he was not true, or not wise, or not powerful, or devoid of life, or of splendour, or of goodness.'[35]

The one and the three

That God is triune does not mean that he is divisible into three. He is one being, the three persons each and together fully God. There are no degrees of deity:

> To us there is one God, for the Godhead is One, though we believe in three persons. For one is not more and another less God; nor is one before and another after; nor are they divided in will or parted in power; nor can you find here any of the qualities of divisible things; but the Godhead is, to speak concisely, undivided in separate persons; and there is one mingling of light, as it were of three suns joined to each other. When then we look at the Godhead, or that first cause, or the monarchia, that which we conceive is one; but when we look at the persons in whom the Godhead dwells, and at those who timelessly and with equal glory have their being from the first cause – there are three whom we worship.[36]

In a passage that Calvin in his *Institutes* said 'vastly delights me', from Gregory's *Oration 40 on Holy Baptism* 41, Gregory spells out brilliantly the equal ultimacy of God as one and as three. We note first that each person is God in himself, obviating any idea that the deity of the Son and the Spirit is derived from the Father. Secondly, entailed in this is the idea of the complete mutual indwelling of the three. Thirdly, his method of refocusing from the unity of God to the Trinity of persons and back again, knowledge of the one and the three coincident, is a vital principle:

> This I give you to share, and to defend all your life, the one Godhead and power, found in the three in unity, and comprising the three separately; not unequal, in substances or natures, neither increased nor diminished by superiorities or inferiorities; in every respect equal, in every respect the same; just as the beauty and the greatness of the heavens is one; the infinite conjunction of three infinite

35. *Oration 29 on the Son* 17.
36. *Oration 31 on the Holy Spirit* 14.

ones, each God when considered in himself; as the Father, so the Son; as the Son so the Holy Spirit; the three one God when contemplated together; each God because consubstantial; one God because of the monarchia. No sooner do I conceive of the one than I am illumined by the splendour of the three; no sooner do I distinguish them than I am carried back to the one. When I think of any one of the three I think of him as the whole, and my eyes are filled, and the greater part of what I am thinking escapes me. I cannot grasp the greatness of that one so as to attribute a greater greatness to the rest. When I contemplate the three together, I see but one torch, and cannot divide or measure out the undivided light.

No illustrations possible for the Trinity

There are no illustrations of this in creation. Each time such an example is cited, Gregory confesses, it falls short of an accurate depiction of the Trinity. An image or illustration may highlight a particular aspect of God as he has revealed himself, but at other points it will lead us astray:

> I have very carefully considered this matter in my own mind, and have looked at it in every point of view, in order to find some illustration of this most important subject, but I have been unable to discover anything on earth with which to compare the nature of the Godhead. For even if I did happen upon some tiny likeness it escaped me for the most part, and left me down below with my example.[37]

> In a word, there is nothing which presents a standing point in my mind in these illustrations from which to consider the object which I am trying to represent to myself, unless one may indulgently accept one point of the image while rejecting the rest. Finally, then, it seems best to me to let the images and the shadows go, as being deceitful and very far short of the truth.[38]

Faith and reason

These factors, the incomprehensibility of God's being and the inadequacy of humanly derived knowledge to lead us to a right understanding of God, were both unacceptable to Eunomius and his supporters, who had a positive view of the capabilities of the human mind. For Gregory, Eunomius risked undermining the gospel, which requires faith and the work of the Holy Spirit. Gregory concludes with a shot across the bows of the rationalists:

---

37. Ibid. 31.
38. Ibid. 33.

> When we leave off believing, and protect ourselves by mere strength of argument, and destroy the claim the Holy Spirit has upon our faith by questionings, . . . what is the result? The weakness of the argument appears to belong to the mystery; and thus elegance of language makes void the cross, as Paul also taught.[39]

Biblical language concerning the lowliness of the Son

Gregory tackles the biblical language about the Son, some of which stresses his humanity, weakness and lowliness. These were cited by Eunomius as reasons to believe that the Son was lesser than the Father. On the contrary, Gregory argues, these passages simply highlight Jesus' human lowliness, his incarnation, without which we could not be saved. Christ was always God; in the incarnation he added human nature for our sake:

> What is lofty you are to apply to the Godhead, and to that nature in him which is superior to sufferings and incorporeal; but all that is lowly to the composite condition of him who for your sake made himself of no reputation and was incarnate.[40]

> What he was he continued to be; what he was not he took to himself . . . While his inferior nature, the humanity, became God, because it was united to God, and became one person because the higher nature prevailed . . . in order that I too might be made God as he is made man. He was born – but he had been begotten: he was born of a woman – but she was a virgin. The first is human, the second divine. In his human nature he had no father, but also in his divine nature no mother.[41]

Here we have the seeds of the later Christological settlement. The person of Christ is one; deity was not abandoned but humanity was added. This was for our salvation, for our deification depends on the assumption of human nature by the Son of God.

The Holy Spirit and deification

This is the point at which the work of the Holy Spirit is so important, in Gregory's view. How could we be deified if the Spirit was less than God; since deification must, by definition, be a work of God, and since the Spirit is the one who makes us to partake of the divine nature, it follows that he is of the status of God, one with the Father and the Son:

---

39. *Oration 29 on the Son* 21.
40. Ibid. 18.
41. Ibid. 19.

> If he is not from the beginning, he is in the same rank with myself, even though a little before me; for we are both parted from Godhead by time. If he is the same rank with myself, how can he make me God, or join me with the Godhead?[42]

> For if he is not to be worshipped, how can he deify me by baptism? but if he is to be worshipped, surely he is an object of adoration, and if an object of adoration he must be God; the one is linked to another, a truly golden and saving chain. And indeed from the Spirit comes our new birth, and from the new birth our new creation, and from the new creation our deeper knowledge of the dignity of him from whom it is derived.[43]

Confusion about the identity of the Holy Spirit

The situation in the 360s and 370s was quite confused, Gregory tells us. There were a variety of opinions on the identity of the Spirit, and some preferred to take a non-committal position on the grounds that they did not want to go beyond Scripture:

> But of the wise men amongst ourselves, some have conceived of him as an activity, some as a creature, some as God; and some have been uncertain what to call him, out of reverence for Scripture, they say, as though it did not make the matter clear either way. And therefore they neither worship him, nor treat him with dishonour, but take up a neutral position, or rather a very miserable one, with respect to him.[44]

The deity of the Holy Spirit

However, Gregory has no such qualms. Where Basil had been allusive about the Spirit's identity, although the evidence is overwhelming that he believed him to be God, Gregory is unequivocal: 'What then? Is the Spirit God? Most certainly. Well then, is he consubstantial? Yes, if he is God.'[45]

The Holy Spirit and prayer

Eunomius and his followers pointed to the absence of biblical references to prayer to the Holy Spirit. This, so the argument ran, proved that he was a lesser being than God. If he were God, it would be clear that there were examples of

---

42. *Oration 31 on the Holy Spirit* 4.
43. Ibid. 28.
44. Ibid. 5.
45. Ibid. 10.

prayer being made to him and worship offered to him. Gregory will have none of it; all our prayers, he insists, are made in the Spirit, while Jesus teaches that true worship is to be offered in him:

> But, he says, who in ancient or modern times ever worshipped the Spirit? Who ever prayed to him? Where is it written that we ought to worship him or pray to him . . .?
>
> . . . for the present it will suffice to say that it is the Spirit in whom we worship, and in whom we pray. For Scripture says, God is a Spirit, and they that worship him must worship him in Spirit and in truth . . . Therefore to adore or to pray to the Spirit seems to me to be simply himself offering prayer or adoration to himself.[46]

Scripture and tradition

Another issue was the paucity of references to the Holy Spirit in comparison with those to the Son and to God as the Father. Why was this so? If he were divine, so Gregory's opponents argued, we should surely find plenty of evidence in the Bible to prove this. They demanded proof texts in support:

> They then who are angry with us on the ground that we are bringing in a strange or interpolated God, viz: – the Holy Ghost, and who fight so very hard for the letter, should know that they are afraid where no fear is; and I would have them clearly understand that their love for the letter is but a cloak for their impiety.[47]

> Over and over again you turn upon us the silence of Scripture. But that it is not a strange doctrine, nor an afterthought, but acknowledged and plainly set forth by the ancients and many of our own day, is already demonstrated by many persons who have treated of this subject, and who have handled the Holy Scriptures, not with indifference or as a mere pastime, but have gone beneath the letter and looked into the inner meaning, and have been deemed worthy to see the hidden beauty, and have been irradiated by the light of knowledge.[48]

This may come as a surprise, perhaps a shock, to some readers. It appears that here the approach taken by Eunomius was a form of biblical fundamentalism. The demand was for chapter and verse from the Bible to prove the point. In contrast, Gregory refuses to play this game. The truth, he says, lies 'beneath the

46. Ibid. 12.
47. Ibid. 3.
48. Ibid. 21.

letter' with 'the inner meaning' of Scripture. Behind this claim lay the events at the Council of Nicaea in AD 325. There it was determined to answer Arius with biblical language. However, Arius and his supporters could agree with the biblical expression that the Son was 'from God'; they simply interpreted it differently from the way the orthodox did. As a result, the council searched for terms that could give expression to 'the sense of Scripture', although they were not to be found in the Bible itself. The dispute was, in the first place, about the meaning of biblical language and required other terms by which its inherent meaning could be brought to expression. Ironically, and with brilliance, Gregory after disposing of this argument, brings his oration to its clinching denouement, with a barrage of evidence from the Bible, overwhelming his opponents with a dazzling tour de force!

Development of revelation of the Trinity in the history of redemption

At this point, Gregory introduces an ingenious argument from progressive revelation. God has revealed himself to us gradually rather than all at once. The reason for this is that people would not have been able to understand it if he had made known everything at an early stage. As the history of redemption unfolded, so, bit by bit, did God reveal who he is:

> For the matter stands thus. The Old Testament proclaimed the Father openly, and the Son more obscurely. The New manifested the Son, and suggested the deity of the Spirit. Now the Spirit himself dwells among us, and supplies us with a clearer demonstration of himself. For it was not safe, when the Godhead of the Father was not yet acknowledged, plainly to proclaim the Son; nor when that of the Son was not yet received to burden us further (if I may use so bold an expression) with the Holy Ghost; lest perhaps people might, like men loaded with food beyond their strength, and presenting eyes as yet too weak to bear it to the sun's light, risk the loss even of that which was within the reach of their powers, but that by gradual additions . . . the light of the Trinity might shine upon the more illuminated.[49]

Criticial evaluation

The contribution of the Cappadocians to the church can hardly be exaggerated. Foremost in significance is, of course, their role in the resolution of the trinitarian controversy of the fourth century. This had wracked the church for

---

49. Ibid. 26.

decades; its settlement was indispensable for the future progress of the gospel. In the course of their work on this matter they, individually and together, brought about a number of positive developments.

First came the simplification of language and its emancipation from a captivity to philosophical terminology. Basil took the lead here. What he did was to define *ousia* and *hypostasis* clearly, words that had meant different things to different people and had usually been understood in the light of their prior use in Greek philosophy. The Cappadocians used the language but stretched it to give it new meaning derived from the Christian gospel. As a result, they enabled the church to think clearly about how God is both one and three. Since the worship and service of God is integral to the Christian faith, the worth of this contribution is immense.

Secondly, the Cappadocians had a consistent stress on the incomprehensibility of God, with a concomitant restriction of the autonomy of human reason. Whereas Eunomius believed that the human mind retained the ability to think very much as God thinks, the Cappadocians knew that God infinitely transcends his creation. Therefore, it is impossible to encompass him by our own thought. In himself, as he is, he is beyond knowledge. Yet we can know him, as he has chosen to reveal himself to us, on our own level, in his attributes and actions, and in the incarnation of his Son. In this they were striking a blow against the rationalism that lies at the root of all heretical developments that occur in the church.

Thirdly, the Cappadocians' theology was rooted in the worship of the church. That is where Basil was brought into the argument. It is no accident that one of the main liturgies in Orthodoxy is the Liturgy of St Basil. This is where theology, especially the theology of God, to be true to itself, must be rooted. As such, the Cappadocians' interests were driven by prayer and worship, and connected integrally to salvation. One of the key issues was how the Holy Spirit could be anything other than God if we are baptized into the one name of the Father, the Son and the Holy Spirit. Following this was the kindred question of how the Spirit could deify us if he were not himself God. In short, philosophy was subdued and put to the service of salvation.

Fourthly, the three Cappadocians are a great example of being steadfast for the truth in the midst of opposition. Each stood his ground and contended for the gospel despite the challenges that presented themselves.

Fifthly, Basil and his colleagues point the church to the centrality of the Trinity for faith and worship. This is a vital principle that has been largely lost in the Western church, although it has recently been rediscovered and so presents hopeful signs for the future. For Gregory of Nazianzus, any mention of God was a reference to the Father, the Son and the Holy Spirit. Nothing less would suffice. If, as the Westminster Shorter Catechism, question 1, has it, man's chief end is to glorify God and enjoy him for ever, this was a focus that can never wear out its welcome.

Sixthly, the principle of the *homoousios* (identity of being) of the Son and the Spirit with the Father was not only crucial in resolving the controversy of the day but is a central truth of the gospel, stressing that the incarnate Son, Jesus Christ, is God manifest among us, and so we can trust him absolutely in all that he says, knowing that his message of salvation is nothing less than the eternal determination of the living God. Thank God for Gregory of Nazianzus for hammering this home!

Seventhly, Basil's example demonstrates that a concern for the organization of the church is not necessarily opposed to theology but is a proper outflow from it. Theology takes place in the church; it is not an abstract pursuit but is aimed at salvation, which in God's purpose takes place in and through the church.

Eighthly, Basil in particular exemplified a genuine concern for discipline in the Christian life. Both he and his brother wrote at length on ascetic issues. Basil established a monastic rule that had profound long-term effect. While conservative Protestants may dismiss monasticism, in view of its later corruptions, yet at the time it was a powerful force for the development of the faith. Indeed, in the West it was the monks who helped preserve biblical and theological scholarship in the following centuries in which both were threatened by cultural deprivation.

Ninthly, Basil's strong pastoral concern comes out forcibly in his letters. These cover a wide range of matters, as would be expected for one who was so active as a scholar, theologian, bishop, monastic leader, organizer and pastor. It is noteworthy that in a life marked by conflict with theological and ecclesiastical foes, Basil found time to write letters to the bereaved offering biblical comfort at a time of grief.

On the other hand, there have been some negative developments stemming from aspects of Cappadocian theology. Principal among them is the distinction, later to be developed by Gregory Palamas, between the essence and energies of God. This was based on the Cappadocian argument that we cannot know God in his essence but only in his energies. There are, as I see it, two major problems with this idea.

First, from the historical perspective it is at odds with the writings of Athanasius, who argued that there is no external development of the Father's essence.[50] If there is anything about or surrounding him which completes the essence so that when we say 'Father' we do not signify the invisible and

50. Athanasius, *On the Decrees* 22, in J.-P. Migne (ed.), Patrologiae cursus completus: Series graeca, 162 vols. (Paris: Cerf, 1857–86), vol. 25.

incomprehensible essence 'but something about it' (*peri auton*) we would be blaspheming. When we say 'Father', we denote his essence itself. Hence, for Athanasius, when we deal with the Son we are dealing with God himself, not something that surrounds him but is a kind of forecourt to who he is. In this the Cappadocians began a process that has led to a situation in which Orthodox liturgies are full of petitions to God for mercy but have little in the way of assurance of salvation. It is difficult to see how we can be confident of ultimate salvation, if we cannot deal with God but only his attributes. Historically, the Cappadocians set the Greek church on a different trajectory.

Secondly, underlying this is a fatal theological objection. If the essence–energies distinction were valid it would undermine the incarnation. In Jesus Christ, the eternal Son himself takes a human nature in a personal, indissoluble union. That could not be if the Cappadocian thesis were correct, for the assumed humanity could never be united to the Son himself but only to his energies. If it is impossible for humans to know God as he is in himself it would be impossible for the incarnate Christ, qua humanity, to know God – still less be personally united to him. That would be no incarnation. In short, the Cappadocian distinction points inexorably in a Nestorian direction, in which the deity and humanity of Christ are kept at a distance. Despite their consistent concern for salvation, this development took away some of their gloss.

In summary, there is an enormous amount we can learn from the Cappadocians. As with all of us, there are also pitfalls in their thought that we should avoid. A critical but appreciative reading of these important theologians and churchmen will do a great deal of good in our own day.

Bibliography

Primary sources in the primary languages

LAMPE, G. W. H. (ed.), *A Patristic Greek Lexicon* (Oxford: Clarendon, 1961). The lexicon to use with Migne (see below), a huge work that took several decades to produce.

MIGNE, J.-P., Patrologiae cursus completus: Series graeca, 162 vols. (Paris: Cerf, 1857–86). For the works of Basil, vols. 29–32; for Gregory of Nyssa, vols. 44–46; for Gregory of Nazianzus, vols. 35–38. This monumental nineteenth-century series is the major source for the works of the Greek fathers.

Primary sources in English

DALEY, BRIAN, *Gregory of Nazianzus*, The Early Church Fathers (London: Routledge, 2000). Contains translations of some of Gregory's writings, as well as a summary biography and introduction to his output.

MEREDITH, ANTHONY, *Gregory of Nyssa*, The Early Church Fathers (London: Routledge, 1999). Provides an introduction and English translations from a variety of Gregory's works.

QUASTEN, JOHANNES, *Patrology*. Vol. 3: *The Golden Age of Greek Patristic Literature from the Council of Nicea to the Council of Chalcedon* (Westminster, MD: Christian Classics, 1992), pp. 203–301. An invaluable source as a springboard for reading in the primary sources.

SCHAFF, PHILIP, *A Select Library of the Nicene and Post-Nicene Fathers of the Christian Church*, 2nd series. Vol. 5: *Gregory of Nyssa: Dogmatic Treatises* (Edinburgh: T. & T. Clark, 1988). The Nicene and Post-Nicene Fathers English translations of select works of the Cappadocians are as good a place as any to begin. While the translations reek of an earlier era than ours, these are available both online and in hard-copy format.

—, *A Select Library of the Nicene and Post-Nicene Fathers of the Christian Church*, 2nd series. Vol. 7: *Select Orations of Saint Gregory Nazianzen* (Edinburgh: T. & T. Clark, 1989).

SCHAFF, PHILIP, and Henry Wace, *A Select Library of the Nicene and Post-Nicene Fathers of the Christian Church*, 2nd series. Vol. 8: *St Basil: Letters and Select Works* (Edinburgh: T. & T. Clark, 1989).

VAGGIONE, R. P., *Eunomius: The Extant Works* (Oxford: Clarendon, 1987). Has an English translation, text and introduction of Eunomius.

WILLIAMS, FREDERICK, and Lionel Wickham (tr.), *St. Gregory of Nazianzus: On God and Christ* (Crestwood, NY: St Vladimir's Seminary Press, 2002). Has a good translation of Gregory of Nazianzus' five theological orations (27–31) and his letters to Cledonius.

Secondary sources

Background to the contribution of the Cappadocians to the trinitarian controversy

AYRES, LEWIS, *Nicaea and Its Legacy: An Approach to Fourth-Century Trinitarian Theology* (New York: Oxford University Press, 2004). A fine work that must not be missed, arguing that Augustine was in basic harmony with the work of the Cappadocians, contrary to the bulk of twentieth-century scholarship.

HANSON, R. P. C., 'The Doctrine of the Trinity Achieved in 381', *Scottish Journal of Theology* 36 (1983), pp. 41–57.

—, *The Search for the Christian Doctrine of God: The Arian Controversy 318–381* (Edinburgh: T. & T. Clark, 1988). This monumental volume puts the Cappadocians into a wider perspective.

KELLY, J. N. D., *Early Christian Creeds* (London: Longman, 1972). For the eventual creed approved at the first Council of Constantinople and the issues surrounding it.

—, *Early Christian Doctrines* (London: Adam & Charles Black, 1968). On the Arian crisis in general.

—, 'The Nicene Creed: A Turning Point', *Scottish Journal of Theology* 36 (1983), pp. 29–39.

LETHAM, ROBERT, *The Holy Trinity: In Scripture, History, Theology, and Worship* (Phillipsburg: Presbyterian & Reformed, 2004). Also considers the Cappadocians against the background of the fourth-century trinitarian crisis.

PRESTIGE, G. L., *God in Patristic Thought* (London: SPCK, 1952). An older book that should still be considered.

YOUNG, FRANCES, *From Nicea to Chalcedon: A Guide to the Literature and Its Background* (London: SCM, 1983). Another standard introductory work.

On Arianism after Arius and, in particular, Eunomius

BARNES, M. R., 'The Background and Use of Eunomius' Causal Language', in M. R. Barnes (ed.), *Arianism after Arius: Essays on the Development of the Fourth Century Trinitarian Conflicts* (Edinburgh: T. & T. Clark, 1993), pp. 217–236. In the same volume, Barnes also contributes an important introduction (pp. xiii–xvii).

KEITH, G. A., 'Our Knowledge of God: The Relevance of the Debate between Eunomius and the Cappadocians', *TynBul* 41(1988), pp. 60–88. A useful introduction to the question.

KOPECEK, T. A., *A History of Neo-Arianism*, 2 vols. (Cambridge, MA: Philadelphia Patristic Foundation, 1979).

LORENZ, R., *Arius Judaizans? Untersuchungen zur Dogmengeschichtlichen Einordnung des Arius* (Göttingen: Vandenhoeck & Ruprecht, 1979).

VAGGIONE, R. P., *Eunomius of Cyzicus and the Nicene Revolution* (Oxford: Oxford University Press, 2000). Indispensable for a study of Eunomius in context and should be read in conjunction with Vaggione's translation of Eunomius' extant works (see above).

WILES, M., 'Attitudes to Arius in the Arian controversy', in Barnes, *Arianism after Arius*, pp. 31–43.

WILLIAMS, ROWAN, *Arius: Heresy and Tradition* (London: Darton Longman & Todd, 1987). A standard work on Arianism, which should be consulted. Hanson, *Search for the Christian Doctrine of God* (see above). From a contrasting perspective, another standard work.

—, 'The Logic of Arianism', *Journal of Theological Studies* 34 (1983), pp. 56–81.

On the Cappadocians in general

MEREDITH, ANTHONY, *The Cappadocians* (Crestwood, NY: St Vladimir's Seminary Press, 1995). A good place to start for a concise survey of the three and their contribution.

On Basil

DRECOLL, V. H., *Die Entwicklung der Trinitätslehre des Basilius von Cäsarea* (Göttingen: Vandenhoeck & Ruprecht, 1996).

HILDEBRAND, STEPHEN M., *The Trinitarian Theology of Basil of Caesarea: A Synthesis of Greek Thought and Biblical Truth* (Washington, DC: Catholic University of America Press,

2007). Considers the biblical foundations of Basil's trinitarianism in the context of his straddling the worlds of the Bible and Greek culture.

LARSON, MARK J., 'A Re-examination of De Spiritu Sancto: Saint Basil's Bold Defence of the Spirit's Deity', *Scottish Bulletin of Evangelical Theology* 19 (2001), pp. 65–84.

RIST, J. M., 'Basil's "Neoplatonism": Its Background and Nature', in P. J. Fedwisk (ed.), *Basil of Caesarea: Christian, Humanist, Ascetic: A Sixteen-Hundredth Anniversary Symposium* (Toronto: Pontifical Institute of Medieval Studies, 1981), pp. 137–220.

ROUSSEAU, PHILIP, *Basil of Caesarea* (Berkeley: University of California Press, 1994). A superb biography.

On Gregory of Nyssa

BARNES, MICHEL RENÉ, *The Power of God: Δύναμις in Gregory of Nyssa's Trinitarian Theology* (Washington, DC: Catholic University of America Press, 2001). Focuses on Gregory's use of power.

LAIRD, MARTIN, *Gregory of Nyssa and the Grasp of Faith: Union, Knowledge and Divine Presence*, Oxford Early Christian Studies (Oxford: Oxford University Press, 2007). An important work.

LUDLOW, MORWENNA, *Universal Salvation: Eschatology in the Thought of Gregory of Nyssa and Karl Rahner*, Oxford Theological Monographs (Oxford: Oxford University Press, 2009).

MEREDITH, ANTHONY, 'The Idea of God in Gregory of Nyssa', in H. R. Drobner (ed.), *Studien zur Gregor von Nyssa und der Christlichen Spätantike* (Leiden: Brill, 1990), pp. 127–147.

RADDE-GALLWITZ, ANDREW, *Basil of Caesarea, Gregory of Nyssa and the Transformation of Divine Simplicity*, Oxford Early Christian Studies (Oxford: Oxford University Press, 2009). Argues that the two Cappadocians used divine simplicity not from philosophical interests but soteriological ones, as an expression of the consistency of God.

On Gregory of Nazianzus

BEELEY, CHRISTOPHER, *Gregory of Nazianzus on the Trinity and the Knowledge of God: In your Light Shall we See Light*, Oxford Studies in Historical Theology (Oxford: Oxford University Press, 2008). An extensive scholarly account of Nazianzus' trinitarianism, arguing that this is the heart of his entire theology.

MCGUCKIN, JOHN A., *St Gregory of Nazianzus: An Intellectual Biography* (Crestwood, NY: St Vladimir's Seminary Press, 2001). A full-length placement of Gregory in the cultural and intellectual context of his day, indispensable as a basis for work on his writings.

REUTHER, ROSEMARY, *Gregory of Nazianzus: Rhetor and Philosopher* (Oxford: Oxford University Press, 1969). Required reading for serious work.

On the trinitarian crisis

AYRES, *Nicaea and Its Legacy* (see above).

DAVIS, LEO Donald, *The First Seven Ecumenical Councils (325–787)* (Collegeville, MN: Liturgical, 1990).

HANSON, *Search for the Christian Doctrine of God* (see above).

HARRISON, VERNA, 'Perichoresis in the Greek Fathers', *St Vladimir's Theological Quarterly* 35 (1991), pp. 53–65.

KANNENGIESSER, CHARLES, *Arius and Athanasius: Two Alexandrian Theologians* (Aldershot: Variorum, 1991).

KELLY, *Early Christian Creeds* (see above).

—, *Early Christian Doctrines* (see above).

LIENHARD, J. T., 'Ousia and Hypostasis: The Cappadocian Settlement and the Theology of "One Hypostasis"', in S. T. Davis *et al.* (eds.), *The Trinity: An Interdisciplinary Symposium on the Trinity* (Oxford: Oxford University Press, 1999), pp. 99–121.

LOHR, W. A., 'A Sense of Tradition: The Homoiousion Church Party', in Barnes (ed.), *Arianism after Arius*, pp. 81–100.

MARGERIE, BERTRAND DE, S. J., *The Christian Trinity in History*, tr. E. J. Fortman, S. J. (Petersham: MA: St Bede's, 1982).

O'CARROLL, MICHAEL, CSSp, *Trinitas: A Theological Encyclopedia of the Holy Trinity* (Collegeville, MN: Liturgical, 1987).

STEAD, G. C., *Divine Substance* (Oxford: Clarendon, 1977).

STUDER, BASIL, *Trinity and Incarnation: The Faith of the Early Church*, ed. M. Westerhoff and A. Louth (Collegeville, MN: Liturgical, 1993).

On deification

MCGUCKIN, JOHN A., 'The Strategic Adaptation of Deification in the Cappadocians', in M. J. Christensen and J. A. Wittung (eds.), *Partakers of the Divine Nature: The History and Development of Deification in the Christian Traditions* (Grand Rapids: Baker Academic, 2007), pp. 95–131. An important study in how the two Gregories received and adapted the inheritance passed on from Origen. He argues that the primary driving force was not Platonism but the Christian mission.

RUSSELL, NORMAN, *The Doctrine of Deification in the Greek Patristic Tradition* (Oxford: Oxford University Press, 2004). A brilliant book that explores the variety of interpretations of *theosis* in the Greek fathers. It is an indispensable starting point for a consideration of a topic that has come to the forefront of attention in recent years.

6. AUGUSTINE

Bradley G. Green

Augustine: a brief survey of his life

Augustine, the most prominent 'Latin' or 'Western' church father, sowed the seeds of virtually the entire Western theological edifice that has been built from his day forward. Gregory the Great once described his own work as a 'despicable little trickle', but could speak of the 'deep torrents' of the work of Augustine and Ambrose.[1] And Henry Chadwick is surely right when he speaks of Augustine as 'the greatest figure of Christian Antiquity'.[2]

Augustine was born in the small town of Thagaste in northern Africa on 13 November 354 (present day Souk-Ahras, in Algeria). African by birth and Roman by culture,[3] Augustine's parents had a decisive influence upon him. His father, Patricius, although a man of modest means, was eager to provide for his son's education. Augustine's mother, Monica, has become the paradigmatic concerned mother, praying earnestly for her son's salvation during his years

1. As quoted in R. A. Markus, *The End of Ancient Christianity* (Cambridge: Cambridge University Press, 1990), p. 11.
2. Henry Chadwick, in his foreword to Serge Lancel, *St Augustine*, tr. Antonia Nevill (London: SCM, 2002), p. 14.
3. This phrase is taken from ch. 1 of Lancel, *St Augustine*.

of spiritual wandering and profligacy. However, some have pointed out that she also had grand ambitions for her son.

Augustine received his first formal (roughly 'grammar' school) education in Madauros (near Thagaste). After a year of idleness in Thagaste (369–70) he moved to Carthage for further study (370–373). During this year he read Cicero's *Hortensius*, which inspired Augustine to love wisdom and pursue it. But it was also during his time in Carthage that Augustine 'joined' the Manichean sect, and spent some nine years wrestling with their claims.[4] Augustine's wrestling with Manicheism will be dealt with more fully below, but briefly (and perhaps too simply), Manicheism was a dualistic and Gnostic system of belief. Spirit and Matter, Good and Evil, Light and Dark – all once separate from one another – had been combined due to the machinations of the Prince of Darkness, who had tried to invade the kingdom of Light. The human state was one where physicality (Material) and immateriality (Spirit) were joined, and physicality/materiality were seen as explicitly evil. Through a secret *gnōsis* (knowledge) the initiate could become aware – over time – of his true state or being. God was at work to rescue or liberate the Light embedded in Darkness.[5]

During his time at Carthage Augustine took a mistress, with whom he remained from 372 to 385. Together they had a son, Adeodatus ('given by God'), born in 372. After spending a year in Rome (383–4), Augustine went to Milan as a teacher of rhetoric and met Ambrose, the bishop of Milan. Ambrose's teaching and preaching influenced Augustine greatly. Besides the bishop there was an influential intellectual circle of friends (including Flavius Manlius Theodorus) in Milan who exercised a significant influence on Augustine. It is also in Milan that Augustine was exposed to the *Libri platonicorum* (the books of the Platonists). Most likely mainly writings of Plotinus, Augustine wrote that he was 'on fire' reading these books, and that – similar to the reading of *Hortensius* – reading these books further inspired him in his quest for the truth.[6] In 385, while in Milan, Monica arranged a more 'suitable' marriage for Augustine, one which would be more conducive to a successful career. Augustine was compelled to send his mistress away – back to North Africa, certainly a painful decision. Adeodatus stayed with Augustine, and the marriage planned by Monica did not take place. In fact, Augustine never married.

---

4. 'Join' because in 373 Augustine became a 'hearer', someone who associated with the Manicheans and listened to their teachings but was not fully bound to the group.
5. Manicheism had its own cosmogony, one that sought to incorporate all other explanations of reality. For a helpful summary see Lancel, *St Augustine*, pp. 31–36.
6. *The Happy Life* 1.4 and *Against the Sceptics* 2.5. Cf. Lancel, *St Augustine*, p. 84.

Augustine's conversion is perhaps the most famous in history. Having wrestled with the truth claims of the Christian faith, and with his own desires (as I recount below in some detail), Augustine was walking in a garden in Milan in August of 386. He heard a voice from a nearby house ('of a boy or girl I do know not') calling *tolle lege, tolle lege* (take read, take read; see in more detail below). Finding a Bible, Augustine turned to Romans 13 and read, 'Not in riots and drunken parties, not in eroticism and indecencies, not in strife and rivalry, but put on the Lord Jesus Christ and make no provision for the flesh in its lusts' (Rom. 13:13–15). As he recounts in *Confessions*, 'I neither wished nor needed to read further. At once, with the last words of this sentence, it was as if a light of relief from all anxiety flooded into my heart. All the shadows of doubt were dispelled.'[7]

Following his conversion Augustine resigned his post as professor of rhetoric, and with his mother, brother (Navigus) and some friends decided to 'retreat' to Cassiciacum (a small town outside Milan) during the autumn of 386. During that time he and his compatriots engaged in discussion and debate, and three key works came out of that period (*Against the Sceptics*, *The Happy Life* and *On Order*). Twenty-first-century readers might see this as an academic seminar led at someone's house by a very intelligent friend or relative – Augustine!

Returning to Milan in early 387 Augustine was baptized by Ambrose (April 387). His life had changed radically during his two or so years in Milan, and Augustine determined to return to Africa. Thus, in summer or early autumn of 387, Augustine and his family and friends left Milan to go to Africa. Monica died en route in Ostia, where the party had stopped for a while.

For a variety of reasons Augustine and his fellow-travellers returned to Rome (instead of going to Africa), and by then it was the autumn of 387. Here Augustine wrote such anti-Manichean polemics as *Morals of the Catholic Church* and *Morals of the Manicheans*. He also wrote *The Greatness of the Soul* and (parts of) his *On Free Will* during this stay in Rome. By the autumn of 388 it was time to return to Africa, and Augustine and his son, Adeodatus, did so.

During this time in Africa Augustine wrote such works as *On True Religion* and *The Teacher*. He was 'forced' in 391 to become a priest of Hippo (he was not yet the bishop, for Valerius would remain in that position until 395/396, when Augustine was ordained as bishop of Hippo). While visiting Hippo (in North Africa, some forty miles north of Thagaste) in order to exhort a friend to the monastic life, Valerius told the congregation he needed assistance. The people immediately ordained the unwilling Augustine as bishop.

---

7. *Confessions* 8.29. All quotations from *Confessions* are from Henry Chadwick's translation (Oxford: Oxford University Press, 1991).

He was somewhat overcome with all that being a bishop entailed. He also probably mourned that his ongoing hope of living in a monastic/study community would not – at least for the present – come to pass. During his years as bishop he engaged in a number of key theological and ecclesiastical struggles, most of which are 'chronicled' in his vast literary output: the Donatist controversy, the lengthy conflict with Pelagianism, lingering Manicheism and his monumental *The City of God*, in which he 'responds' to certain arguments linking the sack of Rome in 410 to the empire's acceptance and adoption of Christianity (see below).[8] Since much of the rest of this chapter summarizes Augustine's key theological insights, I will deal later with such issues as Donatism, Pelagianism, Manicheism and his response in *The City of God* to pagans.

As Serge Lancel has written, 'Augustine was not an "egghead" theologian, poring over texts.'[9] However, while he certainly did 'pore over texts', he was not a cloistered scholar. Rather, much of Augustine's time was spent refereeing squabbles, managing different personalities in his realm and navigating the world of ecclesiastical skirmishes – some of great importance and others of lesser importance. Nonetheless, as one spends more and more time with Augustine the pastor one sees clearly that his pastoral ministry was always theologically driven, and that his ministry was animated by theological concerns.

Augustine engaged in pastoral ministry and theological writing – much of it polemical – until the end of his days. His last major theological skirmish was related to Pelagianism, this time in response to Julian of Eclanum. Julian was erudite and hostile to Augustine, and the conflict lasted the last twelve years of Augustine's life.[10]Augustine spent the rest of his days in Hippo serving as bishop, and his writings were voluminous and wide-ranging. He lived to be seventy-six years of age, dying in 430. He had certain psalms copied and hung on the walls in the room where he lay dying. According to Possidus, Augustine 'wept freely and constantly' as he read the sacred words.[11] Augustine died without a will, for, as Possidius notes, except for his books (left

---

8. I have put 'responds' in quotes because whereas in his writings against the Manicheans, the Donatists and Pelagians he was countering specific persons and arguments, *The City of God* appears to have been directed towards a more loose collection of arguments by generally unspecified persons.
9. Lancel, *St Augustine*, p. 440.
10. Lancel refers to Julian as 'this hotheaded youngster who could have been his son' (*St Augustine*, p. 418).
11. Possidus, *The Life of Saint Augustine*, tr. Herbert T. Weiskotten, Christian Roman Empire Series, vol. 6 (Merchantville, NJ: Evolution, 2008), p. 57.

for the church at Hippo) Augustine had no possessions.[12] Let us now turn to a more detailed look at the thought of this greatest church father of the West.

The theology and theologizing of Augustine

God

How should we talk about God?

Augustine is aware that one must be humble and careful when speaking about God.[13] Indeed, as Augustine continues:

> In any case, when we think about God the trinity we are aware that our thoughts are quite inadequate to their object, and incapable of grasping him as he is; even by men of the calibre of the apostle Paul he can only be seen, as it says, *like a puzzling reflection in a mirror* (1 Cor. 13:12).[14]

And ultimately one must begin one's thinking and speaking about God in prayer, in hope that one will speak rightly and truthfully about God.[15]

Augustine wants to approach God correctly: 'there is no effrontery in burning to know, out of faithful piety, the divine and inexpressible truth that is above us, provided the mind is fired by the grace of our creator and savior, and not inflated by arrogant confidence in its own powers.'[16]

Language used at the human level cannot simply be simplistically applied to God:

> God does not repent as a human being does, but as God. So too, he is not angry as a human being is or merciful as a human being is or jealous as a human being is, but

12. Ibid.
13. At a few points – mainly here on Augustine's doctrine of God – I have reworked material from my dissertation, now published as *Colin Gunton and the Failure of Augustine: The Theology of Colin Gunton in Light of Augustine* (Eugene: Wipf & Stock, 2010).
14. *Trinity* 5.1. All quotations from *The Trinity* are from *The Works of Saint Augustine: A Translation for the 21st Century*, vol. 11, ed. John E. Rotelle, OSA, tr. Edmund Hill, OP (Hyde Park, NY: New City, 1992).
15. Ibid.
16. Ibid.

> does all things as God. God's repentance does not follow upon a mistake, and the wrath of God does not include the agitation of a mind in turmoil.[17]

The triune God

Augustine was thoroughly trinitarian, for he accepted the doctrine of God as Trinity on the basis of Scripture and tradition:

> The purpose of all the Catholic commentators I have been able to read on the divine books of both testaments, who have written before me on the trinity which God is, has been to teach that according to the scriptures Father and Son and Holy Spirit in the inseparable equality of one substance present a divine unity; and therefore there are not three gods but one God; although indeed the Father has begotten the Son, and therefore he who is the Father is not the Son; and the Son is begotten by the Father, and therefore he who is the Son is not the Father; and the Holy Spirit is neither the Father nor the Son, but only the Spirit of the Father and of the Son, himself coequal to the Father and the Son, and belonging to the threefold unity.[18]

Augustine realizes that the quest for adequate construals and conceptions of God is fraught with difficulty, and the analogies Augustine would soon be discussing should be seen against such trepidation and reticence.[19]

For Augustine, when we *truly* speak of God we have to use substance words. Why? Because whereas *we* (humans) sometimes possess certain characteristics and sometimes do not (I am sometimes kind and sometimes not), God possesses all of who he is all the time:

> The chief point then that we must maintain is that whatever that supreme and divine majesty is called with reference to itself is said substance-wise; whatever it is called with reference to another is said not substance – but relationship-wise; and that such is the force of the expression 'of the same substance' in Father and Son and Holy Spirit, that whatever is said with reference to self about each of them is to be taken as adding up in all three to a singular and not to a plural.[20]

---

17. *Answer to an Enemy of the Law and the Prophets* 40. In *The Works of Saint Augustine: A Translation for the 21st Century*, vol. 1.18, introduction, tr. and notes Roland Teske, SJ, ed. John E. Rotelle, OSA (Hyde Park, NY: New City, 1995).
18. *Trinity* 1.2.7.
19. Cf. *On Christian Doctrine* 1.5. In *The Works of Saint Augustine: A Translation for the 21st Century*, vol. 1.11, introduction, tr. and notes Edmund Hill, OP, ed. John E. Rotelle, OSA (Hyde Park, NY: New City, 1996).
20. Ibid. 5.9.

Augustine's central point here is that Father and Son can in some sense be different without being of different substance. To demonstrate this, Augustine is labouring to show that 'Father' and 'Son', though different words, do not denote different substances. Why? Because the words/titles denote different *relationships* without denoting different substances.

Augustine proceeds to speak of the Holy Spirit, and it is clear that 'making sense' of the Holy Spirit is a bit more difficult.[21] To speak of 'father' and 'son' as terms of relation seems rather normal, but to speak of 'Holy Spirit' as a relationship term seems a bit awkward. The Father is the Father of the Son, and the Son is the Son of the Father. But, while the Holy Spirit is the Holy Spirit of the Father, the Father is not the 'Father' of the Holy Spirit. Augustine struggles with the proper name for, and place of, the Holy Spirit virtually to the end of *The Trinity*.

Augustine, though, happily affirms the co-equality and full deity of the three persons:

> we have demonstrated as briefly as we could the equality of the triad and its one identical substance. So whatever may be the solution of this question, which we have put off for more searching examination, there is nothing now to prevent us from acknowledging the supreme equality of Father, Son, and Holy Spirit.[22]

The external works of the Trinity are undivided

Augustine and the tradition that follows him are credited with the Latin maxim *opera trinitatis ad extra sunt indivisa* (the external works of the Trinity are undivided). That is, all three persons of the Godhead are involved in all that God does 'outside' himself – in relation to the world in terms of creation, redemption and governance/providence:

> For the Catholic faith teaches and believes that this Trinity is so inseparable – and a few holy and blessed men also understand this – that whatever this Trinity does must be thought to be done at the same time by the Father and by the Son and by the Holy Spirit. The Father does not do anything that the Son and the Holy Spirit do not do, nor does the Son do anything that the Father and the Holy Spirit do not do, nor does the Holy Spirit do anything that the Father and the Son do not do.[23]

---

21. Ibid. 5.13.
22. Ibid. 6.10.
23. *Letter 11* (Augustine to Nebridius) 2. In *The Works of Saint Augustine: A Translation for the 21st Century*, vol. 2.1, tr. and notes Roland Teske, SJ, ed. John E. Rotelle,

Augustine affirmed the simplicity of God and the idea that all apparent accidental predicates are actually either substantive or relative predicates. Thus nothing in God 'changes' or is complex, but there are nonetheless things that can be said of God, without being said according to substance (*substantialiter*). Thus when we speak of 'Father' and 'Son', we are speaking in terms of relation, or what can be called 'relative predications'. Edmund Hill summarizes Augustine as follows: 'God is one in respect of substantive predications, yet three in virtue of certain relative predications which, following the scriptural revelation, we make of him.'[24]

If one does not want to say three 'substances', and Augustine does not, perhaps it is best to say three 'persons'. What Augustine writes related to this may sound a bit startling:

> So the only reason, it seems, why we do not call these three together one person, as we call them one being and one God, but say three persons while we never say three Gods or three beings, is that we want to keep at least one word for signifying what we mean by trinity, so that we are not simply reduced to silence when we are asked three what, after we have confessed that there are three.[25]

Simplicity and immutability

Historically, when Christian theologians have spoken of divine 'simplicity', they have essentially meant that God is not a compound being. That is, God is not a bunch of different 'things' brought together to make one 'thing'. Augustine can write about God, 'There is, accordingly, a good which is alone simple, and therefore alone unchangeable, and this is God. By this Good have all others been created, but not simple, and therefore not unchangeable.'[26] Augustine goes on to define simplicity:

> And this Trinity is one God; and none the less simple because a Trinity. For we do not say that the nature of the good is simple, because the Father alone possesses it, or the Son alone, or the Holy Ghost alone; nor do we say, with the Sabellian heretics, that it is only nominally a Trinity, and has no real distinction of persons; but we say it is simple, because

---

OSA (Hyde Park, NY: New City, 2001). Cf. *Handbook on Faith, Hope and Love* 12.38: 'the operations of the Trinity are inseparable' (*opera trinitatis ad extra sunt indivisa*).

24. Edmund Hill, *The Mystery of the Trinity* (London: Geoffrey Chapman, 1985), p. 100.
25. *Trinity* 7.11.
26. *City of God* 11.10. All quotations from *The City of God* are from the translation by Marcus Dods (New York: Modern Library, 1950).

> it is what it has, with the exception of the relation of the persons to one another.[27]

Augustine clearly affirms immutability. He speaks of 'the unchangeable substance of God'.[28] Indeed, 'there is no unchangeable good but the one, true, blessed God; that the things which He made are indeed good because from Him, yet mutable because made not out of Him, but out of nothing'.[29] Likewise, 'For since God is the supreme existence, that is to say, supremely is, and is therefore unchangeable, the things that He made He empowered to be, but not to be supremely like Himself.'[30]

Augustine deals with God's wrath or anger and relates it to God's immutability:

> The anger of God is not a disturbing emotion of His mind, but a judgment by which punishment is inflicted upon sin. His thought and reconsideration also are the unchangeable reason which changes things; for He does not, like man, repent of anything He has done, because in all matters His decision is as inflexible as His prescience is certain.[31]

God and time

Augustine repeatedly and consistently teaches that God is eternal and is Lord over time. Indeed, time is a created reality: 'For, though Himself eternal, and without beginning, yet He caused time to have a beginning; and man, whom He had not previously made, He made in time, not from a new and sudden resolution, but by His unchangeable and eternal design.'[32] Indeed, 'God always has been, and that man, whom He had never made before, He willed to make in time, and this without changing His design and will.'[33]

In *Confessions* Augustine takes up the question 'What was God doing before He created the world?' His answer:

> Before God made heaven and earth, he was not doing anything; for if he was doing or making something, what else would he be doing but creating? And no creature was made before any creature was made. I wish I could know everything that I desire to

---

27. Ibid.
28. Ibid. 11.2.
29. Ibid. 12.1.
30. Ibid. 12.2.
31. Ibid. 15.25.
32. Ibid. 12.14.
33. Ibid.

> know to my own profit with the same certainty with which I know that.[34]

And ultimately for Augustine time itself is a creation of God: 'There was therefore never any time when you had not made anything, because you made time itself.'[35]

God and knowledge

For Augustine, God certainly knows all things. When Augustine quotes from Genesis, 'And God saw that it was good,' he then writes, 'For certainly God did not in the actual achievement of the work first learn that it was good, but, on the contrary, nothing would have been made had it not been first known by Him.'[36]

For God does not know like we know:

> For not in our fashion does He look forward to what is future, nor at what is present, nor back upon what is past; but in a manner quite different and far and profoundly remote from our way of thinking. For He does not pass from this to that by transition of thought, but beholds all things with absolute unchangeableness; so that of those things which emerge in time, the future, indeed, are not yet, and the present are now, and the past no longer are; but all of these are by Him comprehended in His stable and eternal presence.[37]

Augustine, of course, does not see God as being 'in' time. And thus God knows things differently from the way we know things. Augustine writes that it would be a mighty miracle if a mind were to know all things in the way a human mind knows. But God's knowledge of all things is even greater, since God *does* know all things but does *not* know like we humans know:

> But far be it from us to suppose that you, the creator of the universe, creator of souls and bodies, know all things future and past in this fashion! Perish the thought! . . . Nothing can happen to you in your unchangeable eternity, you who are truly the eternal creator of all minds. As you knew heaven and earth in the beginning, without the slightest modification in your knowledge, so too you made heaven and earth in the beginning without any distension in your activity.[38]

---

34. Ibid.
35. *Confessions* 14.17.
36. *City of God* 11.21.
37. Ibid.
38. *Confessions* 31.41.

Creation

The goodness of creation

Given his Manichean background – where creation is *not* ultimately and intrinsically good – Augustine was intent on affirming the goodness of creation. At one point he writes, 'We know, therefore, that we should attribute to the creator, not defects, but natures, but one who wants to resist Mani must say where the defects come from.'[39] In short, if one is to 'resist Mani' – that is, if one is to resist the notion that defects or evil can be attributed to the created order itself – one must provide a coherent account of 'defects' or evil within a Christian construal of reality. And this construal must affirm the existence of an eternal and completely good God who is the creator of all things, and where creation is likewise *completely* good.

Augustine can write of the created order, 'with respect to their own nature . . . the creatures are glorifying to their Artificer'.[40] Augustine can also say, 'All natures, then, inasmuch as they are, and have therefore a rank and species of their own, and a kind of internal harmony, are certainly good. And when they are in the places assigned to them by the order of their nature, they preserve such being as they have received.'[41]

Augustine, in wanting to affirm that God truly is the creator of all, makes recourse to a notion of 'seminal seeds'. Augustine's argument is that, when God created the world, he both created actual 'stuff' – animals, vegetation and so on. But God also created these 'seminal seeds' by which (later in time) 'new' things would come forth. Thus, at some point *after* the original creation, we really do see 'new' creatures, 'new' vegetable life and so on. But when animals reproduce, or when the seeds of a plant lead to the existence of a new plant, there is no *autonomous* creating going on. Rather, God is still the *ultimate* creator, because within humans, and within other living things there exists these 'seminal seeds' *created by God*, and only through these seminal seeds does new life come into being. [42]

---

39. *Against Julian, an Unfinished Book* 4.123. In *The Works of Saint Augustine: A Translation for the 21st Century*, vol. 1.25, introduction, tr. and notes Roland J. Teske, SJ, ed. John E. Rotelle, OSA (Hyde Park, NY: New City, 1999).
40. *City of God* 12.4.
41. Ibid. 12.5.
42. *Trinity* 3.13. Augustine speaks of *rationes seminales* or *causales* in his work *The Literal Interpretation of Genesis* 5, 6.

Creation and time

Augustine's teaching that 'time' began with creation has generally prevailed among Christians. Augustine argues that 'the world was made, not in time, but simultaneously with time'.[43] Indeed, 'Since then, God, in whose eternity is no change at all, is the Creator and Ordainer of time, I do not see how He can be said to have created the world after spaces of time had elapsed, unless it be said that prior to the world there was some creature by whose movement time could pass.'[44] Augustine can write, 'For, though Himself eternal, and without beginning, yet He caused time to have a beginning . . .'[45] Indeed, 'But if they say that the thoughts of men are idle when they conceive infinite places, since there is no place beside the world, we reply that, by the same showing, it is vain to conceive of the past times of God's rest, since there is no time before the world.'[46]

Creation and the goodness and will of God

God knows beforehand that what he is going to create is going to be good. Augustine writes, 'certainly God did not in the actual achievement of the work first learn that it was good, but, on the contrary, nothing would have been made had it not been first known by Him'.[47] That is, God creates out of his goodness. This point is most clearly illustrated from Augustine's chapter on creation in *Confessions* (Book 13). Augustine writes, 'Your creation has its being from the fullness of your goodness.'[48]

Evil as a privation of the good

For Augustine, evil is ultimately a privation of the good, or a *privatio boni.* He writes in one of his anti-Pelagian writings:

> Those things which we call evil are either the defects of good things, which cannot exist anywhere by themselves outside of good things, or they are the punishments of sins, which arise from the beauty of justice. Even the defects bear witness to the goodness of the natures. For what is evil by reason of its defect is good by reason of its nature. A defect is against nature, because it harms a nature, and it would not harm

43. *City of God* 11.6.
44. Ibid.
45. Ibid. 12.14.
46. Ibid. 11.5.
47. Ibid. 11.21.
48. *Confessions* 13.2.2.

> it if it did not lessen its goodness. Therefore, evil is only a privation of good. Thus it never exists except in some good thing, which is not supremely good, for something supremely good, such as God, lasts without corruption or change. Still, evil exists only in something good, because it does harm only by diminishing what is good.[49]

Augustine also writes, 'For evil has no positive nature; but the loss of good has received the name "evil."'[50]

Providence

That God sovereignly rules over all of the created order is manifestly clear in Augustine's writings. He writes, 'that God can never be believed to have left the kingdoms of men, their dominations and servitudes, outside of the laws of His providence'.[51] To deny such providence is indeed foolish: 'For he who denies that all things, which either angels or men can give us, are in the hand of the one Almighty, is a madman.'[52] And God's providence is exhaustive: 'You see, dearly beloved, there is nothing that escapes providence.'[53]

Augustine can even argue that God has sovereignly arranged the various trees – including the wild olive trees and the natural olive trees – to serve as a reminder of how Christians have been brought, or engrafted into, the people of God:

> Divine providence has carefully provided certain trees which visibly exemplify these invisible realities which are incredible for those without faith, but are nonetheless true. After all, why should we not believe that this was the reason why he arranged it so that a wild olive tree is born of a domesticated one? Ought we not to believe that in something created for human use the creator provided and arranged what might serve as an example of the human race?[54]

---

49. *Answer to an Enemy of the Law and the Prophets* 1.5.7.
50. *City of God* 11.9.
51. Ibid. 5.11.
52. Ibid. 10.14.
53. *Sermon 8, On the Plagues of Egypt and the Ten Commandments of the Law*. In *The Works of Saint Augustine: A Translation for the 21st Century*, vol. 3.1, introduction Michele Pellegrino, tr. and notes Edmund Hill, OP, ed. John E. Rotelle, OSA (Hyde Park, NY: New City, 1998).
54. *Marriage and Desire* 19.21. In *The Works of Saint Augustine: A Translation for the 21st Century*, vol. 1.24, introduction, tr. and notes Roland J. Teske, SJ, ed. John E. Rotelle, OSA (Hyde Park, NY: New City, 1998).

For Augustine, one must not only affirm God's providence in terms of God's rule over the (non-human) order of nature,[55] but Christians must affirm that God rules over the lives of people as well. Augustine writes:

> Given all this, given too that in everything that goes on in the earth what goes on among human beings takes pride of place, just as human beings themselves do, it is surely the last word in absurdity to deny in great matters that divine provision and forethought which we admire in small ones – unless of course we are to understand that the one who takes so much trouble in making and decreeing the definite number of totally insignificant hairs leaves the lives of men and women free from any judgment![56]

God's providence over evil

Augustine teaches that God is sovereign over all things, including evil and sin. Augustine makes a distinction between God's *creating* and *ruling*:

> But God, as He is the supremely good Creator of good natures, so is He of evil wills the most just Ruler; so that, while they make an ill use of good natures, He makes a good use even of evil wills. Accordingly, He caused the devil (good by God's creation, wicked by his own will) to be cast down from his high position, and to become the mockery of His angels – that is, He caused his temptations to benefit those whom he wishes to injure by them.[57]

Augustine writes:

> It is amazing and yet true that little ones are kindled with intense and hopeful enthusiasm to live upright lives, by the negative example of sinners. As part of the

---

55. Of course, Augustine does affirm that God's providential rule extends to all things. He mentions God's providential rule over animals in his *Exposition of Psalm 145* 13 (as well as Ps. 148). In *Exposition of the Psalms 121–150*, *The Works of Saint Augustine: A Translation for the 21st Century*, vol. 3.20, tr. and notes Maria Boulding, OSB, ed. Boniface Ramsey (Hyde Park, NY: New City, 2004). In his *Exposition of Psalm 148* Augustine (commenting on v. 8) writes, 'everything happens on earth by God's providence'.
56. *Sermon on God's Providence*, Sermons 3/11. In *The Works of Saint Augustine: A Translation for the 21st Century*, vol. 3.2, editorial consultant F. Dolbeau, tr. Edmund Hill, OP (Brooklyn, NY: New City, 1997).
57. *City of God* 11.17.

> same mystery it happens that even heresies are allowed to exist, not because heretics themselves intend it so but because divine providence brings this result from their sins. It is providence which both makes and orders the light, but does no more than order the darkness.[58]

Notice the distinction: (1) providence *makes and orders* the light, but (2) providence 'no more than' *orders* the darkness.

Man

Man as created

Each person is a created being, even if (obviously) each person is brought into being by the union of mother and father: 'For even parents cannot make a human being; rather, God makes one by means of the parents.'[59] Augustine is forthright in speaking of Divine Providence in the creation of new people, even if sin is at times involved in the conception of a new person:

> I do not deny that 'the hand of divine providence is present in the genital organs of sinners.' After all, it reaches from one end to another and arranges all things with might and gentleness, and nothing defiled touches it. For this reason it does what it wants with the unclean and infected, while itself remaining clean and uninfected.[60]

Augustine affirms that God created the first man, and that man was meant to be 'a mean between the angelic and bestial'.[61] The first man was created and placed in the garden, given all he needed, and was called to obey. Augustine writes that if man

> remained in subjection to his Creator as his rightful Lord, and piously kept His commandments, he should pass into the company of the angels, and obtain, without the intervention of death, a blessed and endless immortality; but if he offended the Lord his God by a proud and disobedient use of his free will, he should become

---

58. *Exposition of Psalm 9* 20. In *Exposition of the Psalms 121–150, The Works of Saint Augustine: A Translation for the 21st Century*, vol. 3.20, introduction Michael Fiedrowicz, tr. and notes Maria Boulding, OSB, ed. Boniface Ramsey (Hyde Park, NY: New City, 2004).
59. *Answer to Julian* 3.18.34. In *The Works of Saint Augustine*, vol. 1.24.
60. Ibid.
61. *City of God* 12.21.

> subject to death, and live as the beasts do – the slave of appetite, and doomed to eternal punishment after death.[62]

Adam, grace and the garden

Although it would be developed in the later Protestant tradition (particularly in the Reformed wing), Augustine clearly teaches that if Adam had obeyed God in the garden, he would have brought himself and his posterity into a condition of eternal blessedness. Augustine writes that God 'had so made them, that if they discharged the obligations of obedience, an angelic immortality and a blessed eternity might ensue, without the intervention of death; but if they disobeyed, death should be visited on them with just sentence . . .'[63]

Augustine summarizes what is entailed in Adam's sin:

> the first men were indeed so created, that if they had not sinned, they would not have experienced any kind of death; but that, having become sinners, they were so punished with death, that whatsoever sprang from their stock should also be punished with the same death. For nothing else could be born of them than that which they themselves had been.[64]

Augustine speaks specifically of 'merit' in terms of Adam's disobedience. God 'created man with such a nature that the members of the race should not have died, had not the two first (of whom the one was created out of nothing, and the other out of him) merited this by their disobedience . . .'[65]

Man as fallen

Augustine is rightly and properly viewed as that theologian who gave structure and depth to the doctrine of original sin. We come into the world already 'in Adam', and are caught up in Adam's transgression. Augustine's first mention of 'original sin' is found in his first anti-Pelagian writing, *The Punishment and Forgiveness of Sins*: 'they [the Pelagians] refuse to believe that in the case of little children original sin is removed by baptism, since they maintain that there is no sin at all in

---

62. Ibid.
63. Ibid. 13.1.
64. Ibid. 13.3.
65. Ibid. 14.1.

newborns'.[66] The immediate concern Augustine addresses is whether post-Adam people experience the 'death' of Romans 5:12 due simply to (1) imitation (the Pelagian view) or by (2) propagation (Augustine's view). Augustine does not deny that fallen man does indeed imitate Adam. But Augustine argues that we are 'in' Adam because we inherit our sinful nature and so *of course* imitate him. We do not participate in Adam's transgression primarily due simply to 'imitation'. As Augustine writes, 'Of course, all those who through disobedience transgress God's commandment imitate Adam. But it is one thing for him to be an example for those who sin by their will; it is something else for him to be the origin of those born with sin.'[67] Indeed, 'One man, Adam, has filled the whole wide world with his progeny. The human race, as if it were a single individual, is lying like a great big sick patient from the furthest east as far as the extreme west, and in need of a cure.'[68] Augustine could refer to all of the fallen human race as a 'mass of the damned' (*massa damnata*).[69]

Augustine distinguishes between (1) being sinful in the sense of being in Adam and caught up in Adam's transgression, the notion of 'original sin', which Augustine calls *peccator originaliter* (original sin), and (2) being sinful in the sense of committing sins in our own space and time in history, which Augustine calls our 'actual sins', *peccator actualiter* (actual sin). Indeed, Augustine is explicit: 'Original sins, however, are the sins of others because there is in them no choice of our own will, and yet they are, nonetheless, also found to be our sins because of the infection contracted from our origin.'[70] But the distinction between sin *originaliter* and *actualiter* should not lead us to diminish the importance of the notion that all people are bound up in Adam's transgression. As Augustine notes, 'it is certainly clear that personal sins of each person by which they alone sinned are distinct from this one in which all have

---

66. *The Punishment and Forgiveness of Sins* 9. In *The Works of Saint Augustine: A Translation for the 21st Century*, vol. 1.23, introduction, tr. and notes Roland J. Teske, SJ, ed. John E. Rotelle, OSA (Hyde Park, NY: New City, 1997).

67. Ibid. 10.

68. *Sermon 374, Sermon of Saint Augustine Preached on the Epiphany* 16. In *The Works of Saint Augustine: A Translation for the 21st Century*, vol. 3.10, introduction Michele Pellegrino, tr. and notes Edmund Hill, OP, ed. John E. Rotelle, OSA (Hyde Park, NY: New City, 1998).

69. *To Simplicianus* 2.16. In *Augustine: Earlier Writings*, ed. John H. S. Burleigh, in *The Library of Christian Classics* (Louisville, KY: Westminster John Knox, 2006).

70. *Against Julian, an Unfinished Book* 3.57.

sinned, when all were that one man', but nonetheless, 'from the one man all are born destined for a condemnation, from which only the grace of Christ sets them free'.[71]

God the cause of evil?

For Augustine, sin and evil come into the world through the act of human and angelic willing. God is certainly not the cause of evil, and indeed God created *all* things good. So what is the cause of evil? In the context of speaking about angels, Augustine argues that there is certainly no *efficient* cause of evil. And neither can we say that there evil is *eternal*, for that would bring into doubt the goodness and sovereignty of God:

> If the further question be asked, What was the efficient cause of their evil will? There is none. For what is it which makes the will bad, when it is the will itself which makes the action bad? And consequently the bad will is the cause of the bad action, but nothing is the efficient cause of the bad will.[72]

So the angels fell away because they willed to, and to seek a 'cause' outside the angels' wills is to invite serious error. Why do some angels fall while others do not? They turned from God to themselves.[73] A little later Augustine writes:

> There is, then, no natural efficient cause, or, if I may be allowed the expression, no essential cause, of the evil will, since itself is the origin of evil in mutable spirits, by which the good of their nature is diminished and corrupted; and the will is made evil by nothing else than defection from God – a defection of which the cause, too, is certainly deficient.[74]

Augustine and the grace of God

Augustine is properly called the 'Doctor of Grace'.[75] If contemporary Christians want to understand various contemporary debates and discussions about the doctrine of grace, they must understand Augustine, and particularly

---

71. *The Punishment and Forgiveness of Sins* 13.
72. *City of God* 12.6.
73. Ibid.
74. Ibid. 12.9.
75. N. R. Needham's book *The Triumph of Grace: Augustine's Writings on Salvation* (London: Grace, 2000) is an extremely valuable resource.

his theology as it was hammered out in the 'debates' with Pelagius.[76] Pelagius heard a snippet from *Confessions* that concerned him greatly:

> My entire hope is exclusively in your very great mercy. *Grant what you command, and command what you will.* You require continence. A certain writer has said (Wisd. 8:21); 'As I knew that no one can be continent except God grant it, and this very thing is part of wisdom, to know whose gift this is.' By continence we are collected together and brought to the unity from which we disintegrated into multiplicity. He loves you less who together with you loves something which he does not love for your sake. O love, you ever burn and are never extinguished. O charity, my God, set me on fire. *You command continence; grant what you command, and command what you will.*[77]

Pelagius heard language like 'Grant what you command, and command what you will' and was seriously alarmed. Augustine seemed to be saying that the ability to obey God must somehow come from God. Pelagius (and fellow Pelagians) would criticize Augustine's position in print, leading to an astonishing literary output on Augustine's part.

To understand something of Augustine as the 'Doctor of Grace', we now turn to his story of his own struggle with sin, his resistance to trusting in Christ, and his eventual conversion – all recounted in *Confessions.*

Augustine the recipient of grace

Augustine resists the gospel

Augustine at first claims to have had intellectual problems with the Christian faith (the apparent unsophisticated nature of the Old Testament, the problem

---

76. In *The Deeds of Pelagius* (11.23) (in *The Works of St Augustine*, vol. 1.23) Augustine lists the key tenets of Pelagianism as culled from the Pelagian Caelestius, condemned at the Council of Carthage. They are (1) 'Adam was created mortal so that he would die whether he sinned or did not sin.' (2) 'The sin of Adam harmed him alone and not the human race.' (3) 'The law leads to the kingdom just as the gospel does.' (4) 'Before the coming of Christ there were human beings without sin.' (5) 'Newly born infants are in the same state in which Adam was before his transgression.' (6) 'The whole human race does not die through the death or transgression of Adam, nor does the whole human race rise through the resurrection of Christ.'

77. *Confessions* 10.29.40; emphasis mine.

of evil and so on). But the problem for Augustine was deeper – a matter of the will, desire and affections:

> But now I was not in vanity of that kind. I had climbed beyond it, and by the witness of all creation I had found you our Creator and your Word who is God beside you and with you is one God, by whom you created all things (John 1:1–3). . . . And now I had discovered the good pearl. To buy it I had to sell all that I had; and I hesitated (Matt. 13:46).[78]

Augustine was caught between two sets of competing desires:

> I sighed after such [Christian] freedom, but was bound not by an iron imposed by anyone else but by the iron of my own choice. The enemy had a grip on my will and so made a chain for me to hold me a prisoner. The consequence of a distorted will is passion. By servitude to passion, habit is formed, and habit to which there is no resistance becomes necessity. . . . So my two wills, one old, the other new, one carnal, the other spiritual, were in conflict with one another, and their discord robbed my soul of all concentration.[79]

Augustine compares his bondage to sin, his lethargy to sleep:

> The burden of the world weighed me down with a sweet drowsiness such as commonly occurs during sleep. The thoughts with which I meditated about you were like the efforts of those who would like to get up but are overcome by deep sleep and sink back again. . . . Though at every point you showed that what you were saying was true, yet I, convinced by that truth, had no answer to give you except merely slow and sleepy words: 'At once'–'But presently'–'Just a little longer, please'. But 'At once, at once' never came to the point of decision, and 'Just a little longer, please' went on and on for a long while.[80]

Grant me chastity, but not yet

Augustine begins to hear of the Christian faith of others (Ponticianus and Antony), and wishes to break from his sinful desires. He writes about his struggle:

---

78. Ibid. 7.1.2.

79. Ibid. 8.5.10.

80. Ibid. 8.5.12.

> But I was an unhappy young man, wretched as at the beginning of my adolescence when I prayed you for chastity and said: 'Grant me chastity and continence, but not yet.' I was afraid you might hear my prayer quickly, and that you might too rapidly heal me of the disease of lust which I preferred to satisfy rather than suppress.[81]

The truthfulness of Christianity no longer the issue

As he nears his conversion, Augustine continues to reiterate his dilemma: the problem is no longer the truthfulness of Christianity; the problem is his will, desires and affections:

> The arguments [against Christianity] were exhausted, and all had been refuted. The only thing left to it was a mute trembling, and as if it were facing death it was terrified of being restrained from the treadmill of habit by which it suffered 'sickness unto death' (John 11:4).[82]

A battle of two wills

Augustine was clearly locked in a battle of will, as he describes repeatedly in *Confessions*:

> In my own case, as I deliberated about serving my Lord God (Jer. 30:9) which I had long been disposed to do, the self which willed to serve was identical with the self which was unwilling. It was I. I was neither wholly willing nor wholly unwilling. So I was in conflict with myself and was dissociated from myself. The dissociation came about against my will.[83]

Take read, take read

Finally, after recounting his struggle over a number of pages, Augustine recounts his conversion in the garden in Milan:

> From a hidden depth a profound self-examination had dredged up a heap of all my misery and set it 'in the sight of my heart' (Ps. 18:15). That precipitated a vast storm bearing a massive downpour of tears. . . . I threw myself down somehow under a certain fig tree, and let my tears flow freely. . . . As I was saying this and weeping in the bitter agony of my heart, suddenly I heard a voice from the nearby house chanting as if it might be a boy or a girl (I do not know which), saying and repeating

---

81. Ibid. 8.7.16–17.
82. Ibid. 8.7.18.
83. Ibid. 8.10.22

> over and over again 'Pick up and read, pick up and read.' At once my countenance changed, and I began to think intently whether there might be some sort of children's game . . . . I checked the flood of tears and stood up. I interpreted it solely as a divine command to me to open the book and read the first chapter . . . . I seized it [the Bible], opened it and in silence read the first passage on which my eyes lit: 'Not in riots and drunken parties, not in eroticism and indecencies, not in strife and rivalry, but put on the Lord Jesus Christ and make no provision for the flesh in its lust' (Rom. 13:13–14). I neither wished nor needed to read further. At once, with the last words of this sentence, it was as if a light of relief from all anxiety flooded into my heart. All the shadows of doubt were dispelled.[84]

Augustine the doctor of grace

With Augustine's conversion story in the background we are better prepared to grasp his understanding of grace.

The fallen will, and what it means to be free

Augustine views the freedom of pre-fall and post-fall Adam (and his descendents) very differently. For Augustine, fallen man makes no movement towards God apart from God's grace: 'we must fiercely and strongly oppose those who think that the power of the human will can by itself, without the help of God, either attain righteousness or make progress in tending toward it'.[85] 'Freedom' while we are unregenerate is ultimately only freedom to sin: 'For free choice is capable only of sinning, if the way of truth remains hidden.'[86]

It is with man's 'first freedom' (using his *will*) that he actually destroyed his own will. Augustine writes:

> For those who may not fully understand then, those words of the Apostle would seem to eliminate free will. But how can he eliminate it, when he says, 'the will is present'? It is certain, indeed, that the will itself is within our power; but powerlessness to accomplish good is the result of the fault due to original sin.[87]

---

84. Ibid. 8.12.28–29.
85. *The Spirit and the Letter* 4.
86. Ibid. 5.
87. *To Simplicianus* 1, First Question, 1. All quotations of *To Simplicianus* are from *Augustine: Earlier Writings*, Library of Christian Classics, selected and tr. John H. S. Burleigh (Philadelphia, PA: Westminster John Knox, 1979).

When Augustine tries to articulate the plight of the unregenerate person, he often speaks in terms of the sinner's *desires*:

> The price of deadly pleasure includes the sweetness which deceives, and gives delight in doing contrary to the law, which is all the more pleasant the less it is lawful. No one can enjoy that sweetness as the price of his condition without being compelled to serve lust as a chattel-slave. He who knows that an act is prohibited and rightly prohibited, and yet does it, knows that he is the slave of an overmastering desire.[88]

Election, predestination and the grace of God in initiating salvation

Augustine cautioned that election is extremely difficult to ponder, and that it is a mystery. In one letter he writes:

> But if there is something less clear about the gift of free choice and grace and its outcome, or about the secret depth of God's judgment and about his providence and his secret dispensation regarding various human beings, let no one be disturbed, if he does not understand. Let us believe that the Lord is just and that there is no injustice in him, and let us save for the next life what we do not understand in this life.[89]

In his *Reconsiderations* of his *To Simplicianus* Augustine writes concerning Romans 9:10–29, 'I have tried hard to maintain the free choice of the human will, but the grace of God prevailed.'[90]

Augustine can write clearly of divine election at numerous points. For example, in *The City of God* he writes:

> Now, therefore, with regard to those to whom God did not purpose to give eternal life with His holy angels in His own celestial city, to the society of which that true piety which does not render the service of religion, which the Greeks call *latreia*, to any save the true God conducts, if He had also withheld from them the terrestrial glory of that most excellent empire, a reward would not have been rendered to their good arts – that is, their virtues – by which they sought to attain so great glory.[91]

---

88. Ibid. 7.
89. *A Letter of Bishop Evodius to Abbot Valentine*. In *The Works of Saint Augustine: A Translation for the 21st Century*, vol. 1.26, introduction, tr. and notes Roland J. Teske, SJ, ed. John E. Rotelle, OSA (Hyde Park, NY: New City, 1997).
90. *Reconsiderations* 2.1.
91. *City of God* 5.15.

In his *To Simplicianus* Augustine, in taking up Romans 9:10–29, wrestles with the situations of Jacob and Esau, respectively. Why did Jacob believe and Esau did not? Augustine circles around the question for some time. Finally he turns to Philippians 2:12–13: 'Therefore, my beloved, as you have always obeyed, so now, not only as in my presence but much more in my absence, work out your own salvation with fear and trembling, for it is God who works in you, both to will and to work for his good pleasure' (ESV). Augustine concludes, 'There he clearly shows that the good will itself is wrought in us by the working of God.'[92] Getting to the heart of things, Augustine writes, 'For the effectiveness of God's mercy cannot be in the power of man to frustrate, if he will have none of it. If God wills to have mercy on men, he can call them in a way that is suited to them, so that they will be moved to understand and to follow.'[93]

Indeed, 'He calls the man on whom he has mercy in the way he knows will suit him, so that he will not refuse the call.'[94] Augustine writes elsewhere about Philippians 2:12–13:

> the true interpretation of the saying, 'It is not of him that willeth, nor of him that runneth, but of God that showeth mercy,' is that the whole work belongs to God, who *both* makes the will of man righteous and thus prepares it for assistance, and assists it when it is prepared. For the man's righteousness of will precedes many of God's gifts, but not all; and it must itself be included among those which it does not precede.[95]

Augustine argues that there is no injustice in allowing rebellious humanity to remain in their sin, and there is not injustice if God chooses to have mercy on some:

> Sinful humanity must pay a debt of punishment to the supreme divine justice. Whether that debt is exacted or remitted there is no unrighteousness. It would be a mark of pride if the debtors claimed to decide to whom the debt should be remitted and from whom it should be exacted; just as those who were hired to work in the vineyard were unjustly indignant when as much was given to the others as was duly paid to themselves (Matt. 20:11 ff.).[96]

---

92. *To Simplicianus* 2.12.
93. Ibid. 2.13.
94. Ibid.
95. *Handbook on Faith, Hope and Love* 31.
96. *To Simplicianus* 2.16.

As Augustine continues, note that he – at least here – frames the issue of God's not showing mercy to some more in terms of simply passing over them than in 'driving' such people to sin:

> So the apostle represses the impudent questioner. 'O man, who art thou that repliest against God?' A man so speaks back to God when he is displeased that God finds fault with sinners, as if God compelled any man to sin when he simply does not bestow his justifying mercy on some sinners, and for that reason is said to harden some sinners; not because he drives them to sin but because he does not have mercy upon them.[97]

Augustine and justification

It is right and proper for evangelicals to note the difference between Augustine and the Protestant Reformers in their respective doctrines of justification.[98] It is standard to point out that Augustine would construe justification in the sense of 'make righteous' (Latin: *justifico*, 'I justify, or make righteous') rather than the evangelical understanding of 'to declare' or 'to reckon' righteous (from the Greek term in the New Testament, *dikaioō*). The difficulty here is that Augustine was not embroiled in the Catholic–Protestant debates and should not be interpreted in the light of that distance from such debates. Interestingly, he can at times speak of justification as having a punctiliar type of meaning – which is an understanding with which most evangelicals would resonate. Thus he can write, 'For sins alone produce the separation between human beings and God, and they are removed by the grace of him through whom we are reconciled, when he makes the sinner righteous (Rom 4:5).'[99] Interestingly, here Augustine is dealing with baptism, and so not only does Augustine affirm baptismal regeneration, but justification can be said to occur at the point of baptism – which denotes something like a punctiliar understanding of justification.

Similarly, in *To Simplicianus* Augustine seems to speak of justification in a more past-tense, punctiliar sense:

> So no one does good works in order that he may receive grace, but because he *has received* grace. How can a man live justly who *has* not *been justified*? How can he live

97. Ibid.
98. Among other works, see David F. Wright, 'Justification in Augustine', in Bruce L. McCormack, *Justification in Perspective: Historical Developments and Contemporary Challenges* (Grand Rapids: Baker Academic; Edinburgh: Rutherford House, 2006).
99. *The Punishment and Forgiveness of Sins* 25.

> holily who *has* not *been sanctified*? Or, indeed, how can a man live at all who *has* not been *vivified*? Grace justifies so that he who is justified may live justly.[100]

Notice how receiving grace, justification and sanctification all appear to be past tense and punctiliar. While Augustine is certainly not a Protestant, his punctiliar emphases when speaking of things like receiving grace, justification and sanctification, resonate with later Protestant concerns.

The Christian life and perseverance

Augustine gives great emphasis to the grace of God in initiating our salvation, helping Christians to grow in grace, and in preserving his people. He writes, 'the grace of God both for beginning and for persevering up to the end is not given according to our merits, but is given according to his most hidden and at the same time most just, most wise, and most beneficent will'.[101]

Whereas before conversion people do not *want* – ultimately – to believe, in a similar way *after* conversion we obey God because we *want* to. Augustine writes:

> We, on the other hand, say that the human will is helped to achieve righteousness in this way: Besides the fact that human beings are created with free choice of the will and besides the teaching by which they are commanded how they ought to live, they receive the Holy Spirit so that there arises in their minds a delight in and a love for that highest and immutable good that is God.[102]

He continues, 'unless we find delight in it and love it, we do not act, do not begin, do not live good lives. But so that we may love it, the love of God is poured out in our hearts, not by free choice which comes from ourselves, but by the Holy Spirit who has been given to us (Rom 5:5).'[103] We *want* to do godly things, for God has transformed our *desires*. Augustine writes in his *Against Two Letters of the Pelagians*, 'For the good begins to be desired when it begins to become sweet.'[104]

Christians persevere because they *want* to persevere, even if – for Augustine – *all* they can ultimately do is persevere:

---

100. *To Simplicianus* 1, Second Question, 3; emphases mine.

101. *The Gift of Perseverance* 13, 33.

102. *On the Spirit and Letter* 5.

103. Ibid.

104. *Against Two Letters of the Pelagians* 21. In *The Works of Saint Augustine*, vol. 1.24.

> Now in the case of the saints who are predestined to the kingdom of God by the grace of God, the assistance of perseverance which is given is not that [granted to the first man], but that kind which brings the gift of actual perseverance. It is not just that they cannot persevere without this gift; once they have received this gift, they can do nothing except persevere.[105]

The Christian's future

Augustine wants to point out that the blessedness of the Christian in his future state is a greater blessedness than that blessedness experienced by pre-fall Adam:

> Accordingly, so far as present comfort goes, the first man in Paradise was more blessed than any just man in this insecure state; but as regards the hope of future good, every man who not merely supposes, but certainly knows that he shall eternally enjoy the most high God in the company of angels, and beyond the reach of ill – this man, no matter what bodily torments afflict him, is more blessed than was he who, even in that great felicity of Paradise, was uncertain of his fate.[106]

Augustine at numerous points speaks of man's ultimate end. While in *The Trinity* Augustine speaks in terms of the vision of God as man's ultimate end, at other points he emphasizes the Christian's future peace. In *The City of God* Augustine writes, 'But this is true virtue, when it refers all the advantages it makes a good use of, and all that it does in making good use of good and evil things, and itself also, to that end in which we shall enjoy the best and greatest peace possible.'[107]

Augustine, the incarnation and the cross of Christ

The incarnation

Augustine intentionally and forthrightly affirms a Chalcedonian, two-natures Christology, and self-consciously seeks to resist the Arian error (of denying the full deity of Christ). He affirms the full deity and humanity of Christ, and the centrality of his death for sinners:

---

105. *On Admonition and Grace* 12.34. In *The Works of Saint Augustine*, vol. 1.26.
106. *City of God* 11.12.
107. Ibid. 19.10.

> But if, as is much more probable and credible, it must needs be that all men, so long as they are mortal, are not also miserable, we must seek an intermediate who is not only man, but also God, that by the interposition of His blessed mortality, He may bring men out of their moral misery to a blessed immortality. In this intermediate two things are requisite, that He become mortal, and that He do not continue mortal. He did become mortal, not rendering the divinity of the Word infirm, but assuming the infirmity of flesh. Neither did He continue mortal in the flesh, but raised it from the dead; for it is the very fruit of His mediation that those, for sake of whose redemption He became the Mediator, should not abide eternally in bodily death.[108]

Augustine clearly affirms the sinlessness of Jesus: 'For we were men, but were not righteous; whereas in His incarnation there was a human nature, but it was righteous, and not sinful.'[109] The Word took on a full humanity: 'For, to prevent us from seeking one purgation for the part which Porphyry calls intellectual, and another for the part he calls spiritual, and another for the body itself, our most mighty and truthful Purifier and Saviour assumed the whole human nature.'[110]

In his incarnation the Word remains unchangeable, and Augustine links this with God's grace and our salvation: 'but the incarnation of the unchangeable Son of God, whereby we are saved, and are enabled to reach the things we believe, or in part understand, this is what you refuse to recognize'.[111] Indeed:

> The grace of God could not have been more graciously commended to us than thus, that the only Son of God, remaining unchangeable in Himself, should assume humanity, and should give us the hope of His love by means of the mediation of a human nature, through which we, from the condition of men, might come to Him, who was so far off – the immortal from the mortal; the unchangeable from the changeable; the just from the unjust; the blessed from the wretched.[112]

The atoning work of Christ

Augustine speaks about the atonement in a number of ways. The sacrifice of Christ is offered to the Father: 'The true sacrifice is owed to the one true

---

108. Ibid. 9.15.
109. Ibid. 10.24.
110. Ibid. 10.32.
111. Ibid. 10.29.
112. Ibid.

God.'[113] Augustine mentions the death of Christ in terms of expiation: 'For he was able to expiate sins by dying, because He both died, and not for sin of His own.'[114] Interestingly, also like Anselm, Augustine speaks of the atoning work of Christ redeeming 'a people so numerous, that He thus fills up and repairs the blank made by the fallen angels, and thus that beloved and heavenly city is not defrauded of the full number of its citizens, but perhaps may even rejoice in a still more overflowing population' (although Augustine does not linger long here).[115]

For Augustine, Jesus is both the one who sacrifices and the sacrifice itself:

> Thus He is both the Priest who offers and the Sacrifice offered. And He designed that there should be a daily sign of this in the sacrifice of the Church, which, being His body, learns to offer herself through Him. Of this true Sacrifice the ancient sacrifices of the saints were the various and numerous signs; and it was thus variously figured, just as one thing is dignified by a variety of words, that there may be less weariness when we speak of it much. To this supreme and true sacrifice all false sacrifices have given place.[116]

Augustine argues that it is not the flesh which (by itself) purifies, but the Word who has taken on flesh: 'The flesh, therefore, does not by its own virtue purify, but by virtue of the Word by which it was assumed, when "the Word became flesh and dwelt among us".'[117]

The atonement is not *either* substitutionary *or* a 'victory'. Rather, Augustine can link penal substitution to the defeat of the devil. Our relation to the devil (in terms of the devil's power over us) is a *penal* reality:

> I mean now to speak of the blessings which God has conferred or still confers upon our nature, vitiated and condemned as it is. For in condemning it He did not withdraw all that He had given it, else it had been annihilated; neither did He, in penally subjecting it to the devil, remove it beyond His own power.

---

113. *Sermon 374, Sermon of Saint Augustine Preached on Epiphany* 16. In *The Works of Saint Augustine: A Translation for the 21st Century*, vol. 2.10, introduction, tr. and notes Edmund Hill, OP, ed. John E. Rotelle, OSA (Hyde Park, NY: New City, 1995).
114. *City of God* 10.24.
115. Ibid. 20.1.
116. Ibid. 10.20.
117. Ibid. 10.24.

Augustine is often considered a representative of the 'Christus Victor' approach. However, Augustine sees the victory over the devil fundamentally in terms of *justice*. That is, the devil's influence over people, and the *reason* the devil has such influence, is fundamentally a *justice* issue, and hence the devil must be defeated in terms of justice: 'So it pleased God to deliver man from the devil's authority by beating him at the justice game, not the power game, so that men too might imitate Christ by seeking to beat the devil at the justice game, not the power game.'[118] For Augustine, payment appears to fit under the rubric of justice. Augustine asks, 'What then is the justice that overpowered the devil?' His answer: 'The justice of Jesus Christ – what else?'[119]

Augustine, the church and the sacraments

The nature of the church

Augustine speaks of a 'heavenly church' and a 'pilgrim church'. The 'heavenly church' consists of all the redeemed in heaven, as well as angels, while the 'pilgrim church' consists of the redeemed on earth, those 'wandering on earth'.[120]

Augustine's 'Catholic' doctrine of the church can be seen when he speaks of the forgiveness of sins: 'Indeed, outside the Church they [actual sins] are not forgiven, for it is the Church that has received the Holy Spirit as her own as a pledge without which no sins are forgiven in such a way that those to whom they are forgiven receive eternal life.'[121]

Augustine speaks of the church as 'the rational part of creation which belongs to the free city of Jerusalem'. He goes on:

> Here the whole Church should be understood to be meant, not only the part that is on pilgrimage on earth, praising the name of the Lord from the rising of the sun to its setting and singing a new song after its old captivity, but also that part which has remained with God in heaven ever since its foundation and has never suffered any fall into evil.[122]

---

118. *Trinity* 13.17. Cf. Henri Blocher, '*Agnus Victor*: The Atonement as Victory and Vicarious Punishment', in John G. Stackhouse, Jr (ed.), *What Does it Mean to Be Saved? Broadening Evangelical Horizons on Salvation* (Grand Rapids: Baker, 2002), pp. 67–91.
119. *Trinity* 13.18.
120. *Handbook on Faith, Hope and Love* 17.61.
121. Ibid. 17.65.
122. Ibid. 15.56.

The Christian church is, for Augustine, a pilgrim community travelling to the City of God. But it is at the same time the presence of Christ in this world:

> The universal Church, then, which is now found on the pilgrimage of mortality, awaits at the end of the world what has already been revealed in the body of Christ, who is the firstborn from the dead, because his body, of which he is the head, is also none other than the Church.[123]

Sacraments

Augustine laid the groundwork for later medieval developments (and beyond) of a theology of the sacraments. It is difficult to summarize his understanding of the sacraments briefly. Nonetheless, he writes, 'A sacrifice, therefore, is the visible sacrament or sacred sign of an invisible sacrifice.'[124] The eternal destiny of Christians is for them one day to see God face to face (1 Cor. 13:12), and Augustine's understanding of sacraments must be seen in the light of that face-to-face vision. The sacraments are means by which we are drawn *through* visible and earthly things *to* invisible things (God).[125]

For Augustine, all of creation in some sense testifies to its creator, but only some things should properly be called 'sacraments':

> Thus with the freedom of Christians we use the rest of creation, the winds, the sea, the earth, birds, fishes, animals, trees, and human beings in many ways for speaking, but for the celebration of the sacraments we use only a very few, such as water, wheat, wine, and oil. In the servitude, however, of the old people they were commanded to celebrate many sacraments that are handed on to us only to be understood.[126]

Interestingly, Augustine can have a broad understanding of 'sacrifice': 'Thus a true sacrifice is every work which is done that we may be united to God in holy fellowship, and which has a reference to that supreme good and end in which alone we can be truly blessed.'[127]

---

123. *Letter 55* 2.3. In *The Works of Saint Augustine*, vol. 2.1.
124. *City of God* 10.5.
125. *Letter 55* 5.8.
126. Ibid. 7.13.
127. *City of God* 10.6.

Baptism

Augustine is clear in teaching that baptism removes sin. And Augustine argues that infants who die without baptism are therefore lost. Augustine can use related illustrations to speak of God's sovereign grace: a believer's child who dies apart from baptism is lost, while the child of most wicked unbelievers is by God's grace saved:

> And yet the providence of God, for whom the hairs of our head are numbered and without whose will not even a sparrow falls to the earth, is not subject to fate, nor is it impeded by chance events or defiled by any injustice. Yet his providence does not take care of all the infants of his own children so that they may be reborn for the heavenly kingdom but does take care of the infants of some unbelievers. This infant, born of believing parents and welcomed with the joy of parents, suffocated by the sleepiness of its mother or nurse, becomes a stranger to and is excluded from the faith of his parents; that infant is born of wicked adultery, exposed by the cruel fear of its mother, taken up by the merciful goodness of strangers, baptized out of their Christian concern, and becomes a member and partaker of the eternal kingdom.[128]

Augustine is clear that baptism is necessary to take away original sin.[129] He argues strenuously that since Christians bring their infants to be baptized, this shows that these adults do in fact know at some level that even infants are sinful. And since this sinfulness is not due to the sinful actions or behavior of infants, such infants must in fact be subject to original sin. As Augustine writes:

> if they are not held by any bond of sinfulness stemming from their origin, how did Christ, who died for the sinners, die for these infants who obviously have done nothing sinful in their own lives? If they are not afflicted by the disease of original sin, why do those caring for them bring them out of a holy fear to Christ the physician, that is, to receive the sacrament of eternal salvation?[130]

The challenge of Donatism

The Donatists had argued that the ministry of those church leaders (*e.g.* pastors or bishops) who had been 'traitors' during times of persecution (they

---

128. *Letter 194* (to Sixtus) 32. In *The Works of Saint Augustine: A Translation for the 21st Century*, vol. 2.3, tr. and notes Roland Teske, SJ, ed. Boniface Ramsey (Hyde Park, NY: New City, 2004).

129. *Handbook on Faith, Hope and Love* 64.

130. *The Punishment and Forgiveness of Sins* 23.

had 'handed over' copies of the Scriptures when told to by the authorities) was not valid. Thus, if a 'traitor' had baptized someone, the baptized person had to be rebaptized, for the extreme moral failure (being a 'traitor') in effect nullified the efficacy of the pastor's/bishop's ministry (here, baptizing).[131] While the Donatists argued for a 'pure' church, Augustine argued for a 'mixed church' in the here now, and he utitilized the parable of the wheat and tares to illustrate that God will separate believer and unbeliever at some future date. It can be argued that, for Augustine, only believers in Christ can truly be considered part of the church, but there is little benefit in making hard and fast judgments in the present on who is truly a member of the body of Christ and who is not.

In response to Donatism, Augustine argues that the efficacy of the sacraments does not in fact depend on the moral or spiritual state of the priest, because the *real* or *ultimate* minister ministering the sacrament is Christ himself, who ministers *through* the 'lower' or earthly minister. Augustine writes that the person 'whom the drunkard baptized, those whom a murderer baptized, those whom an adulterer baptized, if it were the baptism of Christ, Christ baptized'.[132] Augustine continues, 'Jesus still baptizes; and as long as we must be baptized, Jesus baptizes. Let a man approach confidently to a lesser minister; for he has a superior teacher.'[133]

The Lord's Supper

There is some debate as to whether Augustine held to what would become a fully 'Roman Catholic' position at some point later in church history.[134] Pamela Jackson notes that Augustine speaks of three different realms as being 'sacraments': (1) rites (both Old Testament rites and New Testament realities like baptism and the Lord's Supper); (2) symbolic figures (*e.g.* the Red Sea as a 'type' of God's rescuing his people); (3) mysteries (*e.g.* the Trinity or resurrection). And since Augustine saw Scripture as a divine collection of various 'signs',

131. Lancel, *Augustine*, pp. 164–165.

132. *Tractates on the Gospel of John 1–10* tr. John W. Rettig, vol. 78 in *The Fathers of the Church: A New Translation* (Washington DC: The Catholic University of America Press, 1988), 5.18.

133. *Tractates on the Gospel of John 11–27*, in *The Fathers of the Church*, vol. 79. Emmanuel J. Cutrone's 'Sacraments', in Allan D. Fitzgerald (ed.), *Augustine Through the Ages: An Encyclopedia* (Grand Rapids: Eerdmans, 1999), pp. 741–746, is helpful in outlining Augustine on the sacraments.

134. See Cutrone, 'Sacraments'.

signs that point to God, the 'signs' of Scripture could virtually be viewed as sacraments.[135]

Perhaps one of the most famous places where Augustine speaks of the Lord's Supper is in *The City of God* 10.6. Speaking of the sacrifice of Christ, he writes, 'Thus a true sacrifice is every work which is done that we may be united to God in holy fellowship, and which has a reference to that supreme good and end in which alone we can be truly blessed.'[136] Thus, for Augustine, when we act as we ought, and act in such a way as to glorify God, that is a 'sacrifice'.[137] Augustine writes about the 'sacrifices' we as Christians offer:

> true sacrifices are works of mercy to ourselves or others, done with a reference to God, and since works of mercy have no other object than the relief of distress or the conferring of happiness, and since there is no happiness apart from that good of which it is said, 'It is good for me to be very near to God,' it follows that the whole redeemed city, that is to say, the congregation or community of the saints, is offered to God as our sacrifice through the great High Priest, who offered Himself to God in His passion for us, that we might be members of this glorious head, according to the form of a servant.[138]

Augustine in this section is speaking of sacrifice, and of how all we do that is directed towards God is a kind of sacrifice. Then Augustine writes, 'And this also is the sacrifice which the Church continually celebrates in the sacrament of the altar.' He has just quoted Romans 12:3–6, on how Christians are the body of Christ. Thus, when Augustine writes that '*this* is the sacrifice', he seems to have in mind the church existing as the body of Christ. Augustine goes on to write that the 'sacrament of the altar' is likewise a sacrifice, for in this sacrament (the Lord's Supper), 'she herself [the church] is offered in the offering she makes to God'.[139] A Roman Catholic interpreter may see the seeds (even the explication of) a Roman Catholic understanding of the 'real presence' of Christ in the Lord's Supper. A Protestant might look at this passage and conclude, (1) all that we do – if done for God – can be, or is, a 'sacrament'; and (2) in the Lord's Supper the Christian church herself

---

135. Cf. *On Christian Doctrine*, *Responses to Januarius* 54.
136. *City of God* 10.6.
137. Ibid.
138. Ibid.
139. Ibid.

is offered to God. To the extent that one emphasizes Augustine's notion that all things done for God are sacraments, one will be less likely to see Augustine as 'catholic'. To the extent that one emphasizes that the church's self-sacrifice in the sacrament of the altar is also a sacrifice where Christ is really present – and is sacrificed again – one would see Augustine as more 'catholic'.

Augustine and the Bible

The nature and authority of Scripture

Augustine speaks of the divine origin, inspiration and authority of Scripture. In *The City of God* he writes of Christ, the Holy Spirit and the Scriptures:

> This Mediator, having spoken what He judged sufficient, first by the prophets, then by His own lips, and afterwards by the apostles, has besides produced the Scripture which is called canonical, which has paramount authority, and to which we yield assent in all matters of which we ought not to be ignorant, and yet cannot know of ourselves.[140]

In the same letter Augustine writes, 'I most firmly believe that none of their authors erred in writing anything.'[141] Indeed, 'with regard to their writings [the writings of the prophets and the apostles] it is wicked to doubt that they are free from all error'.[142]

The authority of Scripture and the nature of the church

Perhaps one of Augustine's most famous statements on how he came to believe Scripture is as follows: 'For my part, I should not believe the gospel except as moved by the authority of the Catholic Church.'[143] While it might be tempting to some to take this passage as sure-fire support for some sort of two-source view of divine authority, or as a 'proof text' of sorts for papal

---

140. Ibid. 11.2.
141. *Letter 82* (Augustine to Jerome) 3, 1.3. In *The Works of Saint Augustine:*, vol. 2.1.
142. Ibid. 1.3.
143. *Against the Epistle of Manichaeus Called Fundamental* 5.6, tr. Richard Stothert. In Philip Schaff (ed.), *A Select Library of the Nicene and Post-Nicene Fathers of the Christian Church* [*NPNF*] (Edinburgh: T. & T. Clark; Grand Rapids: Eerdmans, 1887), vol. 4.

infallibility, other passages from Augustine mitigate against such a move. Augustine ultimately looks to the Scriptures as his ultimate authority, giving evidence (at the risk of being anachronistic) of a version of *sola scriptura.* He writes, 'I owe this complete obedience only to the canonical scriptures, and by it I follow them alone in such a way that I have no doubt that their authors erred in them in absolutely no way and wrote nothing in them in order to deceive.'[144] Likewise Augustine speaks of the 'lofty supremacy' and authority of Scripture:

> there is a distinct boundary line separating all productions subsequent to apostolic times from the authoritative canonical books of the Old and New Testaments. The authority of these books has come down to us from the apostles through the successions of bishops and the extension of the Church, and, from a position of lofty supremacy, claims the submission of every faithful and pious mind.[145]

The unity of Holy Scripture

Augustine writes of the unity of Scripture: 'the words they hated to see ascribed to God in the Old Testament were righteous enough to be found in the New, and those they praised and celebrated in the New Testament were also to be found in the Old'.[146] Similarly,

> (Among the people who had received the Old Testament) there were so many signs and such preparation for the New Testament that we can find in the Gospel and the apostles' preaching no precept, no promise, however difficult and divine they may be, that is missing from those ancient books.[147]

In affirming the unity of the Bible Augustine writes, 'in the Old Testament the New is concealed, and in the New the Old is revealed'.[148]

---

144. *Letter 82* (Augustine to Jerome) 3.24. In *The Works of Saint Augustine:*, vol. 2.1.
145. *Against the Epistle of Manichaeus Called Fundamental* 5, *NPNF*, vol. 4.
146. *Against Adimantus* 4. *Against Adimantus* is one of Augustine's anti-Manichaean works that has not yet been translated into English. I am relying at this point on the translation from Lancel, *St Augustine*, p. 272.
147. Ibid. 3.4.
148. *The First Catechetical Instruction* 4.8, tr. Joseph Christopher, *Ancient Christian Writers* (New York: Newman, 1978).

The interpretation of Scripture

Readers of Scripture are attempting 'to discover the thoughts and will of the authors it was written by, and through them to discover the will of God, which we believe directed what such human writers had to say'.[149]

God has *intentionally* made Scripture difficult to understand, so that we must *work* at understanding Scripture:

> This [the difficulty of understanding and interpreting Scripture] is all due, I have no doubt at all, to divine providence, in order to break in pride with hard labor, and to save the intelligence from boredom, since it readily forms a low opinion of things that are too easy to work out.[150]

Augustine also writes about his former efforts to approach Scripture from an unbelieving heart. This cannot be the case if one is to understand Scripture:

> if you have no qualms about believing, there's nothing you need be ashamed of. I am speaking to you as one who was myself caught out once upon a time, when as a lad I wanted to tackle the divine scriptures with the techniques of clever disputation before bringing to them the spirit of earnest inquiry. In this way I was shutting the door of my Lord against myself by my misplaced attitude; I should have been knocking at it for it to be opened, but instead I was adding my weight to keep it shut. I was presuming to seek in my pride what can only be found by humility.[151]

Augustine and the possibility of knowledge

Augustine and St Anselm (1033–1109) are properly viewed as advocates of 'faith seeking understanding'. For Augustine 'faith seeking understanding' is first and foremost a term which describes how we know God. We have *faith* in Christ, believing that we will one day see God face-to-face and have a fuller *understanding* of him. That is, 'faith seeking understanding' has a type of historical-redemptive undertone: we have *faith* as we walk in this temporal/earthly realm, believing that we will in the future *understand* more and more the God

149. *On Christian Doctrine* 2.6.7.

150. Ibid.

151. *Sermon 51* 6. In *The Works of Saint Augustine: A Translation for the 21st Century*, vol. 3.111, tr. Edmund Hill, OP, ed. John E. Rotelle, OSA (Hyde Park, NY: New City, 1990).

in whom we have placed our trust. Thus, Augustine can write: 'understanding refers to everlasting sight, while faith in temporal things as a kind of cradle is, so to say, nourishing little ones on milk; now, however, we are walking by faith and not by sight (2 Cor 5:7), but unless we walk by faith, we shall never be able to reach the sight which does not pass away but endures, when with our understanding purified we cleave to Truth.'[152] This – like virtually all shorthand summaries of theological insights and convictions – is prone to misunderstanding. One thing 'faith seeking understanding' does *not* mean is that there is some sort of hostility between faith and understanding. Also, it is not the case that 'faith' here can simply be first and foremost a non-cognitive (or non-thinking) reality. Rather, Augustine can write that 'believing' is actually *always* preceded by 'thinking':

> everything which is believed should be believed after thought has preceded; although even belief itself is nothing else than to think with assent. For it is not every one who thinks that believes, since many think in order that they may not believe; but everybody who believes, thinks – both thinks in believing, and believes in thinking.[153]

For Augustine, the state of our hearts affects our ability to truly *know* or *see* something. Hence, because of disordered loves, some people do not always see the beauty in creation: 'Yet by love of created things they are subdued by them, and being thus made subject become incapable of exercising judgment.' Through a type of disordered love, certain people are 'subdued' by the rest of the created order. 'Moreover, created things do not answer those who question them if power to judge is lost.'[154]

Interestingly, Augustine, while affirming 'faith seeking understanding', nonetheless affirms a high place for reason. There are two ways to know things: (1) authority and (2) reason. However, while authority is first *temporally*, reason is first in order of *reality* (in the sense of being of most importance). We may enter into the truths of Christianity by *authority*, but 'after one has entered, then without any hesitation he begins to follow the precepts of the perfect life'. For *reason*, 'now strong and capable after the cradle of authority' allows us actually to understand what *reason itself* is.[155]

---

152. *On Christian Doctrine* 2.17.

153. *Predestination of the Saints* 5. In Vernon J. Bourke, *The Essential Augustine*, 2nd ed. (Indianapolis: Hackett, 1974), p. 22.

154. *Confessions* 10.6.10.

155. *On Order* 2.9.26 (from Bourke, *Essential Augustine*, p. 26).

Augustine and divine illumination

For Augustine, it is God who illuminates the human mind in every act of knowing. He writes:

> the intellectual mind is so formed in its nature as to see those things which by the disposition of the Creator are subjoined to things intelligible in a natural order, by a sort of incorporeal light of a unique kind; as the eye of the flesh sees things adjacent to itself in this bodily light, of which light it is made to be receptive, and adapted to it.[156]

Augustine argues that we *learn* nothing from signs; rather, we learn from the 'inner Teacher' – Christ. Augustine writes that when Christ is teaching someone, this person is 'taught not by my words but by the things themselves made manifest within when God discloses them'.[157] That is, God (Christ in the person) must 'enlighten' or 'illuminate' the person, allowing them to learn. People have an 'inner light of Truth', which results in illumination and rejoicing.[158] To determine 'whether truths have been stated', students look 'upon the inner Truth'.[159] Indeed, the ultimate goal of teaching is 'to be inwardly turned toward Him'.[160]

Augustine writes:

> Regarding, however, all those things which we understand, it is not a speaker who utters sounds exteriorly whom we consult, but it is truth that presides within, over the mind itself. . . . And He who is consulted, He who is said to 'dwell in the inner man,' He it is who teaches – Christ – that is, 'the unchangeable Power of God and everlasting Wisdom.'[161]

For Augustine, the human person 'is taught not by my words, but by the realities themselves made manifest to him by God revealing them to his inner self'.[162] Thus it is *Christ himself* who teaches us, who illuminates the human mind.

---

156. *Trinity* 12.15.24.
157. Ibid. 12.40.38–39.
158. Ibid. 12.40.31–33.
159. Ibid. 14.45.5–10.
160. Ibid. 15.46.24–27.
161. *Teacher* 11.38. All quotations of *The Teacher* are from *Augustine: Earlier Writings*, Library of Christian Classics (Philadelphia, PA: Westminster John Knox, 1979). The seminal work on Augustine's doctrine of illumination is still Ronald H. Nash, *The Light of the Mind: St Augustine's Theory of Knowledge* (Lexington: University of Kentucky Press, 1969).
162. *Teacher* 12.40.

Augustine, education and the liberal arts

Augustine is a wealth of insight on the nature of liberal arts, and on learning more generally. He is quite clear that one can find truth in non-Christian sources:

> while the heathen certainly have counterfeit and superstitious fictions in all their teachings, and the heavy burdens of entirely unnecessary labor, which everyone of us must abominate and shun as we go forth from the company of the heathen under the leadership of Christ, their teachings also contain liberal disciplines which are more suited to the service of the truth, as well as a number of most useful ethical principles, and some true things are to be found among them about worshiping only the one God.[163]

Augustine famously writes, 'all good and true Christians should understand that truth, wherever they may find it, belongs to their Lord'.[164] Augustine uses the exodus and how the Israelites 'plundered the Egyptians' as a metaphor to portray the Christian use of the liberal arts.[165]

Augustine registers his concern regarding the liberal arts when he writes of the potential danger of pride for those engaged in study (and pagans in particular in view), when he speaks of those people encamped on the 'mountain of pride'.[166] And at least at times Augustine could register a certain caution regarding the liberal arts.[167]

Augustine on words and signs

Augustine is the first Christian thinker to give sustained attention to the nature of words and signs.[168] In Book 1 of *On Christian Doctrine* Augustine explicitly

---

163. *On Christian Doctrine* 2.40.60.
164. Ibid. 18.28.
165. Ibid. 2.60.
166. *Sermon* 198 (Dolbeau 26) 59, in *Works of St Augustine: A Translation for the 21st Century*, vol. 3.11, tr. Edmund Hill, OP, ed. Francoise Dolbeau, ed. John Rotelle, OSA (Hyde Park, NY: New City, 1997).
167. *Letter 101* 2.
168. David Lyle Jeffrey notes, 'For Augustine even a theory of signs is therefore ultimately based on considerations of intention and the ordering of value.' That is, Augustine's theory of signs is rooted in his ethical views, which are part of Augustine's larger Christian vision. See David Lyle Jeffrey, *People of the Book: Christian Identity and Literary Culture* (Grand Rapids: Eerdmans, 1996), p. 83.

correlates 'words' and the Incarnate 'Word'.[169] In Book 2 of *On Christian Doctrine* he defines 'sign': 'a sign, after all, is a thing, which besides the impression it conveys to the senses, also has the effect of making something else come to mind'.[170] Augustine offers a philosophy of signs that grounds our words in *the* Incarnate Word, and directs our signs (words) to the ultimate thing – God – giving our language an eschatological focus and meaning. Words, language and signs for Augustine are inherently tied to the nature and purposes of God. We can plunder from Augustine his formulation of a doctrine of words, language and signs in explicitly Christian and theological terms.

Augustine and the nature of civil authority

The emergence of civil government

Augustine argues that civil government is not necessarily sinful, but its *need* emerges due to sin. God's intention was not that man should rule over man, but that man should simply rule over the rest of the created order:

> He did not intend that His rational creature, who was made in His image, should have dominion over anything but the irrational creation – not man over man, but man over the beasts. And hence the righteous men in primitive times were made shepherds of cattle rather than kings of men, so intending thus to teach us what the relative position of the creatures is, and what the desert of sin.[171]

The authority and nature of the government of the earthly city

Augustine distinguishes between the peace of the earthly city and the peace of the heavenly city. When he does so, he is using 'earthly city' in the sense of the authorities and structures of this temporal realm. Thus he writes, 'The earthly city, which does not live by faith, seeks an earthly peace, and the end it proposes, in the well-ordered concord of civic obedience and rule, is the combination of men's wills to attain the things which are helpful to this life.'[172] The heavenly city is different: 'The heavenly city, or rather the part of it which sojourns on earth and lives by faith, makes use of this peace only because it must, until this mortal condition which necessitates it shall pass away.'[173] And while the

169. *On Christian Doctrine* 1.13.
170. Ibid. 2.1.1.
171. *City of God* 19.15.
172. Ibid. 19.17.
173. Ibid.

heavenly city is sojourning amidst the earthly city, the citizens of the heavenly city are fine to obey the laws of the earthly city (within proper limits):

> Consequently, so long as it lives like a captive and a stranger in the earthly city, though it has already received the promise of redemption, and the gift of the Spirit as the earnest of it, it makes no scruple to obey the laws of the earthly city, whereby the things necessary for the maintenance of this mortal life are administered; and thus, as this life is common to both cities, so there is a harmony between them in regard to what belongs to it.[174]

Interestingly, Augustine also compares the civil government to a band of robbers.[175]

Just war

Augustine did not write a treatise per se on 'just war', and his thoughts must be culled from his various works. For Augustine, war arises due to sin, even if there are times where it is 'just' to engage in war. He is critical of those who think of war in a flippant way, and do not realize its horrors. His hypothetical interlocutor says that the wise man will wage just wars. Augustine does not deny this, but expresses concern about not grasping the misery of war:

> But, say they, the wise man will wage just wars. As if he would not all the rather lament the necessity of just wars, if he remembers that he is a man; for if they were not just he would not wage them, and would therefore be delivered from all wars. For it is the wrong-doing of the opposing party which compels the wise man to wage just wars; and this wrong-doing, even though it gave rise to no war, would still be a matter of grief to man because it is man's wrongdoing. Let every one, then, who thinks with pain on all these great evils, so horrible, so ruthless, acknowledge that this is misery. And if any one either endures or thinks of them without mental pain, this is a more miserable plight still, for he thinks himself happy because he has lost human feeling.[176]

Augustine apparently uses the term 'just war' only once, where he writes, 'just wars are usually defined as those that avenge injuries'.[177] Ultimately, for

---

174. *City of God* 19.17.
175. Ibid. 4.4.
176. Ibid. 19.7.
177. *Questions on the Heptateuch* 6.10. *Questions on the Heptateuch* has not been translated or published in English. This quotation is from Frederick H. Russell, 'War',

Augustine war is undertaken to preserve peace:

> Your will ought to aim at peace; only necessity requires war in order that God may set us free from necessity and preserve us in peace. For we do not seek peace in order to stir up war, but we wage war in order to acquire peace. Be, therefore, a peacemaker even in war in order that by conquering you might bring to the benefit of peace those whom you fight.[178]

Referencing Matthew 5:39, 'Do not resist one who is evil' (ESV), Augustine argues that we should not delight in vengeance.[179] A Christian – including a solider or governmental ruler – is to *love* his enemies, even in times of war, and seek the best interests of those enemies: 'if this earthly state keeps the Christian commandments, even wars will not be waged without goodwill in order more easily to take into account the interests of the conquered with a view to a society made peaceful with piety and justice'.[180] Even in war the Christian ruler must keep in mind the interests of the 'conquered'.

War is not always wrong, for Jesus (Luke 3:14) counsels the soldier who approaches him how to live while remaining a soldier (not that it is necessary to resign from the military). However, Christian soldiers should be of a certain type – those who honour and love Christ.[181] War can be morally acceptable and even appropriate, although it can be conducted only by proper authorities, and not by individual Christians.[182] And even in war Christians are – ultimately – to love their enemies and seek what is best for them. Indeed, war is to be conducted with a recognition that it is always a sign and reminder of the reality of living in a fallen and sinful world.

---

in Allan D. Fitzgerald (ed.), *Augustine Through the Ages: An Encyclopedia* (Grand Rapids: Eerdmans, 1999), pp. 875–876. Cf. Russell's *The Just War in the Middle Ages*, Cambridge Studies in Medieval Life and Thought, 3rd series (Cambridge: Cambridge University Press, 1977).

178. *Letter 189* 6. In *The Works of Saint Augustine*, vol. 2.3.
179. *Letter 47* 5. In *The Works of Saint Augustine*, vol. 2.1.
180. *Letter 138* 2.14. In *The Works of Saint Augustine: A Translation for the 21st Century*, vol. 2.2, tr. and notes Roland Teske, SJ, ed. Boniface Ramsey, OSA (Hyde Park, NY: New City, 2003).
181. Ibid. 2.15.
182. *Letter 47* 5.

Augustine, history and the two cities

Problems with the pagans

The City of God is clearly Augustine's *magnum opus*. He wrote *The City of God* from 413 to 427. In 410 Alaric and the Visigoths had successfully invaded Rome, and it seemed the great city was no longer impenetrable.[183] But why was Rome susceptible to defeat? Augustine wrote *The City of God* – in part – to counteract certain people who wanted to blame Rome's adoption of the Christian faith for the city's susceptibility:

> The glorious city of God is my theme in this work . . . . I have undertaken its defence against those who prefer their own gods to the Founder of this city – a city surpassingly glorious, whether we view it as it still lives by faith in this fleeting course of time, and sojourns as a stranger in the midst of the ungodly, or as it shall dwell in the fixed stability of its eternal seat, which it now with patience waits for, expecting until 'righteousness shall return unto judgment,' and it obtain, by virtue of its excellence, final victory and perfect peace.[184]

How could someone who saw all people as fellow image-bearers and saw fellow-Christians as spiritual 'brothers' or 'sisters' give meaningful allegiance to their own particular and earthly city? How could someone who believed his *true* citizenship was to be found in some *heavenly* city be able to be a good citizen in *this* city?[185] Augustine writes that he has 'things to say in confutation of those who refer the disasters of the Roman republic to our religion, because it prohibits the offering of sacrifices to the gods':

> For this end I must recount all, or as many as may seem sufficient, of the disasters which befell that city and its subject provinces, before these sacrifices were prohibited; for all these disasters they would doubtless have attributed to us, if at that time our religion had shed its light upon them, and had prohibited their sacrifices. I must then go on to show what social well-being the true God, in whose hand are all kingdoms, vouchsafed to grant to them that their empire might increase. I must show why He did so, and how their false gods, instead of at all aiding them, greatly

---

183. However, Rome was not 'conquered' by the Visigoths, who withdrew after three days.
184. *City of God* 1.pref.
185. See Ernest Fortin, '*Civitate Dei, De*', in Fitzgerald, *Augustine Through the Ages*, p. 197.

> injured them by guile and deceit. And, lastly, I must meet those who, when on this point convinced by irrefragable proofs, endeavour to maintain that they worship the gods, not hoping for the present advantages of this like, but for those which are to be enjoyed after death.[186]

Augustine spends Books 1–10 laying out his critique of various pagan arguments against Christianity. Then in Books 11–22 he outlines 'the origin, history, and deserved ends of the two cities'.[187]

Augustine's arguments against the pagans are manifold. Rome suffered many attacks and evils before Christianity was the dominant religion. Rome has never been able to achieve justice, even *before* Christianity emerged. The Roman gods have a long and sordid track record of capriciousness, pettiness and immorality.[188] In many ways Christianity has been *good* for the city of Rome. Thus Augustine asserts that when barbarians attacked Rome, many Romans survived because they took refuge in Christian churches, which – Augustine argues – the barbarians refused to attack.[189] Augustine also argues that the only reason *any* city – including Rome – achieves any success or stability of happiness is due to the providential workings of God.[190] Augustine writes:

> we do not attribute the power of giving kingdoms and empires to any save to the true God, who gives happiness in the kingdom of heaven to the pious alone, but gives kingly power on earth both to the pious and the impious, as it may please Him, whose good pleasure is always just.[191]

Augustine summarizes his overarching purpose for *The City of God* as follows:

> In truth, these two cities are entangled together in this world, and intermixed until the last judgment effect their separation. I now proceed to speak, as God shall help me, of the rise, progress, and end of these two cities; and what I write, I will write for the glory of the city of God, that, being placed in comparison with the other, it may shine with a brighter luster.[192]

---

186. *City of God* 1.36.
187. Ibid. 10.32.
188. These arguments are found in Books 2 and 3 of *The City of God.*
189. Ibid. 1.1.
190. Ibid. 4.2.
191. Ibid. 5.21.
192. Ibid. 1.35.

Two cities, two loves

In Book 11 of *The City of God* Augustine begins to trace out 'the origin, history, and destinies of the two cities, the earthly and the heavenly'.[193] Augustine of course finds the imagery for the 'city of God' from Scripture itself. He makes recourse to Psalms 87:3 and 48:1, among others. In the opening section of Book 11, Augustine writes these summative words about the two cities:

> I will endeavor to treat of the origin, and progress, and deserved destinies of the two cities (the earthly and the heavenly, to wit), which, as we said, are in this present world commingled, and as it were entangled together. And, first, I will explain how the foundations of these two cities were originally laid, in the difference that arose among the angels.[194]

What are the two 'cities'? The definitions can shift a bit throughout *The City of God*, as well as throughout Augustine's other writings. At times the 'earthly city' denotes the typical affairs of this temporal realm: politics, for example.[195] At other times, the 'heavenly city' can represent Christians, while 'earthly city' often means something like the lost, unsaved or reprobate.[196]

The two cities are intermingled in the present:

> During the present age these two cities are mingled together, but they will be separated at the end. They are in conflict with each other, one fighting on behalf of iniquity, the other for justice; one for what is worthless, the other for truth. This mixing together in the present age sometimes brings it about that certain persons who belong to the city of Babylon are in charge of affairs that concern Jerusalem, or, again, that some who belong to Jerusalem administer the business of Babylon.

The two cities have their origin – ultimately – in Adam himself. For at first there would only have been the city of God, and no earthly city – for the earthly city truly comes into being only with sin.[197]

At the heart of the two cities are two loves. At the very end of Book 14 of *The City of God* Augustine gives perhaps the clearest summary of how the two cities are most centrally rooted in two loves: either (1) love of self or (2) love of God:

---

193. Ibid. 11.argument.
194. Ibid. 11.1.
195. This is the meaning in *Commentary on Psalm 61* 8.
196. *City of God* 14.1.
197. Ibid. 12.27.

> Accordingly, two cities have been formed by two loves: the earthly by the love of self, even to the contempt of God; the heavenly by the love of God, even to the contempt of self. The former [the love of self], in a word, glories in itself, the latter [the love of God] in the Lord. For the one seeks glory from men; but the greatest glory of the other is God, the witness of conscience. The one lifts up its head in its own glory; the other says to its God, 'Thou art my glory, and the lifter up of mine head.' In the one, the princes and the nations it subdues are ruled by love of ruling; in the other, the princes and the subjects serve one another in love, the latter obeying, while the former take thought for all. The one delights in its own strength, represented in the persons of its rulers; the other says to its God, 'I will love Thee, O Lord, my strength.'[198]

All of history can be understood in terms of the origin, growth and end of these two cities: 'For this whole time or world-age, in which the dying give place and those who are born succeed, is the career of these two cities concerning which we treat.'[199]

Ultimately, the true founder of the earthly city is Cain, who founds the earthly city in slaying his brother.[200] And there are thus two lines – one proceeding from Cain (the earthly city) and the other from Seth (the heavenly city), and these two lines constitute the two cities.[201] Adam is then the father of these 'two lines, proceeding from two fathers, Cain and Seth, and in those sons of theirs whom it behoved to register, the tokens of these two cities began to appear more distinctly'.[202]

The 'two cities', then, can be understood as one way of simply tracing out the history of redemption. Instead of thinking of 'history' (in an almost 'neutral' or 'secular' sense), and thinking of God's actions in history as a supplement to or part of that, it is probably better to think of all of history as encompassed within the more fundamental story of the history of redemption – which Augustine traces out in terms of the two cities.

The end of the city of God

Augustine teaches that the end of the city of God is eternal blessedness. He spends a large portion of Book 22 (the last book) of *The City of God* dealing with this state of blessedness. Key to this final state is of course the resurrection. In

---

198. Ibid. 14.28.
199. Ibid. 15.1.
200. Ibid. 15.5–8.
201. Ibid. 15.8.
202. Ibid. 15.17.

the resurrection, all of the inhabitants of the city of God will be raised up and transformed without deformity, in perfect proportion. Indeed, 'all that is wrong is corrected, and all that is defective supplied from the resources the Creator wots of, and all that is excessive removed without destroying the integrity of the substance'. In short, there is continuity between our pre-resurrection and post-resurrection body (really the same body), but there is also discontinuity, in that there is a transformation and perfecting of the body.[203] This transformation of the body – due to the power of God – will even include bodies or body parts that have disintegrated (or for example that have been cremated).[204]

All through Augustine's thought he emphasizes the centrality of our desires (whether for good or bad), and returns to this at the end of *The City of God*. Our ultimate desire is for God, so it is fitting that God of course will be radically present in the future heavenly city: 'He shall be the end of our desires who shall be seen without end, loved without cloy, praised without weariness.'[205]

In this future state it is most certainly the case that free will is *not* lacking. Rather, 'It will, on the contrary, be all the more truly free, because set free from delight in sinning to take unfailing delight in not sinning.'[206] Hence, while the first man – Adam before the Fall – had *posse non peccare* (the ability *not* to sin) and *posse peccare* (the ability *to* sin), in our future and heavenly state we will be *non posse peccare* (not able to sin). As Augustine argues, being unable to sin does not mean one is not free. Indeed, 'Are we to say that God Himself is not free because He cannot sin?' 'Free will' indeed will be a reality in heaven: 'In that city, then, there shall be free will, one in all the citizens, and indivisible in each, delivered from all ill, filled with all good, enjoying indefeasibly the delights of eternal joys, oblivious of sins, oblivious of sufferings, and yet not so oblivious of its deliverance as to be ungrateful to its Deliverer.'[207]

Appropriating Augustine

It is hard to overstate Augustine's importance in the development of the Christian theological tradition. He is claimed as a patriarch by both Catholics and Protestants, and understandably so. When one speaks of someone being

203. Ibid. 22.19.
204. Ibid. 22.20.
205. Ibid. 22.29.
206. Ibid. 22.30.
207. Ibid.

an 'Arminian', 'Lutheran' or 'Calvinist' and so on, certain key doctrinal convictions and theological commitments come to mind. It is somewhat different when one speaks of an 'Augustinian'. Augustine's influence is so significant and broad that 'Augustinian' can almost seem to be shorthand for being a traditional Christian. In this evaluative section we will ask how evangelicals might appropriate the thought of Augustine. Why does Augustine matter? Why should evangelicals read him?

Approaching God

There are a number of things we could say about Augustine's approach to God. We noted earlier in the chapter that in *The Trinity* Augustine argues that in order one day to see God face to face one must be changed by the atoning work of Christ. Thus, while the Christian will one day see God, and know fully and be fully known (1 Cor. 13:12), the only way to arrive at this face-to-face vision is by being cleansed by the atoning work of Christ. Such a gospel-centred understanding of knowing God should resonate with all evangelicals as they think about the nature of theology and of our future destiny (when we will see God face to face). It is appropriate to see in Augustine a type of theological forerunner to Luther's *theologia crucis* (theology of the cross) and Calvin's teaching that Christians should be reticent about probing into the essence of God, and should rather be satisfied in knowing God through what he does in sending the Son and the Spirit. Calvin warned about avoiding the 'foolish speculation of the schoolmen',[208] for he feared such 'schoolmen' (certain medieval theologians or thinkers) were irreverently and inappropriately approaching God. That is, Augustine's gospel-centred understanding of approaching God seems to stand in the same theological line of thinking as that seen in the later Reformers, and can and should be appropriated by evangelicals as we think about what it means to approach God.

The nature of knowledge

Augustine wrestled at length with the nature of knowledge, and this interest stretches back to one of his earliest works, *Against the Academics*. Augustine fleshed out an understanding of the nature of knowledge that can be very fruitful for the contemporary Christian. He believed that in every act of human knowing, God is illuminating the human mind. This is briefly but

---

208. John Calvin, *Institutes of the Christian Religion*, tr. Ford Lewis Battles, ed. John T. McNeill (Philadelphia: Westminster, 1960), 1.4.5, 3.24.3, 3.25.6, 10, 11.

explicitly dealt with in *The Teacher*. It is important to grasp the radical nature of what Augustine is saying. For Augustine, *every time we know or acquire knowledge, Christ is the Teacher who is illuminating the mind and allowing such knowledge to take place.* Thus *every* act of knowing is one that takes place due to God's goodness towards us. As contemporary Christians wrestle with the question of the possibility of knowledge, Augustine is worthy of serious attention. His insight seems fundamentally right and biblical, in that God is Lord of all things, and when this lordship is applied to the question of knowledge, Augustine is led to construe the reality of knowledge in a radically God-centred (and in particular, a radically Christ-centred) way. Modern and so-called postmodern people are (at times) told by the larger and dominant culture that knowledge (of the natural or supernatural orders) is impossible, or that claims of knowledge are ultimately simply results of the 'will to power'. Augustine provides a Christ-centred understanding of the nature of knowledge, both of the natural and of the supernatural order. Besides his understanding of divine illumination, Augustine can also provide wisdom in the way he links our ability to know to the state of our hearts or wills. As discussed above, Augustine believes that our disordered loves (our sin) often keeps us from truly 'seeing' things – that is, our sin keeps us from grasping the nature of reality. As Christians think through the nature of knowing and learning, it is important to realize that the life of the mind must be seen as a subset of the life of discipleship. That is, learning is a fundamentally spiritual reality that can never be sequestered from the nature of our wills and hearts, and from the reality of our sin.

What Augustine argues for, which is sorely missing in our contemporary context, is a construal of the life of the mind in which our intellectual life is bound up with our ultimate loves. Whereas modernity has often seemed to construe the life of the mind as a 'neutral' endeavour, Augustine rightly links to the state of our loves our ability to interpret, understand and 'see' things. Along these lines, as Stephen Williams has noted, Pascal criticized Montaigne, not because Montaigne lacked certain intellectual powers, but because Montaigne was simply not open to hearing and knowing the truth. That is, Montaigne was *indifferent* to eternal matters, and this indifference – in Augustinian terms – kept Montaigne from *seeing* what was really *there*.[209] Thus for Pascal – in this sense thoroughly Augustinian – moral degradation would keep one from knowing the truth. As Pascal writes, 'Our inability to know the truth is the consequence

209. Stephen N. Williams, *Revelation and Reconciliation: A Window on Modernity* (Cambridge: Cambridge University Press, 1995), p. 21 (referencing Pascal, *Pensées*, §427).

of our corruption, our moral decay.'[210] Fools really *do* hate knowledge (Prov. 1:22).

The Trinity

Augustine was crucial in the development of the doctrine of the Trinity. Although there is no room to argue the point in detail here, I suspect it is unhelpful to drive too big a wedge between the Eastern church fathers and Augustine – and then turn to the East as the locus of theological right thinking. Augustine's maxim *opera trinitatis ad extra sunt indivisa* (the external works of the Trinity are undivided) is still worth mining and, where it has been lost, worth recovering. Augustine believed in the Trinity because of Scripture and tradition. He also believed that one day he would see the trinitarian God. But what would this God be like? In working through his understanding of the Trinity, Augustine forged an understanding of the centrality of love. Love was at the heart of the Godhead, and hence love must be central as we try to understand who the Trinity is. By emphasizing love at the centre of the Godhead Augustine was led to think of God fundamentally in *relational* terms.[211] Augustine thus bequeaths to the Western theological tradition the tendency to explore what it means to say 'God is love', and the Western church continues to benefit from this trajectory and influence to the present day.

Additionally, in Augustine's *The Trinity* we find what I think are helpful insights as to how to think and talk about God. For example, Augustine contends that ultimately all words about God are 'substance-words', and therefore it is *not* simply the case that 'God is loving', but that ultimately 'God *is* his love'. The benefit for contemporary evangelicals (and, I think, for any traditional Christian) is that biblical language about God, while not giving us *exhaustive* knowledge, nonetheless gives us *real* knowledge. The Christian who goes to the Scriptures and reads in 1 John 4:8, 'God is love', can trust that in such a passage the Christian reader is getting insight into who God *really* is, and who God *fundamentally* is – and that unlike other competing deities (whether past or present), God is *always* what the Scriptures say he is. Here (1 John 4:8), God is *fundamentally* and *always* 'love'.

---

210. Quoted in Friedrich Nietzsche, *The Will to Power*, tr. Walter Kaufmann and R. J. Hollingdale (New York: Vintage, 1968), 1.83.

211. Cf. my *Colin Gunton and the Failure of Augustine* (see n. 13 above). A condensed version of my argument can be found in my 'The Protomodern Augustine? Colin Gunton and the Failure of Augustine', *International Journal of Systematic Theology* 9.3 (June 2007), pp. 328–341.

The reality of sin

While not inventing the doctrine of original sin, it is certainly Augustine who developed and fleshed it out – and the influence of the fundamental structure of his thought on this issue continues to be felt today. However, does Augustine's understanding prevail in the contemporary church? While he 'won' the arguments in the formal sense during his day, it is an open question as to whether the contemporary evangelical church is 'Augustinian' in its doctrine of sin. For those of us on the whole sympathetic to Augustine at this point, it seems that he is simply working within fundamentally Pauline thinking here. That is, Augustine was working within a commitment to the Adam–Christ parallel so fundamental to Paul's thought. Both the Reformed and Lutheran branches of the Reformation are fundamentally Augustinian in their doctrine of sin.

It can be argued that Christians (evangelical or otherwise) will never truly grasp the reality of grace until they have some sense of the reality of sin. And Augustine is extremely helpful here. What young man cannot relate – at a fundamentally existential level – to Augustine's struggles as portrayed in *Confessions*? Augustine can remind evangelicals that the doctrines of free grace and justification by faith alone will never be as joyously and rightly understood until Christians have some sort of grasp of the nature of their own sin, and hence the radical nature of God's grace in rescuing us from our plight.

The two cities

Augustine's *The City of God* is certainly one of the most significant works in the Western canon, and it is virtually impossible to summarize its significance in a few sentences. The notion of 'two cities' has proved to be a pregnant metaphor that has provided grist for many Christian thinkers. In the Protestant world, Lutherans have tended to move in the direction of 'two kingdoms' – and have often been criticized for severing too radically the ability of Christian principles to influence statecraft. The Reformed have tended to affirm 'two cities', but see both as subject to the same God – and there is great diversity within Reformed thinking on this score.

As Christians have wrestled with the way in which the church is to exist within, and relate to, the broader and dominant culture, Augustine is a necessary conversation partner, and attention to *The City of God* always repays careful reading. There is something to be said for the power of an image – here the two cities – to provoke thought, and Augustine's *magnum opus* has proven to be the place (after Scripture) where one generally begins in thinking through the ways in which Christians and the Christian church are to live within, reach out to and confront the broader culture.

In a little different direction, the notion of the 'history of redemption' is a staple of Reformed theology, and owes at least some inspiration to Augustine's notion of the 'two cities'. His understanding of the historical flow of redemption is felt today in numerous ways, and it is significant. Indeed, the current fascination with 'whole-Bible' theology or 'Biblical Theology' is fundamentally 'Augustinian', in that the current 'whole-Bible' or 'Biblical Theology' movement moves in the same theological trajectory as Augustine does.

The centrality of grace in the Christian life

Often when people reference Augustine on grace, the context is the initiation of salvation – whether in terms of election or in terms of conversion. These are extremely important issues, and Augustine is very helpful in those areas. But I suspect there is another component of his understanding of grace that is equally important. Augustine speaks about the way God's grace works in the midst of the Christian life and in drawing us on to obedience in our Christian life. And this is where I suspect he might be of particular help to evangelicals.

I come into contact with many students who have some understanding that God saves by grace, and that their salvation rests on the grace of God. But – to put it simply – they have a notion of how grace *gets* them 'in', but little understanding of how God's grace *keeps* them 'in'. That is, grace is often seen as that which gets the salvific process started. But then there is not much of a theological framework for how we continue to walk, obey and persevere by grace.

Augustine speaks repeatedly of how God's grace changes and transforms us, and how his grace so shapes our desires that we *want* to obey and do the right thing. If evangelicals are to keep from falling into various forms of legalism, it will probably be because they have discovered something like Augustine's understanding of how a gracious God saves us – where God's grace is fundamental to the beginning, the continuing and the completing of our salvation. That is, God continues to transform our *desires* and *affections* so that we actually *desire* what we *ought* to desire, and we *want* to do those things which *ought* to be done.

Conclusion

At one level all of Western theology has been – in a sense – a long series of footnotes to Augustine. He bequeathed to the church deep reflection on how to talk and think about God, how language works when speaking about

God, and on the nature of the triune God. Augustine's understanding of the knowing process is a rich mine of resources as Christians wade through the challenges of modern and so-called postmodern thought forms, which are so often sceptical about the possibility of knowledge – whether of God or of the created order. Augustine's *The Trinity* (at times an ignored text when people are summarizing his significance) is still a treasure of insight, and worthy of sustained attention. Augustine wrestled with what this trinitarian God is going to be like, whom Christians will one day see. His insights as to how one must affirm one God in three divine persons – where the three are understood in terms of relationship and love – is seminal. The tradition that followed Augustine continued to wrestle with the reality and implications of his belief that God is fundamentally love. Augustine's doctrine of man as sinner – and hence in need of radical grace – is central to understanding Scripture, and every evangelical must still come to terms with his view of original sin. Augustine's perception of the 'two cities' has informed Christian thinking on the nature of politics, culture and many similar issues. Finally, Augustine is rightfully considered to be the Doctor of Grace, for it is in Augustine's understanding of grace that he has perhaps made his greatest mark on the church. The grace of God, set upon us from all eternity, that moves us to trust in and believe God, that transforms our hearts, that efficaciously moves us to obey God as we travel as pilgrims on our way to the city of God, and that so moves in us that we persevere to the end – this is a grace worth believing and promulgating in the world today. For these and many other reasons, Augustine is worthy of our attention, and can help evangelicals as we strive to understand and serve the God of Scripture.

Bibliography

Primary sources in Latin

There are several ways to access Augustine's writings in the language in which he wrote (Latin):

CETEDOC Library of Christian Latin Texts (CLCLT). This is the most recent attempt to provide digital access to Christian Latin texts.

Corpus Augustinianum Gissense a Cornelio Mayer editum (Basel: Schwabe, 1995). This is perhaps the finest digital collection of Augustine's works in Latin, comparable to the CLCLT.

Corpus Christianorum: Series latina (Turnhout: Brepels, 1953–). This series of Latin texts, originally available in printed form, is now available digitally as well.

Corpus scriptorum ecclesiasticorum latinorum (Vienna: Tempsky, 1865–). An older collection of Christian Latin texts, also available digitally.
Loeb Classical Library (London: William Heinemann, 1912–). A number of Augustine's works are featured in this series, which features Latin and English on opposite pages.
Patrologiae cursus completus: Series latina, ed. J.-P. Migne (Paris: Cerf, 1844–64). For many years this was the main way to access Christian Latin texts. It is now available digitally as the Patrologia latina Database.

Primary sources in English

A number of collections and series contain the writings of Augustine in English, but none contains *all* of his writings in English:

Ancient Christian Writers, ed. J. Quasten and J. C. Plumpe (Westminster, MD: Newman, 1946–). A series of classic Christian texts in English translation with helpful introductory essays and explanatory footnotes.
Cambridge Texts in the History of Political Thought (Cambridge: Cambridge University Press). Their edition of *The City of God*, tr. R. W. Dyson, was published in 1998.
Fathers of the Church (Washington, DC: Catholic University Press). This series, ed. R. J. Deferrari, contains a number of Augustine's works.
Library of Christian Classics (Louisville: Westminster John Knox). This series contains English translations of various Christian writers from across the span of Christian history. It contains volumes with a selection of Augustine's writings.
Oxford Library of the Fathers (Edinburgh: T. & T. Clark; Grand Rapids: Eerdmans). This series, ed. Marcus Dods, contains a number of works by Augustine.
A Select Library of the Nicene and Post-Nicene Fathers of the Christian Church (Grand Rapids: Eerdmans, 1994 repr.). This collection contains many of Augustine's writings and, while not exhaustive, is still helpful. The translation is dated, but has served English readers for many years.
Self-standing volumes. There are a number of self-standing or independent translations of Augustine's works that readers may want to obtain. For example, there are translations of *The City of God* (Henry Bettenson [London: Penguin, 2003]; and Marcus Dods [New York: Modern Library, 1950]). Similarly, Henry Chadwick's translation of *Confessions* (Oxford: Oxford University Press, 1991) is excellent.
Works of Saint Augustine (Brooklyn, NY: New City). New City has engaged in an ambitious effort to translate all of Augustine's writings into English, currently under the editorship of Boniface Ramsey. (Also available digitally.)

Where in Augustine might a reader start?

Confessions (either the New City ed. [Brooklyn, NY: 1991] by Maria Boulding, or the Henry Chadwick translation). *The City of God* is a treasure that cannot be mined enough

(Bettenson or Dods are both good; see above). If a reader wants a shorter introduction to the 'big picture' of Augustine's thought, I would recommend *The Augustine Catechism: The Enchiridion on Faith, Hope, and Love*, tr. Bruce Harbert (Hyde Park, NY: New City, 1999).

Here is a list of some seminal works of Augustine that might serve as a good summary of his thought. I have used the common English titles, with Latin titles in parentheses (and where there is some disagreement I have used the English titles from the tables in Allan D. Fitzgerald [ed.], *Augustine Through the Ages: An Encyclopedia* [Grand Rapids: Eerdmans, 1999]):

Against Two Letters of the Pelagians (*Contra duas epistulas Pelagianorum*)
On Christian Doctrine (*De doctrina christiana*)
The City of God (*De civitate Dei*)
Confessions (*Confessiones*)
On the Gift of Perseverance (*De dono perseverantiae*)
A Handbook on Faith, Hope and Love (*Enchiridion ad Laurentium de fide spe et caritate*)
On the Spirit and Letter (*De spiritu et littera*)
To Simplicianus (*Ad simplicianum*)
The Trinity (De Trinitate)

Where the novice student might start

There is a growing list of writings on Augustine. One might start with the following:

BROWN, PETER, *Augustine of Hippo: A Biography*, rev. ed. (London: Faber & Faber, 2000). This is probably still the classic volume on Augustine.

CHADWICK, HENRY, *A Very Short Introduction to Augustine* (Oxford: Oxford University Press, 2001). A helpful slim volume (sometimes what is most helpful!) by a senior scholar.

FITZGERALD, ALLAN D., *Augustine Through the Ages: An Encyclopedia* (Grand Rapids: Eerdmans, 1999). For the person who wants to get to know the thought of Augustine, it would be hard to improve upon the essays in this volume. Excellent bibliographies.

KNOWLES, ANDREW, and Pachomios Penkett, *Augustine and His World*, IVP Histories (Downers Grove: IVP, 2004). A wonderful introduction to Augustine, featuring a nice layout with beautiful artwork.

LITFIN, BRYAN, 'Augustine', in *Getting to Know the Church Fathers: An Evangelical Introduction* (Grand Rapids: Baker, 2007), pp. 213–237. A helpful introduction to Augustine.

NEEDHAM, N. R., *The Triumph of Grace: Augustine's Writings on Salvation* (London: Grace, 2000). Needham has provided readers with a true treasure, a collection of Augustine's writings on sin, grace and salvation.

Additional key studies and resources

This list is by nature impartial and incomplete, but I hope it will point interested readers to some of the key works on Augustine. Besides the studies below, interested readers should be aware of the main Augustine scholarly journal, *Augustinian Studies*.

BERNARDINO, ANGELO D., and Johannes Quasten, *Patrology*. Vol. 4: *The Golden Age of Latin Patristic Literature from the Council of Nicaea to the Council of Chalcedon* (Westminster, MD: Christian Classics, 1991). This series, while somewhat dated, is still an excellent place for the student to start who wants to get a sense of the issues and history of scholarship related to Augustine.

ARNOLD, D. W. H., and P. Bright (eds.), *'De doctrina Christiana': A Classic of Western Culture* (Notre Dame: University of Notre Dame Press, 1995). A helpful companion to *On Christian Doctrine.*

AYRES, LEWIS, *Augustine* (Oxford: Oxford University Press, 2010). This forthcoming volume promises to become a standard in the field.

BONNER, G., 'Augustine as Biblical Scholar', in *The Cambridge History of the Bible*, vol. 1, ed. P. R. Ackroyd and C. F. Evans (Cambridge: Cambridge University Press, 1970), pp. 541–563. A helpful summary of Augustine's approach to and appropriation of the Bible.

—, *St. Augustine of Hippo: Life and Controversies*, rev. ed. (Norwich: Canterbury, 1986). A classic work on the thought of Augustine.

BURNABY, JOHN, *Amor Dei: A Study in the Religion of St. Augustine* (London: Hodder & Stoughton, 1938). A classic study on Augustine, with attention to the centrality of love.

CHADWICK, HENRY, *Augustine: A Life* (Oxford: Oxford University Press, 2009). This is an overview of Augustine by a prominent Augustine scholar.

CLARK, MARY T., *Augustine*, Outstanding Christian Thinkers (London: Geoffrey Chapman, 1994). A helpful one-volume survey of Augustine's thought.

GILSON, ETIENNE, *The Christian Philosophy of Saint Augustine* (New York: Random House, 1960). A seminal work by a twentieth-century 'neo-Thomist'.

LANCEL, SERGE, *St Augustine*, tr. Antonia Nevill (London: SCM, 2002). A magisterial work, translated into English not long before Lancel's death. Full of helpful and fascinating historical background.

MARKUS, R. A., *Augustine's Theory of Signs* (Liverpool: University of Liverpool, 2003). Augustine was the first Christian thinker to develop a 'theory' of signs, and Markus is an able guide.

—, *Saeculum: History and Society in the Theology of St. Augustine* (Cambridge: Cambridge University Press, 1970; repr. 1989). A seminal work on a crucial aspect of Augustine's thought.

NASH, RONALD H., *The Light of Mind: St. Augustine's Theory of Knowledge* (Lexington: University of Kentucky Press, 1969). Essentially Nash's doctoral dissertation, and still the seminal work in the field. Recently reprinted by Academic Renewal, Lima, Ohio, 2003.

O'CONNELL, R. J., *Images of Conversion in St. Augustine's 'Confessions'* (New York: Fordham University Press, 1995). O'Connell has written a number of important studies, and this is one of his latest.

O'DONNELL, J. J., *Augustine: Confessions*, 3 vols. (Oxford: Clarendon, 1992). This three-volume commentary is essential for one wanting to explore *Confessions* in depth.

O'MEARA, JOHN J., *The Young Augustine: The Growth of St. Augustine's Mind up to his Conversion*, rev. ed. (London: Longmans, 1954). An important work on the pre-conversion Augustine.

PORTALIE, E., *A Guide to the Thought of Saint Augustine*, tr. R. J. Bastian (Chicago: Henry Regnery, 1960). A little older, but still a helpful introduction.

RIST, JOHN M., *Augustine: Ancient Thought Baptized* (Cambridge: Cambridge University Press, 1994). A collection of various essays by a prominent scholar.

TESELLE, EUGENE, *Augustine the Theologian* (London: Burns & Oates, 1970). A good overview by an established scholar.

WRIGHT, DAVID F., 'Justification in Augustine', in Bruce L. McCormack, *Justification in Perspective: Historical Developments and Contemporary Challenges* (Grand Rapids: Baker Academic; Edinburgh: Rutherford House, 2006). A helpful analysis of Augustine on justification, from a Protestant scholar.

It is also worth drawing attention to James J. O'Donnell's web page, which is a helpful holding place for many things Augustinian: <http://www.georgetown.edu/faculty/jod/augustine>, accessed 4 Dec. 2009.

7. ANSELM

David Hogg

Approaching Anselm

It is not always an easy task to reconstruct the events pertinent to and surrounding the life of people who lived in the European Middle Ages. There are several reasons for this. The most common reason is that biographies and autobiographies were not part of the mainstream of literature at that time. Until the later Middle Ages, writing an autobiography was considered an exercise in vanity and self-aggrandizement. Who would be so arrogant as to think that their life was worth so much? The great counter example to this was none other than Augustine, the famous bishop of Hippo. His autobiography, though, was not written in what we today might consider the usual manner. The purpose of his work was to trace out a spiritual pilgrimage in which God's hand was evident only in hindsight. Augustine's purpose was more didactic than informative. Nevertheless, even this example of autobiography was considered throughout much of the medieval period as a special case. It was fine for Augustine to write what he did, in part, because he was a truly great man and, in part, because he was remarkably humble, but he was the exception and not the rule.

While autobiographies were rather scarce, biographies were slightly more popular. We should be careful not to assume, though, that biographies were written with pure or objective motives. Many times, a biography was written to highlight and publicize the virtues and godly character of someone with the hope that there might at least be an increased awareness of their life and a concomitant awareness of the monastery, convent, church or town with which they had been associated before dying. Such awareness could bring any number of benefits. This does not mean, of course, that biographers were self-centred charlatans seeking to trade on another's integrity for their own benefit, far from it. Rather, we should think of these chroniclers as standing in a tradition originally influenced by Augustine's *Confessions*, but directed and developed in different ways over time. Just as Augustine was not content simply to pass on a chronological account of the events of his life, but provide a clear interpretation of pertinent events that highlighted points of intersection between the human and the divine, so medieval biographers sought to do the same for others. The exegetical skill required in the examination of the text of Scripture was a skill that transferred to the analysis of an individual's life. There are multiple levels of interpretation for a given text in the Bible, and there are multiple levels of interpretation for specific events in someone's life.

Does this mean we cannot trust autobiographies or biographies from the Middle Ages? No, but it means we must read them intelligently, as they were intended. It is easy for us to forget that medieval biographers were writing for an audience who shared, for the most part, their knowledge, their world-view, their appreciation for the use of various literary devices, allusions and intimations. We do not share very many of these things and so must take greater care and exert more effort to understand not only the content of these works, but the purpose and intention of the parts that make up the whole.[1]

With these considerations in mind we can begin to approach Anselm, whose biography was written by his devoted student and friend, Eadmer. It is the general consensus that this biography falls just short of what we now refer to as an authorized or official biography. It cannot claim to be authorized since Anselm did not give it his imprimatur. In fact, when Anselm discovered that one of his close friends was writing a biography he asked if the rumours were true. Eadmer reluctantly admitted to the project and gave Anselm the wax tablets on which he had been writing his secret biography. Initially, Anselm's response to the work was positive. He even offered some help, advice and an editorial hand. It was not long, however, before Anselm commanded Eadmer to destroy the tablets on which Eadmer had been working. As deep

1. For more reflection on this see Michael Staunton, 'Eadmer's *Vita Anselmi*: a reinterpretation', *Journal of Medieval History* 23 (1997), pp. 1–14.

as Anselm's desire was to make every effort to help guide others, he appears to have realized the inherent hubris in writing an autobiography.

Despite this early disappointment, Eadmer indulged in some creative thinking that, on reflection, might better be described as cunning. Although he had taken a vow of obedience (not only to God, but to his superiors) that required he destroy the tablets on which he had begun writing Anselm's biography, he could not bear to destroy the fruits of such labour. In a weak or perhaps devious moment, Eadmer determined that sufficient obedience would be achieved if he followed the letter of Anselm's command, even if he did not follow its spirit. Strictly speaking, Anselm had commanded that the wax tablets Eadmer had been using be destroyed, and they were, but not before their contents had been copied onto other wax tablets![2]

Given that Anselm did not know what Eadmer had done, and would become suspicious had Eadmer asked too many questions about Anselm's past and experiences, where and how did Eadmer obtain and compile the information that became his biography? We know that the material detailing Anselm's early life came directly from Anselm himself, most likely before the destruction of the original written drafts. Additional material, and especially the particulars surrounding the many recorded miracles, came from interviews or correspondence with several monks at Anselm's former monastery in Bec (northwest France). The later material covering Anselm's reign as Archbishop of Canterbury is provided by Eadmer's own experience.[3] Clearly, Eadmer was intent on providing an accurate and reliable account of Anselm's life that would elicit appropriate appreciation for the man, and due praise to God. Nevertheless, as has already been mentioned, we must take care lest we glibly assume that Eadmer has provided a purely objective work. As with all biographies (medieval or not), the purpose is not simply to retell events in chronological sequence, but to provide an interpretation of those events. In the case of dignitaries or other significant figures, the details are often juxtaposed with broader developments in political, social or intellectual arenas in order to offer further interpretation on issues of contemporary concern. As we look at Anselm's life, then, we must take care to recognize that facts are not given merely as discrete pieces of information, but are part of a larger whole intended to convince the reader of positions and beliefs the author has deemed important.

---

2. Eadmer, *The Life of St Anselm Archbishop of Canterbury*, tr. R. W. Southern (Oxford: Clarendon Press, 1972), p. 151.
3. Ibid., p. 149.

Introducing Anselm

Anselm was born in 1033 in the small town of Aosta, in what is now northern Italy. At the time of Anselm's birth it was on the border between Lombardy and Burgundy. His Burgundian mother, Ermenberga, was a devout Christian who desired that her son should grow in the nurture and admonition of the Lord. His father Gundulf, on the other hand, is described as given to a secular way of life.[4] By this is meant that Gundulf was a man of the world who gave little heed to the things of God or the Christian faith. It was in this state that Gundulf remained until very near his death when he converted and became a monk.

At some point when Anselm was still a teenager his mother died. As difficult as the grief of such a loss would have been to bear, Anselm had to bear the added grief of living with his father. There is every indication that the two men did not get along particularly well, and this ultimately led to Anselm deciding to leave home when he was in his early twenties. For the next few years of Anselm's life we know almost nothing. He appears to have wandered around Europe, but it is reasonable to assume that his wanderings were not entirely random. Recall that his mother was from Burgundy and still had family there. We cannot be sure of this, but it is more than possible that the young man headed for a happier homestead in the company of those who, like his mother, would care for him and encourage his interests.

Whatever Anselm spent his time doing and wherever he may have spent it, we do know that he eventually decided to investigate monastic living. Again, why he should have decided to pursue this lifestyle is a matter of some speculation, but he did find the academic possibilities and opportunities appealing. In the mid to late eleventh century, European university education was not yet possible. The precursor to universities, the cathedral schools, were just getting started, but they required what Anselm lacked, money. We might also speculate from Anselm's later life that he was a somewhat reclusive and quiet young man. This is not to suggest that he was poorly gifted at leading or unable to do well in various administrative tasks, but it is to suggest that his preference in lifestyle was to remain quiet and enjoy long periods of undisturbed privacy.

For anyone aware of Anselm's later life this could appear to be an incorrect assessment given his impressive epistolary output and interaction with many people from every walk of life. It is true that Anselm became a busy man with a lot of responsibility, but accepting responsibility and carrying it out with

4. Ibid., p. 3.

integrity does not mean a man needs to change his personality. Although there are certainly examples to the contrary, when monks looked for leaders they preferred to choose men according to the quality of their life and character rather than for their industry in leadership. The character of one's life then, as now, is something that is not developed through busyness, but through meditation on and obedience to God's word. It was only as the integrity of Anselm's life became evident that he was asked to take on more and more responsibility and leadership.

Anselm's monastic context

Returning to Anselm's early desire to join a monastery, we are told that he visited and considered a number of options including one of the great monasteries of his day, the Abbey of Cluny. By the time Anselm was old enough to consider joining a monastery, Cluny had been operating for about 150 years. Like every other monastery before it, Cluny began amidst humble circumstances and with a desire to remain in such circumstances. Ironically, it was this desire that some would argue was both Cluny's greatest strength and its greatest weakness.

The group at Cluny had committed to a revitalization of the Benedictine Order, the Order started by Benedict of Nursia in the sixth century. After a period of time adjusting to solitary life, Benedict eventually established himself at Monte Cassino in Italy. He had many followers who desired to live a similar lifestyle and it soon became apparent to Benedict that he needed to organize this band of brothers more formally and strictly. Borrowing from a number of monastic rules, some of them already well known and followed, Benedict formulated his own version of what proper ascetic existence should look like. Over time, as other monasteries were formed and chose to adopt Benedict's Rule the interpretation of the Rule became quite diverse. Some houses held to a quite strict interpretation and even added to the Rule, while others preferred a freer interpretation, allowing for the pursuit of more diverse activities.

The diversity of interpretation and practice within the Benedictines becomes especially apparent during the Carolingian Renaissance of the ninth century. During that time Charlemagne attempted to make sweeping reforms in a number of different areas, including the church. Initially, he was helped in this task by Alcuin of York who was, in turn, helped by like-minded church leaders. Among those who continued the agenda of reform and unity in the Carolingian church was Benedict of Aniane. This Benedict was given the task of unifying the practice and interpretation of the Benedictine Rule among all the monasteries within the borders of the Carolingian Empire. Benedict of Aniane worked successfully towards this task, but after his death the unity he accomplished was not so equally maintained. It was from a desire to return to this state of affairs that led to the foundation of the monastery at Cluny in 909.

The Cluniac Order prided itself on a strict adherence to the Benedictine Rule in the tradition of Benedict of Aniane. In fact, their adherence went beyond what Benedict had suggested to the point where manual labour was reduced to a minimum and the amount of time spent in services was demanding. From the perspective of the ruling classes, this group looked very committed and was, for that reason highly sought after. It was not long before other monasteries aligned themselves with Cluny and their members were being asked to found new monasteries throughout Europe. On the one hand, the opportunity to establish monasteries and even churches was a very good thing, but on the other hand, it meant that they grew ever more powerful and wealthy. Over time Cluny would fall to the fate of so many houses before them; they would become ever more like the world and the aristocrats they served and ever less tied to the principles of their foundation.

It was as Cluny's reputation was rapidly expanding that Anselm considered joining them. In the end, he decided not to because the demands they laid on their members for services was so great that the time remaining in the day for study was slight. Anselm was impressed, but it was a group that did not comport either with his desires or his abilities. The monastery at Bec was, however, a different story.

Anselm was drawn to this relatively new and minor monastery mainly because of the reputation of its prior, Lanfranc. Lanfranc was one of the intelligentsia of his day and well respected by monarchs as much as by monks. When Anselm arrived at the monastery he was immediately impressed with Lanfranc's learning, not to mention the quality of his life. What is more, the monks at Bec held to a slightly less rigorous interpretation of Benedict's Rule which allowed for plenty of study time should a monk so please. In 1060, then, Anselm joined the monks at Bec and began living a life from which he would eventually be called, but for which he never lost his love.

Only three years after Anselm joined the community at Bec, Lanfranc left to become abbot of the monastery in Caen. Although there were other men with more experience and seniority, Anselm was elected to replace Lanfranc as prior. In such a short time Anselm was already proving the mettle of his mind and the quality of his character to those more seasoned in life than himself. It is most likely during his time as prior that Anselm composed some of his first prayers and meditations as well as his two works on the existence of God, the

Monologion and the *Proslogion*. He also began what would become an extensive correspondence.

After the Abbot of Bec died, Anselm was elected to succeed him in 1078. It was during this next portion of his life that Anselm would write works on the nature of truth and free will. He also tackled the rather difficult subject of the origin of evil and how Satan came to be. These works tend to be more philosophical in nature, but they must not be thought of as philosophy. Anselm was adamant that all of his works were an example of exegetical and theological method. Many in our day would question this, but their doubt about this matter stems more from a shift in focus. Whereas our contemporary theologians and exegetes tend to emphasize the analysis of the minutiae of the biblical text, often to the exclusion of broader theological considerations throughout the canon, the medieval theologian preferred to think and write with a view to a broader understanding of the canon. In practice this generally means that commentaries from the Middle Ages are replete with intertextual links, while commentaries from our own day are replete with grammatical and historical analysis. The point here is not to claim one is better than the other, but simply to point out that different emphases do not necessarily constitute superior outcomes.[5]

Connecting context to corpus

To this point, Anselm's biography seems fairly straightforward, perhaps even a bit mundane, and possibly even irrelevant to the task of addressing his theology. There is, though, a great deal of relevance to this history because, as we have noted, it was during this time of monastic existence that Anselm wrote some of his works. It could almost go without saying that the reason Anselm was able to write the prayers that he did was because he spent so much time in a place of prayer, surrounded by men whose life was devoted to prayer. Moreover, the monastery was full of men persistently and consistently studying the Bible and the theology handed down to them by the church fathers and other great luminaries. As every monk knew, the way to grow in depth of

---

5. For more on Anselm's theological method and manner of exegesis see Stanley G. Kane, '*Fides Quaerens Intellectum* in Anselm's Thought', *Scottish Journal of Theology* 26 (1973), pp. 40–62. The reader will also find Robert Crouse's article helpful: 'Anselm of Canterbury and Medieval Augustinians', *Toronto Journal of Theology* 3 (1987), pp. 60–68.

prayer was to grow in depth in the knowledge of God. The more one knew God and about God, the more one prayed and wanted to pray. Anselm was in the ideal situation to be able to pen prayers for those less able.

The most important reason to be aware of Anselm's early history and pedigree, however, has to do with understanding the *Proslogion*. As we will see, the *Proslogion* is the work in which Anselm sets out to prove, or perhaps to put it more accurately, to probe the existence of God. Countless articles and chapters and essays have been written essentially arguing that Anselm has done a poor-to-mediocre job of defining and defending the possibility of God's existence. What these authors so often miss is that Anselm sets his investigation into God's existence squarely and openly in the context of prayer. Anselm wrote the *Proslogion* as a monk, not as a philosopher, nor as a disinterested or objective academic. It is vital to grasp the fact that Anselm never believed theology was something that could or should be pursued merely as one subject amidst an array of disciplines. Theology is different. Theology is unique. For Anselm what sets theology apart from any other subject is its object. The object of theology is God, and, at the risk of stating the obvious, there is nothing like God in all creation. He is, after all, the Creator.

Since God is unique in every way, we cannot approach God as we like, but only in the way or ways he has permitted. It is this foundational premise that underlies Anselm's great and oft-repeated dictum that, 'I do not understand so that I might believe, but I believe so that I might understand; for I also believe that unless I believe I cannot understand.'[6] Proofs for the existence of God would take slightly different forms in the centuries to come as universities developed and the expectations of both pedagogy and culture began to change the way theologians expressed themselves. Here it is tempting to say that to judge Anselm by the standards and expectations of later periods in history is both anachronistic and unfair, but while this is true, there is a far more dangerous issue at stake. To judge Anselm's theological method, his conviction that belief is the foundation for understanding, by methodologies developed after his time is to run the risk of chronological snobbery.[7] Is all change in time progress? Are all new ideas superior to old ones? An affirmative answer to such questions would make no sense of theologians' continual return to the past as

---

6. See below for this quote in context in the first chapter of the *Proslogion*.

7. For more on this see James E. Bradley and Richard A. Muller, *Church History: An Introduction to Research, Reference Works and Methods* (Grand Rapids: Eerdmans, 1995) and David Bebbington, *Patterns in History: A Christian Perspective on Historical Thought* (Grand Rapids: Baker Book House, 1990).

the source for what is written in the present. Anselm's method was not only the method of a monk meditating in a monastery, but of a Christian steeped in the revelation of God to humanity.

There are many more details to Anselm's life worth noting, not to mention some humorous ones, but the detail that matters most for our purposes is his appointment as Archbishop of Canterbury in 1093. There is no evidence at all that Anselm desired or even thought about the possibility of becoming archbishop. He was more than happy to remain Abbot of Bec, tending to his students, helping others as he had opportunity and living out a quiet life. How, then, did he attain such high office?

After William the Conqueror died his son William Rufus took the throne. The most efficient way to describe Rufus' reign is to compare him to Reheboam, son of Solomon, son of David, king of Israel. We read of Reheboam that he acted foolishly, refused to listen to the elders of the land, refused to keep his father's counsellors in his court and did what was pleasing in his own sight. The result was disaster for Israel. The same is true of Rufus. He was kept in check for the first two years of his reign only because Lanfranc, former Prior of Bec and Abbot of Caen, had been appointed by William the Conqueror as Archbishop of Canterbury and was still alive and sufficiently powerful to keep the young king from some of his grander follies. When Lanfranc died, however, Rufus began living immorally and with reckless abandon. Although there is disagreement amongst historians as to his motives, one of the things Rufus did that impoverished the English people spiritually was to keep Lanfranc's position empty. By doing this Rufus could collect the revenue from that office and use it for his own purposes rather than doing what should have been done, namely, to redistribute the money to redress needs and poverty throughout the land.

The situation looked grim on several fronts and did not appear to be improving until Rufus became very ill. It looked to all that the king was on his deathbed and for that reason he asked the bishops present what he should do to make amends for his wicked ways. They answered that he should appoint an archbishop who could lead the church as well as the nation. The man they called upon to fulfil this task was Anselm. Despite his objections of being too old (he was now 60) the bishops prevailed and won the day. All might have improved had not Rufus recovered from his illness. Newly invigorated and emboldened, he carried on in his old ways with greater vigour than before. Anselm objected to many of the king's decisions and, after a lengthy stalemate and much frustration, he decided that he needed to leave the country to seek the greater counsel and aid of the pope. So began Anselm's first exile that lasted for three years.

Anselm would eventually return to England after Rufus died under suspicious circumstances. Rufus' successor and brother, Henry I, asked Anselm to return in order to help bring peace and stability to the country. Anselm did so in 1100, only to leave for a second exile in 1103 because of difficult relations with the monarchy yet again. To everyone's relief and joy the rift between king and archbishop was mended and Anselm returned to England in 1106 where he remained until his death in 1109.

These final details are, like the details of Anselm's early life, not insignificant with respect to his writing. It was in the years leading up to and during his first exile that Anselm wrote *Cur Deus Homo*, addressing the question of Christ's atonement. It must be admitted that Anselm may have written on the atonement for the simple reason he states at the beginning of the work, that he is helping some of his fellow monks with a difficult question. It is curious, though, that amidst the many requests we know he received for help on different topics, that he should chose this one, at a time when England was suffering spiritually and Normandy (northeastern France) was not doing so well either. What was needed at the end of the eleventh century was a reminder that sin was a weighty matter, that the Devil was not in charge, that God was still on his throne, that God was holy and just and that the only way of salvation possible was through faith in Jesus' atoning death and resurrection. This is what *Cur Deus Homo* delivers. Judging another man's motives is not easy when that man is living; judging a man's motives nine hundred years after the fact is no easier. Nevertheless, there are enough similarities between the spiritual needs of the day, about which Anselm was keenly aware, and the subjects and ideas that he addressed in *Cur Deus Homo*, to make a good case that Anselm was writing a piece of theology that dealt with the issues of his immediate context, and has continued to speak to the church and the world in which we live.

We turn now to consider the content of the three most significant and enduring aspects of Anselm's theology. We will look first at his prayers, then at his arguments for God's existence in the *Proslogion*, and finally at his theology of the atonement in *Cur Deus Homo* and his *Meditation on Human Redemption.*

Theological analysis

The prayers

Anselm stands in a long tradition of pastors and theologians who have written prayers for the edification of believers in private and public worship. While Anselm's prayers were (and still are) sometimes used in public worship, his desire was that they be used most assiduously in private. In Anselm's letters we discover that he wrote many of his prayers for aristocratic women who had more time on their hands than most other women of their day. Granted, such women were not wallowing in idleness all day long, but they did have the luxury of ordering their day and using their servants in such a way that they could set aside time for private meditation and prayer. In addition to these women, Anselm also wrote prayers for men and women who, whether they had entered the cloistered life or not, were living in relative seclusion for the purpose of giving themselves over to prayer and the pursuit of piety. In an effort to direct their thoughts and aid them in their reflections, these people would ask leaders in the church and holy men and women to give them help. Anselm answered such calls by writing prayers.

Now the most obvious question centres on the content of these prayers. What, in other words, did Anselm write for these women and others who hoped to lift their souls to God in devotion? For many years after Anselm died this was not such a straightforward question. It appears that Anselm's prayers were so highly thought of that a number of now anonymous writers copied his style as best they could and then credited what they wrote to Anselm. If emulation is among the highest forms of flattery then here, surely, is the measure of the man. For those who wish to distinguish the originals from the copies, however, pseudonymous works are the proverbial thorn in the flesh. Thankfully, though, during the early decades of the twentieth century scholars such as F. S. Schmitt, A. Wilmart, R. W. Southern and others worked assiduously to distinguish what was written by Anselm from what had been later written by others in his name.

In what follows, I have not provided a complete translation of all of Anselm's prayers even though there are only nineteen.[8] I have instead provided translations of portions of the prayers that highlight certain characteristics or points of interest. We begin, then, with Anselm's prayer to God.

Prayer to God

Anselm's *Prayer to God* may be his earliest surviving prayer. It is rather brief, much like the prayers produced in the period immediately preceding Anselm's by the Anglo-Saxons and Carolingians. Many of his other prayers are much longer and more elaborate. While the evidence is far from conclusive, it does seem more likely that Anselm moved from the shorter and simpler to the

---

8. For translations of all of Anselm's prayers along with his meditations, see Benedicta Ward's *The Prayers and Meditations of Saint Anselm with the Proslogion* (London: Penguin Books, 1973).

longer and more complex. Indeed, the affinities between this prayer (and one or two others like it) and earlier prayers by Anselm's theological predecessors are strong enough to suggest a conscious mimicking. Furthermore, the *Prayer to God* is a prayer that, as we will see, imitates the Lord's Prayer as given in the sixth chapter of Matthew's Gospel. All of this hints rather heavily that Anselm's concern was to stay within biblical boundaries and to follow the example of his theological forebears.[9]

> Omnipotent God, merciful Father and good Lord, be merciful to me a sinner. Grant me forgiveness of my sins and that I may avoid and conquer all snares and temptations and harmful desires. May I completely shun inwardly and outwardly what you prohibit, yet do and keep what you command. May I believe, hope, love and will in accord with your knowledge and power. Give me complete humility and piety that I might discern between abstinence and the mortification of the flesh. May I love you, pray to you, praise you, meditate upon you in accordance with all that you do and think, purely, soberly, zealously, with a true and effective mind. Grant that I would know your commands, love them and, with readiness, obey them. O Lord, may I always move forward with humility to that which is greater, and never grow faint. And, Lord, do not give me over to my will nor human ignorance and infirmity, nor to what I deserve, nor to anything else other than your holy character. But according to your kindness, do with me and all my thoughts and action what is pleasing to you, so that by me and in me and through me your will alone might always be done. Deliver me from all evil, and lead me into eternal life. Amen.[10]

The first sentence of this prayer sets the tone not only for the rest of the prayer, but also for much of the theology of the prayers as a whole. In the first sentence we are drawn towards God's sovereignty, graciousness and goodness. The reader is then led to consider his or her own state, 'a sinner'. These two themes, the greatness of God and the sinfulness of humanity, dominate much of the prayers and well they should. Throughout Anselm's prayers, not

---

9. Although these translations cannot do the original Latin justice, the reader ought to bear in mind that Anselm intended his prayers should be read out loud. Reading out loud has many advantages, one of which is that the reader adds another sense, hearing, to the experience of seeking God.

10. Cf. Ward, pp. 91–92, ll. 1–32. All translations of Anselm's works are my own. I will, however, include page and line references to Benedicta Ward's published translation so that readers can gain access to more than what can be incorporated into this chapter.

to mention his other works, Scripture is woven into the very fabric of his prose. This is not a deliberate action, but the result of a mind that naturally pours out what has been supernaturally poured in.

Consider the general outline of the above prayer in relation to what is commonly called the Lord's Prayer in the sixth chapter of Matthew's Gospel. The reader is led to consider some of the names and attributes of God. Here is a hallowing, a declaration of the holiness of God. From this consideration Anselm moves seamlessly to contrition for sins as he enjoins us to beg for forgiveness. Anselm pauses over the depth of sin. This is no easy confession. There is no place for familiarity with God, as though he owes us anything, only familiarity with sin that breeds contempt. Next Anselm makes numerous and frequent requests that he would be able to follow God's commands. In this prayer the commands are not simply hurdles over which the believer must jump, but objects of love. What is done in heaven with rejoicing must surely be mirrored on earth. Finally, and most obviously, the connection with Matthew 6 is cemented in the closing lines as the request is made for deliverance from all evil into eternal life. The comparison between this prayer and the biblical text is not exact, but then it is not intended to be exact. Anselm's prayers frequently recall Scripture, not in a wooden manner, but in such a way as to spur the reader to a deeper appreciation of what is contained in Scripture. Much as a preacher seeks to explain and draw out for the listener the expansive meaning of a smaller portion of revelation, so Anselm hoped to do the same for his readers.

Prayer to Christ

It does not take the reader long to see that in these prayers, as elsewhere, whether Anselm is addressing God or the saints directly, he never loses his sense of the sovereignty, grandeur and glory of God that is infused and suffused in believers. It is this sense of the divine that leads Anselm to write as he does when addressing Christ.

> Lord Jesus Christ, my redeemer, my mercy, my salvation; I praise you, I give you thanks. Yet how immensely unequal are such in comparison to your blessings, and how much more does the worthiness of devotion demand, for how great is the leanness of my desire and abundant the sweetness of your love: nevertheless, by some sort of praise, by some sort of thanks, not equal to what I know I owe; but as I am able, my soul will pay its debt to you.[11]

---

11. Cf. Ward, p. 93, ll. 1–11.

In these opening words Anselm begins characteristically by drawing his and our attention to the magnitude of God and the majesty of his holy nature. He does this effectively by considering God's nature and activity and comparing that with the lowly estate of his creatures. It may sound strange to modern ears, but Anselm believed that prayer should begin with an admission of insufficiency and inadequacy. Some may wish to question this in light of the boldness with which parts of Scripture allow the believer to approach God. Has not the blood of Christ provided access into the very presence of God where once there was a barrier dividing deity from humanity? To this Anselm responds,

> Hope of my heart, strength of my soul, help of my weakness, by your powerful kindness complete what in my powerless weakness I attempt. My life, the end to which I strive, although I have not yet attained to love you as I ought, still let my desire for you be as great as my love ought to be.[12]

Here Anselm is reminding the reader that however inadequate her or his prayers may be, and whatever sin may cloud their vision, the mighty grace of God is sufficient to overcome such shortcomings and faults. To this end Anselm continues his prayer.

> My light, you see my conscience because, Lord, before you is all my desire, and if my soul wills any good you gave it to me. O Lord, if what you inspire is good, or more precisely, because it is good that I wish to love you, give me what you make me want, so that I might love you to the degree that you command. I give you praise and thanks for the desire you have inspired. I offer praise and prayer so that the gift which you freely gave to me may not be unfruitful. Perfect what you began, and give to me what you have made me desire, turning my apathy into your fervent love which comes unmerited.
>
> To this, most merciful Lord, my prayer is directed: remembering and meditating on your blessings so that you might stir up your love in me. O Lord, your goodness created me, your mercy cleansed creation from original sin, your patience has so far endured and nourished and waited for me even when I willed to commit many sordid sins after the cleansing of baptism. You wait, good Lord, for my correction. My soul waits for the breath of your grace that I may be sufficiently repentant and live well.
>
> My God, my Creator, who tolerates and nourishes me, be my help. I thirst for you, I hunger after you, I desire you, I long for you, I eagerly yearn for you. Just as an orphan who is deprived of the presence of a wonderful father, weeping and wailing

12. Cf. Ward, p. 93, ll. 12–19.

> incessantly, embraces the thought of his father's face with his whole heart, so too, though not as much as I ought, but as much as I am able, remember your passion, how you were slapped, your scourging, your cross, your wounds, how you were slain for me, how you were prepared for burial and buried, while simultaneously recalling your glory, resurrection and marvellous ascension. This I hold with unflinching faith, and I weep for the affliction of exile, hoping in the solitary consolation of your return, passionately longing for the glorious contemplation of your face.
>
> Alas! I was not able to see the Lord of the Angels humbled to speak with man, so that men might be exalted to speak with angels, when God, the offended one, died of his own free will that the sinner might live. Alas! I did not deserve to be astounded in the presence of such admirable and inestimable love. Why, O my soul, were you not present to be pierced by that most sharp and painful sword when you could not bear the lance piercing the side of your Saviour, when you could not see the shame of the nails in the hands and feet of your creator, when the blood of your Redeemer drained away? Why were you not drunk with tears of bitterness when he drank the gall of bitterness? Why did you have no compassion on the most pure Virgin and most worthy mother of your most blessed Lord?[13]

None but the hardest of hearts could read such a prayer and fail to be moved. Truly, Anselm could mine the depths of contrition in order to animate the imagination like few of his contemporaries. Even a casual reading of this opening section reveals a strategy that seeks to use language powerfully yet sparingly. Note carefully the repeated desire to see the face of God, to know the glory of God and to experience the presence of God through the incarnate Son. In the Middle Ages readers would have immediately recognized that they were being led in pursuit of the beatific vision. Simply put, the beatific vision is the desire to see, that is to understand, God to ever greater degrees in a never ending pursuit of closer union with him. While there were some who interpreted this idea in a mystical fashion, seeking God through self-inflicted suffering, theologians made it clear that the beatific vision is attained through the joyful study and comprehension of the Bible.

The goal of the beatific vision, of growing ever closer in union with Christ, was tantamount to being recast into the image of the Son of God. It is not enough to know *that* God exists, that there is a being through whom creation was made. Equally, it is not enough to believe that God is omnipotent. Anselm spent much time and effort seeking to convince his readers that a knowledge of God that is devoid of an understanding of who he is, his person and character,

---

13. Cf. Ward, pp. 93–95, ll. 20–91.

is a deficient, indeed insufficient knowledge. Knowing that God exists has little or no value if we do not also know who God is. Pursuing the beatific vision is the road along which both believer and unbeliever alike must travel if they wish to answer that most fundamental question, does God exist? We will see shortly that when Anselm answers this question more fully and directly he does so in the context of prayer. What this particular prayer adds to that discussion is a Christological starting point. If we wish to see God, to know God as he has made himself known then we must turn to the one who is the exact representation of his nature and character. We must turn to Jesus Christ.

Prayer to the Holy Cross

Placing Christ at the centre was not, however, always Anselm's concern, or so it might seem. Consider what he says as he draws the worshipper's attention to the cross.

> Holy cross, which calls to mind that cross on which our Lord Jesus Christ died that we, through his death, are being lead away from eternal death to which all our misery was leading us, and has raised us to eternal life which we were losing through our sinning. I adore, I venerate and I glory in that cross which you represent to us, and in that same cross our merciful Lord and what he has done for us by that mercy. O worthy cross in which is our salvation, life and resurrection! O precious wood through which we are saved and set free! O sign to be revered through which we are sealed for God! O glorious cross, we ought solely to glory in you![14]

For those in many Protestant traditions this prayer is rather disturbing. There are overt hints of relics and the veneration of objects. To be sure, we should not deny that Anselm was writing and thinking in a context where relics and the veneration of objects associated with saints or even Jesus himself were believed to carry spiritual benefits. We should, however, bear the direction of thought in mind and recognize that it is, once again, Christological. In other words, while this prayer is clearly occasioned by the sight of a replica cross calling to mind the real cross, the point of the prayer is to concentrate on the purpose of the cross and on the one who died on that cross. This is, in fact, what Paul does in the New Testament. The word 'cross' is the term often used by the apostle to indicate all that Christ accomplished in his incarnation and life. Consider Galatians 6:14, 'May it never be that I should boast, except in the cross of our Lord Jesus Christ through which the world has been crucified

---

14. Cf. Ward, p. 102, ll. 1–15.

to me and I to the world.'[15] Note how the rest of the prayer, though mingled with elements of veneration for the object itself, is thoroughly saturated in a theology of the cross that ultimately draws attention to Christ. This attention on Christ, even through the lens of a symbol, remains throughout Anselm's prayers, and must be borne in mind to appreciate his prayers to saints, and especially his prayers to Mary.

Prayer to Mary (1)[16]

Modern Evangelicals continue to feel uncomfortable with Anselm's prayers to saints and Mary, and given the absence of evidence for or instruction on this practice in the Bible their disquiet is understandable. Moreover, Anselm does blur the line of thanksgiving and appropriation of salvation at times. It is for this reason that Anselm has been associated with rejuvenating the practice of venerating Mary. The person who deserves more of the credit for this development in the mid to late Middle Ages is Bernard of Clairvaux, but as the following excerpt shows, Anselm was not far behind.

> Holy woman, among the saints most holy after God, Mary, mother of wonderful virginity, virgin with wonderful fertility, you bore the Son of the Most High, you gave birth to the Saviour of depraved humanity. Lady, shining with such great holiness, unsurpassed in dignity, it is beyond doubt that you are not least endowed with power and piety. To you, O giver of life, O mother of salvation, O temple of piety and mercy, my miserable soul endeavours to present itself to you, weak with the sickness of sin, cut with the wounds of crimes, putrid with the ulcers of disgrace. On you my soul depends to the degree that death calls me. I ask that you might deign to heal me by the power of your merits and your holy prayers. For, holy woman, there is no end to the stupidity that alienates me from you, so that I have almost no sense of the enormity of my sickness. I am so polluted by filth and such a stench that I fear you will turn your merciful face from me. Thus, I look to you for conversion even though I am racked with despair such that even my mouth has been silenced of prayer.
>
> My sin, my wicked ways, since you have destroyed my soul with your poison, why do you make it a horror with your filth, so that none are able to look upon my misery? If your burden hides any hope of a favourable answer to prayer, why do you block the voice of my prayer with your shame? If you have made my mind mad with love for you, why have you rendered my senses senseless with your apathy? Alas, how

15. Author's translation.
16. Anselm wrote three prayers to Mary. He did so not because he was obsessed with Mary, but because he was not satisfied with what he had written the first two times.

deep is the shame of sin in the presence of shining holiness! Alas, how confused is the sullied conscience in the sight of gleaning purity![17]

God's Existence: The **Proslogion**

Although we began by looking at Anselm's prayers, which he regarded as the foundation of his pastoral ministry and were a continual source of encouragement and consolation to those who received them, he is better known for two other works. The names of these works are not always so well remembered, but their content has endured the test of time. The first of these works is called the *Proslogion.* This brief treatise has perpetually stirred up much thinking and debate about the existence of God right up to the present day. Anselm's purpose was, as you will soon see, to try to figure out if there was a single argument that could be used to prove God's existence. Anselm had already written a slightly longer treatise on the matter called the *Monologion*, but he considered that work too unwieldy; there were too many intertwining arguments and lines of thought for it to be useful. Consequently, at the continued urging of his fellow monks at Bec and in conjunction with his own desire to produce a more effective work on the subject of God's existence, Anselm set to work. The opening chapters below comprise the foundation of his thinking and require some work on the reader's part, but the effort paid in comprehending Anselm's argument is repaid with dividends to those who persevere.

Prologue

After I wrote a little work at the request of certain brothers, in which I desired to provide an example of meditating according to reason that is consistent with the faith, and in which I assumed the position of someone silently reasoning with himself who investigates what he does not know, it occurred to me that I had constructed an argument consisting of many links as though in a long chain. I began to wonder, then, if it were possible to find one argument which required no other arguments for proof and was sufficient in itself, and would be able to show that God truly exists, and that he is the greatest good requiring nothing else for existence, yet on whom all things rely for their existence and well-being, and whatever else we believe about the divine nature. To this end I often and with diligence turned my thoughts. Now sometimes it seemed to me that it was possible to attain what I sought, whereas at other times the answer escaped from my mind's eye so that eventually, in desperation, I decided to stop. I decided not to seek after something that could not be found. But when I tried to prevent the matter from entering my thoughts, lest my mind be occupied in vain

---

17. Cf. Ward, pp. 107–108, ll. 1–39.

and from other matters in which I might be able to accomplish something, again and again the idea began persistently to force itself upon me against my wishes and efforts to the contrary. Then one day, when I was growing weary of vehemently resisting its persistence, in the midst of my conflicting thoughts, the answer of which I had despaired of resolving presented itself so that I eagerly embraced the thought which I had with anxiety rejected.

Therefore, thinking that what I had rejoiced to find might please a reader if it were written down, I wrote down this very matter along with some others in the little work that follows under the persona of one trying to raise his mind to the contemplation of God, and seeking to understand what he believes. It is my judgment that neither the work I mentioned above nor this one are worthy to be called books, nor to bear the name of the author. Nevertheless, I do not think that either should be sent out without some sort of title so that when they come into the hands of readers they might be encouraged in some measure to read them. Consequently, I gave each one a title. To the first I gave the title, 'Meditating according to Reason that is Consistent with the Faith'. The second one I called, 'Faith Seeking Understanding'.

Now since both of these works have been transcribed with these titles, I was encouraged by a number of people (especially by the Most Reverend Archbishop of Lyons, and Apostolic Legate to Gaul, Hugo, who ordered me by his apostolic authority) to append my name to them. I have also named them more aptly. The first I called the *Monologion* which means a speech directed at oneself. The second I called *Proslogion* which means a speech given to another.

Chapter 1: Raising the mind to the contemplation of God

Come now little man, flee from your trifling occupations and turn away for a short time from the turbulence of your thoughts. Cast away your burdens and cares, and set aside your distractions. Clear a little space for God and rest for a little while in him. Enter into the closet of your mind and exclude everything except God and that which helps you to seek him. When you have closed the door, seek him. Speak now, my whole heart, speak now to God. I seek your face, your face, O Lord, I seek.

Come now, O Lord my God. Teach my heart where and how it may seek you, where and how it may find you. O Lord, if you are not here, where shall I seek you if you are absent? If you are everywhere, why do I not see you if you are present? But surely you dwell in light inaccessible. And where is inaccessible light? How am I to approach such inaccessible light? Who will lead me to it so that I might see you in it? By what signs am I to seek your face? At no time have I seen you, O Lord my God. I do not know your face.

What shall he do, O Most High Lord, what shall he do who is a distant exile from you? What shall your servant do, troubled by love for you yet cast far away from your face? He longs to see you but your face is too far away from him. He desires to approach you but your dwelling is inaccessible. He wants to find you, but does not know where you are. He tries to seek you, but does not know your face.

O Lord, you are my God and my Lord; yet I have never seen you. You have made and remade me, and all my good you have given to me, and yet I still do not know you. I was created that I might see you, but I have not yet done that for which I was created.

O what misery is the fate of humanity! They have lost that for which they were created. O how hard and calamitous was their fall! Alas, what have they lost and what have they found? What has departed and what has remained? They lost the blessedness for which they were created, and found misery for which they were not created. They lost that without which there is no happiness, and kept what brings nothing but misery. They have eaten the bread of angels, but now are hungry; now they eat the bread of anguish that, then, they did not know. Alas, the common sorrow of humanity, the universal lament of the children of Adam! He was fully satisfied; we sigh with hunger. He had abundance; we beg. He possessed such abundance happily, and abandoned it in misery; we are unhappily without the same, and we desire such abundance in misery. Alas, we remain empty. Why did he not protect what we now so deeply lack, since he was easily able to do it? Why did he prevent the light from reaching us, and cover us with darkness? Why did he take life from us and inflict death? Wretched as we are, we have been expelled, yet to where have we been driven? To where have we been cast down? Where have we been cast in ruin? We have been cast from our proper country into exile, from the vision of God into blindness, from happy immortality to bitterness and the horror of death. What a miserable change from so much good to such great evil! O what a heavy loss and heavy grief for all is oppression.

But alas my misery, one among the sons of Eve, far from God! What have I begun? What have I accomplished? For what purpose am I striving? In what circumstances am I sighing? Where have I arrived? To what did I aspire? I have sought the good and, behold, confusion. I am striving toward God and I stumbled upon myself. I sought peace in the midst of privacy, and found tribulation and grief in my innermost thoughts. I wished to laugh in the joy of my mind, yet I was compelled to bellow from the groaning of my heart. Gladness was my hope, but behold, deep sighs were multiplied.

And you, O Lord, how long? How long, Lord, will you forget us, turning your face from us? When will you turn back to us and hear us? When will you illumine our eyes and reveal your face to us? When will you restore us? Look upon us, Lord; hear us, illumine us, turn yourself to us. Restore yourself to us so that it may be well for us; for without you our lot is bad. Take pity on our labour and efforts to reach you, for nothing goes well for us apart from you. You invite us, so help us. I pray, Lord, that I might not despair in my groaning, but that I might breathe in hope. Lord, my heart is becoming bitter through its desolation; I pray you would make it sweet through your consolation. Lord, in hunger I began to seek you; I pray that my hunger for you would not end. I have come to you famished, may I not go away hungry. I came as a pauper to a rich man, in misery to the one who is merciful; do not let me turn away empty and despised. And if before I eat I sigh, after my sighing, feed me yet. Lord, I am not able to bend down except to look down; raise me, therefore, that I might stretch upward. My iniquities have surpassed my head, they have covered me and like a heavy burden, they weigh me down. Extricate me, remove this burden from me lest the pit of my iniquities close itself over me. Permit me to look upon your light, even from afar, even from the depths. Teach me to seek you, and show yourself to me when I seek you because it is not possible to seek you unless you teach me. It is impossible to find you unless you show yourself. Let me seek you longing; let me long for you in seeking; let me find you in loving; let me love you in finding.

I acknowledge you, O Lord, and give you thanks because you created your image in me that I might be mindful of you, think on you and love you. This image has, however, been obliterated and obscured by sins, and obfuscated by the smoke of my sins, that it cannot do that for which it was created unless you renew and refashion it. I do not try, O Lord, to penetrate your great heights because my understanding is in no way comparable to the task; yet I desire to understand some degree of your truth which my heart believes and loves. For I do not seek to understand so that I might believe, but I believe so that I might understand. For this also I believe, that unless I have believed I will not understand.

Chapter 2: That God truly exists

Therefore, Lord, you who give understanding to faith, grant me, as far as you know it is expedient, to understand that you exist as we believe you exist, and that you are what we believe you to be. We believe that you are that than which nothing greater can be conceived. Or is there no such nature? For the fool has said in his heart there is no God. But surely this very fool, when he hears the statement I just made – you are that than which nothing greater can be conceived – understands what he hears, and what he understands is in his mind even if he does not understand that it exists. It is one thing for something to exist in the mind, but another thing altogether to understand that that same thing exists in reality. For when a painter imagines what he will paint, he has the subject in his mind, but what he has not yet painted he does not yet understand to exist in reality. Now when he has painted his picture, and he also has the idea in his mind, he understands that it exists in reality because he has now made it.

Thus, even the fool is convinced that that than which nothing greater can be conceived exists in the mind because he has heard the statement and understands it. What he understands is in his mind. Surely that than which nothing greater can be conceived is not able to exist in the mind alone. For if it exists in the mind alone it is possible to conceive of its existence in reality as well, which is greater. If, therefore, that than which a greater cannot be conceived exists in the mind alone, that being, than which nothing greater can be thought, is actually that than which a greater can be conceived. This cannot be possible. It is therefore beyond doubt that a being exists, greater than which cannot be conceived, either in the mind or in reality.

Chapter 3: That God cannot be thought not to exist

This being exists so truly that he cannot be thought not to exist. For it is possible to think something exists that cannot be thought not to exist, which is greater than that which can be thought not to exist. Therefore, if that than which nothing greater can be conceived can be thought not to exist, then it is surely true that that than which nothing greater can be thought is not that than which nothing greater can be thought, which cannot be. Consequently, that than which nothing greater can be thought truly exists such that it cannot be thought not to exist.

This is who you are, O Lord our God. So truly do you exist, O Lord, my God, that it is not possible to conceive of you not existing, and rightly so. For if some mind could conceive of something greater than you, the creature would rise above the Creator and judge the Creator, which is clearly absurd. Whatever exists, except for you alone, can be thought not to exist. Therefore, you alone of all have existence that is the greatest and most true because whatever else exists does not exist truly and on that account has a lesser existence. Why, then, has the fool said in his heart there is no God since it is so very evident to a rational mind that you exist most greatly of all. Why, apart from the fact that he is not only a fool, but stupid as well!

Chapter 4: How the fool has said in his heart what cannot be thought

How then has the fool said in his heart what cannot be thought? Or how can he not think what he has said in his heart, since to say something in one's heart is to think it? If he truly, or rather because he truly thought this, because he has said it in his heart, he did not say it in his heart because it is not possible to think it, there must be more than one way of 'saying in one's heart' or 'thinking'. In one sense, a thing is thought when the word signifying that thing is thought; while in another sense, what a thing is is understood as the thing itself. God can be thought not to exist in the first sense, but in the second sense, not at all. So then, no one who understands what God is is simultaneously able to understand that God does not exist even though he may say the words in his heart without any signification or with a rather peculiar signification. God is that than which nothing greater can be thought. Whoever understands this properly surely understands that this God exists such that it is not possible to think that he does not exist. Therefore, whoever understands that this is the nature of God's existence is not able to think that he does not exist.

> Thanks be to you, good Lord, thanks be to you, for what I first believed you have now granted that I should understand by the light of your illumination so that even if I did not want to believe that you exist, it would impossible to understand that you exist.[18]

Assessing the argument

At this stage a few words of clarification may be in order. The first point all readers must fix firmly in their minds is what Anselm is not doing. Anselm is not trying to argue for the existence of God apart from a consideration of God's nature. In other words, it is not enough to address the existence of a supreme being whose nature is not known apart from being greater than creation. Such a being would be worthy neither of praise nor of worship because such a being would not be known personally or may not have the capacity or desire to be known personally. The crux of the matter, then, is not to begin with existence and then move to nature, but to begin with nature and then move to existence. To many, such an argument seems backwards, but to Anselm it is the only way to approach the question of God's existence. If God is a transcendent being, a being who is above and beyond creation, then how could we say anything meaningful about such a being unless he first reveals himself to us? To put this another way, Anselm believed that knowing that God exists must be connected to the far more important question of who he is. That this is so is clear from at least two parts of the opening four chapters. First, it is clear from the way Anselm begins his investigation. Second, it is clear from the definition Anselm gives for God. Let's look at these two aspects in turn.

As Anselm introduces his readers to the topic of God's existence he makes two requests. First, he asks that they take the time to set aside any and all distractions so that their concentration might not be impeded as they think about the God of the Bible. That Anselm is specifically interested in the God of the Bible to the exclusion of any other god is evident from his citation of passages from the Bible. He quotes, for instance, from the sixth chapter of Matthew's Gospel when he asks the readers to enter into the closet of their minds. In that passage Jesus is giving instructions to believers on how to pray.

The second, and more important, request Anselm makes draws directly on Psalm 27:8 (Psalm 26 in the Vulgate) when he cries out, 'I seek your face, your face, O Lord, I seek'. This second request is directed to God alone. Anselm carries on in this vein and adds further pleas that God should reveal himself

18. *Proslogion*, Prologue and chapters 1–4.

and aid the meditating monk in his efforts. It is this second request that proves most disturbing to many readers. How can Anselm claim to be proving the existence of God if he begins by asking this God to help him find that proof? Has Anselm not begged the question? Surely his argument is circular since he begins by assuming the very thing he wishes to prove! As noted already, these questions and accusations misunderstand what Anselm is trying to accomplish. He does not begin with the assumption that what he desires to prove exists does not exist, for in the case of deity, which is by nature transcendent, such a starting point would be no starting point. God is not a creature who can be investigated according to the methods applied to the rest of creation. God, as Anselm says much later in a reply to one man who disagreed with him, is in a category of one.[19] The category in which we might place God (if it is even appropriate to place God within a category) is a category in which existence is not something added to God, but something that is a necessary and inseparable part of him.

If we consider any part of creation, whether it be an animal, a human or even an inanimate object, we readily understand that existence is not a necessary part of that object's nature. A person comes into existence and then dies. An animal comes into existence and then dies. A rock was not always a rock, but was formed by processes external to it. At some point in history everything that we now know in creation did not exist. The reason for this is that existence is not a necessary or inseparable part of everything that falls into the category of creation. God, on the other hand, has always existed because existence is part of what it means to be God.

This line of argument brings us to the second of the above mentioned considerations, the definition of God. Although it may initially be difficult to get one's mind around the statement that God is that than which nothing greater can be conceived, the meaning is deceptively simple. Anselm's point is that whatever may be the highest and best thought anyone can have, God is yet higher. Regardless of how much human thinking and understanding may develop, Anselm's definition states that God is still greater. We may come to a new and better understanding of power or of goodness or of compassion or of love, but God is still greater in all these areas and more than even our latest and greatest conceptions.

---

19. After Anselm wrote the *Proslogion*, he received a reply from another monk named Gaunilo who challenged him on a number of points. What I have written here reflects part of Anselm's reply. Gaunilo's famous rejoinder and Anselm's response is included in the English translation identified in the bibliography.

There is, however, a little more to Anselm's definition. If the definition of God is that he is greater than anything that can be conceived, that means that, in order for the definition to be true, he must be greater than even the most magnificent being one could imagine who is perfect in every way. But if this being we have imagined is perfect in every way, how could God be greater? He is greater in that he exists, which is the one perfection lacking in the being who exists in our minds. Here Anselm's critics raise their protests once again and claim that just because Anselm has said that existence must be a necessary or inseparable part of God's existence, that does not prove that it actually is. The being Anselm has claimed exists is just as much in his imagination as is the perfect being in anyone else's imagination. In short, the method is flawed.

True, Anselm is not doing a very good job of following the scientific method nor is he following a psychological method very well either. Then again, Anselm never claimed to be following either of those disciplines, so why would he follow their methodology? Is the method of investigation for mathematics the same as that pursued in biology? Is the method of investigation for astronomy the same as that pursued in music? Anselm is writing theology and so the method he is using is a theological one. Each subject, each area of inquiry must progress in their study in a manner that is consistent with and derived from the nature of their subject. How can a theologian address the nature and existence of a transcendent being apart from the aid that being offers? God may be the author of the universe, but he is not the subject of astronomy. God may have created matter, but he is not the subject of physics. God's fingerprints, as it were, may be visible throughout his creation, but it is the Christian alone who has the means to say anything meaningful or accurate about God. In fact, judging from how Anselm begins and ends the *Proslogion*, he would add that it is the praying Christian who alone can say anything meaningful about God because it is to such that God reveals himself most fully. For Anselm, it is on the grounds of knowing God that one comes to understand the nature of God and from that, the necessity of his existence. The fool, the unbeliever, is the one who either fails to understand this or to admit it.

To this point the argument is that God's nature is of an entirely different order than anything known in creation. God's nature is inseparable from his existence. If God is God than he must exist by virtue of all that it means to be God. But is there any further confirmation that Anselm is arguing in this way? Indeed there is. The excerpt included above is only the prologue and first four chapters of a twenty-six chapter treatise. The remaining twenty-two chapters deal with God's attributes. This preponderant emphasis on God's nature again highlights for us that what matters most to Anselm is who God is. Here is how

Anselm transitions from his opening, somewhat opaque argument, to the rest of the work.

> **Chapter 5: That God is whatever it is better to be than not to be, and that he alone exists through himself, and makes all things from nothing**
> What, therefore, are you, Lord God, except that than which nothing greater can be thought? But what are you except the greatest of all which alone exists through itself, and has made everything else from nothing? For whatever is not this, is less than what can be thought, but it is not possible to think you are this. Therefore, what good is lacking in the supreme good, through which every good exists? Thus you are just, truthful, blessed and whatever it is better to be than not to be. For it is better to be just than unjust and blessed rather than lacking in blessing.[20]

The central theme in this section that arises again and again throughout the rest of the *Proslogion* is that God is all that it is better to be than not to be. This line of thought flows directly out of the initial definition of God, that he is that than which nothing greater can be conceived. The God who fulfils Anselm's definition is the God who not merely has, but is perfection. We can think of a being in our imagination that is perfect, but that being will never be truly perfect until it exists, and it will never reach perfection properly speaking until perfection is its nature rather than something it can achieve by the power inherent to it. On this basis, Anselm begins to show how God is, among many other things, good, just, ineffable, holy and real. The force of all this is, once again, to remind the reader that the question of God's existence is not a question about existence *per se* but about the kind or nature of God's existence since it is nothing like everything else we do or will ever know.

Christ's atonement: Cur Deus Homo

One of the great doctrines of the church has always been the atonement. This is not to say that other doctrines such as the doctrine of revelation or the doctrine of God are unimportant; rather that they find their beginning or end in this aspect of Christology. What point would there be in God revealing himself to sinful humanity if there was no hope that we should be extricated from the morass of sin that keeps us from union with our creator? Apart from the atonement there would be no ecclesiology, no eschatology worth worrying about and no soteriology.

Theologians in the Middle Ages recognized this and spent much time

20. *Proslogion*, ch. 5.

explaining not only the centrality of the atonement, but also the manner in which atonement was accomplished. During the first centuries of the early church numerous perspectives on the atonement were propounded. Some theologians emphasized the fact that Jesus nullified the effects of sin (Rom. 5:17), others that Jesus removed the just judgment of God's wrath from those who believed (Rom. 8:1), still others that Jesus defeated the Devil (1 John 3:8) as part of a cosmic battle finally won. As we move out of the early church into the early Middle Ages we discover that the most prominent, though not the only perspective on the atonement, was the ransom theory. Drawing on passages such as Mark 10:45 along with others, theologians and leaders of the church such as Pope Gregory the Great (597-604) taught that Jesus' death was a ransom paid to the Devil that permitted the release of those held in bondage. The obvious response to this was that the Devil would surely know that what he was receiving as payment for those he held in bondage, namely Jesus, was something he could never hope to keep. How could the Devil ever have power over God? How could death maintain any hold over the one who is life and in whom there is no sin or cause of death?

The usual explanation for this was that Jesus' incarnation was not unlike bait on a hook. Prior to the incarnation, the Devil could never have dreamed that he would have the opportunity to hurt God or defeat him in some way; with the incarnation, though, the Devil had the opportunity to kill the one who was strong, now made weak. In his great arrogance and self-presumption the Devil seized the opportunity to kill the Son of God, to take the bait as it were. Much like a hungry fish, the Devil realized too late that he had been tricked and was now unable to get away. Unlike the fish, however, the Devil could not keep the bait and so rather than death swallowing up the Son of God in victory, death was itself swallowed up by the Son of God when he rose from the grave on the third day. At this stage different accounts of salvation begin to take shape, but common to all of them is the view that with Christ's resurrection we see the first of many who are led out of the grip of death into eternal life.

To be sure, this account has much about it that is appealing. The Devil is given his due. God demonstrates his sovereignty and power over the greatest of adversaries. Humanity is not lost forever, doomed to an eternity in hell, but freed through victory in Christ to dwell eternally in paradise. For centuries this was the accepted perspective on the atonement. Anselm, however, would begin churning up the winds of change with his *Cur Deus Homo* (*Why God Became a Man*), for in this work he not only dismisses the idea that Jesus was a ransom paid to the Devil, but replaces it with the idea that Jesus did for humanity what humanity could not do for itself. Jesus satisfied God's just demand for obedience, and in making that satisfaction on our behalf put us in the position of being acceptable to God once again.

Among the details Anselm gives us about the history of how this work came to be, there is one piece of information to which every reader ought to pay close attention. Anselm is clear about the fact that because he finished this work faster than he would have liked it turned out to be shorter than he would have liked. What else he would have included we shall, of course, never know. What is important for contemporary readers to bear in mind, however, is that Anselm did not consider this work exhaustive. *Cur Deus Homo* certainly addresses a number of salient points related to the doctrine of the atonement, but he is under no illusions as to the limitations of his discussion.

One of the complaints against *Cur Deus Homo* is that it only deals with one perspective: satisfaction. Anselm dismisses the idea that Jesus' death was a ransom paid to the Devil, but says nothing about to whom he thinks the ransom was paid. He does not address Jesus' atonement as victory over sin and death. There are a number of omissions that could be mentioned, but to make a list of them or to criticize Anselm for them would be to misrepresent his intention and design. As will become clear, Anselm is interested in bringing a particular perspective on the atonement to light; a perspective he believed was not only a good corrective to the prevailing view, but also one that would speak most directly to his own context. Before he broaches the subject, though, Anselm reminds us that the atonement is a weighty doctrine that ought not to be treated lightly or by theological neophytes.

> I have been asked many times and with great earnestness by many people, both in word and by letter, if I would write down the reasons for some of the questions relating to our faith to which I am in the habit of responding to those who ask. These people say that my answers are pleasing to them and are considered satisfactory. When they ask their questions, they are not seeking to add to faith through reason, but to delight in contemplating and understanding what they already believe, and that, as far as it is possible, they may always be ready to give a satisfactory answer to all who ask for the reason for the hope that is in us.
>
> The question which is constantly put before us by unbelievers who deride the simplicity of Christianity as foolishness is one which is not only used as an objection, but is also a question that is mulled over in many believers' minds. It is the question of the necessity or reason why God became a man and restored life to the world by his death just as we believe and confess. This is a curiosity when it seems plausible that he could have accomplished the same through another being or an angel or another human or simply by an act of his will. With respect to this question the educated as well as many uneducated inquire into and desire to find an answer. Since,

therefore, many seek to engage in this discussion even though it seems a very difficult matter, nevertheless, I will undertake to explain to these inquirers what God has seen fit to reveal to me. The solution is plainly understandable and even attractive in its beauty and reasonableness. I should say, however, that what the holy fathers have said on this matter ought to be considered sufficient.

Now since investigations which are framed in the form of question and answer are both more pleasant and plain, especially to those who are slow of mind, I will have as an opponent one who argues importunately and who insistently stirs up the argument against me. Boso is the name of the one who will ask the questions and Anselm is the one who will respond.

Boso: In one sense, right order demands that we believe profundities of the Christian faith before we presume to discuss its rationality; however, it seems to me that we would be negligent if, after we have been confirmed in the faith, we do not study in order to understand what we believe. Indeed, it is by the prevenient grace of God that I believe I hold to the faith of our redemption such that even if I were not able to comprehend a single reason for what I believe, nevertheless, nothing could uproot me from my convictions. Thus, I ask that you uncover what, as you know, many have asked of me; namely, by what necessity or for what reason did God, who is all powerful, assume the humility and infirmity of human nature for its restoration.
Anselm: What you ask from me is above me, and therefore I dread to treat such lofty matters lest someone should think or see that I have not satisfied him and believe that I have either failed to explain the truth or my intellect is not sufficient to grasp it.
Boso: You should not fear what I ask for and recall that it often happens during discussion of some question or other that God opens what at first was hidden. You should, then, hope for the grace of God because if you freely impart what you have freely received, you will arrive at better things, things to which you have not yet attained.
Anselm: There is another reason which I see will stop us from amply dealing with, indeed scarcely dealing fully with this matter now. It is essential that we consider the nature of power and necessity and will and other such realities which are interconnected and rely on one another for a proper understanding of each one. Each one of these ideas requires its own work which, it seems to me, would not be an easy undertaking, yet not wholly futile. The reason is that ignorance on these matters makes for difficulties which can become less troublesome if they are understood.
Boso: You could address these particular issues briefly as they arise so that we might understand what is sufficient for the present work, and we will defer to another time whatever else needs to be addressed.
Anselm: I yet remain disinclined to acquiesce to your request because the material is weighty and concerns he who is beautiful in form beyond the sons of men. In

> fact, there is a beauty to the reason to which your question points that is above human understanding. On account of this I fear that, in the same way, I always grow indignant with bad painters when they paint our Lord in an ugly way, so it will be with me if I presume to write on such a beautiful topic in an amateurish and thus contemptible fashion.
> **Boso**: You ought not to draw back from this because, just as you allow anyone who can say it better than you to do so, so you prohibit no one who does not like your work from writing something more beautiful. But, so that I might exclude all your excuses, you will not be doing what I ask for the learned, but for me and for those who make the same request with me.[21]

A theological foundation

The first question many readers have on their mind when they begin reading *Cur Deus Homo* is whether or not there really was a man named Boso. While some scholars have tried to deny that Boso was a real person, there is every reason to believe that even though such a name would be less than desirable today, it was an acceptable name in the Middle Ages and, in this case, belonging to a real student.

Apart from the banter that might seem a bit contrived, Anselm is already weaving into his discussion a theme that will recur throughout the rest of the work. The theme is the beauty of theology broadly, and the beauty of Christ's redemptive work more specifically. Anselm introduces this idea by referring to the one who is 'beautiful in form beyond the sons of men'. This is an allusion to Psalm 45:2 (Ps. 44:3 in the Vulgate), the purpose of which is to remind the reader of the grandeur of the Messiah in the midst of the humble estate of the incarnation. There is nothing about the atonement that is not beautiful. At first, this might seem an odd statement to make given the gruesome details of the crucifixion, but Anselm's idea of beauty is not primarily one of aesthetic pleasure for the eyes, but of fittingness and propriety. The atonement is beautiful in so far as it is the right, the proper, the most fitting response and answer to the problem of sin. God's redemptive response to the fall takes into account the manner and means by which that first sin occurred.

> **Anselm**: In light of your importunity, and the importunity of those who, along with you, make this request out of love and religious devotion, I will try, as far as I am able (and helped by God and your prayers which you have often promised when I asked for them in light of this task), not to show you what you seek, but to seek it with you.

---

21. *Cur Deus Homo* 1.1.

I want everything that I say to be accepted according to the following stipulation: if I say anything which is not confirmed by a greater authority, then even though I appear to prove it in a reasonable manner, it will be accepted as certain only in the sense that it seems certain for now and until God reveals something better to me. And in so far as I am able to satisfy your inquiry to some extent, then it must be the case that someone wiser than me will be able to provide a better response. Nevertheless, regardless of what man can say or know about this topic, the rationale for such a lofty matter will remain hidden.

Boso: Allow me to represent the position of unbelievers, for since we desire to seek after the reason for our faith it seems fair that we present the objections of those who are not at all willing to accept our faith without reason. For although they seek the rational basis of our faith because they do not believe, while we seek the same because we believe; nevertheless, it is exactly the same thing that we both seek. If you should say something that sacred authorities appear to oppose, let me bring that authority to your attention, so that you may clear up any supposed contradiction.

Anselm: If that seems best to you, it is acceptable to me.

Boso: The unbelievers who mock our simplicity raise this objection: that we offend and insult God when we assert that he descended into the womb of a woman, was born of a woman and that he grew as he was nourished by common victuals such as milk and food. In addition, we also offend and insult God when we assert other things which do not seem appropriate to God's nature including weakness, hunger, thirst, beatings and was hung on a cross and died between robbers.

Anselm: We do not offend and insult God at all, but, giving thanks with our whole heart, we praise him and proclaim the ineffable height of his mercy. For he has shown us how great is his love and devotion toward us by the grandeur of the marvellous and inexplicable restoration of us from the deserved evil in which we exist to such undeserved good which we had lost. For if these unbelievers would consider how fitting is this mode of restoring humanity, they would not deride our simplicity, but praise this wise and kind God with us. For it was fitting that just as through one man's disobedience the human race entered into death, so through the obedience of one man life was restored. Moreover, it was fitting that the sin which was the cause of our damnation, was initiated through a woman, so the author of our justification and salvation should be initiated through a woman. Furthermore, it was fitting that the Devil who conquered man by persuading them to eat of the tree should be conquered by a man whose suffering on a tree was inflicted by the Devil. There are many more things which, when carefully considered, demonstrate the ineffable beauty of our redemption that was thus procured.[22]

---

22. *Cur Deus Homo* 1.2–3.

Anselm's remarks certainly give one pause. It is remarkable that the plan of salvation worked out by God should have answered and addressed so well not only humanity's sin, but also the very means by which sin entered into the world. Anselm's perspective sheds new light on the manner in which God chose to bring about redemption. Here there is no cold reason or calculating mind that is interested merely in accomplishing restoration, but a God who desires that Jesus' life should be the life Adam ought to have lived. It is no wonder that Paul, among others, should identify Christ as a second Adam. Adam's birth was miraculous in that the union of a man and woman were not required. Adam's sin did not affect only himself, but spread to the rest of humanity. Yes, the details of how that sin and guilt are passed on is a matter of continuing debate, but no matter what one decides on this issue, it is clear that in some way Adam was the fountainhead of a race that would, because of its ties to him, be ever more mired in sin apart from an act of divine grace. How wonderful, then, to consider that Jesus, the second Adam, should live the life of obedience Adam failed at in order to procure restitution for us. Finally, Anselm introduces his readers to a rich vein of thought that runs throughout the history of the church. He reminds us that while there was a tree in the Garden of Eden on which hung an object of desire that would lead to the degradation of humanity, there was another tree on which hung the object of derision that would lead to the exaltation of humanity.

Although Anselm never leaves the idea of the fittingness or beauty of God's saving activity, he does carry on to address some other concerns unbelievers may have.

> **Boso**: All that you say must be acknowledged and recognized as beautiful pictures, but if there is nothing solid supporting them, they do not appear to unbelievers to be sufficient reason why we ought to believe, as we contend, that God was willing to suffer these things. For he who wishes to paint a picture chooses something solid on which to paint so that what he paints will become permanent. For no one paints with water or in the air because nothing of what is painted remains. Therefore, when we set out to unbelievers these ideas of fittingness, which you call pictures, as they relate to a real event in history, since they do not believe that what you are talking about is a real event in history, as we believe it is, but a figment of the imagination, they think that we are painting on a cloud. Therefore, we must first demonstrate the rational foundation of the truth, that is to say, sound reasoning that proves that God ought to have humbled himself for the purpose we proclaim. Then, so that this body of truth might shine all the more, these arguments for fittingness should be set out as pictures of this body of truth.

Anselm: Does it not seem that what we have said is sufficient reason for why God ought to have done what he did? After all, the human race, which is surely his precious work, had been wholly ruined and it was not fitting that what God planned for humanity should be completely annihilated, not to mention that this very plan could not be brought into effect unless the human race were freed by its own Creator.
Boso: If it were said that this liberation of which you just spoke was accomplished by someone other than a divine being, whether that be an angel or a human, the human mind would accept this far more easily. For God could have created another human being without sin, who was created neither out of the sinful mass currently in existence, nor from another human, but created just as Adam was and through whom it seems this work of redemption could have been accomplished.
Anselm: But do you not understand that should any other person ransom humanity from eternal death, humanity would be rightly judged his servant? Were this the case, then humanity would have by no means been restored to the dignity which it had, had he not sinned in the first place. For man, who was created to serve no one except God and to be equal to the good angels in everything, would serve this specially created person who is not God and whom the angels do not serve.
Boso: This is what really perplexes unbelievers, that we call this liberation ransom. They ask us, 'In what captivity or in what prison or in whose power were you being held from which God was not able to liberate you except by redeeming you with such great effort and, ultimately, by his own blood?' We answer: he redeemed us from sin and from his wrath and from hell and from the power of the Devil over whom we have no power. He came to conquer the Devil for us and brought the kingdom of heaven back for us. In doing all of this in this way he has shown how great is his love for us. They then respond by saying, 'If you say that God could not have done all of this by a simple command, and he was the one whom you say created all things by his command, then you are contradicting yourselves because you make this God out to be powerless. But if you admit that he is, in fact, able to do this, but that he does not wish to redeem humanity by the power of his word, then how can you demonstrate that he is wise when, without any reason at all, he willed to suffer so many unfitting things? For everything which you have been setting forth derives from his will. The wrath of God, for instance, is a matter of his will to punish. If, therefore, he does not will to punish human sin, man is free from sins and from the wrath of God and from hell and the power of the Devil and everything he suffers on account of sin and he recovers what he lost on account of his sin. For who has power over hell or the Devil or to whom does the kingdom of heaven belong except to the one who made all these? Consequently, whatever you fear or love are subject to his will which no power can resist. So, if he is not willing to save humanity except in the way you have outlined, even though he could have accomplished salvation through an act of his will, to say it most mildly, do you not see how you are belittling his wisdom?

If a human could perform an action easily, but, for no reason at all, performed that action in a difficult and roundabout way, he would certainly not be judged by anyone to be acting wisely. Of course, you say that God is showing how great is his love for you, but this is not a defensible position if it cannot be shown that he was unable to save humanity in any other way. For if he could not have accomplished salvation by another way, then it was necessary for him to display his love in precisely this way. Since, however, he could have saved humanity by another way what reason is there that he should do and suffer the very things that you say he did? Does he not show the good angels how much he loves them even though he does not suffer so much for them? As for your statement that he came to conquer the Devil on your behalf, on what grounds do you dare to make this claim? Does not God's omnipotence reign everywhere? How, therefore, can it be that God needed to descend from heaven in order to conquer the Devil?' These are the objections unbelievers raise before us.

Now as we carry on in this argument, we are in the habit of saying that God, in order to free man, had to oppose the Devil in the context of what is just rather than in sheer power. In this way, when the Devil killed him in whom there is no reason for death and who was, by nature, God, he justly lost the power which he had over sinners. Otherwise, God would have acted in unjust violence against the Devil since the Devil justly possessed humanity whom he had not come to possess through violence, but man himself, by his own free will, submitted to the Devil. For myself, Anselm, I do not see the power of this argument.

For if the Devil or a man were his own master or belonged to someone other than God or remained in the power of someone other than God, perhaps this claim could be justly made. Since, however, neither the Devil nor man belong to anyone except God, and neither of them exist outside God's power, what did God need to do in the case of that which was his own except to punish his own servant who persuaded his other servant to desert his Lord and cross over to join him and, like the traitor he is, received this fugitive and as a thief received this second thief along with what was stolen from their Lord? They were both thieves since one was stealing himself from his Lord at the persuasion of the other. If God were to do this, could he be any more just?

Or if God, who is the judge of all, were to find humanity in the Devil's possession and seize him from the power of the one unjustly holding him, either to punish him in some way other than through the Devil or to spare him, would this be unjust? For although humanity was being justly tormented by the Devil, the Devil was unjustly tormenting humanity. Humanity deserved to be punished and there was no one more fitting to do this than the one to whom he had consented to sin. But the Devil had no merit whereby he should punish humanity. Instead of being dragged along to act according to the love of justice, he was compelled at the instigation of malice, which made his actions all the more unjust. The Devil was not acting this way at God's command, but with God's incomprehensible wisdom by which he ordains even evil things for good.[23]

The beauty of the atonement

Boso is certainly doing a good job of raising as many objections and problems as he can! Patient as always, Anselm works through them all, but takes his time in doing so. The first objection Boso raises on behalf of unbelievers is that Anselm has not yet proven that God had to follow the plan of salvation that he did. The critical point here is that it is unfitting that deity should stoop to the level of humanity. Whenever this objection or one closely related to it, is raised, Anselm's response is as simple as it is brief. Humanity may have fallen into sin, but humanity was and remains the most precious part of all creation. Moreover, when God created humanity, he did so for a specific purpose and the character of God requires that he accomplish what he set out to do, while his power guarantees that none can stop God from realizing his plans. For this reason, the first question must be how God could *not* redeem humanity since man and woman are the centrepiece of God's creative activity.

To this the unbeliever remains either unsatisfied or only partially satisfied. God's omnipotence and love may require that he do something, but surely whatever God does it should be consistent with his character and nature. There must have been a better way to save humanity than the one espoused by Christians. But here too, Anselm is remarkably brief as he cuts through the Gordian knot of possibilities presented by Boso. Boso's first objection is that it would be far more palatable to believe that God created another being to save humanity than that the Creator succumbed to the ignominy of joining himself to created flesh. Second, Boso points out that if God were truly omnipotent he could have commanded or willed that sin be no more. Would such a solution not be more worthy, more honourable, more fitting to God's character than incarnation, suffering, bloodshed and death? In addition to these two proposed improvements, Boso broaches the idea accepted by many theologians of Anselm's day that God saved humanity as he did because he needed to pay a ransom to the Devil. In other words, though it would have been better to save humanity in either of the two ways just suggested, God was put in the position of saving humanity as he did because of the power the Devil held over humanity.

In short, Anselm is being asked, simultaneously, to respond to two objections and one possible explanation. This may seem to be a case of too much

---

23. *Cur Deus Homo* 1.4–7a.

too fast, but Anselm knows that the best way to counter falsehood is not to match it point for point, but simply to present the truth. As Anselm's argument unfolds he draws attention to two components that must be present in any answer to why God redeemed humanity in the way that he did. The first component is that when humanity was created we were created to obey God. The obedience owed to God, however, is not given to him, because sin stops us from being obedient. What makes this disobedience so poignant is that an act of disobedience is tantamount to dishonouring the one who is disobeyed. This is best explained by analogy with children and parents.

When children disobey their parents, especially in a public place, parents usually become self-conscious of the fact that not only is their child's act of disobedience problematic in itself, but this public display of defiance and rebellion is also a demonstration of dishonour toward their authority. In a similar fashion, this is what humanity has done to God. By being disobedient, and constantly disobedient at that, we are continually not giving God what we owe him and are thereby dishonouring him. Given this offense, the question then becomes a matter of the extent of the offense. In a stunning stroke, Anselm informs us that the offense is proportionate to the nature of the one offended. It may take a moment to sink in, but the reader is faced with the dilemma of wondering how she or he can redress an offense in a way that is comparable to an infinite God.

It is at this moment that the second component of Anselm's argument becomes necessary. In light of the impossibility of finite sinful beings not only giving God what they owe (obedience) but also redressing the weight of dishonour already incurred against an infinite God, is there any hope for humanity? Even a humanity of billions of people comes woefully short of measuring up to an infinite God. If the offense against God is going to be addressed, it must be addressed by one who is able to pay an infinite price on behalf of all humanity. Who could pay such a price? What finite human could accomplish a task of infinite proportions? This is where the beauty of Anselm's thinking on the atonement comes into its own. He has led the reader to realize that a human needs to address humanity's sin. No other part of the creation can solve humanity's dilemma. A lamb is not a human. It cannot take away humanity's sin. Equally, though, a human in the Adamic line cannot save humanity because no human in Adam's line can redress an infinite problem.

Like an early Sherlock Holmes, Anselm is pushing the reader to see that after all possibilities have been eliminated, whatever remains, no matter how improbable, must be the solution. The solution is a God-Man. But where can we find such a one? We find him in the womb of a virgin, in the temple courts teaching, on the cross bleeding, from the tomb rising, in the clouds ascending.

Without mentioning Jesus throughout his argument, Anselm arrives at the only possible answer to why God became a man. He alone is the one whose infinite nature would not only be proportionate to the dishonour incurred, but would also cover all humanity. Satisfaction lived in Christ becomes satisfaction applied to all who believe in him.

What makes Anselm's articulation of the atonement even more astounding is that inherent in this answer as to why God became a man, why God accomplished atonement in this way, is a rejection of the idea that God was using his Son to pay a ransom to the Devil. In that model of the atonement the problem is how to satisfy the Devil; whereas in Anselm's model the problem is how to satisfy the holiness of God. In a masterful way, Anselm has answered the criticisms of unbelievers as well as corrected the accepted wisdom of his peers.

Meditation on Human Redemption

The companion piece to the *Cur Deus Homo* is a brief and all too often ignored meditation on human redemption. The *Meditation on Human Redemption* is among Anselm's later works. It was almost certainly written after *Cur Deus Homo*. It is the result of mature reflection on the subject of the atonement in particular, and salvation more broadly. A work of tremendous passion and verve, it is not difficult to imagine – and this is an act of imagination – that this meditation was penned at a single sitting after attending a service of corporate worship in which the liturgy emblazoned afresh on Anselm's heart the weight of glory.

Anselm begins by addressing the 'Christian soul', and then describing what it means for a soul to be Christian. For Anselm the Christian soul is one that has been ransomed or redeemed from eternal death, and has been liberated for service to the one whose blood was shed on his or her behalf. Here is a monk who is mindful of how meditating on the cost of redemption is transformative. Much like Augustine, Anselm is ever pressing his readers to be self-conscious about the reflection–action dynamic in a believer's life. That is to say that the believer's doing proceeds out of the believer's being. If the Christian is not kindled with love for the Saviour from within through chewing 'the honeycomb of his words' and thereby savouring its sweet flavour, then how has a Christian any claim to being different from the world? Indeed, Anselm would ask, how can the Christian claim to be a Christian, for this is what it means to be a Christian.

> Christian soul, soul brought to life again from under the weight of death, soul redeemed and freed from the misery of bondage by the blood of God, stir up your mind and forget not your new life. Recognize your redemption and liberation for

what it is. Consider anew the strength of your salvation and from where it comes. Continue to meditate upon it and delight in that contemplation. Shake off your pride and focus your heart and mind on this. Taste the goodness of your redemption and kindle love within you for your Saviour. Chew the honeycomb of his words, suck on its sweet flavour, swallow its sweet wholeness. Chew by thinking, suck by understanding, swallow by loving and rejoicing. Be glad to chew, be thankful to suck, be delighted to swallow.

Wherein is the power and strength of your salvation? It is surely in the fact that Christ has brought you back to life. He is the good Samaritan who healed you. He is the good friend who redeemed and freed you by giving his own life on your behalf. Christ has done this. Therefore, the strength of your salvation is the strength of Christ. Wherein is the strength of Christ? As the prophet Habakkuk says, 'Horns are in his hands, there is his strength hidden.' Horns are in his hands because his hands were nailed to the arms of the cross. What strength could there be in such weakness? What height could there be in such humiliation? What veneration could there be in such contempt? Surely there is something hidden in his weakness, hidden in his humiliation, hidden in his contempt. O the strength that is hidden! The man who hangs on a cross lifts the sentence of eternal death on which humanity was hanged. The man who was fastened to the cross with nails breaks apart the bonds that held the world in eternal death. O hidden power! The man condemned with thieves saves men condemned with demons. The man stretched out on a gibbet draws all to himself. O hidden strength! One soul is hurled into torment and innumerable souls are released from hell. The man who accepts the death of the body is the one who destroys the death of souls.

Why good Lord, blessed Redeemer, powerful Saviour, why did you conceal such power by such humility? Was it that you might deceive the Devil who deceived man resulting in him being cast out of paradise? But truth deceives no one. He who is ignorant, who does not believe the truth, deceives himself. He who sees the truth but responds with contempt deceives himself. Truth does not deceive anyone. Or was the truth given so that the Devil might deceive himself? But just as the truth does not deceive, so its intention is that no one should deceive themselves, although it could be said to do so when such is permitted. For you did not assume humanity so that you might conceal what is known about you, but so that you might reveal what was unknown. You declared yourself to be true God and true man and showed the evidence of it. That which was hidden was not hidden on purpose, for what took place did not happen in order to hide something, but so that his plan might be fulfilled. He did not deceive anyone, but did what was fitting. And if God's saving activity is identified as something concealed, it is only thought so because it is not revealed to everyone. For even if truth does not manifest itself to everyone, nevertheless, it does not deny itself to anyone. Therefore, O Lord, neither did you

> deceive anyone, nor did your revelation cause anyone to deceive themselves. Through all of this you never departed from the truth, but accomplished what you did in the way it had to be done. Consequently, he who is deceived by your truth is not deceived by your truth; let him complain against his own falsehood.[24]

There is a wealth of theological depth even in this brief excerpt and only prolonged meditation on its contents will ever do it justice. In fact, we would do well to remind ourselves that Anselm intended that not only his prayers, but also his meditations would be read slowly, deliberately, repeatedly and prayerfully. Even so, there are a number of points that demand our attention.

First, the reader cannot but notice how the contemporary theological background is again finding its way into Anselm's work. Anselm had already argued that the atonement ought not to be viewed as a ransom paid to the Devil, yet this image was powerful and sufficiently pervasive in medieval Europe that Anselm had repeatedly to address it.

Second, Anselm never got away from the idea that God's actions in history are the outworking of his nature. That is to say, since God is beautiful, so are his works. God only does what is fitting and right. In *Cur Deus Homo* Anselm made sure his students and future readers would understand that, for all we can say about the atonement, the most fundamental statement we can make is that, in all its details, it was a fitting act, a beautiful act. It was fitting not only with respect to the nature of God, but also with respect to the nature of the dilemma caused by sin. Unlike parents who tend to have a limited repertoire of punishments for their children despite the diversity of their disobedience, God's forgiveness and salvation as much as his punishments are always appropriate to the sin.

Third, Augustine's influence is never very far from anything Anselm wrote. Augustine struggled throughout his life with the juxtaposition of God's sovereignty and humanity's will. In the early days of his theological development the accent fell on the priority of human choice, but he soon shifted and for most of his mature Christian life the accent fell decidedly on the utter ruin and sinfulness of the whole person such that nothing but the grace of God could save humanity. This meant that Augustine was a strong proponent of election and the necessity of God's prevenient grace before anyone could exercise their will in favour of repentance and obedience.

Fourth, as should be clear from the *Proslogion*, Anselm did not favour definitions of God that placed borders around him. Paradoxically, the very purpose

---

24. Cf. Ward, pp. 230–232, ll. 1–57.

of a definition is to set boundaries and borders, but Anselm worked very hard to describe God and speak about his nature and work in a fashion that imparted understanding while maintaining mystery. God is, therefore, not the greatest than can be thought, but greater than can be thought. By using the comparative rather than the superlative the option for ever new vistas of perception are never ending. So here, in this little meditation, Anselm continues along the same lines. He states that the incarnation did not conceal what might be known about God, but revealed what was not known. This statement has fairly obvious connections to the magisterial opening of the book of Hebrews, but additionally, Anselm is confirming the principle that in the incarnation there is a revealing in the concealing while there is a concealing in the revealing. The nature and exact representation of God is enfleshed to walk among men and women in plain sight, and yet the incarnation of deity is itself the rock of stumbling and the height of folly to those who refuse to believe.

Critical evaluation

If we may start with what we have just read, there is certainly room for criticism, but given the spirit in which Anselm wrote, criticism ought not to be our initial impulse. His *Meditation on Human Redemption* ranks among the most moving and insightful short works on the atonement that has ever been written. This is a man for whom theology is not an academic discipline that engages the head apart from the heart. This is a humble monk whose passion for his God and his Saviour form the foundation of his theology, steeped as it is in decades of reflection and refined by edifying repartee. There is no prevaricating between love and learning as though one somehow excludes or eclipses the other. As great as Anselm's legacy is and as profound as some of his theological insights have proven, perhaps his greatest gift to the church is his example of the manner and method by which he pursued truth.

Anselm's Christology

But what of the content of what we have read? Should we accept everything Anselm wrote uncritically? No, there are some points to which a reply is necessary. Take, for example, Anselm's idea in *Meditation on Human Redemption* that hell was emptied by Christ's death. This belief became known later in the Middle Ages as the harrowing of hell. The thought was that even the great saints of the Old Testament were bound in hell until Christ rose from the grave. At that time those saints of old were finally released from their bondage into paradise. Support for this idea is almost exclusively claimed from 1 Peter 3:18–20. The trouble with interpreting this verse in this way is that it ignores the fact that the spirits to whom Christ preached are described as disobedient. Quite apart from any discussion of the timing of Christ's preaching or to whom 'spirits' refers, it is clear that those who heard the message of salvation did not believe. Those who are in view in this passage are, quite decidedly, not believers, not those who are counted among God's obedient followers. The imagery of the harrowing of hell has a certain appeal, but it is an appeal that finds no warrant in Scripture.

As we think about theological ideas that are not founded on a solid scriptural foundation we might be tempted to lay another charge at Anselm's feet. In *Cur Deus Homo*, Anselm agreed to discuss the atonement without any explicit reference to Christ. How can this be? Did he place too much trust in the power of his own reason? Not at all. It could be said that it is precisely in *Cur Deus Homo* where Anselm argues his case *remoto christo*, apart from Christ, that he is at his most biblical. This is so because what Anselm is doing there is to begin with our sinfulness and inability to accomplish salvation on our own. Given this situation, the question is quite naturally raised, how then can humanity be saved or, more accurately, who can save humanity from this predicament? The answer to which Anselm is nudging his readers is, sin is a God-sized problem so is there anything God has done? By removing Christ from the main body of the argument for the atonement Anselm is able to focus his readers' attention rather sharply on the depravity of humanity and the necessity of divine activity. He convinces us that there is no other option than that a fully human, fully divine person stand in our stead, take upon himself the punishment due to us and pay to God a debt he did not owe on behalf of we who owed a debt we could not pay.

In addition to these criticisms, a rather forceful attack against Anselm and those who follow his line of thinking has been levelled by Gustaf Aulén.[25] There is more in Aulén's book than we can discuss here, but with respect to Anselm he argues that *Cur Deus Homo* makes the seminal mistake of neglecting the most prominent aspect of the atonement: the victory of Christ over Satan and sin. Aulén points out that many of the early church fathers describe the atonement within the context of a cosmic battle between God and Satan. There is, of course, no doubt as to who will win, but the drama is thereby no less significant. In this titanic struggle, the death and resurrection of Christ is the final divine blow to the Satanic onslaught.

---

25. Gustaf Aulén, *Christus Victor*, tr. A. G. Hebert (London: SPCK, 1978).

As we saw when we looked at *Cur Deus Homo*, Anselm certainly does not cast his perspective on the atonement in the context of a divine drama between God and Satan. He is more interested in the drama of the divine-human relationship. In this interpretation, Satan plays a minor role. Despite Anselm recasting the context of the atonement, we should take care to note that he does not dismiss the power of the Devil nor does he neglect to address Christ's victory over sin and death. For Anselm, the victory that Christ wins for humanity is the demonstration of the victory that Christ won over the Devil. To set Satan aside is not to ignore the fact that Christ swallowed up death in victory, but identify the primary agents in the plan of redemption. What, or more properly, who, matters most in redemption is God and humanity.

Thinking more broadly about the many perspectives the Bible gives on the atonement, the charge that Anselm has not been exhaustive or has not said enough will always be true. The point that must be borne in mind is that Anselm had no intention of being exhaustive. His goal was the rather modest one of pointing out what he believed was an error in the theological thinking of his day (the atonement was a ransom paid to the Devil) and providing an alternative that expressed the content of Scripture more accurately.

Implications of the doctrine of God

When we turn to the *Proslogion*, the first comment that comes to most people's minds is that it is difficult to understand. In response to this fairly frequent complaint the best advice is to read it again and again. We tend to appreciate those things in life that take the most work, and this is another of those gems worthy of the effort. Having said that, there is more here for present-day Christians than an argument that defends the existence of God. In some respects, the most important contribution of the *Proslogion* may be the reminder that objectivity is not only impossible, but inappropriate. Interpretation is what provides meaning and understanding and to pretend that this is not the case is to play the fool whose folly is so great that he goes so far as to deny what he is suppressing.

It is also worth emphasizing that where the existence of God is concerned we do not begin with the sorts of questions we think are necessary. This is part of what Anselm intended his readers to grasp when he began the *Proslogion* in prayer. The work of saying anything true about God is a work that can only be properly accomplished in the context of a vibrant interaction with God. Moreover, when we consider the one about whom we wish to speak, it should become clear that the creature is not free to make demands of the Creator; rather, it is the Creator who sets the boundaries of what the creature is permitted to know. God is not an impersonal force that can be quantified and qualified at our discretion. God is the supreme being, the one who is greater than what we can imagine and the one than which nothing greater can be imagined.

Along similar lines, as we move from his theological method to his apologetic method, we should note that Anselm is not willing to give up any ground to unbelief. In other words, Anselm will not allow someone who denies God's existence to set the boundaries of what is acceptable in the discussion over God's being and nature. Anselm is right to maintain that God's existence is given and defended on its own terms and not those granted by his creatures. This is certainly not a popular way of defending the faith in a culture saturated with the belief that the scientific method is the supreme means by which truth will be discovered, but it is more consistent with the doctrine of God as it finds expression in his majesty, sovereignty, holiness and power.

Prayer within the bounds of Scripture

Finally, there are Anselm's prayers. About the only criticism that could be levelled against these is his belief that the members of the church militant can speak to and be heard by the members of the church triumphant. While the book of Revelation does indicate that the saints in heaven are to some degree aware of the continued suffering of believers on earth at the hands of Christ's enemies, there is nothing in all of Scripture to warrant the belief of open lines of communication between earth and heaven. Moreover, even if we were to grant some form of communication between believers on earth and in heaven, the nature of that communication would not be mediatorial. The Bible is quite clear that there is one mediator between God and man, the man Christ Jesus (1 Tim. 2:5). Anselm certainly believed this, and should not be considered heretical or unworthy of appreciation on account of his view of the saints' role in prayer. Instead, in a manner similar to what we saw in the *Proslogion* and *Cur Deus Homo*, we should recognize a method of praying that is richly imbued with a zeal for Christ's salvation, an ardour for purity from sin and a fervour to deny the reign of sin in the believer's life because it has been replaced by the reign of Christ.

One of the characteristics that stands out in Anselm's prayers is that he did not address saints at random. He chose saints who were known to have had an experience or personality trait with which later believers could connect. In his prayer to Peter, for instance, Anselm recalls Peter's failure to keep his word and stand by Christ during his trial and crucifixion. This experience is used by Anselm to highlight the fact that believers continue to fail Christ in numerous and significant ways, but that does not mean forgiveness is beyond them. What matters time and again is that the believer repents of sin and relies on God's grace as the only source of forgiveness, salvation and future victory over sin. Although, as we have seen, Anselm goes too far in praising Mary from time to time, when we look at his prayers as a whole and compare them to his other theological works it becomes clear that Jesus Christ stands alone as the author of salvation.

It is in this expression of Anselm's piety that evangelicals identify a tension between his firm conviction in salvation by Christ alone, by faith alone and by grace alone and the commonly accepted practice of seeking solace and help in saints who have passed from this world to the next. In this way, Anselm reminds us how difficult it can be to discern inconsistencies in our own thinking and practice while we are still immersed in those very patterns of thought and life. What is obvious to an observer from outside a given context is not always so obvious to those living within that same context. Were we to talk to Anselm about his prayers, we might wish to ask him why he believed so strongly in praying to saints when we have no example of this practice anywhere in Scripture? Surely Jesus or Paul or Peter or John or others would have either explained the necessity of this practice or led the church by example.

At this point in our imaginary discussion with Anselm we may well be asked about the place and importance of tradition. If praying to saints is a time-honoured expression of faith and is part of how believers deal with their sin, how can we dismiss it so easily? While many may wish to respond that the Bible is our sole standard of authority and anything that does not measure up must be jettisoned or at least held lightly, Anselm's point should be given more careful consideration. It may be that human tradition is subject to the word of God, but we must take care to approach God's revelation with humility. The case of whether or not we should pray to saints is, to be sure, more easily decided on account of the complete lack of evidence for such in both Testaments. Nevertheless, whether wrestling with the nature of prayer or the nature of the atonement, we all must bear in mind that the context in which we live and learn has an effect on how we think, interpret and apply the Bible.

From this sampling of Anselm's life and work, then, we have considered four distinct elements. We have considered his biography and how that can affect the way we understand what he wrote. We have listened to his prayers as he expresses his faith to his Saviour and draws others in so that his solo becomes a much more impressive concert. We have wrestled with Anselm through the existence of God and wondered at the simplicity of his method. Finally, we have soared with him through the reality of salvation accomplished, but only because we have appreciated the deep valley from which sinful humanity has come. Anselm did not get everything right, but in these areas he has remained a faithful witness to the church through the centuries and into a new millennium.

Bibliography

Primary sources in Latin

SCHMITT, F. S. (ed.), *Sancti Anselmi Opera Omnia*, 6 vols. (Edinburgh: Thomas Nelson and Sons, 1946–61). This is the critical edition of Anselm's works. Readers can also find Anselm's works in J. P. Migne, *et al.*, *Patrologia cursus completes: Series Latina* (Paris, 1841–77), vols. 158–159, but are better served with Schmitt's edition.

SOUTHERN, R. W. and F. S. Schmitt, *Memorials of St. Anselm* (Oxford: Oxford University Press, 1991) includes a number of untranslated works that have bearing on Anselm's life and context as well as a number of unfinished works of a more philosophical nature thought to be original to Anselm.

EADMER, *Vita Anselmi*, ed. R. W. Southern (Oxford: Oxford Medieval Texts, 1972).

EADMER, *Historia Novorum in Anglia*, ed. M. Rule (London: Rolls Series, 1884).

Primary sources in English

WARD, BENEDICTA, *The Prayers and Meditations of Saint Anselm with the Proslogion* (London: Penguin Books, 1973) provides an excellent translation of all the prayers believed to be original to Anselm along with his three meditations and, as the title notes, the *Proslogion*.

DAVIES, BRIAN and G. R. Evans (eds.), *Anselm of Canterbury, The Major Works* (Oxford: Oxford University Press, 1998) includes not only Anselm's treatises but also some of what have become known as his philosophical fragments.

The above two volumes provide modern readers who lack a reading knowledge of Latin with everything Anselm wrote apart from his over 400 letters for a very reasonable price. An older and more expensive translation which should also be consulted is Jasper Hopkins and Herbert Richardson, *Anselm of Canterbury*, 4 vols. (Toronto: Edwin Mellon Press, 1976).

FRÖLICH, WALTER, *The Letters of Saint Anselm of Canterbury*, 3 vols. (Kalamazoo: Cistercian Publications, 1990).

EADMER, *The Life of St Anselm, Archbishop of Canterbury*, ed. and tr. R. W. Southern (Oxford: Clarendon Press, 1972). This volume is somewhat unique in that it provides the Latin text of Eadmer's biography on the left page with a translation on the right page.

EADMER, *History of Recent Events in England*, tr. Geoffrey Bosanquet (London: The Cresset Press, 1964).

Secondary sources

Biographies

SOUTHERN, R. W., *Saint Anselm: A Portrait in a Landscape* (Cambridge: Cambridge University Press, 1990) is the essential modern biography of Anselm. Other biographies that deserve attention include:

EVANS, G. R., *Anselm* (London: Geoffrey Chapman, 1989).

SOUTHERN, R. W., *St Anselm and his Biographer* (Cambridge: Cambridge University Press, 1963).

VAUGHN, SALLY, *Anselm of Bec and Robert of Meulan, the Innocence of the Dove and the Wisdom of the Serpent* (Los Angeles: University of California Press, 1987).

Anselm's theology

BARTH, KARL, *Anselm: Fides Quaerens Intellectum* (London: SCM Press, 1958) remains one of the seminal works on the *Proslogion.*

McINTYRE, J., *St. Anselm and His Critics: A Reinterpretation of Cur Deus Homo* (Edinburgh: Oliver and Boyd, 1954) is the most significant work on Anselm's theory of the atonement.

Anselm's medieval context

BROOKE, R. B. and C. N. L. Brooke, *Popular Religion in the Middle Ages: Western Europe 1000-1300* (London: Thames & Hudson, 1984).

GIBSON, MARGARET, *Lanfranc of Bec* (Oxford: Clarendon Press, 1978) is the most recent biography on Anselm's mentor, but the older work by A. J. MacDonald, *Lanfranc: A Study of his Life, Work and Writing* (London: Humphrey Milford, 1926) should not be ignored, not only for his insight, but also for his excellent writing style.

Further study

General works on Anselm's thought

G. R. Evans has been among the most prolific writers on matters related directly and indirectly to Anselm's life and context. Among her works the following will prove instructive:

EVANS, G. R., *Anselm and Talking About God* (Oxford: Clarendon Press, 1978).

___, *Anselm and a New Generation* (Oxford: Clarendon Press, 1980).

___, *The Language and Logic of the Bible, the Earlier Middle Ages* (Cambridge, Cambridge University Press, 1991).

___, *Philosophy and Theology in the Middle Ages* (London: Routledge, 1993).

Other works providing valuable interaction with Anselm's thought include:

ADAMS, MARILYN MCCORD, '*Fides Quaerens Intellectum:* St. Anselm's Method in Philosophical Theology', *Faith and Philosophy* 9.4 (1992), pp. 409–435.
BARRAL, MARY R., 'Truth and justice in the mind of Anselm', in Jean Pouilloux (ed.), *Les Mutations Socio-culturelles au tournant des XIe-XIIe siécles* (Paris: Centre National de la Recherche Scientifique, 1984).
BROWN, FRANK BURCH, 'The Beauty of Hell: Anselm on God's Eternal Design', *Journal of Religion* 73 (1993), pp. 329–356.
DAVIES, BRIAN and Brian Leftow (eds.), *The Cambridge Companion to Anselm* (Cambridge: Cambridge University Press, 2004).
FORTIN, JOHN (ed.), *Saint Anselm: His Origins and Influence* (Lewiston: Edwin Mellon Press, 2001).
GASPER, GILES E., *Anselm of Canterbury and his Theological Inheritance* (Aldershot: Ashgate, 2004).
HOGG, DAVID S., *Anselm of Canterbury: The Beauty of Theology* (Aldershot: Ashgate, 2004).
HOPKINS, JASPER, *A Companion to the Study of St. Anselm* (Minneapolis: University of Minnesota Press, 1972).
SCHNAUBELT, J. C. *et al.* (eds.), *Anselm Studies: An Occasional Journal*, 2 vols. (New York: Kraus International Publications, 1988).
___, *Twenty-five Years (1969-1994) of Anselm Studies* (Lewiston: Edwin Mellon Press, 1996).
WARD, BENEDICTA, *Anselm of Canterbury: A Monastic Scholar* (Oxford: SLG Press, 1977).
___, *Anselm of Canterbury: His Life and Legacy* (London: SPCK, 2009).

General works on Anselm's context

BARLOW, FRANK, *William Rufus* (London: Methuen, 1983).
KNOWLES, D., *The Monastic Order in England* (Cambridge: Cambridge University Press, 1963).
___, *The Evolution of Medieval Thought* (London: Longman, [2]1988).
LOYN, H. R., *The English Church, 940-1154* (London: Longman, 2000).
DE NOGENT, GUIBERT, *A Monk's Confession, the Memoirs of Guibert of Nogent*, tr. Paul J. Archambault (University Park: University of Pennsylvania Press, 1996).

Specific resources on Anselm's argument for God's existence

The number of books, articles, chapters and essays written on this topic is almost innumerable. Many of these touch on either the so-called ontological argument (a name applied by later philosophers to the argument initially formulated by Anselm but also developed by others) or deal directly with Anselm's *Proslogion* itself. The interested reader would do well to read the collection of essays in J. Hick and A. McGill, *The Many-Faced Argument* (London: Macmillan, 1968). While there are many fine essays in this book, by far the best is the entry by Anselm Stolz entitled, 'Anselm's Theology in the *Proslogion*'. Additional works worth consulting include E. J. Butterworth, *The Identity of*

Anselm's Proslogion Argument for the Existence of God with the Via Quarta of Thomas Aquinas (Queenston: Edwin Mellon Press, 1990); Charles Hartshorne, *Anselm's Discovery* (La Salle: Open Court, 1965).

Specific resources related to Anselm's theory of the atonement

Aulén, Gustaf, *Christus Victor*, tr. A. G. Hebert (London: SPCK, 1978).

Balthasar, Hans Urs von, *The Glory of the Lord: A Theological Aesthetic*, vol. 2, tr. Andrew Louth, Francis McDonaugh and Brian McNeil (Edinburgh: T&T Clark, 1982).

Evans, G. R., 'The *Cur Deus Homo*: The Nature of St Anselm's Appeal to Reason', *Studia Theologia* 31 (2008), pp. 33–50.

Gorringe, Timothy, *God's Just Vengeance* (Cambridge: Cambridge University Press, 1996).

Grensted, L. W., *A Short History of the Doctrine of the Atonement* (Manchester: Manchester University Press, 1962).

McGrath, Alister, 'Rectitude: the moral foundation of Anselm of Canterbury's soteriology', *Downside Review* 99 (1981), pp. 204–213.

Pelikan, Jaroslav, *The Growth of Medieval Theology, 600-1300* (Chicago: Chicago University Press, 1978).

8. THOMAS AQUINAS

Mark W. Elliott

Thomas Aquinas's life began where it would also end, in southern Italy.[1] Born around 1225 at Roccasecca Castle in Aquino, Campagna, he was a young 'oblate' (educated with the prospect of later taking vows) at Monte Cassino from 1230 onwards. The Benedictines who formed this promising boy sent him to Naples for his liberal arts education, as Michael Scot of the Sicilian court had made Greek and Arabic philosophy available in translation (1239) in that city. While in Naples, Thomas was won over to the Dominicans. In 1244 his family tried to divert him, even abduct him from the Dominican novitiate, since it was a social humiliation for a nobleman to be mendicant. Thomas was intercepted while setting out for study in Paris and had to escape from Roccasecca Castle where his family had attempted through (unsuccessful) seduction to entice him into marriage. At Paris no member of a religious order could be enrolled in the Arts faculty, so in 1245 he probably just heard (audited) lectures of the Dominican master, Albert the Great, who was incepting as a master there. However J.-P. Torrell thinks that a dispensation to study

---

1. A helpful eight-page overview of Aquinas' life, with his works listed in chronological order, can be found in N. Kretzmann, *The Metaphysics of Theism: Aquinas's Natural Theology in Summa Contra Gentiles* (Oxford: Clarendon; New York: Oxford University Press, 1997), pp. 255–262.

Arts formally would have been quite possible and that before these studies were finished Thomas started his five years of theology.[2]

Certainly in 1248 he moved with Albert to Cologne, where there was no university, to found the first Dominican *studium generale* (a house of study) that would fill this intellectual gap, although that was not its primary aim. There Augustine was consulted for theology, Aristotle for physics and Galen for medicine. Albert's verdict on Thomas was as encouraging as it was affectionate: 'We call him the Dumb Ox, but the bellowing of that ox will resound throughout the whole world.'[3] Albert pushed Thomas towards philosophy (Aristotle's *Ethics* had just been translated by Robert Grosseteste of Lincoln, and this became his course of lectures). Thomas was also ordained to the priesthood around 1250.

From 1252 to 1256 Thomas was based in Paris at the Dominican House of St Jacques, a little out from the main conglomeration of study houses on the left bank of the Seine. This house had been supported by Pope Honorius III and King Louis IX, despite Parisian resistance from the cathedral of Notre Dame and its school, the hub of the new university (although St Jacques was always open to non-Dominicans). Thomas became chief lecturer on Peter Lombard's *Sentences* (*Sententiarus*). These were a collection of patristic texts ordered around the great themes, 'a rearrangement of patristic views (*sententiae Patrum*), touching on all major Christian teaching following the order of the Creed: the Trinity, creation and creatures, Christ and the virtues, and finally the sacraments and the four last things'.[4] However, when he incepted as Master in 1256, Thomas was no longer bound to teach the *Sentences*. Apart from being caught up in the struggle for Dominicans to have the second chair at Paris University (to some it seemed that the friars were bringing the monastery into the city), this marked the beginning of his peaceful creativity, and hence maturity as a theologian.

Masters were required to hold *quaestiones disputatae* a number of times a year. These were the foundation, or rather the building blocks, for Thomas' major works, with the first of these being the *De veritate* (1260). When he moved to Naples, and then Orvieto in 1260, he embarked on writing the *Summa contra gentiles* (*SCG*), which he completed in 1265 after a lot of revising. The Aristotle

---

2. J.-P. Torrell, *Saint Thomas Aquinas*. Vol. 1: *The Person and His Work* (Washington, DC: Catholic University of America Press, 1996), pp. 22–23.

3. Ibid., p. 26.

4. J. Weisheipl, *Friar Thomas D'Aquino: His Life, Thought, and Works* (Oxford: Blackwell, 1975), p. 67.

translation used had not been available in Paris. The first three books, which interact with the world of non-Christian thought, rely heavily on Aristotle and Avicenna: Book 2, emanation; Book 3, return; Book 4, four truths beyond unaided reason (the Trinity, incarnation, sacraments and resurrection of the body). One can still see this as a form of apologetic philosophical theology on its way to a full systematic theology – it was about proving the truths of faith given through Scripture by rational reasoning, in order to deepen the faith of believers. He also had time to compose his only work of political theology, the *De regno*, taking a mediating position on papal authority, two generations before the explosive polarization on the issue (Bonfatius VIII's *Unam sanctam* [1301], for which temporal power is essential to a pope's authority, and Marsilius of Padua's *Defensor fidei* [c. 1335]). In Rome after finishing his *Commentary on Dionysius' Divine Names* and the *De potentia* (1264; dealing with divine power, creation and the Trinity – developing and sharpening the first *Summa*), he started work on the *Summa theologiae* (*ST*) in Rome at Santa Sabina during 1265.

From this time comes the *Compendium of Theology* (a handbook like Augustine's *Enchirdion*), which spells out the content of the faith by following the articles of the creed. The theological content of the virtue hope is then dealt with by a treatment of the petitions of the 'Our Father'. Charity is explored in terms of the Ten Commandments. So if one is to know truth in the creed, one has to pursue the good end, and observe justice. He returned to Paris as Master in 1269. There he had some problems to address, as one who espoused Aristotle in a way that for his opposite number in the Franciscan order, Bonaventura, seemed suspect. Thomas seemed to tend towards allowing for the eternity of the world, the necessity of 'fate' and the idea that all intellectual creatures share in one 'Intellect'. Indeed, around this time Thomas wrote, '"that the world is not eternal" can only be held by faith and cannot be proven, just as with the Trinity' (*ST* 1, Q46, a2).[5] The Franciscan Pecham opposed this. Thomas himself answered that something's being held on faith did not make it less true.

Worse was to follow when Archbishop Tempier's thirteen propositions (10 Dec. 1270) included some idea that Thomas had entertained eternity of the world or denial of God's universal providence or unicity of intellect or determinism, even if, unlike Siger of Brabant and Boethius of Dacia, he did not finally accept these positions as in any sense true.

5. Unless stated otherwise, I have used the translation of *ST* completed in 1265 that is available from New Advent at <http://www.newadvent.org/summa>.

The famous first part of the second part of the *Summa theologiae* was written in Paris, as he used Aristotle's *Rhetoric* in William Moerbeke's translation. It followed Thomas's completion of his *On Evil*. The affective side of Thomas came to the fore in his last years. He became arguably more 'Augustinian' as he got older.[6] In his course on Pauline epistles, he sees these texts as providing a whole theology. His move in 1272 from Paris to the Dominican house of studies at Naples was no real promotion. However, his worth was recognized in the Pope's request that he write against the Greeks in defence of the *filioque* and related matters for the upcoming ecumenical Council of Lyons, even though unlike Bonaventura, whose gifts were also administrative, he was not made a cardinal.

On 6 December 1273 Thomas seems to have experienced a 'stupefying' vision while at mass. He wrote no more of the unfinished *Summa* and is said to have wished to burn his works, since they were no better than 'straw'. His sister visited him and found only silence. It is perhaps fitting rather than ironic that he had just finished the section on the Eucharistic sacraments as the 'relics of Christ's passion' that cause grace to be drawn out from the potential of the human being, and was in the middle of his treatment of penance. Somewhat recovered in February 1274, he set out for Lyons with his *Contra errores Graecorum*. Not far from home he struck his head on a tree near Borgonuovo, and died on 7 March at the Cistercian Fossanova Abbey.

Thomas and theology

Thomas is often regarded among Protestants as the chief of scholastics, or chief of sinners. Scholastics are viewed with suspicion as those who switch the focus of attention from God to 'God-talk'. 'According to Aquinas, the object of faith is in fact God himself; but since in this life our minds cannot comprehend God directly or immediately, the object of faith is more correctly considered as propositions about God.'[7] Perhaps this should be interpreted not as a preference for dry doctrine over the living God, but rather humility when it comes to making statements about God and his character and action.

It is extremely important that God is love, such that his necessary or essential action takes place, as it were, within the Trinity and that his only real relations are those within himself. God's Persons are his nature and vice versa

6. Torrell, *Thomas Aquinas*, vol. 1, p. 187. Cf. *ST* 1.2, Q4, a2, ad3.
7. Eleonore Stump, *Aquinas* (London: Routledge, 2003), p. 363.

(*ST* 1, Q33, a3, ad1), so any distinctions within him are of relation. God is not three because as Good he has to be diffusive of that good, but because there is something in him analogous to thinking and will or 'intellectual appetite' (unlike with knowledge we love because of what is in the beloved). Yet relation also unites God in himself, even as it means there are distinctions of Father, Son and Holy Spirit within him, since in relation God has an ecstatic character. To be pure act and not static essence, in other words to be fully himself, God is three. Scripture tells us God is eternally the Father and as such has the Son eternally, and since he cannot be Father to the Spirit (or else there would be two sons) is related to the Spirit by another way. God is more like a verb than an adjective. 'God's act of understanding is the very substance of the one who understands. . . . For both the Word that comes forth spiritually and its source are contained in the perfection of the divine existence' (Q27, a2, ad2, ad3). This means there is no real relation of God to creatures, even though creatures as dependent do have a real relation to God (Q28, a1, ad3). Relation in God is not within his nature but in his action. Thomas shows (e.g. in *ST* 1, Q29, a4) that each divine Person subsists in relation to the other two. 'To read the treatise on the Trinity in the Summa requires knowledge of biblical revelation, of the liturgy, and, to an extent, knowledge of Christian tradition.'[8] Within God himself there is a movement towards that which is non-identical or 'other'. As Thomas puts in *ST* 1, Q27, a4:

> The procession of love in God ought not to be called generation. In evidence whereof we must consider that the intellect and the will differ in this respect, that the intellect is made actual by the object understood residing according to its own likeness in the intellect; whereas the will is made actual, not by any similitude of the object willed within it, but by its having a certain inclination to the thing willed. Thus the procession of the intellect is by way of similitude, and is called generation, because every generator begets its own like; whereas the procession of the will is not by way of similitude, but rather by way of impulse and movement towards an object. So what proceeds in God by way of love, does not proceed as begotten, or as son, but proceeds rather as spirit; which name expresses a certain vital movement and impulse, accordingly as anyone is described as moved or impelled by love to perform an action.

---

8. G. Emery, *The Trinitarian Theology of St Thomas Aquinas* (New York: Oxford University Press, 2007), p. 51.

Aquinas and Scripture

At the height of his career Albert the Great wanted to turn to write more biblical commentaries and finish his commentary on Lombard's *Sentences*. This career plan was however interrupted by his elevation to the See of Regensburg, which included a good deal of Crusade preaching. Thomas Aquinas filled the gap Albert left. He had already become a Bachelor at Cologne, taking the role of respondent in Albert's disputations, and also by 1256, as master of sacred sentences, able to lecture on Bible (*cursor biblicus*), giving paraphrases and a light gloss of difficult passages. Given the limited nature of the goal, it is accurate, if uncharitable, for Sixtus of Siena to judge that these (on Isaiah and Jeremiah) have *doctrinae sterilitas*. Aidan Nichols claims that one can nevertheless spy spiritual exegesis in the marginal notes (as scriptural connections were made in the margin).[9] J.-P. Torrell is even more revisionist and positive. Some of Thomas's contemporaries skipped serious study of the Bible on the way to becoming Bachelors on the *Sentences*, but not Thomas. This account does not intend to deny that he was serious about his philosophical investigations – far from it. However, if philosophy and the Bible were sources for his theology, then the biblical–theological side of Thomas deserves consideration, although of course Bible and philosophy worked together.

It must also be remembered that while Thomas was a philosopher his career started with Scripture and ended with a flourish. He did not confuse the two disciplines. One sees a similar structure in the *Summa theologiae*: where Scripture can be a guide, Thomas makes its voice heard. There are things for which one needs revelation and thus grace to know (theology), but many other things are knowable by the careful exercise of reason (philosophy, and its application to many 'sciences'). Obviously these two become intertwined,[10] but the sources are distinct. Also, while in the *Summa*, Thomas states his own conclusions, often not very long; in terms of content, almost 80% of the material comes from other sources and the persistent form is that of question, proposed answer, objection, counter-objection and resolution. The structure of the *Summa* is such that it moves from knowing and speaking about God to the Trinity, creation and fundamental anthropology to ethics, the soul and its passions, history and law, nature and grace (*ST* 1.2), then on to faith, love, hope, the cardinal virtues

---

9. Aidan Nichols, *Discovering Aquinas: An Introduction to His Life, Work, and Influence* (Grand Rapids: Eerdmans, 2003), p. 5.
10. See Brian Davies, *The Thought of Thomas Aquinas* (Oxford: Oxford University Press, 1992), p. 14.

(*ST* 2.2), then Christology and the sacraments. One might want to discern an *exitus–reditus* scheme (according to which God goes out of himself into the other he creates, in order to redeem it by bringing it back to himself). So at the centre stands the human being in becoming, from creation to fulfilment in Christ. The *Summa* is thus in one sense a practical theology, written for trainee pastors, not theological peers. Torrell has insisted that the commentaries and even the *Compendium* are fuller on many theological points.[11]

Thomas's love for Scripture is often reinforced by anecdotes such as his claim that when studying Isaiah, he said he had been in discussion with Peter and Paul at night, which seems to mean more than simply that he read their epistles.[12] Or that one evening as Thomas and a colleague gazed on Paris in the distance, he stated that he would give Paris in exchange for a copy of Chrysostom's commentary on Matthew. But although he did not own it until as late as his second period in Paris, he did get a copy![13] And it would seem that Thomas increasingly allowed the Bible to mould his theology: he allowed Paul to challenge him on his ecclesiology 'even to the point that he reverses his usual order of theological priority so as to allow human reconciliation and unity pride-of-place, even over sanctification. He also reverses this order in regard to the superiority of preaching over sacraments.'[14] The idea is that Paul allows him to see the church as primarily a network of relationships wherein people are addressed, challenged and encouraged, and only secondarily as a medium of personal holiness, with the sacrament itself having an inner word of instruction to the receiver. After all, 'only canonical Scripture is the rule of faith'.[15] Thus the pope can interpret and apply but not supplement,[16] not adding to but extending the range of scriptural truth.

The *Commentary on Isaiah* of course confirms Thomas's early taste for exegesis that gives preference to the literal sense.[17] Curiously, this characteristic

---

11. Torrell, *Thomas Aquinas*, vol. 2, p. 330.
12. Weisheipl, *Friar Thomas D'Aquino*, p. 119.
13. Ibid., p. 215.
14. Christopher T. Baglow, *'Modus et Forma': A New Approach to the Exegesis of Saint Thomas Aquinas with an Application to the Lectura super Epistolam ad Ephesios* (Rome: Biblical Institute Press, 2002), p. 274.
15. 'Sola canonica Scriptura est regula fidei' (in *Commentary on John 21*, lect. 6, 2, n 2656, S488; cf. 4 *Sentences* 25, 3, 2, and *ST* 3 Q55, a5).
16. As he made clear in *De veritate* 14, 10.
17. See J.-P. Torrell and D. Bouthillier, 'Quand saint Thomas méditait sur le prophète Isaïe', *Revue Thomiste* 90 (1990), p. 28.

was even at the origin of a dispute over this work's authenticity: for how could a theological doctor be *so* literalist in his approach? So, in his interpretation of Isaiah 8:4, Thomas thought that the *puer* announced there was the son of the prophet and his wife. This alone was enough to make Nicholas of Lyra doubt in 1326 the Thomist authorship of the commentary. Torrell sums up the Thomist approach to exegesis as: Listen–believe–meditate (for moral benefit)–communicate–complete. This is not the style of a theologian who wants to bypass the Scriptures.

As Nicholas Healy reminds us, all that Aquinas did he did as a friar with an emphasis on charity and transformation, but also, distinctively, and over against the monastic orders, that there was a calling to get out and engage with the world. Thomas urged a 'passing on to others the fruits of our contemplation through preaching and teaching'.[18] Contemplation *and* proclamation were truly apostolic.[19] Scripture is the material for contemplation, resulting in doctrine, and not just edification for two hours a day, or for three hours a day in Lent. Healy quotes a fine passage from Beryl Smalley, taken in turn from Peter the Chanter on disputation as serving in the digestion of the scriptural 'food', but Thomas should himself be heard on this (*ST* 1.2, Q10):

> it is necessary to dispute in public about the faith, provided there be those who are equal and adapted to the task of confuting errors; since in this way simple people are strengthened in the faith, and unbelievers are deprived of the opportunity to deceive, while if those who ought to withstand the perverters of the truth of faith were silent, this would tend to strengthen error.

If one liked, one could argue that the daily diet of students at the Dominican house of studies in Paris was almost two-thirds 'biblical'. As Torrell puts it, 'In the first hour of the day, Thomas gave his lecture; after that came the lecture of his bachelor; in the afternoon, both gathered with their students to "dispute" on a chosen theme.'[20] The lecture was the foundation; the disputation, the walls of the building; preaching, the roof or 'cover'.

---

18. 'Introduction', in Thomas Weinandy, Daniel Keating and John Yocum (eds.), *Aquinas on Scripture: An Introduction to His Biblical Commentaries* (New York: T. & T. Clark, 2005), p. 6.
19. Cf. Nicholas M. Healy, *Thomas Aquinas: Theologian of the Christian Life* (Aldershot: Ashgate, 2003), p. 6.
20. Torrell, *Thomas Aquinas*, vol. 1, p. 62.

It might come as no surprise that 'Thomas is best at exegeting texts that are more expository than narrative in nature'.[21] Or, put another way, narratives can be reduced to messages, although Thomas was looking not to explain stories but to see how their driving principles could affect the lives of the readers or listeners. The message of Scripture is of salvific significance, a matter of eternal life and death.[22] Hence the moral sense of Ephesians 2:21 is 'not so much illuminative as applicative. It takes a literal sense which is primarily theological, and in explaining its theological ramifications regarding the soul in grace, challenges the recipient through an invitation to comparison.'[23] The 'literal' hermeneutic means seeing Bible reading as leading one upwards as much as leading one forwards in the course of the history of salvation. The attention to the literal sense can be seen in Thomas's exegesis of Genesis 1:6 (in *ST* 1.2, Q68, a3): the 'water' is really formless matter or any kind of transparent body. The literal meaning can include metaphors, prophecies and types.[24]

Chris Baglow has interestingly pointed out the way Thomas in his commentating on *Paul* used a motif verse from a Gospel after introducing the section with a Psalms text.[25] That the origins of this method lie in the liturgy seems very suggestive. Thus John (10:16, 'many flocks') operates as a motto theme-verse through all of his commentary on Ephesians, with Psalm 74:4 only as the 'access' point. Here we see liturgy as fecund for biblical theology, although it may be that a purely lectionary approach would not be sufficient for a 'whole-biblical theology'.

It may be true that revelation originates in God, and Scripture is the channel, yet the sacred words are channels that bring knowledge of higher things, where words of other texts simply point towards, or at best lead the mind.[26] What these things are of course limits the range of meaning of words in Scripture.

21. Baglow, *Modus et Forma*, p. 271.
22. O.-H. Pesch, 'Theologie des Wortes bei Thomas von Aquin', *Zeitschrift für Theologie und Kirche* 66 (1969), pp. 437–465.
23. Ibid.
24. Rowan D. Williams, 'The Literal Sense of Scripture', *Modern Theology* 7 (1991), pp. 121–134.
25. Baglow, *Modus et Forma, passim.*
26. Maximo Arias Reyero, *Thomas von Aquin als Exeget: Die Prinzipien seiner Schrifdeutung und seine Lehre von den Schriftsinnen* (Einsiedeln: Johannes, 1971), pp. 246–247: 'Et sic in homine instruit intellectum et *immediate per sacras litteras, et mediate per alias scripturas (In II Tim 3:3)* ('and thus he instructed the intellect in humans both in an *unmediated way by the sacred scriptures and in a mediated way by other writings*'; my emphasis).

Scripture belongs much more in the world than say Pseudo-Dionysius implied with his notion of it as a store of divine ideas. From *Quodlibet* 7, Q6 onwards, Thomas made it clear that for any spiritual sense of a text that is to be allowed it must be referred to Christ, which, in one sense, earths the interpretation. In a way comparable to Barth, Thomas moved from a principle of revelation to one of Christ. More generally throughout the *Summa* one can conclude, 'Thomas Aquinas relies most strongly upon Scripture in the *argumenta sed contra*, but Scripture is present in every phase of the *quaestio*.'[27] There is an 'allusiveness . . . indicative of an influence of Scripture on theological language itself, in which Scripture is no longer recognized as an external *auctoritas*'.[28] By this Valkenberg means that for Thomas Scripture is something *more* than an external authority. So it is more than the mere 'function of Scripture as an element in logical argumentation', since 'the function of Scripture as encompassing source and framework for theology' should be recognized.[29]

If one may nuance Healy's view,[30] which wants to see *sacra scriptura* and *sacra doctrina* as one and the same thing for Thomas, *sacra doctrina* rather is the ray of colourful light that happens when revelation 'shines through' *sacra scriptura*. Revelation is indeed in the first instance the understanding of Jesus by the apostles, in a similar but fuller way to that which the prophets received: it is an event in the mind, strengthening of reason, but *doctrina* is what comes out the other side of the Bible to the post-biblical reader. Aidan Nichols insists that Thomas saw revelation not to exist in events 'out there', but in the mind. Thus *lumen naturale* gets us through the world in intelligent fashion, but *lumen propheticum*

> is given by God the Redeemer, to enable human beings (a few of them directly, all of them indirectly) to locate and interpret aright the ultimate goal of human life, a goal entirely supernatural because consisting in the open vision of the Trinity, and hence transcending finite, created nature altogether.[31]

Divine light is given so that they can communicate things. The Bible writers see things both commonplace and supernatural as mediating understanding of

27. Pim Valkenburg, *Words of the Living God: Place and Function of Holy Scripture in the Theology of St. Thomas Aquinas* (Leuven: Peeters, 2000), p. 36.
28. Ibid., p. 43.
29. Ibid., p. 47.
30. Healy, *Thomas Aquinas*, p. 18.
31. Nichols, *Discovering Aquinas*, p. 24.

salvation. The knowledge as 'input' is thus less important than the prophetic mind that interprets. As Persson (see *De veritate* 12, 7) in his classic and yet-to-be-surpassed work puts it, 'lumen propheticum [is] . . . the constitutive element of revelation, for this "light" is in fact nothing other than a divine strengthening of the power of reason to interpret and judge knowledge'.[32] It becomes revelation only when the observing or perceiving subject can classify and interpret it in an intelligible way. To cite Persson further:

> External events may be the material for the judgment of the illuminated reason, and consequently there is a relationship between the two, but these events are not in themselves revelation. Revelation, therefore, according to Thomas, cannot consist, for example, in events recorded in the Gospels, – the birth, death or resurrection of Christ, and the like. We may not even regard the incarnation as a divine revelation. Only *knowledge* of the incarnation can be revelation, and this is always something internal to man. . . . If it is possible to speak of 'a revelation of God in Christ' in Thomas – an expression which he himself never uses – this must refer to a knowledge brought about by God in the human soul of Christ, on the ground of which he can be said to be 'the first and foremost teacher of the faith' (*primus et principalis doctor*) (*ST* 3, Q7, a7). The incarnation may indeed be the presupposition of revelation, but because the cognitive viewpoint is all-decisive, the event of the incarnation itself cannot be understood as a *revelatio*. Supernaturally communicated knowledge does not *point to* revelation but as *cognitio* it is itself *the same as* revelation.[33]

Thomas is not quoting to embellish nor to prove a theological point, as if theological knowledge could be attained outside revelation: the latter is indispensable. Of course, quotations from Scripture turn up often to illustrate or confirm the conclusion to a Question and at other times replace syllogisms in the *Summa*, in the *sed contra* section, but their authority in doing this should not be undervalued. 'The theologically primary function of Scripture in these *quaestiones* is that it functions as a framework indicating the limits of the "hypothetical" investigations.'[34] In other words, metaphysical Christology takes place

---

32. Per Erik Persson, *Sacra doctrina: Reason and Revelation in Aquinas* (Oxford: Blackwell, 1970), p. 24.
33. Ibid., p. 25.
34. Valkenberg, *Words of the Living God*, pp. 146–147. Valkenberg starts his book by reminding the reader that M. D. Chenu, *Introduction à l'étude de saint Thomas d'Aquin* (Montreal-Paris: Publications de l'Institut d'études médiévales, 1954), 'characterizes

within the framework of the history of salvation, such that the question 'how fitting was the incarnation for our salvation?' gets framed. Valkenberg argues that Aquinas got round the back of Chalcedon, in that Scripture tends to get quoted in the last article of each question. For Aquinas, 'although theology is not restricted to the words of Scripture itself, all insights and language developed by theologians have to be tested for their faithfulness to Scripture as the Word of God'.[35] Valkenberg concludes that it was his expositions on Scripture that make the later *Summa* differ from the earlier *Scriptum*.[36] He worked on Bible commentaries, the *Summa* and Aristotle simultaneously. This is because Scripture for Thomas was source and framework, not proof and garnish.

The apostles compared to the prophets have a clearer revelation, since they were taught by Christ himself, and the Spirit's descent on them completed it.[37] Salvation hinges on the intellect: get that right and the sinful will should come round. Faith is about an infused possession through the light of divine faith (*habitus per lumen fidei divinitus infuses* [a disposition infused by the light of faith]; *ST* 2.2, Q2, a3) – where the object is not perceived directly but through another's testimony, yet, all the same, it is a knowledge. Finally, the content of revelation is then passed on in *spoken* words. 'Sacred doctrine is a knowledge which has a practical end and even works for salvation' (*ST* 2.2, Q2, a1). Hermeneutics then means interpreting the sacred writers' minds where that knowledge held its purest form. So one starts and restarts with Scripture. A key text is to be found in *ST* 3, Q1, a3: the divine will is made known to us in the Scriptures. Faith rests on the content of the Bible (*ST* 2.2). Only the truth manifested in the canonical scripture is the formal object of faith (3a, Q55, 5). In *Commentary on John 21*, lecture 6 (20), Aquinas is explicit that only canonical scripture is the rule of faith; that is, tradition is more to be kept (*servanda*) as things to be done, not believed. It is quite clear that tradition has nothing to do with doctrine, but only specific practices (*ST* 3, Q64, a2, ad1). Persson confirms, 'This means for Thomas that the subject of theology is pre-eminently *biblical theology*, and *sacra doctrina* may be regarded,

---

Footnote 34 (*cont.*)

his [Aquinas's] theology on the mysteries of the life of Christ in *Summa Theologia III* 27–59 as a specimen of biblical theology' (*Words of the Living God*, p. 1, quoting Chenu, Introduction, p. 222).

35. Valkenberg, *Words of the Living God*, p. 151.

36. Ibid., p. 188.

37. *De veritate* 14, 11, 6.

to use an apt expression of Etienne Gilson, as "holy scripture received in a human intellect.'"[38]

Of course, for Aquinas, Scripture was always so cased in tradition of its interpretation that it is often hard to distinguish between the two. Most markedly in the *Catena aurea* on the Four Gospels, the Scriptures come clothed in the fathers' interpretations.[39] Often the use of Scripture is allusive; but biblical citations in the third 'Christological' part of the *Summa* are also 25–30% up on the rest of that work; almost twice as much as in Lombard. In Thomas's own *Scriptum* on the *Sentences* there is perhaps more discussion with fathers and philosophers. 'In the *Summa*, however, Aquinas concentrates on the proper nature of theology in its dependency on God's revelation. Accordingly he focuses on the proper authorities in theology: Scripture in the first place, but the Fathers as well.'[40] Now 'the amount of Scriptural quotation is still greater in soteriological than Christological part', for the former deals with 'questions concerning the connection of contingent events with the will of God to save humankind'.[41] Thus, in the Christological part of the *Summa* at *ST* 3, Q53, a2 (and also at 3 *Sentences* 21, 2, 2), *conveniens* (fitting) is used in that the resurrection's being on the *third* day fits both the Old Testament Scriptures (Hos. 6:2 and the sign of Jonah per Matt. 12:40) and the facts of human life. (The mention of the third day as suitable [*congruens*] is to show that Christ was indeed dead.) Events can be contingent and yet have theological and soteriological significance.[42] Scripture describes a real world in all its depth and potential for glory.

Another way of putting this is to say, 'the clearer revelation happened in the New Testament' (*ST* 2.2, Q174, a6, ad3); the Word in the Old Testament was often veiled; in the New Testament the Word has become visible. John the Baptist is a witness to the light illuminated by that very Light. Right teaching directs the gaze to the Christ who was becoming fully manifest. Christoph Berchthold shows how Aquinas did not understand the Bible as codebook or sourcebook for theological themes as much as that which documented the history of salvation as expanding to include the Gentiles: the unclean shepherds saw the baby before the worthy ancients of the old faith.[43] There was

38. Persson, *Sacra doctrina*, p. 89.
39. *Catena aurea*, tr. John Henry Newman, 8 vols. (Eugene: Wipf & Stock, 2005).
40. Valkenburg, *Words of the Living God*, p. 28.
41. Ibid., p. 33.
42. Ibid., p. 83.
43. Cf. Thomas's nuanced translation of Isa. 64:4, 'without you no eye has seen what you have prepared for those who love you' (Vulgate 'besides you . . . who wait on you').

an 'openness' principle at work in Thomas's biblical theology, such that the parables are only secret in an introductory, propaedeutic way. Manifestation is then something more than revelation: after the resurrection, disciples hear of him but also encounter him.[44]

What we get with Aquinas is possibly a preference for ideas over events, but without the events to be perceived there would be no being grasped by God in the mind and hence no informing and guiding of the will. And it is the event of the coming of Christ that makes all the difference to the quality of the content made available to the mind. The words of Scripture show the mind of the writers as reflective of the will of God. This is what the literal sense meant. The Spirit draws us immediately to God, and the oracular words of Moses and the Prophets touch us. Now of course the *Summa* is more of a mystical or spiritual theology, in that it sketches a movement from creation and God to human existence at its best, ending up driven to consider Christ and then encounter him. Yet all this is indeed biblical theology.

A living and practical theology: the *Summa theologiae*

This is the first and the last of Thomist theology: first because it is the most widely published, translated and commented on of Aquinas's works, and last because it belongs to the later, more mature expression of his theology (1265–73), with only a few things coming later: the Romans commentary, the final version of the Psalms commentary and *Against the Errors of the Greeks*. So the *Summa theologiae* is his crowning glory and as such most accessible in terms of its words (e.g. see the full translation on the New Advent website; details in n. 5 above). Yet its structure makes its purpose and interpretation far from clear. The *Summa*, according to the fine summary of A. Nichols, describes a covenant of creation leading humans up towards God, and a covenant of saving revelation, which is descending (katabatic). And yet these two are 'ultimately unitary', with an 'ordering to the new and everlasting covenant in Jesus Christ'.[45]

Sandwiched within all this however is treatment of anthropology in ethics: in *ST* 1.2, Man's Last End, Human Acts, Passions, Habits, Vice and Sin, Law and Grace. Then, in *ST* 2.2, Faith, Hope, Charity, Prudence, Justice, Fortitude,

---

44. Christoph Berchthold, *Manifestatio Veritatis: Zum Offenbarungsbegriff bei Thomas von Aquin* (Münster: LIT, 2000), pp. 238–247.

45. Nichols, *Discovering Aquinas*, p. 34.

Temperance, Acts Which Pertain to Certain Men. The question to ask is why *ST* 2.2 precedes rather than follows the Christological and sacramental. A brief examination of the theological virtues will show that the language is extremely Christian: 'faith' (in *ST* 1.2, Q1) is in Christ, propositions about him as well as the reality. Yet for Thomas, *ST* 1.2 is about the Christian's 'walking with Jesus', whereas *ST* 3 is about receiving from him. The two go together, but that which he says about the active and contemplative life is instructive (*ST* 3 Q182, ad3). Sometimes a man is called away from the contemplative life to the works of the active life, on account of some necessity of the present life, yet not so as to be compelled to forsake contemplation altogether. Hence Augustine says (*City of God* 19.19), 'The love of truth seeks a holy leisure, the demands of charity undertake an honest toil,' the work namely of the active life.

> If no one imposes this burden upon us we must devote ourselves to the research and contemplation of truth, but if it be imposed on us, we must bear it because charity demands it of us. Yet even then we must not altogether forsake the delights of truth, lest we deprive ourselves of its sweetness, and this burden overwhelm us.[46]

Hence it is clear that when a person is called from the contemplative life to the active life, this is done by way not of subtraction but of addition. The active life still matters as an important natural end: the natural end of human life, that is, the attainment of specific perfection as a human being is not rendered otiose or irrelevant by the fact that we are directed towards a supernatural end. The specific natural ideal of humanity remains the proximate norm of morality. That is why Aquinas insists that while the theological virtues transform the cardinal virtues, they do so in such a way as to leave intact the rational structure of the latter (ST 2.2, Q26, a6), which is itself derived from their orientation towards the natural human good (ST 1.2, Q62, a1; 1.2, Q63, a2), that is, natural perfection in accordance with the specific kind of humanity (ST 1, Q62, a1). At the same time, the theological virtues do add something to the moral life, beyond a new motivation for moral behaviour that 'inner harmony and unity of life that all things naturally desire'.[47] Porter here is right to stress how different beatitude is in kind from any 'unlimited enjoyment of finite goods' as Thomas describes it in

---

46. *City of God*, tr. H. Bettenson (Harmondsworth: Penguin Classics, 2003).
47. Jean Porter, *The Recovery of Virtue: The Relevance of Aquinas for Christian Ethics* (Louisville: Westminster John Knox, 1990), p. 67.

Summa contra Gentiles (*SCG*) 3.63. In the blessed state the society of friends will not be needed (ST 1.2, Q4, a8), even if in the meantime friends are very much needed. Thomas viewed *tristitia* (depression) as one of the seven deadly sins, for it would block off friendship with God, which is the state of grace, and he offers remedies as gentle in practice (company, baths, wine) as determined and serious in intent. A sadness that becomes joylessness in the Christian life from so many struggles is what he particularly means by *tristitia*, and the emphasis is not so much on the sinfulness of self-pity as on self-correction.[48]

So this is a practical theology, even while being more theocentric than Lombard's, it is less cosmocentric than Albert's. Aquinas will not speculate. 'In principle, for Aquinas, Scripture sets an upper bond on soteriological speculation: assertions should not venture beyond explicit Biblical claims and what clearly follows from them.'[49] Whereas for Scotus it is better to praise Christ too much than too little; for example, the incarnation would have happened even without sin (as Bonaventura), Aquinas remains with the actuality of the world and God's economy as they are.

Example: sin and salvation in relation to Augustine

It is important to recognize that Aquinas promoted a living orthodoxy not least because of his commitment to biblical theology. True, Aquinas wanted not merely to describe theology but to explain it,[50] and in this he made use of the tradition of theological interpretation. Gilles Emery observes that Aquinas allows a rather nice co-operation of Scripture and some fitting arguments in establishing and understanding doctrine.[51] In this matter one should not underestimate the importance of Augustine on Aquinas for his understanding of John, Romans and the Psalms. 'The two thousand citations of Augustine in the Summa attest to an uninterrupted dialogue with him.'[52] Thus he is able in his theological works to 'go behind Lombard' to say that the divine essence does not generate itself. This living theology means that he

48. Pesch, 'Theologie', p. 231.
49. Marilyn McCord Adams, *What Sort of Human Nature? Medieval Philosophy and the Systematics of Christology* (Milwaukee: Marquette University Press, 1999), p. 67.
50. Torrell, *Thomas Aquinas*, vol. 2, pp. 9–10.
51. G. Emery, *Trinity in Aquinas* (Ypsilanti, MI: Sapientia, 2003), p. 225.
52. L. Elders in Torrell, *Thomas Aquinas*, vol. 2, p. 380, n. 21.

understands Augustine because, unlike Lombard, he does not simply 'cut and paste' his source, but gets into the spirit of the theology. This means of course that Augustine sets him on paths, but is not the end of the path. Indeed, over against Augustine there is a certain 'biblical' hylomorphism in which the soul as form of the body is not a free-floating entity detached from it.[53] Likewise, in Aquinas's account, Romans 5:12 describes not so much Augustine's 'original sin' as the idea of corporate identity in Adam, and yet in this Aquinas thinks more Platonically (organically) than Aristotelian (causally), while agreeing with Peter Lombard that the 'tinder' (*fomes*) of sin is what remains in the baptized. Also, in John 15:5 the idea of indwelling grace takes Augustine's view a good deal further. John Rist is surely right to attack Robert Pasnau for insisting that according to Aquinas humans are simply free to choose the good, and that a certain amount of happiness is possible by using the resources given in creation (secondary causation).[54] Aquinas uses Augustine to desecularize Aristotle's ethics, such that our free will needs to be helped by God's grace, while Aquinas remains a bit more optimistic than Augustine about the natural capacity of humans for virtue. There is an apparent puzzle here: why, in *ST* 1.2, Q81, a1 on inherited sin (below), did Thomas ignore Augustine?

> Therefore we must explain the matter otherwise by saying that all men born of Adam may be considered as one man, inasmuch as they have one common nature, which they receive from their first parents; even as in civil matters, all who are members of one community are reputed as one body, and the whole community as one man . . . In this way, then, the disorder which is in this man born of Adam, is voluntary, not by his will, but by the will of his first parent, who, by the movement of generation, moves all who originate from him . . . so original sin is not the sin of this person, except inasmuch as this person receives his nature from his first parent, for which reason it is called the 'sin of nature,' according to Ephesians 2:3: 'We were by nature children of wrath.'

---

53. 'Hylomorphism' is the notion that a thing is composed of 'matter' and 'form' (*hylē* is a Greek word meaning 'wood' or 'matter', while *morphē* is a Greek word generally translated as 'form'), to the point that these cannot exist independently of each other.

54. *De veritate* 24, 14; see John Rist, 'Augustine, Aristotelianism and Aquinas: Three Varieties of Philosophical Adaptation', in M. Dauphinais, B. David and M. Levering (eds.), *Aquinas the Augustinian* (Washington, DC: Catholic University of America Press, 2007), pp. 79–99.

In the *Summa*, as Mark Johnson notes,[55] even this defect seems to be 'somebody else's'. We are members of a body that can be moved by Adam's will. His sin was mortal sin; ours needs to be cleansed by baptism but does not make us liable to damnation – we are not culpable for it; so Aquinas has to be silent about Augustine's view if he does not want to seem out of line. In locating Adam's and our sin in the will rather than 'deeper' in our being, he is here arguably more like Paul in this respect than Augustine, although he probably would not have got there without the apostle. In Eleonore Stump's casting of this, 'When *we* love someone, Aquinas says, we take account of some good, real or apparent, in that person; but when *God* loves someone, he is causing, not taking account of good in that person', so that even 'imputing' means changing something within. 'Grace that is the source of the meritorious acts that a person performs is cooperating grace, but grace that justifies or heals a person's soul is operating grace', and in the matter of justification it is all operating grace.[56] Augustine's Sermon 169.11.13 gets quoted to effect in *ST* 1.2, Q111, a2, ad2: 'God who made us without our will will not justify us without it.' Any act of free will comes with infusion of grace simultaneously (though *logically* secondary) after a long providential build-up. Grace acts on the soul with only formal, not efficient, causality.

The beginning of being made righteous is when one believes God will make one righteous and then desires him to do so. God can change first-order volition in a person without removing second-order volition (i.e. the will to command); and God would not implant such a first-order volition without the second-order volition wanting the same thing. Thomas is faithful to Augustine's lead here: 'Making a sinner righteous then, will be a process in which a believer's specific volitions are brought into harmony with the governing second-order volition assenting to God's bringing her to righteousness, with the consequent gradual alteration in first-order volition.'[57] Grace is more than just the mental illumination that Pelagians thought it was, to be gained for example from reading the Bible. It is the atonement that cracks the will's resistance to grace. Thus the intellect's being flooded by grace causes a free response. There can be no compulsion of the will. 'God can change the will with necessity, but he cannot compel it.' Grace inheres in its subject as a form – and alters our configuration (*De veritate* 22, 8). Thus, 'Aquinas says that divinely infused grace operates on the will in the manner of a formal cause and not in the manner of

55. Mark Johnson, 'Augustine and Aquinas on Original Sin: Doctrine, Authority and Pedagogy', in Dauphinais, David and Levering, *Aquinas the Augustinian*, pp. 145–158.

56. Stump, *Aquinas*, p. 376.

57. Ibid., p. 381.

an efficient cause,'[58] for the latter remains with the agent. At the moment of the infusion of grace the will is in neutral; that is, no longer for God or against him; and an absence of refusal means God can act. But the human being is free to get herself 'there' where God can touch her, or to remove obstacles at least. It is not so much like reconfiguring a stone so that it inclines upwards instead of being pulled down by gravity, for, if anything, God gives back to human wills their original, natural inclination. The giving of the law has both an outward (Old Testament) and an inward sense (New Testament). Behind all this lies a Christological model of the One who was perfectly obedient.

The fullest expression of Thomas's exposition of the Pauline teaching was completed in Naples in 1272. Whereas in the *Summa* reprobation came at the same time as the merits that were foreseen, by now in the Romans commentary he is closer to Augustine: although predestination causes the merits of the elect, reprobation comes after foreseen merits (*post praevisa merita*), even if in such cases there is also a withdrawal of grace.[59] The difference from Augustine is that Thomas plays down the role of original sin and therefore leaves the decree more a mystery than Augustine did. One could say he has gone beyond Augustine to Paul.[60] As God is the cause of all actions in as much as they are actions, he also determines that which is bad action by causing it in as much as it is *action*. Thus sinners are 'without excuse'.

God and creation

The doctrine of God and the doctrine of creation could be viewed as Thomas's big contributions to the history of Christian theology. For Aquinas, Aristotle was the philosopher. Norman Kretzmann was correct to say that Thomas loved Aristotle not so much for his physics but for his metaphysics – that there was more to creation than the world of sense and myths. Or, as McInerny puts it, 'For Thomas, there is one great division in reality, that between God and creatures.'[61] On this rests Thomas's famous assertion of a relationship of analogy between the Creator and the creature (*ST* 1, Q13, a5):

58. Ibid., p. 393.
59. Michal Paluch, *La profondeur de l'amour divin: La prédestination dans l'oeuvre de Saint Thomas d'Aquin* (Paris: Vrin, 2004), p. 261, with reference to Rom. 9:13, 16.
60. Ibid., p. 314.
61. Ralph McInerny, *Aquinas and Analogy* (Washington, DC: Catholic University of America Press, 1999), p. 66.

> I answer that: Univocal predication is impossible between God and creatures. The reason of this is that every effect which is not an adequate result of the power of the efficient cause receives the similitude of the agent not in its full degree, but in a measure that falls short, so that what is divided and multiplied in the effects resides in the agent simply, and in the same manner; as for example the sun by exercise of its one power produces manifold and various forms in all inferior things. In the same way, as said in the preceding article, all perfections existing in creatures divided and multiplied, pre-exist in God unitedly. Thus when any term expressing perfection is applied to a creature, it signifies that perfection distinct in idea from other perfections; as, for instance, by the term 'wise' applied to man, we signify some perfection distinct from a man's essence, and distinct from his power and existence, and from all similar things; whereas when we apply to it God, we do not mean to signify anything distinct from His essence, or power, or existence. Thus also this term 'wise' applied to man in some degree circumscribes and comprehends the thing signified; whereas this is not the case when it is applied to God; but it leaves the thing signified as uncomprehended, and as exceeding the signification of the name. Hence it is evident that this term 'wise' is not applied in the same way to God and to man. The same rule applies to other terms. Hence no name is predicated univocally of God and of creatures. Neither, on the other hand, are names applied to God and creatures in a purely equivocal sense, as some have said. Because if that were so, it follows that from creatures nothing could be known or demonstrated about God at all; for the reasoning would always be exposed to the fallacy of equivocation. Such a view is against the philosophers who proved many things about God, and also against what the Apostle says: 'The invisible things of God are clearly seen being understood by the things that are made' (Romans 1:20). Therefore it must be said that these names are said of God and creatures in an analogous sense, i.e. according to proportion.

So there is a 'no' to double truth, for things on earth and in heaven correspond as well as interact. The message is of the dependent autonomy of creation, with penultimate ends of earthly flourishing as good. A sacramental universe means that things in creation have meaning in relation to themselves and also to the bigger cosmic picture. As the theologian of creation there is a reminder of a certain humility. 'Our experience of things is not a confrontation with something utterly alien, but a way of absorbing, and being absorbed by, the world to which we naturally belong.'[62]

---

62. Fergus Kerr, 'Beyond Subject and Object: NeoThomist Reflections', in D. Z. Phillips (ed.), *Whose God? Which Tradition? The Nature of Belief in God* (London: Ashgate, 2008), pp. 21–34, 33.

Thomas is often and rightly understood as a theologian of creation, and this status is seen in his understanding of Romans as providing a large degree of revelation. Romans 1:20 shows how creation invites us into God's wisdom, power and goodness, which we are to consider but also to worship (*SCG* 2.860):[63]

> Therefore, since the Christian faith principally teaches (*instruit*) a human being about God, and through the light of divine revelation makes the human being one who cognises created things, a kind of likeness of divine wisdom is brought about in the human being.[64]

This is the state of humanity before the Fall. Human beings have been given all the wisdom they need but they usually ignore it. So Thomas can be viewed as providing a sort of theodicy: 'Whatever happens on earth, even if it is evil, turns out for the good of the whole world. Because, as Augustine says in the Enchiridion, God is so good that he would never permit any evil if he were not also so powerful that from any evil he could draw out a good.'[65]

His allowing the possibility that philosophically the world could be explained as without a beginning in time, thus avoiding the problem of 'infinite regress', was complemented by his adding the contribution of revelation – Genesis 1:1 settles matters: creation itself began (*SCG* 2.16.13). Yet this beginning can be explained as somehow timeless: 'For creation is not a change, but the very dependency of the created act of being upon the principle from which it is produced. And thus, creation is a kind of relation; so that nothing prevents its being in the creature as its subject. Creation is not a motion' (*SCG* 2.18.2). In other words, Thomas is adding to Augustine's conclusion that if time is logically posterior to the divine act of creation, then it comes out of nothing, and so creation does not come at some point in 'divine time'. *Ex nihilo* is a way of saying that creation does not come from anywhere or 'any-when'. Thomas, like Augustine, had a problem with *creatio ex nihilo* in time, since even time is

---

63. Normann Kretzmann, *The Metaphysics of Creation: Aquinas's Natural Theology in Summa contra gentiles II* (Oxford: Clarendon, 1999), p. 22.
64. *The Summa Contra Gentiles of Saint Thomas Aquinas*, tr. English Dominican Fathers (London: Burns Oates & Washbourne, 1923–9). All subsequent quotations from *SCG* are taken from this edition.
65. In Rom. 6; Thomas d'Aquin, *Commentaire de l'epitre aux Romains* (Paris: Cerf, 1999), p. 463 (*SCG* 3.20).

necessarily dependent on God.[66] Creation is called to aim to make its existence its essence inasmuch as much as it can resemble its Creator (*ST* 1, Q54, a3). Thomas was used to discussing metaphysical and physical matters together; God's making individual things comes from his creating or individuating particulars according to their essence. The structure of being according to grades of being was inspired by Platonizing influences, not least that of the *Divine Names* of Dionysius. What creatures share with God is existence (*esse*) rather than essence (*ens*). Potential is in matter and form actualizes it, not least in the case of the human soul as the form of the body, with for example 'humankind' as form individuated through a number of individuals. Substance is the two of these together that goes on towards its natural end and uses accidental features that depend on the material to get there (*De principiis naturae*). Thomas was able to mould Aristotle's teleology (each natural thing tends towards its end) to Christian eschatology (each rational creature has an end beyond the limits of the 'natural' lifespan). *Felicitas* becomes *beatitudo*.[67] We read the foundation of Thomas's dynamic ontology when he writes (*ST* 1, Q45, a1):

> I answer that, As said above (Question 44, Article 2), we must consider not only the emanation of a particular being from a particular agent, but also the emanation of all being from the universal cause, which is God; and this emanation we designate by the name of creation. Now what proceeds by particular emanation, is not presupposed to that emanation; as when a man is generated, he was not before, but man is made from 'not-man,' and white from 'not-white.' Hence if the emanation of the whole universal being from the first principle be considered, it is impossible that any being should be presupposed before this emanation. For nothing is the same as no being. Therefore as the generation of a man is from the 'not-being' which is 'not-man,' so creation, which is the emanation of all being, is from the 'not-being' which is 'nothing.'

But in article 7 of the same question comes an affirmation of creation's goodness, owing to traces of the Creator to be found in creation:

> I answer that, Every effect in some degree represents its cause, but diversely. For some effects represent only the causality of the cause, but not its form; as smoke represents fire. Such a representation is called a 'trace': for a trace shows that

66. See M. Dauphinais (ed.), *Aquinas the Augustinian* (Washington, DC: Catholic University of America Press, 2007).
67. Cf. Volker Leppin, *Thomas von Aquin* (Münster: Aschendorff, 2009), p. 66.

> someone has passed by but not who it is. Other effects represent the cause as regards the similitude of its form, as fire generated represents fire generating; and a statue of Mercury represents Mercury; and this is called the representation of 'image.' Now the processions of the divine Persons are referred to the acts of intellect and will, as was said above (Article 27). For the Son proceeds as the word of the intellect; and the Holy Ghost proceeds as love of the will. Therefore in rational creatures, possessing intellect and will, there is found the representation of the Trinity by way of image, inasmuch as there is found in them the word conceived, and the love proceeding.
>
> But in all creatures there is found the trace of the Trinity, inasmuch as in every creature are found some things that are necessarily reduced to the divine Persons as to their cause. For every creature subsists in its own being, and has a form, whereby it is determined to a species, and has relation to something else. Therefore as it is a created substance, it represents the cause and principle; and so in that manner it shows the Person of the Father, Who is the 'principle from no principle.' According as it has a form and species, it represents the Word as the form of the thing made by art is from the conception of the craftsman. According as it has relation of order, it represents the Holy Ghost, inasmuch as He is love, because the order of the effect to something else is from the will of the Creator. And therefore Augustine says (*De Trin.* vi 10) that the trace of the Trinity is found in every creature . . .

As 'being itself' God does not relate to creation as one thing to another. (Even the atonement does not change God's position towards creation, but reconciles it to him: 2 Cor. 5:19.) Thomas avoids any idea of emanation of creation from out of God, but the cause of all is the divine will, and the creation has its distinctiveness in its essence, although not autonomy in its existence. Creation can be itself although it is free also to rise to higher things with the power of God's grace.

Faith and knowledge

Although theology is about 'faith seeking understanding', there was in Augustine also the theme of 'understanding preceding faith', in the sense of doctrine as providing a knowledge that faith can hold on to. And it could be that for Thomas it was contemplation, rather than what we might mean by 'understanding', that the faithful sought.[68]

---

68. Thomas Aquinas, *Commentary on the Epistle to the Hebrews*, tr. Chrysostom Baer (South Bend, IN: St Augustine's Press, 2006), p. 270.

> Likewise he is the consummation of faith in two ways. In one way by confirming it with miracles. Jn 10:38. In the other way by rewarding faith. For since faith is imperfect knowledge, its reward consists in the perfection of that knowledge Jn 14:21 *I will love him, and will manifest myself to him.* This was signified in Zech 4:9, where it is said, *the hands of Zorobabel have laid the foundations of this house*, namely the church, whose foundation is faith, *and his hands shall finish it.* For the hands of Christ, Who descended from the line of Zorobabel, founded the Church in faith and consummates that faith with glory. (1 Cor 13:12). Augustine says in *On the Trinity* (I,10) 'Contemplation is the reward of faith, for which reward hearts are cleansed by faith, as it is written, *Cleansing their hearts by faith.*'

And yet theology is a science because it relates to reality as it really is.[69] Since 'although on Aquinas's view it would be a mistake to suppose that faith is *acquired* by an exercise of reason, reason may nonetheless clear away some intellectual obstacles that bar the believer's way to faith'.[70] Revelation then comes in to draw the person:

> The propositions of faith present the ultimate good under both these descriptions, namely as the happiness of eternal life in union with God; and they present it as available to the believer. For a person coming to faith, the will is drawn to the great good presented in the propositions of faith; and in consequence it influences the intellect to assent to them.[71]

Thomas (*ST* 1, Q1, a2) calls on Augustine (*De Trinitate* 14) to reinforce the idea of theology as a science, even though not founded on first principles. As in the early commentary on Boethius' *On the Trinity* or the *Commentary on the Sentences*, so also Thomas insisted in the *Summa* (*ST* 1, Q12, a32, ad1) that the Trinity cannot be known or shown from the things of creation, but there can be a fittingness of the revealed mystery of the Trinity with what can be discerned from the world about God's power, wisdom and goodness. On the grounds of fittingness and correspondence there cannot be real contradiction between the things of faith and the things of reason – there is no place for the Averroist 'double truth', as Thomas wrote in his *De unitate intellectus* of 1270. Grabmann insisted that reason did not just serve Thomas in theological preamble and in

---

69. M. Grabmann, *Die theologische Erkenntnis- und Einleitungslehre des hl. Thomas von Aquin auf Grund seiner Schrift in Boethium de Trinitate im Zusammenhang der Scholastik des 13. Und beginnenden 14. Jarhunderts dargestellt* (Freiburg, CH: Paulusverlag, 1948), p. 98.
70. Stump, *Aquinas*, p. 374.
71. Ibid., p. 364.

apologetics (although it is important that theology correspond to the world), for reason is used to deduce other doctrines from one principal doctrine.[72]

This is significant, for it does seem that scholastic theology built on the Bible so as to construct its theological systems;[73] from the letter of the text to its sense (*sensus*) on to theological judgment (*sententia*), involving philosophical means to understand the text properly so as to arrive at the divine truths. Thomas on the basis of Exodus 3:14 gives 'another kind of biblical theology' or doctrine of God – as pure existence, not just Augustine's 'unchanging one'. The question is whether Thomas finds in Scripture what his metaphysics, from as early as *On Being and Existence* (*De ente et esse*), had already asserted. Certainly what the believer is to aim for is a knowledge that does not dispense with faith but perfects it. In his *On Truth* (*De veritate* 14, 8) Scripture means for Thomas that truth is personal; but the consideration of 'God as love' in the Dionysian sense is quite different from what Pope Gregory IX complained about when he attacked Aristotelians in 1228 for an 'impersonal' view of God (in his *Letter to the Paris theologians*).[74] Scripture did not have a worked-out metaphysic and was not going to claim one, so there was room for a faithful graced philosophy to be added. Yet Scripture and its teaching could rule some metaphysical positions out; for example, some version of Averroism which taught that the agent intellect was a power of the soul seemed a safer bet than Avicenna's view of that intellect as a separate power and thus existing independently of individual human beings. Aquinas accused this position of being a betrayal of Aristotle *and* the Christian faith.[75] And Scripture could encourage certain thinking about God as pure *esse*, not least the witness of Exodus 3:14 as mulled over by some Greek traditions of interpretation of which Thomas was aware. Therefore Aquinas does test his 'speculation' by the measure of faith that is handed to him as Christian reflection on some key verses.

It seems unfair to accuse him of privileging the Oneness of God simply because he treats the One God and the Triune God in distinct questions. Both Albert and Thomas tempered their negative theology by remembering that the divine essence would be visible in the life to come. Yet it reminded Thomas of the need for care when speaking of God, to recall that there is something implicitly trinitarian about God as source, means and fulfiller of divine action in the world.

---

72. Grabmann, *Theologische Erkenntnis*, pp. 181–182.
73. M. Chenu, 'Lecture de la Bible et Philosophie', *Mélanges Gilson* (1974), pp. 161–171.
74. Heinrich Denzinger (ed.), *Enchiridion Symbolorum definitionum et declarationum* (Freiburg: Herder, [26]1998), p. 824.
75. See A. de Libera, *L'Unicite de l'intellect contre les averroistes* (Paris: Flammarion, 1994).

There is thus no dogmatic–mystical theology divide, in which Franciscans see the latter as that which persuades, and leads one into knowledge of God. Any mysticism Thomas admits to is not one that stops us from forming judgments about God (*ST* 2.2, Q45, a1, 2).[76] Yet theology is about putting one's mind in the place near enough to God where he can surprise us. Theology does not take us all the way, as for some inheritors of the Dionysian tradition. On earth there is revealed the mysteriousness of 'the name of God' and the figure of Jesus, and yet at the beginning and end of the theological task there is contemplation.[77] Theology puts the believer in a place where contemplation becomes possible.

God as pure act or agent does not have passions, though he can be said to have affections such as joy (*SCG* 1.89), analogous to ours. It is proper to say God is self-satisfied and takes pleasure in creatures approximating to him. Willing the good for another is benevolence, while love is more about spending time with, or making time for, as God does in his providence that reaches out to all individual people and causes them to be – it is not enough to say (with Maimonides) that God cares only for humanity as a species. Here again a small piece of Scripture seems to haunt him, as per Romans 13:1 (Vulgate), 'all that comes from God is ordained by him', and this happens according to the measure creatures share in (his) existence (*ST* 1, Q22, a2). The whole thrust of Thomas's argument in *SCG* 3 shows God ironing out the creases of evil in creation through his patience; he has the principle of every creature (including for rational creatures their free will to make non-necessary choices) factored into his plans, while allowing each creature still to determine to what extent it realizes its purpose (*ST* 1, Q8, a1). This is reinforced by quoting 1 Corinthians 9:9 – that God's care is much greater towards humans than towards beasts (like oxen). Then, at *ST* 1, Q22, a2, ad4: there are things foreseen by God that come about freely through us.

If God is simple, this does not mean only that he is unitary but that 'there are no sides' to God. All that he is he is fully, which includes love. God's will is necessitated by his nature as goodness as to whether to create, but he is free as to what to create.[78] Of course here Aquinas cannot escape revealed ideas of love, of a fixing in God's attitude that yet preserves God's transcendent 'otherness'. God is part of creatures' being in his sustaining them but wants them to will a completer union (*ST* 1.2, Q26, a2, ad2). This is where predestination in

76. Thierry-Dominique Humbrecht, *Théologie negative et noms divins chez saint Thomas d'Aquin* (Paris: Vrin, 2005), p. 777.
77. Ibid., p. 781.
78. Kretzmann, *Metaphysics of Theism*, p. 225 (cf. *SCG* 1.87.724).

the sense of God's 'sending' towards a *super*natural end comes in. Since God is the cause of all who will be elect, and the one who permits sinners to trap themselves in sin, Thomas has no place for the good or merits of anyone to count in their reaching this goal, but those things can be yet very much for the common good of the natural ends of human society. In both the predestined and the reprobate, God shows his goodness under the aspect of mercy and justice respectively (*ST* 1, Q23, a5, ad3).

Analogical thinking argues from what everybody already knows, and builds up from there: it is 'folksy' in the same way the Bible is, since it uses everyday language (not least the parables of Jesus). The names we use about creatures and God are used analogically *secundum proportionem* (*ST* 1, Q13) as 'healthy' can be used of 'medication' and 'body'. But as this is only about the medication because it owes its health to what it does in the body, so too is what is said about humans derived from what is said about God (cf. Eph. 3:14) as *cause* of all that is health in us. It does not suggest for a moment that we can climb up to God by this means, as perhaps Luther feared.[79]

Nature and grace

Here I attempt a quick sketch of what was fundamental to Thomas's anthropology.

God moving us in nature does not stop us being free, so, he asks, why should we lack freedom when he moves us in grace, by a special inward moving of human souls to a special end? Whether in the original pre-Fall state or in the present, humans have always needed grace. Against Lombard, Bonaventura and the majority, Thomas taught that Adam was created in grace, not later given grace to help him do acts of merit. At *ST* 1.2, Q109, a2 he speaks of the human nature in its state of integrity. The point of contention lies in the existence of a phrase attributed to Augustine (*Stare Adam poterat, pedem movere non poterat* [Adam (in paradise) was able to stand, but he was unable to progress]),[80] which Peter Lombard interpreted as meaning that pre-fallen Adam could avoid

79. This is contrary to the view of Milbank and Pickstock, *Truth in Aquinas* (London: Routledge, 2000), p. 63, for whose reading of Aquinas the hominization of the Son is 'appropriate' as restoring the deification of humanity, and this shows that what it restores is 'analogical ascent' through various degrees of *esse ipsum*.

80. Although see his *De natura et gratia* 43, 50–55, 65, in Bibliotheque Augustinienne 21 (Paris: Desclée de Brouwer, 1967), pp. 614–622.

evil but not do good, and that the latter only happened in a second moment when Adam turned to God. The pre-fallen man could however at least have kept all the content of natural law, since moved to do so by the causative *esse* of God; but in neither state could man have truly loved God without grace and thus have eternal life with him: in order not to sin, that grace was required. Thomas insists that even in paradise Adam needed operative grace from the very beginning, to achieve anything.[81] And in that sense Adam was able to sin because his will was not yet confirmed in the good. The Fall was less a flaw of nature (created good after all) than humans choosing to dispense with grace. Grace in paradise was the relationship to God, a connection to him, and after the Fall it includes healing. In their fallen state humans can do some good but not the original whole good. However, in that fallen state one needs grace not just to be elevated but to be healed in the first place, for there is a need for grace to redirect the will. *ST* A6 of Q109 asks, can we prepare for grace? Yes, but only if we have habitual grace in us; but to get that in the first place we need God's grace as particular help, for we cannot resist sin otherwise. That grace needs to find us. Now grace given freely, which transforms, makes us people who, with 1 Corinthians 12:7 in mind, can pass on grace to others. Grace is as a direct, initiating help from God to us 'operative', and when our will responds it becomes cooperative. One speaks of God's grace as 'operative' in as much as God justifies or heals, but also as 'cooperative' as far as it is the principle of a meritorious action coming also from our free will. God must be regarded as the external principle of human action, who instructs us by law and helps us by grace (Q90); for if we are to see God we need elevating. 'Grace does not remove nature but perfects it' (*ST* 1, Q8, a1, ad 2):

> There is a huge gap between the human being and the God who is the human's end, the gap that separates what is not God from God. Through grace and the theological virtues, God has bridged the gap by raising the person to God's own level. Acting out of this grace and these virtues will bring the person to the end promised by God, namely God.[82]

Wawrykow seems to overinterpret when he comments on this famous saying. Perhaps it would be more precise to say that the promised end is 'the vision of

---

81. *Commentary on the Sentences* 2, 29, 1, 2; see discussion by J.-P. Torrell, *Nouvelles recherches Thomasiennes* (Paris: Vrin, 2008), pp. 100–103.

82. Joseph P. Wawrykow, *The Westminster Handbook to Thomas Aquinas*, Westminster Handbooks to Christian Theology (Louisville: Westminster John Knox, 2005), p. 98.

God' rather than 'God himself', if by that we mean some sense of 'possessing God'.

We find in the DeLubacian reading of Thomas, according to which Thomas's view was that in original nature there was already the grace of a relationship with God, the capacity for beatific vision slides into some natural right to beatific vision. As Milbank paraphrases this unfortunate overemphasis of De Lubac: nature longs to see a cause and such an urge must be fulfilled.[83] However, Aquinas is quite clear (*Commentary on the Sentences* 2, 29, 1) that grace was there from the beginning, but that does mean it is there in postlapsarian nature. (And in prelapsarian nature this gift was hardly so much part of nature that it became something close to an enforceable right.) The story of Adam however shows that humans do not in fact find this impulse overwhelming, such that any grace comes to them after a hiatus (however short) of disconnection with that source and goal, and it comes as some sort of new law (*nova lex*), instituted by and with reference to Christ the Redeemer, and not as such given in nature. What is there in nature is indeed a capacity for grace.

The general contrast of the old law that restrains or patches up sin, and the new seems in this regard, helpful (*ST* 1.2, Q 107, a1):

> We must therefore say that, according to the first way, the New Law is not distinct from the Old Law: because they both have the same end, namely, man's subjection to God; and there is but one God of the New and of the Old Testament, according to Romans 3:30: 'It is one God that justifies circumcision by faith, and uncircumcision through faith.' According to the second way, the New Law is distinct from the Old Law: because the Old Law is like a pedagogue of children, as the Apostle says (Galatians 3:24), whereas the New Law is the law of perfection, since it is the law of charity, of which the Apostle says (Colossians 3:14) that it is 'the bond of perfection.'

Thomas then adds that while the Old Law was to be obeyed out of fear, the New is couched in terms of love. Yet he admits that the inwardness of the

83. 'Today, catholic conservatives like J.-H. Nicolas (*Revue Thomiste* [1995], pp. 399–418), who wish to back away from de Lubac's revolution, try to claim that only the fulfilment is granted by grace, while the impulse to the beatific vision is purely natural. Yet this cannot be the case, because a nature is fulfilable as a nature; it demands as of right fulfilment and hence if we are naturally orientated to the supernatural this can only be because our original and "most proper" nature is a paradoxically superadded nature (a supreme instance of "second act"), giving us more than our due as our due and pulling us naturally beyond our nature in an *ecstasies* at the outset' (Milbank and Pickstock, *Truth In Aquinas*, p. 38).

'New Law' was present among believers before Christ (*ST* 1.2, Q107, a1, ad 2):

> Nevertheless there were some in the state of the Old Testament who, having charity and the grace of the Holy Ghost, looked chiefly to spiritual and eternal promises: and in this respect they belonged to the New Law. In like manner in the New Testament there are some carnal men who have not yet attained to the perfection of the New Law; and these it was necessary, even under the New Testament, to lead to virtuous action by the fear of punishment and by temporal promises. But although the Old Law contained precepts of charity, nevertheless it did not confer the Holy Ghost by Whom 'charity . . . is spread abroad in our hearts' (Romans 5:5).

There is also parity in his account of the New's being contained in the Old (ST 1.2, Q107, a3, ad1, ad2):

> Whatsoever is set down in the New Testament explicitly and openly as a point of faith, is contained in the Old Testament as a matter of belief, but implicitly, under a figure. And accordingly, even as to those things which we are bound to believe, the New Law is contained in the Old.
>
> The precepts of the New Law are said to be greater than those of the Old Law, in the point of their being set forth explicitly. But as to the substance itself of the precepts of the New Testament, they are all contained in the Old.

Then in article 4, after admitting that the Old Testament law was more burdensome for having such a great number of commands, whereas the New Testament added only a few to the Natural Law, he balances this by adding that in another respect the New Testament is more burdensome since it requires inner virtue, which will be the whole theme of the II-II section, which is just about to follow (ST 1.2, Q107, a 4):

> The other difficulty attaches to works of virtue as to interior acts: for instance, that a virtuous deed be done with promptitude and pleasure. It is this difficulty that virtue solves: because to act thus is difficult for a man without virtue: but through virtue it becomes easy for him. In this respect the precepts of the New Law are more burdensome than those of the Old; because the New Law prohibits certain interior movements of the soul, which were not expressly forbidden in the Old Law in all cases, although they were forbidden in some, without, however, any punishment being attached to the prohibition. Now this is very difficult to a man without virtue: thus even the Philosopher states (Ethic. v, 9) that it is easy to do what a righteous

> man does; but that to do it in the same way, viz. with pleasure and promptitude, is difficult to a man who is not righteous. Accordingly we read also (1 John 5:3) that 'His commandments are not heavy': which words Augustine expounds by saying that 'they are not heavy to the man that loves; whereas they are a burden to him that loves not.'

Overall then it seems that the Old Testament had a primary earthly goal with a secondary heavenly goal, yet the New Testament reverses that. Nevertheless that earthly goal, even in the Old Testament context, required a consideration of 'the good' as including heavenly beatitude as a goal to which it points: it is like the railway line from Edinburgh to St Andrews, Scotland: it is the line for *St Andrews*, even though it stops four miles short of that goal, such that a new form of grace is needed to get there. The II-II section of the Summa records that, while at the same time realizing that the letter of the Old Testament law has fallen away, to be replaced by the internalized spiritual law that provides grace and infused virtues for any virtuous life on its way freely and lovingly to meet Christ, who is 'met' in the final, third part.[84]

Christology

To begin with trinitarian theology, there is a temptation to argue that Thomas was more properly trinitarian; that is, that he believed in the priority of God as three rather than as one, by arguing that he followed less Augustine and more a personalism informed by the Greeks.[85] The Son is an intellectual procession, and the Spirit not so much the act as the fruit of love.[86] It is also worth remembering that the *Sentences* commentary shows how Scripture informs trinitarian theology, which in turn informs the reading of Scripture. The Trinity is not a necessity arising from first principles. 'For Thomas, it is only in the basis of revelation in salvation history that we can recognize a Trinity in oneness.'[87] A divine person is a subsisting relation; 'relation here has an ecstatic character', which is proven by the procession and also return of creatures.

Yet Thomas is *not less* than Augustinian. Following Augustine's analogy

84. I have found the study by Ulrich Kühn, *Via caritatis: Theologie des Gesetzes bei Thomas von Aquin* (Berlin: Evangeliese Verlaganstalt, 1964), to be illuminating.
85. Emery, *Trinity in Aquinas*, p. 177.
86. J.-P. Torrell, 'Preface', in ibid., p. xvi.
87. Ibid., p. 24.

from *De Trinitate*, in the same manner as knowledge engenders love in the human soul, which enables better knowing, so in the Trinity's action the sending of the Son accompanies the gift of the Spirit, which allows humans to know God's mystery. This accords with the Spirit's coming through the Son, who in turn is received by Christ and led back to the Father. The idea of the Son and the Spirit in parallel originations from the Father seems deficient, and the Spirit is not the cause of the Father–Son love, but its fruit (*ST* 1, Q37, a2, ad3). It might seem a little hard to think of a person as the fruit of love (*ST* 1, Q27, a4); the expression of the Father–Son nature is expressed in a link found to be the Holy Spirit, which moves beyond likeness towards otherness. *ST* 1, Q37, a1, ad3 contains something of the thought of Richard of St Victor, for whom love had to be threefold if it were not be mere 'mutual admiration'. If Chrysostom (*Tractate on John* 75,1; *Patrologiae cursus completus: Series graeca* 59, 403) is the one who reminded Thomas (*Commentary on John 14:16*, lect. 4) to think of the Holy Spirit not just as paraclete-advocate but as 'another comforter', then that Greek father's view of the glorification on the cross was all-important for Thomas (*Commentary on John 7:39*, lect. 5), as distinct from Augustine for whom the cross was only the prelude to glorification (*Tractate on John* 63, 3).[88] In other words one can see the fullness of glorious trinitarian love towards the other in the 'oddest' of places – the dereliction of humanity on the cross.

The incarnation was contingent in that there was no antecedent necessity of events, not even Christ's death, not least because this was an event within the free life of the Trinity. For when Thomas asks (*ST* 3, Q46, a1), 'In what sense was Christ's suffering "necessary"?' the answer is that, since he willed it, it was not a necessity of a force from God, but a necessity that arrives from the end: to deliver others, in order to be exalted and for God's sake (thus fulfilling Scripture: e.g. Luke 24:46).

Thomas's Christology pays a large amount of attention to the *life* of Christ, as well as to the metaphysics of his incarnation and death. As he moves to interpret Hebrews 8 Aquinas makes it clear that this theology concerns Christ as perfect priest. If 'throne of greatness' means the Father, then 'he sits' means the Son sits at the same level as God the Father. Yet this is not as likely as the following interpretation:

> Or it can be taken as He is a man, and this is more properly the intention of the Apostle, because he speaks of the priesthood of Christ, Who is a priest inasmuch

88. D.-D. Le Pivain, *L'Action du Saint-Esprit* (Paris: Croire et Savoir, 2006), pp. 88, 138.

> as He is a man. And thus he sits, because His assumed humanity has a certain association with the deity and sits to judge.

For Aquinas, Christ ministers grace now and glory in the future. Where the text then has 'If then [that being offered/He] were on earth, He would not be a priest,' Aquinas needs to meet the objection: 'But was not the flesh of Christ earthly?' This gives Aquinas some trouble, yet the point is that Christ as priest is not still on earth.[89]

Dealing with the phrase 'unto the example' (Heb. 8:5), Aquinas asserts that this does not mean the Old was prior, but that on earth it served as a demonstration model of the invisible. The law indeed had fault in that it did not have power to purge those things which had been committed, and second, because it does not give the helping grace to avoid sin, but only to know it, and thus it was an occasion of sin.[90] Yet Thomas sees the motion set by the Old Testament as a forward and thus positive one, creating desire for the perfect: *a place should not indeed have been sought.*

> For just as a body never perfectly rests, but is always moved, until it attains to its place, so it is that while something is had imperfectly, desire does not rest, but always tends further, until it will come to the perfect. Therefore a place for this was sought by the man who desired: but more by God, Who is said to seek on account of the desire for our salvation.[91]

The perfection of the New consists, as the quotation from Jeremiah 31 suggests, in its internal power: 'And in this way the NT was given because it consists in the infusion of the Holy Spirit Who instructs interiorly.' So it does not just guide the intellect with precepts, even new ones, but also inclines the heart to act well.[92] There are still teachers in New Testament, Aquinas is pleased to note. Of course in heaven no one will need to be taught knowledge of the divinity. 'And perhaps there will be teaching even to the end of the world while the execution of the effects of God perdures.'[93]

In a strong sense the life of Christ is what links the faith or religion of the Old Testament with that of the New and through into the church. Ecclesiology

---

89. Aquinas, *Hebrews*, p. 165.
90. Ibid., p. 168.
91. Ibid., p. 170.
92. Ibid., p. 172.
93. Ibid.

means what the sacraments do: it is an ecclesiology in act with sacraments as instruments of God's causal power, whose 'character' allows this to happen in a certain way. The character received in baptism (which is the *habitus* or ongoing disposition of the Son's serving and receptive attitude towards the Father[94]) enables reception of all other sacraments; it requires some intrinsic natural causal power for God to work with, and this quality and power happen through participating in the priesthood of Christ (*ST* 3, Q36, a3).

Thomas's Christology leads just as seamlessly into his teaching on salvation (soteriology) as it does into his ecclesiology. The *Summa* presents Christ as 'the whole Christ' (employing a phrase of Augustine), who is to be the vehicle to the goal of blessedness. Predestination begins with that of Christ, for it is he who is the head of the Book of Life (and this can be seen in his commentary on Heb. 1:7). It is about exemplarity rather than causality such that there remains room for human free choice to accept or reject. Christology therefore is hardly detached from eucharistic theology, when the latter follows from the former in Thomas's account. Thus indeed it was fitting that Christ was the humble penitent who ended on a cross, because Adam's sin was essentially to do with pride. Yet to argue that for Thomas, God 'seeks also positively to *forgive* us, by tracing as only an innocent man can, the perfect ways of penitence which we are to imitate' and he comes like prelapsarian Adam who was predestined to deification,[95] this goes much further than Thomas would, for Christ's work as a human being does not have that individual agency distinct from that of the divine person in Christ. Christ as a (hu)man did not win by merit grace or knowledge or beatific vision or divinity – all those things were with him from the beginning of his earthly life, but he did win immortality of the body, without which we could not experience personal immortality (*ST* 3, Q19, a4). What he merits is its effect for the church, which is of course his body. The assumption seems to be that the soul of humans as such does not need to be made immortal, and any saving of it is done by Christ's divinity working on Christ's human soul.

Thomas continued with a Chalcedonian Christology based on Cyril of Alexandria, while recasting it. It is less about deification of humanity so as to become our instructor. If anything the one *esse* in Christ guarantees his

---

94. See J.-M. Garrigues, 'La doctrine de la grace habituelle dans ses sources', *Revue Thomiste* 103 (2003), pp. 179–202, 202: it is the Greek fathers from whom Aquinas draws his teaching on the habitual, constant side of grace, to complement the insistence of Augustine on 'actual grace' from God's immediate activity.

95. Milbank and Pickstock, *Truth in Aquinas*, p. 62.

humanity as a concrete man, like a Peter or a James (*ST* 3, Q17 a2). Nothing can be added to the divine *esse*, and it is this existence that is shared in, not the divine essence. The one hypostasis or *esse* is not a way of being; rather it is simply an existence that both natures share. It is not that there is a touching of natures or even a one-way seeing.[96]

What is acquired by God in the incarnation is not a new person or existence but a new *habitudo* or accustoming of that pre-existent personal being to the human nature. Imperfections can be predicated of God but only through his human nature, and when 'God' is used, it is shorthand for 'Son of God'. There is a nice use of 'revelation' and 'reason' together when John 1:14 ('The Word was made flesh') is understood as not meaning that God changed, but that he changed position in relation to something else as that something else changed position with regard to him. Likewise the psalmist (89:1 Vulgate) sings, 'O Lord you have become a refuge for us' (*ST* 3, Q16, a6). One could say 'it was brought about that man is God' but not that 'man became God'. (*ST* 3, Q16, a7). Christ as this man is God, but not 'Christ as man is God' (*ST* 3, Q16, a11, ad3).

While Ambrose (*Super Lucam* 10: *Patrologiae cursus completus: Series latina* 15, 1819) taught that in Gethsemane 'my will' was that of the human nature and 'your will' was that of the divine nature, Aquinas (*ST* 3, Q18, a1) prefers to see Christ's human will as integrated. His human will could choose yet not deliberate to the point of doubting or hesitating.

Thomas is happy to speak of a predestination of the union of natures from eternity, not some plan that God came to devise. It is the person of Jesus Christ who was predestined and we should not force the plain sense of Paul's words 'predestined to be the Son of God' to mean anything other than 'predestined to be revealed [in man] as the Son of God'. The humanity of Christ can appropriately be reverenced (with *hyperdoulia*) whenever taken together with worship of the Lord's/Christ's divinity (*ST* 3, Q25, a2). Hence, following John of Damascus, an image of Christ can also be reverenced, for since the incarnation it is fitting to show God in an image. For a Western theologian, in the tradition of Cyril of Alexandria, Thomas grasps the point of the fullness of God's self-revelation in Jesus, even while preserving a strong sense of mystery.

---

96. Richard Cross, *The Metaphysics of the Incarnation* (Oxford: Oxford University Press, 2002), touches the nerve that Thomist Christology allows humanity no existence, since it is only a part or property of the Word, but whatever the advantages of the rival Scotist account, this does not seem like a fair criticism of Thomas.

According to *ST* 3, Q49, a2, Christ offered more to God than the offence; not only sufficient but a superabundant *satisfaction* (not as in the Blackfriars translation, 'atonement'; see bibliography below), though our own confession and contrition need to be added. For the love of the suffering Christ outweighed the wickedness of his killers; indeed 'it was in fact the flesh of God and on this account of infinite value' (*ST* 3, Q49, a2). The following article (3) raises the question: Was Christ's death actually a sacrifice? In this article the clinching authority that overrules the arguments against answering this in the negative is Ephesians 5:2 ('Christ . . . a fragrant offering and sacrifice to God' Vulgate). For, Thomas adds, sacrifice is that which humans offer to God in token of the special honour due to him and to please him. The sacrifice of the man Jesus Christ is like that which prefigured it in the Israelite cult, yet it was much higher in kind. As Augustine has it, 'what could be so fitly chosen by men to be offered for them as human flesh, and that so pure?' (*De Trinitate* 4.14; as cited by Thomas). Yet in the final analysis what that reality did was to symbolize a moral reality of obedience that we as humans owed, even while the image of God remained in us. The bond of love was broken and in article 4 Thomas concludes we are indebted to God as judge, for even if the devil was executioner, the price of our life was to be paid to God alone. Thus 'it was more fitting (*conveniens*) that we be liberated by Christ's passion rather than by God's will alone' (*ST* 3, Q46, a3).

So it makes sense to accentuate Christ's life of obedience as that which redeems. His penance is the foundation of ours, his baptism, the ground, form and content of ours. Grace is twofold: as trinitarian, it is personal, not material assistance; secondly, Christ as a man is an exemplary cause of our salvation,[97] providing all except for our own response for faith, since Jesus who had a christic-prophetic knowledge and not just faith was in that way different from believers (*ST* 3, Q11, a5). His life is a mystery not in the sense of our not getting it, for his mystery is now open and is only hidden *in us* as something to be lived out; that is, the life of Trinity, as Jesus had within him.[98]

Now the topic of the mediation of Christ is discussed, and yet article 3, Q26 is the shortest in the third part of the *Summa*, and seems to have one eye on Christian priesthood. Thus other men can be mediators as they minister in a co-working way, even though 1 Timothy 2:5 teaches Jesus is the sole mediator.

---

97. Gerd Lohaus, *Die Geheimnisse des Lebens Jesu in der Summa theologiae des heiligen Thomas von Aquin* (Freiburg: Herder, 1985), pp. 255–256.

98. Torrell, 'Saint Thomas d'Aquin et la science du Christ', in *Recherches Thomasiennes*, pp. 198–213.

Christ indeed was mediator as (hu)man, being set apart from God in as much as he was a creature, and set apart from human beings due to his amount of grace, and thus poised equidistant between the two (*ST* 3, Q26, a2). Perhaps it seems disproportionate that 'the death of Christ' is just one small question (Q50), surrounded by a number of other questions concerned with Christ's *passion*; only the last article, 6, asks whether it had anything to do with our salvation. To this the answer comes that the death is to be considered (1) 'as it was taking place' in which case it is part of his passion and so makes a contribution, and (2) 'as an accomplished fact', which as instrument of the death of death contributed 'negatively' by taking those two hindrances away, though not contributing anything positively. Likewise the abandonment of Christ: 'He [God] withdrew his protection, but maintained the union' (*ST* 3, Q50, a2, ad1).

The emphasis on the sacraments can be seen as the reason why the cross is less in view: they rather than the holding up of the cross are what in fact communicate the benefits of Christ's death. Thomas gives his reason, that actions speak louder than words, yet what they have to say is checked by right doctrine or understanding of such signification (*ST* 3, Q60, a6):

> Thirdly, a sacrament may be considered on the part of the sacramental signification. Now Augustine says (*De Doctr. Christ.* ii) that 'words are the principal signs used by men'; because words can be formed in various ways for the purpose of signifying various mental concepts, so that we are able to express our thoughts with greater distinctness by means of words. And therefore in order to insure the perfection of sacramental signification it was necessary to determine the signification of the sensible things by means of certain words. For water may signify both a cleansing by reason of its humidity, and refreshment by reason of its being cool: but when we say, 'I baptize thee,' it is clear that we use water in baptism in order to signify a spiritual cleansing.

Here we see how Thomas anticipates the question that the liturgy of the ritual can become 'mindless'. Ritual actions need to be 'perfected' by words. How much words matter to the point of being indispensable is seen in article 8:

> The other point to be considered is the meaning of the words. For since in the sacraments, the words produce an effect according to the sense which they convey, as stated above [*ST* 3, Q7, ad 1], we must see whether the change of words destroys the essential sense of the words: because then the sacrament is clearly rendered invalid. Now it is clear, if any substantial part of the sacramental form be suppressed, that the essential sense of the words is destroyed; and consequently the sacrament is invalid.

> Wherefore Didymus says (*De Spir. Sanct.* ii): 'If anyone attempt to baptize in such a way as to omit one of the aforesaid names,' i.e. of the Father, Son, and Holy Ghost, 'his baptism will be invalid.' But if that which is omitted be not a substantial part of the form, such an omission does not destroy the essential sense of the words, nor consequently the validity of the sacrament. Thus in the form of the Eucharist – 'For this is My Body,' the omission of the word 'for' does not destroy the essential sense of the words, nor consequently cause the sacrament to be invalid; although perhaps he who makes the omission may sin from negligence or contempt.

Yet there can be no doubt that without the sacraments our faith is, in Thomas's view, empty (*ST* 3, Q61, a1):

> I answer that, Sacraments are necessary unto man's salvation for three reasons. The first is taken from the condition of human nature which is such that it has to be led by things corporeal and sensible to things spiritual and intelligible. Now it belongs to Divine providence to provide for each one according as its condition requires. Divine wisdom, therefore, fittingly provides man with means of salvation, in the shape of corporeal and sensible signs that are called sacraments.
>
> The second reason is taken from the state of man who in sinning subjected himself by his affections to corporeal things. Now the healing remedy should be given to a man so as to reach the part affected by disease. Consequently it was fitting that God should provide man with a spiritual medicine by means of certain corporeal signs; for if man were offered spiritual things without a veil, his mind being taken up with the material world would be unable to apply itself to them.

The third reason is taken from the fact that man is prone to direct his activity chiefly towards material things. Lest, therefore, it should be too hard for man to be drawn away entirely from bodily actions, bodily exercise was offered to him in the sacraments, by which he might be trained to avoid superstitious practices, consisting in the worship of demons, and all manner of harmful actions, consisting in sinful deeds.

> It follows, therefore, that through the institution of the sacraments man, consistently with his nature, is instructed through sensible things; he is humbled, through confessing that he is subject to corporeal things, seeing that he receives assistance through them: and he is even preserved from bodily hurt, by the healthy exercise of the sacraments.

Article 2 makes it clear that the Old Testament saints were in a sense saved through visible signs. For in his Reply to Objection 3 he says:

> The sacrament of Melchisedech which preceded the Law is more like the Sacrament of the New Law in its matter: in so far as 'he offered bread and wine' (Genesis 14:18), just as bread and wine are offered in the sacrifice of the New Testament. Nevertheless the sacraments of the Mosaic Law are more like the thing signified by the sacrament, i.e. the Passion of Christ: as clearly appears in the Paschal Lamb and such like. The reason of this was lest, if the sacraments retained the same appearance, it might seem to be the continuation of one and the same sacrament, where there was no interruption of time.

Thomas's teaching here is quite revolutionary when at *ST* 3, Q62, a1 he writes:

> Some, however, say that they are the cause of grace not by their own operation, but in so far as God causes grace in the soul when the sacraments are employed. And they give as an example a man who on presenting a leaden coin, receives, by the king's command, a hundred pounds: not as though the leaden coin, by any operation of its own, caused him to be given that sum of money; this being the effect of the mere will of the king. Hence Bernard says in a sermon on the Lord's Supper: 'Just as a canon is invested by means of a book, an abbot by means of a crozier, a bishop by means of a ring, so by the various sacraments various kinds of grace are conferred.' But if we examine the question properly, we shall see that according to the above mode the sacraments are mere signs. For the leaden coin is nothing but a sign of the king's command that this man should receive money. In like manner the book is a sign of the conferring of a canonry. Hence, according to this opinion the sacraments of the New Law would be mere signs of grace; whereas we have it on the authority of many saints that the sacraments of the New Law not only signify, but also cause grace.
>
> We must therefore say otherwise, that an efficient cause is twofold, principal and instrumental. The principal cause works by the power of its form, to which form the effect is likened; just as fire by its own heat makes something hot. In this way none but God can cause grace: since grace is nothing else than a participated likeness of the Divine Nature, according to 2 Pet 1:4: 'He hath given us most great and precious promises; that we may be [Vulgate: 'you may be made'] partakers of the Divine Nature.' But the instrumental cause works not by the power of its form, but only by the motion whereby it is moved by the principal agent: so that the effect is not likened to the instrument but to the principal agent: for instance, the couch [piece of furniture] is not like the axe, but like the art which is in the craftsman's mind. And it is thus that the sacraments of the New Law cause grace: for they are instituted by God to be employed for the purpose of conferring grace. Hence Augustine says (*Contra Faust.* xix): 'All these things,' viz. pertaining to the sacraments, 'are done and pass away, but the power,' viz. of God, 'which works by them, remains ever.' Now

> that is, properly speaking, an instrument by which someone works: wherefore it is written (Titus 3:5): 'He saved us by the laver of regeneration.'

A sacrament then is more like a channel than a reservoir, an instrument that can do nothing without its operator, but the Operator has seen it convenient not to do without this instrument to achieve the imparting of grace, just as no less than Christ's humanity was indispensable in the redemption. The concreteness of Christ means he is available for 'touching' in some sense through the sacrament, although as universal he is not just one other thing in the universe but is that which binds and holds it together.[99] There was no real imparting of grace in and through the Old ceremonies, circumcision included: the best these could do was to point to Christ as signs and thus encourage forward-looking faith in him, despite it saying (*ST* 3, Q 62, a6, obj 2):

> Objection 2. Further, there is no sanctification save by grace. But men were sanctified by the sacraments of the Old Law: for it is written (Leviticus 8:31): 'And when he,' i.e. Moses, 'had sanctified them,' i.e. Aaron and his sons, 'in their vestments,' etc. Therefore it seems that the sacraments of the Old Law conferred grace.

Sacraments then give more than can be received by faith (i.e. justifying grace). This sanctification operates in a dual way, defensive against sin, and advancing (*ST* 3, Q63, a1):

> I answer that, As is clear from what has been already stated [*ST* 3, Q62, a5] the sacraments of the New Law are ordained for a twofold purpose; namely, for a remedy against sins; and for the perfecting of the soul in things pertaining to the Divine worship according to the rite of the Christian life. Now whenever anyone is deputed to some definite purpose he is wont to receive some outward sign thereof; thus in olden times soldiers who enlisted in the ranks used to be marked with certain characters on the body, through being deputed to a bodily service. Since, therefore, by the sacraments men are deputed to a spiritual service pertaining to the worship of God, it follows that by their means the faithful receive a certain spiritual character.

In ad 2 to the second objection he explains just what he means by 'character'. 'Nevertheless from a kind of likeness, anything that assimilates one thing to another, or discriminates one thing from another, even though it be not sensible, can be called a character or a seal.' They are all remedies against sin, but

---

99. To affirm the insight of Milbank and Pickstock, *Truth in Aquinas*, p. 82.

not all (e.g. penance) are positive in the sense of moving forward in the divine worship. However, one could argue, although Thomas does not, that being 'restored to a former state' is nevertheless some sort of improvement in the penitent's condition, and hence an advance.

The priest's role according to Q64 is not central to the efficacy of the sacraments that work by the power within them (*ex opere operato*), yet 'nor is there any reason why the devotion of a just man should not contribute to this effect'. There is no extra power that can be given to the sacrament by priest or praying people, since Christ's passion is the all-sufficient driving force (*ST* 3, Q62, a5). However, a praying minister can be used by God to change the *receiver* of the sacrament.

The main answer (*ST* 3, Q75) on the Eucharist is moving and worth quoting at length:

> I answer that, The presence of Christ's true body and blood in this sacrament cannot be detected by sense, nor understanding, but by faith alone, which rests upon Divine authority. Hence, on Luke 22:19: 'This is My body which shall be delivered up for you,' Cyril says: 'Doubt not whether this be true; but take rather the Saviour's words with faith; for since He is the Truth, He lieth not.'
>
> Now this is suitable, first for the perfection of the New Law. For, the sacrifices of the Old Law contained only in figure that true sacrifice of Christ's Passion, according to Hebrews 10:1: 'For the law having a shadow of the good things to come, not the very image of the things.' And therefore it was necessary that the sacrifice of the New Law instituted by Christ should have something more, namely, that it should contain Christ Himself crucified, not merely in signification or figure, but also in very truth. And therefore this sacrament which contains Christ Himself, as Dionysius says (Eccl. Hier. iii), is perfective of all the other sacraments, in which Christ's virtue is participated.
>
> Secondly, this belongs to Christ's love, out of which for our salvation He assumed a true body of our nature. And because it is the special feature of friendship to live together with friends, as the Philosopher says (Ethic. ix), He promises us His bodily presence as a reward, saying (Matthew 24:28): 'Where the body is, there shall the eagles be gathered together.' Yet meanwhile in our pilgrimage He does not deprive us of His bodily presence; but unites us with Himself in this sacrament through the truth of His body and blood. Hence (John 6:57) he says: 'He that eateth My flesh, and drinketh My blood, abideth in Me, and I in him.' Hence this sacrament is the sign of supreme charity, and the uplifter of our hope, from such familiar union of Christ with us.
>
> Thirdly, it belongs to the perfection of faith, which concerns His humanity just as it does His Godhead, according to John 14:1: 'You believe in God, believe also in

> Me.' And since faith is of things unseen, as Christ shows us His Godhead invisibly, so also in this sacrament He shows us His flesh in an invisible manner.
>
> Some men accordingly, not paying heed to these things, have contended that Christ's body and blood are not in this sacrament except as in a sign, a thing to be rejected as heretical, since it is contrary to Christ's words. Hence Berengarius, who had been the first deviser of this heresy, was afterwards forced to withdraw his error, and to acknowledge the truth of the faith.

The Eucharist does not convey Christ by means of his transformed body, but through divine causal power in that sacramental body as a channel or instrument.

Evaluation

Peter Candler has recently lamented the impoverishment of Reformation theology with its hard *sola scriptura* principle. He claims:

> The attempted abstraction of this language in the sixteenth century implies a radical shift in the direction of the divorce of a certain 'text', the Scriptures, from the way in which it is *used* in the community of people whose story it is supposed to tell – indeed, not only from the manner of its presentation, but from the voice of its oration or incantation.[100]

The 'book culture' of the Reformation meant a shift from a 'grammar of participation' to be found in Aquinas, he thinks, to a 'grammar of representation', as well as a loss of corporate reading. Actually, whether the medieval church believed in and practised 'participation' seems questionable, and Thomas was as bookish as the best of them. Commentaries, whether medieval or modern, were things that were written and not readily available, the *Glossa ordinaria* included. A chain of being with hierarchies obtruding between God and humans was something the Reformers had to battle, not least in the recasting of Thomism by Cardinal Cajetan. The Dominicans are blamed by Candler for

---

100. P. Candler, *Theology, Rhetoric, Manduction* (London: SCM, 2006), pp. 9–10. He continues, 'Already with Calvin, the tendency towards a grammar of representation is discernible in the fact that his Eucharistic theology is everywhere composed in terms of a Word to which we must respond, thereby pushing the participation of the body of believers in the triune life of God himself to the margins' (p. 16).

not getting the point that Thomas's work was that of moral theology,[101] but this only reminds one how revered the text was for that very purpose, both in his own order and further afield, especially in the Thomist renaissances of the 1520s and 1880s. To claim that Thomas was not a systematic theologian because he was a moral one is to miss the point: what we have in Thomas is a rich synthesis that overcomes the bifurcation of 'dry doctrine' and 'how-to' manuals. This indeed was the whole thrust of the Dominican 'method' of which Thomas was the outstanding theorist, that Christ as the end of the theological task is both doctrine and practice, for he is Word of God while perfect man, sharing one *esse*.[102]

Protestants might have suspicions that the church was too much of an authority for Thomas as Catholic theologian par excellence. First we should be clear that Thomas spoke of a church that could not err, not of a pope. Councils with the pope decide on new doctrine in the light of arising heresies.[103] Secondly, church tradition was indeed a source for Thomas, as the example of worship of Christ's image at *ST* 3, Q25, a4, ad 4 shows, but it was not a hermeneutic that meant one must try to find in Scripture that which was hardly there and expand it through some 'magnifying-glass' of tradition. Thomas's argument for paying reverence to a picture or icon of Christ on the grounds of the incarnation follows a theological logic suggested to him by John of Damascus, and does not pretend to be scriptural: however, the tradition is a practical one, with some theological justification, but without perhaps serious theological *consequences*.[104] One could say similar things about his rather guarded devotion to Mary. It might be perfectly correct to call Aquinas an 'Augustinian' reader of Scripture, whereby there is a shift of focus in exegesis towards Christ as God the teacher: 'The words of

101. 'Thus the very goal of the Summa – to resituate moral thought within a theology of exit and return – was quickly and perhaps irrevocably subverted by Thomas' own religious Order' (ibid., p. 91).

102. See Kent Emery, Jr, and Joseph Wawrykow (eds.), *Christ among the Medieval Dominicans: Representations of Christ in the Texts and Images of the Order of Preachers* (Notre Dame: University of Notre Dame Press, 1998), particularly the essays by Wawrykow, Horst and Torrell.

103. See Ulrich Horst, *The Dominincans and the Pope* (Notre Dame; University of Notre Dame Press, 2006.)

104. *Contra* the claims of Candler: 'The principle [*sic*] intent of Sacred Doctrine is to "hand over" the knowledge of God . . . as performance, craft, motion – movement of the reader towards God is analogous to the movements of the continual handing on of the *doctrina* of the Church' (*Theology, Rhetoric, Manduction*, p. 124).

Scripture continually point beyond themselves toward the encounter with their divine source; the transformative power of the words is known in their ability to direct the reader or hearer to the divine teacher.'[105] Yet it is also clear that for Thomas, revelation shines through the Scriptures like a light through stained glass, and that he uses church fathers and other authorities as a means of 'cleaning' that glass where it has become 'dirty'.

Two other matters that might seem missing to the eyes of evangelical readers are the cross and the Holy Spirit. First, cultic metaphors, which would be useful for an interpretation of Christ's death as expiatory or propitiatory, are indeed missing, but for one standing in the medieval Anselmian tradition (employing a 'satisfaction of a debt according to civil law' metaphor rather than 'vicarious punishment according to a criminal law' one) this is expected. It is not that he did not understand the seriousness of sin. That is a recurring phrase in Anselm's *Cur Deus homo*, and Aquinas in turn thinks the incarnation would not have occurred but for human sin (*ST* 3, Q1 a2). In *SCG* 3.158 he is clear that Christ leads the Christian will through participation in penance back on the road of virtue to God.[106] It is not the case that his anthropology is 'optimistic' – for every mention of virtue and habits there is as much of vice and passions. Secondly, the Spirit is experienced in the form of love (cf. Rom. 5:5) just as God the Son was experienced in the form of the man Jesus. The Spirit is clearly for Thomas the Spirit of the Son, of obedience and fellowship with God, yet also as one who gives gifts of grace for works of love.

Lastly, as *the* catholic theologian, it is often remarked that Thomas had no article on 'The church'. It goes against the spirit of what Yves Congar claimed but needs to be said that a church which *is* the living of the New Law in the context of the sacramental life is not *both* institutional and mystical in Thomas's account, but *neither* institutional nor mystical.[107] The church lives out

---

105. M. Levering, *Participatory Biblical Exegesis: A Theology of Biblical Interpretation* (South Bend, IN: University of Notre Dame Press, 2008), p. 75. This is a point of L. Elders, 'Aquinas on Holy Scripture as the Medium of Divine Revelation', in *La doctrine de la revelation divine de saint Thomas d'Aquin* (Vatican City: Libreria Editrice Vaticana, 1990), pp. 104–131.

106. I have found R. van Nieuwenhove ('Bearing the Marks of Christ's Passion', in R. van Nieuwenhove and J. Wawrykow [eds.], *The Theology of Thomas Aquinas* [Notre Dame: University of Notre Dame Press, 2005], pp. 277–302, esp. 287–290) to be helpful here.

107. Y. Congar, 'The Idea of the Church in St Thomas Aquinas', in *The Mystery of The Church* (Baltimore: Helicon, 1965), pp. 97–117.

of the present actualizing of the life of her Lord in her. One can truly speak of Thomas's doctrine of the church as both Christological and eschatological, and hence 'provisional' and not triumphalist. The sacraments have causal power in believers, and the Holy Spirit is the soul of the church. It is the Spirit who returns all to God.[108]

To sum up: Aquinas asserted the goodness of creation as participating in the existence of God. Creation has a high capacity for grace, although the realm of grace is not the same as that of nature. God as a Trinity of Love and Might does not need his creation but does not disdain it either. The focus of our access to God is in Christ-centred worship, inspired by the light of revelation shining through the Scriptures and received in the church.

Bibliography

Primary sources in the primary languages

For the *Summa theologiae*: St. Thomas Aquinas, *Summa theologiae*, Blackfriars ed. (New York: McGraw Hill, 1964 onwards; now reprinted by Cambridge University Press). Includes facing English translation.

For the rest: *Corpus Thomisticum* <http://www.corpusthomisticum.org/>, accessed 9 December 2009.

For the existing and forthcoming volumes of the Leonine edition, see <http://www.corpusthomisticum.org/repedleo.html>, accessed 9 December 2009.

Primary sources in English

Again, the Blackfriars edition above for the *Summa theologiae.*

Also <http://www.newadvent.org/summa/>, accessed 9 December 2009. This translation is old and not always based on the best text, but is still serviceable. (I have relied on it often in the above article.)

And Thomas Aquinas' bibliography: <http://www.home.duq.edu/~bonin/thomasbibliography.html>, accessed 9 December 2009.

Aquinas on Creation (*Scriptum super libros Sententiarum Petri Lombardi*) (2 prologue and 2, 1, 1); *De aeternitate mundi contra murmurantes*, tr. Steven E. Baldner and William E. Carrol (Toronto: Pontifical Institute of Mediaeval Studies, 1997).

Catena aurea (*Glossa continua super evangelia*), tr. John Henry Newman, 8 vols. (Eugene: Wipf & Stock, 2005).

---

108. *De veritate* 20, 4; *ST* 3, Q8.

Compendium of Theology (*Compendium theologiae ad fratrem Reginaldum socium suum*), tr. Cyril Vollert (St. Louis: Herder, 1949).

On Evil (*De malo*), tr. Jean Oesterle (Notre Dame: University of Notre Dame Press, 1995).

On the Power of God (*Quaestiones disputatae de potentia dei*), tr. the English Dominican Fathers, 3 vols. in 1 (Eugene: Wipf & Stock: 2004).

On Truth (*De veritate*), tr. Robert W. Mulligan, 3 vols. (Chicago: Henry Regnery, 1952; repr. Indianapolis: Hackett, 1994).

Summa contra gentiles, tr. Anton Pegis (Notre Dame: University of Notre Dame Press, 1975).

Summa theologiae. A concise translation (an abbreviated presentation) in English of the entire *ST*, assembled by T. McDermott (Allen, TX: Westminster, 1989). There is also a collection of philosophical passages from the *Summa theologiae*: P. J. Kreeft, *A Summa of the Summa: The Essential Philosophical Passages of St. Thomas Aquinas' Summa Theologica* (San Francisco: Ignatius, 1990).

Introductory studies

Davies, Brian, *Aquinas: An Introduction* (New York: Continuum, 2004).

Healy, Nicholas M., *Thomas Aquinas: Theologian of the Christian Life*, The Great Theologians Series (Aldershot: Ashgate, 2003).

Nichols, Aidan, *Discovering Aquinas: An Introduction to His Life, Work, and Influence* (Grand Rapids: Eerdmans, 2003).

Wawrykow, Joseph P., *The Westminster Handbook to Thomas Aquinas*, Westminster Handbooks to Christian Theology (Louisville: Westminster John Knox, 2005).

Weinandy, Thomas, Daniel Keating and John Yocum (eds.), *Aquinas on Doctrine* (New York: T. & T. Clark International, 2004).

—, *Aquinas on Scripture: An Introduction to His Biblical Commentaries* (New York: T. & T. Clark, 2005).

Additional key studies and resources

These are mostly in English, but I have included one or two French and German sources where I have found these without equivalent in English:

Adams, Marilyn McCord, *What Sort of Human Nature? Medieval Philosophy and the Systematics of Christology* (Milwaukee: Marquette University Press, 1999).

Baglow, Christopher T., *'Modus et Forma': A New Approach to the Exegesis of Saint Thomas Aquinas with an Application to the Lectura super Epistolam ad Ephesios* (Rome: Biblical Institute, 2002).

Berchthold, Christoph, *Manifestatio Veritatis: Zum Offenbarungsbegriff bei Thomas von Aquin* (Münster: LIT, 2000).

Boyle, Leonard E., 'The Setting of the *Summa Theologiae* of St. Thomas – Revisited', in Stephen J. Pope (ed.), *The Ethics of Aquinas* (Washington, DC: Georgetown University Press, 2002), pp. 68–89.

Cessario, Romanus, *The Moral Virtues and Theological Ethics* (Notre Dame: University of Notre Dame Press, 1991).

Cross, Richard, *Metaphysics of the Incarnation: Thomas Aquinas to Duns Scotus* (New York: Oxford University Press, 2002).

Davies, Brian, *The Thought of Thomas Aquinas* (Oxford: Oxford University Press, 1992).

Garrigues, J.-M., 'La doctrine de la grace habituelle dans ses sources', *Revue Thomiste* 103 (2003), pp. 179–202.

Hall, Alexander W., *Thomas Aquinas and John Duns Scotus: Natural Theology in the High Middle Ages* (New York: Continuum, 2007).

Johnstone, Brian V., 'The Debate on the Structure of the *Summa Theologiae* of St. Thomas Aquinas: From Chenu (1939) to Metz (1998)', in Paul van Geest, *et al.* (eds.), *Aquinas as Authority* (Leuven: Peeters, 2002), pp. 187–200.

Leblanc, Marie, 'Le péché originel dans la pensée de S. Thomas', *Revue Thomiste* 93 (1993), pp. 567–600.

Kretzmann, Norman, *The Metaphysics of Theism: Aquinas's Natural Theology in Summa contra gentiles* (Oxford: Clarendon; New York: Oxford University Press, 1997).

—, *The Metaphysics of Creation: Aquinas's Natural Theology in Summa contra gentiles II* (Oxford: Clarendon; New York: Oxford University Press, 1999).

Kretzmann, Norman, and Eleonore Stump, *The Cambridge Companion to Aquinas* (Cambridge: Cambridge University Press, 1993).

Laporte, J. M., 'Christ in Aquinas's Summa Theologiae: Peripheral or Pervasive?', *Thomist* 67.2 (2003), pp. 221–248.

Levering, Matthew, *Christ's Fulfillment of Torah and Temple: Salvation According to Thomas Aquinas* (Notre Dame: University of Notre Dame Press, 2002).

Nichols, Aidan, 'St Thomas Aquinas on the Passion of Christ: A Reading of *Summa Theologiae* q. 46', *Scottish Journal of Theology* 43 (1990), pp. 447–460.

Nieuwenhove, R. van, and J. Wawrykow (eds.), *The Theology of Thomas Aquinas* (Notre Dame: University of Notre Dame Press, 2005).

Paluch, Michal, *La profondeur de l'amour divin: La prédestination dans l'oeuvre de Saint Thomas d'Aquin* (Paris: Vrin, 2004).

Pelikan, J., 'The Doctrine of the Filioque in Thomas Aquinas and its Patristic Antecedents', in *St Thomas Aquinas, 1274–1974: Commemorative Studies* (Toronto: Pontifical Institute of Medieval Studies, 1974), vol. 1, pp. 322–326.

Persson, Per Erik, *Sacra doctrina: Reason and Revelation in Aquinas* (Oxford: Blackwell, 1970).

Pesch, O.-H., *Thomas von Aquin. Grenze und Grosse mittelalterlicher Theologie* (Mainz: Grünewald, 1989).

Pinckaers, Servais, *The Sources of Christian Ethics* (Washington, DC: Catholic University of America Press, 1995).

Pope, Stephen J. (ed.), *The Ethics of Aquinas* (Washington, DC: Georgetown University Press, 2002).

Ryan, Thomas, *Thomas Aquinas as Reader of the Psalms*, Studies in Spirituality and Theology 6 (Notre Dame: University of Notre Dame Press, 2000).

Stump, Eleonore, *Aquinas* (London: Routledge, 2003).

Torrell, J.-P., *Saint Thomas Aquinas*. Vol. 1: *The Person and His Work* (Washington, DC: Catholic University of America Press, 1996).

—, *Saint Thomas Aquinas*. Vol. 2: *Spiritual Master* (Washington, DC: Catholic University of America Press, 2003).

Torrell, J.-P., and D. Bouthillier, 'Quand saint Thomas méditait sur le prophète Isaïe', *Revue Thomiste* 90 (1990), pp. 5–47.

Valkenberg, Pim, *Words of the Living God: Place and Function of Holy Scripture in the Theology of St. Thomas Aquinas* (Leuven: Peeters, 2000).

Weisheipl, J., *Friar Thomas D'Aquino: his Life, Thought, and Works* (Oxford: Blackwell, 1975).

Westberg, Daniel, *Right Practical Reason: Aristotle, Action and Prudence in Aquinas* (Oxford: Clarendon, 1994).

Williams, Rowan D., 'The Literal Sense of Scripture', *Modern Theology* 7 (1991), pp. 121–134.

INDEX